Treatment Resistant
ANXIETY DISORDERS

Treatment Resistant
ANXIETY DISORDERS

RESOLVING IMPASSES TO SYMPTOM REMISSION

EDITED BY

DEBBIE SOOKMAN

ROBERT L. LEAHY

Routledge
Taylor & Francis Group
New York   London

Routledge
Taylor & Francis Group
270 Madison Avenue
New York, NY 10016

Routledge
Taylor & Francis Group
27 Church Road
Hove, East Sussex BN3 2FA

Printed in the United States of America on acid-free paper
10 9 8 7 6 5 4 3 2 1

International Standard Book Number: 978-0-415-98891-9 (Hardback)

Library of Congress Cataloging-in-Publication Data

Treatment resistant anxiety disorders : resolving impasses to symptom remission / edited by Debbie Sookman, Robert L. Leahy.
    p. ; cm.
  Includes bibliographical references and index.
  ISBN 978-0-415-98891-9 (hardback : alk. paper)
    1. Anxiety disorders--Treatment. 2. Cognitive therapy. I. Sookman, Debbie. II. Leahy, Robert L.
    [DNLM: 1. Anxiety Disorders--complications. 2. Anxiety Disorders--therapy. 3. Cognitive Therapy--methods. 4. Treatment Refusal. WM 172 T7849 2009]

RC531.T686 2009
616.85'2206--dc22
    2009014786

Visit the Taylor & Francis Web site at
http://www.taylorandfrancis.com

and the Routledge Web site at
http://www.routledgementalhealth.com

Dedication

To my parents Bella and Larry Sookman,
who would have read this book with pride,
and to Arthur Landa
for your love and encouragement.
D.S.

Again, for Helen
R.L.

Contents

Contributors

Hal Arkowitz
University of Arizona
Tucson, Arizona

Timothy J. Bruce
University of Illinois College
of Medicine
Peoria, Illinois

Marylene Cloitre
New York University School
of Medicine
New York, New York

Simon Ducharme
McGill University Health Centre
Montreal, Quebec, Canada

Steven C. Hayes
University of Nevada
Reno, Nevada

Christie Jackson
New York University School
of Medicine
New York, New York

Theodore T. Kolivakis
McGill University Health Centre
Montreal, Quebec, Canada

Robert L. Leahy
The American Institute for
Cognitive Therapy
New York, New York

Deborah A. Lee
Berkshire Traumatic Stress Service
University College
London, United Kingdom

Howard C. Margolese
McGill University Health Centre
Montreal, Quebec, Canada

Dahlia Mukherjee
University of Nevada
Reno, Nevada

Kore Nissenson
Montefiore Medical Center
Bronx, New York

Roisin M. O'Connor
Dalhousie University
Halifax, Nova Scotia, Canada

Travis L. Osborne
Anxiety and Stress Reduction
Center of Seattle (ASRC) *and*
University of Washington
Seattle, Washington

Jennifer C. Plumb
University of Nevada
Reno, Nevada

Jayde Pryzgoda
Anxiety and Stress Reduction
  Center of Seattle (ASRC) *and*
University of Washington
Seattle, Washington

William C. Sanderson
Hofstra University
Hempstead, New York

Debbie Sookman
McGill University
Montreal, Quebec, Canada

Gail Steketee
Boston University
Boston, Massachusetts

Sherry H. Stewart
Dalhousie University
Halifax, Nova Scotia, Canada

Michael P. Twohig
Utah State University
Logan, Utah

Stacy Shaw Welch
Anxiety and Stress Reduction
  Center of Seattle (ASRC) *and*
University of Washington
Seattle, Washington

Adrian Wells
University of Manchester
Manchester, United Kingdom

Henny A. Westra
York University
Toronto, Ontario, Canada

Introduction

Debbie Sookman

Anxiety disorders are the single most prevalent category of psychiatric illness. Prevalence is approximately 28% of the general population. Many individuals receive inadequate treatment as defined by empirically based standards or are unable to participate sufficiently to achieve sustained symptom reduction. Although cognitive–behavioral treatments are highly effective for some individuals who stay in treatment and engage in the required exposure and cognitive restructuring, dropout rates are high. Many patients remain symptomatic following treatment or have relapsed at follow-up. Inadequately treated anxiety disorders are commonly associated with long-term psychosocial disability, severe depression, and substance abuse. Although there is clear recognition among therapists of the difficulties that these patients face, there is currently no book we know of that addresses the nature and treatment of "resistant anxiety disorders." This edited book brings together leading cognitive–behavioral therapists from major theoretical orientations to provide clinicians with a source of information, skills, and strategies from a wide range of cognitive–behavioral therapy (CBT) approaches. The aim of treatment for anxiety disorders is complete symptom remission at posttreatment and long-term maintenance of improvement. There is a commensurate need for a set of tools and strategies to address the roadblocks that arise in treatment.

This book describes and illustrates how to combine empirically based findings, broad-based and disorder-specific theoretical models, and individualized case conceptualization to formulate and apply specific strategies for varied aspects of resistance during treatment of anxiety disorders. The contributors discuss strategies for common areas of, or reasons for, resistance that include intolerance of anxiety and other strong feelings, cognitive and metacognitive dysfunction, overvalued ideas, motivational difficulties, interpersonal issues, skills limitations, risk aversion, treatment-interfering behaviors, and substance abuse. Strategies for patient, intervention, and therapist factors that may impede successful application of empirically based treatments for specific anxiety disorders are discussed. Several chapters present interventions for core emotional and cognitive schemas that may be related to intransigence of symptoms. The contributors describe their theoretical and clinical rationale for treatment and provide illustrative clinical examples.

The contributors' chapter summaries are presented next.[1] Chapters 1 to 4 describe specialized theoretical and therapeutic approaches developed to improve outcome for specific anxiety disorders. Chapters 5 to 9 describe the application of therapeutic approaches for various manifestations of intransigent anxiety. Chapters 10 and 11 address comorbid substance abuse and pharmacotherapy for anxiety disorders. Following the chapter summaries, I offer a few additional comments about CBT resistance in anxiety disorders.

In Chapter 1, Wells describes the metacognitive theory of psychological disorder and how this has been applied in the metacognitive model and treatment of generalized anxiety disorder (GAD). Specific treatment strategies are elaborated that focus on modifying maladaptive metacognitive appraisals and beliefs and enhancing more adaptive meta-awareness and mental control. Extended negative thinking is hypothesized to occur because of the activation of styles of processing dominated by worry and rumination, attentional monitoring for threat, and counterproductive coping behaviors. Individuals with GAD tend to overuse worry as a coping strategy which can lead to emotional regulation difficulties such as impaired emotional processing. Metacognitive therapy focuses on challenging beliefs about the uncontrollability of worry. Treatment aims to help patients develop alternative non-worry responses to negative thoughts, challenge beliefs about the danger of worrying, and weaken positive beliefs about the need to worry in order to cope. The process of treatment and metacognitive strategies used for creating change are described and illustrated.

In Chapter 2, Sookman and Steketee discuss and illustrate specialized cognitive behavior therapy for treatment resistant obsessive compulsive disorder (OCD). Empirically based approaches are reviewed with emphasis on varied patient and intervention factors that impede optimal response to treatment. The authors propose comprehensive guidelines for an adequate trial of specialized CBT for OCD, required both for clinical practice and for controlled treatment trials, as well as criteria for recovery/ remission and for CBT resistance after an adequate trial of CBT has been delivered or attempted. Two specialized treatment approaches for OCD

---

[1] The chapter summaries are an edited version of abstracts written by each contributor.

are described and illustrated. The first approach, described by Wilhelm and Steketee, involves Beckian cognitive therapy that includes a variety of cognitive strategies and behavioral experiments to help patients to test their dysfunctional hypotheses. Cognitive therapy may be especially effective for patients with cognitive rituals and for those whose intrusions trigger concerns about over-importance of thoughts, responsibility, and perfectionism with related checking behaviors. The second approach developed by Sookman and colleagues involves a schema-based conceptual model and treatment approach for CBT resistant OCD of different subtypes, formulated to specifically address the heterogeneity of this disorder. Schema-based interventions expand upon standard cognitive therapy methods and are intended to facilitate exposure and response prevention (ERP), improve generalization and maintenance of change, and reduce relapse rates. Treatment outcome results for both these specialized approaches are promising.

In Chapter 3, Jackson, Nissenson, and Cloitre discuss treatment for complex posttraumatic stress disorder (PTSD). Treatments for PTSD were originally proposed to address the consequences of a specific traumatic event, such as a rape or a motor vehicle accident. PTSD related to chronic and repeated forms of trauma (e.g., childhood abuse, domestic violence, being a witness to genocide) is associated with a more complex constellation of symptoms that can be especially resistant to treatments that are otherwise quite successful. This chapter describes PTSD in its more complex forms and introduces a modular sequential treatment approach. Traditional therapies for PTSD implement some type of traumatic memory processing (e.g., imaginal exposure, narrative exposure therapy, cognitive processing therapy), and these have been demonstrated to be effective in resolving PTSD. The treatment described in this chapter introduces an initial phase that focuses on skills training in affective and interpersonal regulation (STAIR) to target clinically salient problems such as anger management and relationship difficulties that often co-occur in complex forms of PTSD and interfere with the successful application of exposure work. This type of approach might also be useful for patients with a range of other psychiatric comorbidities that involve impaired self-regulatory functioning such as bipolar disorder, borderline personality disorder, eating disorders, and substance use disorders. This approach is consistent with a movement in clinical research and treatment that considers emotion or self-regulatory difficulties as a shared underlying construct explaining vulnerability to a spectrum of psychiatric disorders.

In Chapter 4, Bruce and Sanderson discuss conceptualization and management of treatment resistant panic disorder (PD). Cognitive–behavioral therapy is recognized as an effective psychological treatment for PD; however, the literature on prediction, prevention, and management of suboptimal response is not well developed. Considering this lack of empirical guidance, these authors conducted a survey of expert cognitive–behavioral therapists about what they had found in their practices that contributed to a poor treatment response and what strategies they found helpful in managing these problems. Ten factors associated with a poor treatment response were identified: lack of engagement in behavioral experiments, noncompliance with treatment, presence of comorbid conditions, inadequate case formulation or misdiagnosis, external support for dysfunctional behavior, problems with cognitive restructuring, presence of negative life events, medication complications, poor delivery of CBT, and therapeutic relationship barriers. The authors discuss each of these factors in detail and offer a practical set of recommendations for addressing common causes of treatment-resistant PD.

In Chapter 5, Leahy discusses emotional schemas and resistance to change in anxiety disorders. Each anxiety disorder is hypothesized to reflect the patient's theory of emotional dysregulation that underpins resistance to engage in exposure. Emotional avoidance and fear of anxiety can be viewed as a consequence of the "emotional schemas" (that is, interpretations of emotions and strategies engaged for emotion) endorsed by the patient that underlie the anxiety disorder and resistance to change. Each anxiety disorder may be characterized as a set of rules that are employed to avoid the negative effects of anxious arousal, thoughts, or sensations—that is, the "solution" is the "problem." Several strategies are described that are derived from emotional schema therapy to help patients overcome their resistance to exposure and habituation. These include identifying the patient's theory of anxiety, validation, and self-reward for change; clarifying the patient's criteria for improvement; using constructive discomfort by investing in anxiety; establishing comprehensibility and consensus or emotion; building acceptance; encouraging expression; evaluating the duration and variability of emotion; modifying beliefs about the need to control and globalize emotion; reducing shame and guilt; and modifying rumination about emotion. A case of treatment-resistant OCD is presented.

In Chapter 6, Welch, Osborne, and Pryzgoda discuss augmenting exposure-based treatment for anxiety disorders with principles and skills from dialectical behavior therapy (DBT). For clients who are not responding to gold standard CBT treatments for anxiety disorders, a more intensive form of therapy is sometimes warranted. DBT provides several strategies for addressing problems that can hinder progress in therapy. The authors summarize the theory, principles, and strategies of DBT and its relevance to anxiety disorders. Specifically discussed are applications of mindfulness, emotion regulation, and distress tolerance, as well as ideas for improving compliance such as validation techniques. The authors propose a "levels of care" approach to applying components of DBT to the treatment of anxiety and provide recommendations for when to consider each level of care. Clinical examples of how they have integrated components of DBT into the treatment of anxiety disorders in difficult-to-treat cases are discussed. The emerging body of literature in which aspects of DBT have been incorporated into anxiety treatments is reviewed.

In Chapter 7, Westra and Arkowitz discuss how combining motivational interviewing with cognitive–behavioral therapy may increase treatment efficacy for generalized anxiety disorder (GAD). Resistance to change is often encountered in cognitive–behavioral therapy and other types of psychotherapy. While reducing resistance can lead to improved clinical outcomes, there has been surprisingly little research to guide therapists in how to accomplish this. The authors discuss how motivational interviewing (MI), an empirically supported treatment for substance use disorders, can be fruitfully combined with CBT in the treatment of GAD. They describe MI, how and why it may reduce resistance and increase motivation to change, the clinical methods of MI, and how it can be used in combination with CBT. The authors provide an extended case illustration of the use of combined MI and CBT in GAD. The chapter concludes with a discussion of research that points to the value of combining MI and CBT in the treatment of GAD and other anxiety disorders.

In Chapter 8, Lee elaborates compassionate mind therapy. Reported feelings of shame and self-criticism are prevalent in many mental health problems such as PTSD, mood disorders, eating disorders, and substance abuse. Compassion-focused case conceptualization and interventions may offer useful ways to work with comorbid presentations that do not respond to standard CBT treatment protocols. This chapter draws on social mentality theory to explore the nature of negative self-evaluations and presents theory–practice links on how to develop a compassionate mind to foster change. Use of imagery and the generation of compassionate feelings for the self are illustrated with a case of PTSD.

In Chapter 9, Twohig, Plumb, Mukherjee, and Hayes describe the use of acceptance and commitment therapy (ACT) for resistant OCD. ACT for OCD is a form of cognitive–behavioral therapy that focuses on acceptance and stepping back from obsessions and associated anxiety while moving in valued life directions. Focusing on these therapeutic processes may be useful in decreasing the impact of obsessions, reducing compulsions, and increasing quality of life in individuals diagnosed with OCD. The authors offer suggestions on how to address difficult situations that therapists who treat OCD may encounter. They use a case illustration to describe

ACT procedures that can be used to address symptoms such as primary obsessions and hoarding, comorbidity, and treatment refusal, dropout, or poor compliance.

In Chapter 10, Stewart and O'Connor address the treatment of anxiety disorders in the context of concurrent substance misuse. Anxiety disorders frequently co-occur with substance use disorders at rates that far exceed chance. Clients with anxiety comorbid with substance abuse or dependence display poorer treatment outcome for their anxiety disorder. Because substance misuse can perpetuate or even worsen anxiety in the long term, the presence of a comorbid substance use disorder can create an apparently treatment-resistant form of anxiety. In this chapter, for each form of anxiety disorder that is commonly comorbid with substance abuse or dependence, the authors review theoretical explanations for the co-occurrence that can be used to guide case conceptualization; emerging integrative cognitive–behavioral treatment packages that target both disorders and their interrelations; and data on the efficacy of these emerging integrative treatments. The chapter concludes with a case example that illustrates the relationship between anxiety and substance misuse and how an integrative treatment can be employed to resolve a seemingly treatment-resistant case.

In Chapter 11, Kolivakis, Margolese, and Ducharme discuss pharmacotherapy for treatment resistant anxiety disorders in adults in the setting of cognitive–behavioral therapy. Response rates from randomized controlled trials in anxiety disorders are highly variable for pharmacotherapy and psychotherapy, and reported remission rates are a great deal lower. A majority of patients are treatment resistant in that they suffer from residual symptoms that are associated with poor functional outcomes. Over the last decade, there has been increasing emphasis placed on the practice of evidence-based medicine in the provision of mental health services. Studies estimate that a minority of people (<25%) with anxiety disorders receive interventions of proven efficacy. The authors review evidence-based interventions (both pharmacological and combined medication and CBT) specifically in treatment-resistant anxiety disorders and discuss their implications for clinical practice. Clinicians must use an evidence-based approach in treating resistant anxiety disorders. This will increase and hasten the likelihood of achieving response or remission and avoid time-wasting, low-impact trials. Further research is required to examine which patients would respond best to a combination of CBT and pharmacotherapy and how these should be administered. Despite available evidence-based treatments, clinicians often have to manage patients with severe anxiety disorders with significant comorbidity who seem to be resistant or refractory to multiple trials of medications and therapy. Multiple medication trials, even if justified, should never be a barrier to referral for specialized CBT. There may be a bias toward pharmacotherapy in treatment-resistant disorders that interferes with early referral for specialized CBT.

Following from the above chapter summaries, in my view it is useful to conceptualize "treatment resistance" as a myriad of potential intervention factors as well as patient characteristics and/or their interplay. We must know what mainstream specialized interventions are currently empirically demonstrated as effective (and essential) for specific disorders, accounting for heterogeneity within disorders and across individuals. We must be able to collaborate with each patient to generate evolving clinical hypotheses, to formulate complex empirically based interventions, and to create an emotionally meaningful learning experience that fosters multidimensional growth. This task requires a broad conceptual base and scope of technical and relational skills. Effective resolution of impasses to adaptive learning and change during therapy may often involve application of existing mainstream strategies combined with creative new ones. This process, though it may begin with art, must become science. New strategies must be grounded in and subject to empirical examination. Outcome trials with resistant samples are challenging, as research methodology should not impoverish treatment delivery. Multidimensional criteria are required to operationalize treatment resistance and to examine treatment efficacy. For example, standardized and idiographic measures, behavioral observation, and neurobiological correlates of change may help us to understand differences on the continuum from treatment failure to full recovery.

There is, indeed, wide variability in our patients' capacity to accommodate potentially reparative experience, given the anxiety (and other strong feelings) integral to the change process. Undoubtedly, the resources and limitations of each patient are predictive of treatment response. Current research indicates considerable variability in treatment response reported and identifiable patient characteristics that predict outcome; however, the greatest uniformity of outcome and best response rates are generally reported in studies conducted by experts at specialized sites. For example, research on CBT for obsessive–compulsive disorder and its heterogeneous subtypes indicates that some patients previously labeled "treatment resistant" are able to achieve symptom remission when treated at a specialized OCD clinic where expertise and resources focus on this disorder. An essential issue in addressing CBT resistance is treatment delivery and how to best disseminate expertise available at specialized clinics (Sookman & Steketee, this volume). Given that our goal is symptom remission for as many patients as possible, it is an essential clinical skill to know whom to accept for treatment, when to consult or request supervision, and when to recommend timely referral to a specialist colleague or clinic.

We hope this book will prove useful to clinicians and clinical researchers along the spectrum of experience, and to our patients who come with remarkable suffering as well as capacity for adaptive change. Ongoing clinical research should aim to further extend our understanding and skill to effectively address the diverse expressions, meanings, and sources of "treatment resistance."

chapter one

Metacognitive therapy
Application to generalized anxiety disorder

Adrian Wells
University of Manchester
Manchester, United Kingdom

Contents

A central premise of metacognitive theory and therapy (Wells, 2000) is that the control of thought processes determines how long mental suffering lasts. More specifically, sustained processing determines unwanted and extended emotions. In metacognitive theory, the content of thoughts is not seen as central in causing psychological disorder, but the extent to which individuals engage in a specific style of thinking is crucial.

Metacognitive therapy (MCT) (Wells, 1995, 2009) is based on the self-regulatory executive function (S-REF) model (Wells & Matthews, 1994, 1996). A basic principle is that periods of negative thoughts, distressing beliefs, and negative emotions are quite common and normal human experiences, but these inadvertently become elaborated and extended because of the style of a person's subsequent cognition and coping. Disorder is caused (in the sense that it persists) by a toxic style of thinking called the *cognitive attentional syndrome* (CAS), which is the product of metacognition.

1

Before describing in detail the nature of the CAS, we should examine first what is meant by the term "metacognition."

Metacognition is a domain of cognition that is responsible for the regulation and appraisal of thinking. It is cognition applied to cognition and probably involves some discrete architecture, mechanisms, and processes. The field of metacognitive inquiry arose in the context of developmental psychology and memory research (e.g., Brown & McNeill, 1966; Flavell, 1979; Nelson & Narrens, 1990) but remained largely unexplored as an area of fruitful study for understanding psychological disorders.

This situation changed with the advent of the self-regulatory executive function (S-REF) model, which offered a metacognitive account of the development and maintenance of psychological disorder (Wells & Matthews, 1994, 1996). In the S-REF theory, all psychological disorders can be linked to the activation of a style of thinking known as the CAS. This consists of three components: (1) a preponderance of verbal conceptual activity in the form of worry and rumination, (2) the tendency to maintain attention on sources of threat, and (3) coping behaviors that disrupt self-regulation or the acquisition of new information that can modify erroneous knowledge.

The CAS essentially represents the person's response to internal events and is a specific constellation of cognitive and behavioral coping styles. Although the volitional nature of this style remains intact, the person's awareness or knowledge of control and volition over processes such as worry and rumination is often incomplete or erroneous. The initiation of such processes can be reflexive, but sustained processing in the form of worry or rumination is under voluntary control.

Worrying is comprised of long chains of verbal thoughts in which the person seeks answers to questions about how to cope with or avoid potential danger. It is epitomized by triggering thoughts such as "What if I have an accident?" and is followed by an extended inner dialogue in which the person attempts to generate answers. Rumination is a similar conceptual process, but it tends to be past oriented and seeks reasons for failing and ways of understanding and dealing with feelings of sadness and loss.

Another aspect of the CAS, *threat monitoring*, refers to maintaining attention on sources of threat. These may be internal, such as bodily sensation in panic disorder or an impression of the self in social phobia, but they may also be external, such as looking for signs of dirt or contamination in obsessive–compulsive disorder (OCD), or scanning the environment for potential sources of danger in posttraumatic stress disorder (PTSD).

The third constituent of the CAS is other coping or self-regulatory behaviors, including avoidance, using substances to control thoughts and emotions, and more direct attempts to suppress thoughts. These strategies may provide short-term relief from suffering, but they fail to provide a long-term solution. Indeed, they are prone to backfire and maintain or contribute further to stress. For example, thought suppression is not consistently effective and may contribute to fears of loss of control. Strategies such as avoidance remove the opportunity to learn that emotions or situations are safe. Strategies such as alcohol use can have negative physical and social consequences.

What are the other mechanisms linking the CAS to prolonged emotional suffering? Worry and rumination are a problem because they prolong anxiety and negative affect by focusing on danger or by extending thoughts about failure, loss, and sadness. For example, a depressed patient undergoing metacognitive therapy explained how he would analyze reasons for feeling sad in an attempt to find a way to improve his mood. Unfortunately, he was unable to find a cause and concluded he was weak and defective for being like this. Similarly, a patient with PTSD who had been involved in a traffic accident reported that she worried about bad things that could happen in the future because she wanted to avoid them. As a result, she had begun to notice how unsafe the environment was and how much potential there was for danger. This increased her sense of vulnerability and maintained her anxiety when traveling away from home.

Worry and rumination can interfere with other in-built processes necessary for emotional processing and regulating lower level cognitive activity. They use processing resources leading to a reduction in resources that are necessary for executive control of cognition. Worry and rumination continuously present threat-related information to consciousness and maintain the sense of current danger and the anxiety program that accompanies it. Such effects are likely to be dependent on prefrontal modulation of activity in fear and emotion networks in the limbic brain.

Threat monitoring is problematic because it enhances perceptions of danger, thereby increasing the activation of anxiety responses. Many of the threats in emotional disorder are "tentative" in nature and represent "potential threats." For example, the person with obsessive–compulsive disorder scans the environment for possible signs of contaminants, and the individual with hypochondriasis checks his body for unusual signs that could indicate serious illness. As a consequence, normal benign environmental or internal events appear more dangerous and the person feels more vulnerable.

Other coping behaviors are problematic in several ways. Self-regulatory strategies such as trying to suppress thoughts are not particularly effective and may increase intrusions or maintain awareness of unwanted thoughts (Wegner, 1997; Wegner, Schneider, Carter, & White, 1987). However, even when suppression is successful, it can prevent the person from developing a healthier and more flexible relationship with his own cognitions. Thus, the person does not discover that thoughts are simply passing internal events that are unimportant. For example, the person with obsessive–compulsive symptoms believes that some thoughts can cause harm, and successful suppression or neutralization prevents the individual from discovering that thoughts alone have no real influence. Thus, an appropriate and more adaptive metacognitive awareness and model of internal mental experiences is not acquired or strengthened.

Behaviors such as avoidance or saving oneself from threat backfire because they deprive the person of an opportunity to discover that threat is erroneous or that they can cope effectively. For example, an individual with social phobia who mentally rehearses sentences before speaking in order to avoid appearing foolish does not learn that his spontaneous speech does not attract such derision. Moreover, mental rehearsal impedes spontaneity and appropriate attention to the social task. Strategies such as using substances or seeking reassurance are a problem because they can have an adverse interpersonal effect that contributes to relationship pressures and further stress.

As the forgoing describes, the CAS presents a problem in that it compounds and extends dysfunctional ideas and emotional distress. This syndrome arises out of metacognitions, of which two general content categories are identified in the metacognitive model: positive and negative metacognitive beliefs. Positive metacognitive beliefs concern the advantages of engaging in components of the CAS and include beliefs about worry, rumination, threat monitoring, and controlling or avoiding thoughts and emotions. For instance, the person believes: "Focusing on possible threats means I'll be able to remain safe," or "Worrying about harmful events means I won't be taken by surprise," or "Analyzing why I feel so bad will help me overcome my depression." Negative metacognitive beliefs concern the uncontrollability, importance, and danger of thoughts. Examples of these beliefs include: "I have no control over my thinking," or "My thoughts mean I'm losing my mind," or "Some thoughts have the power to make bad things happen."

In particular disorders, it is possible to identify some specificity in these categories. In depression, positive beliefs primarily concern the advantages of rumination, whereas in generalized anxiety disorder (GAD) they concern the advantages of using worry as a coping strategy. In OCD, positive beliefs concern the advantages of worrying as a means of preventing the dangerous consequences of thoughts or preventing contact with possible contamination. Positive beliefs in OCD also include the benefits of engaging in rituals and neutralizing responses in response to obsessions. In PTSD, they concern the advantages of worrying about threats in order to remain safe and the benefits of recounting aspects of the trauma to find answers about causality. As we will see later, positive beliefs in GAD focus on worry as a means of effectively avoiding or dealing with danger in the future.

As for negative beliefs in OCD, these concern "fusion" domains in which the individual believes thoughts have special power or significance to cause negative outcomes. The term *thought–action fusion* (TAF) was introduced by Rachman (1993) in his description of cognitive distortions in OCD. He distinguished probability and morality variants of TAF in which the individual appraises the occurrence of a thought as being morally equivalent to performing an action or as increasing the probability of an occurrence. The metacognitive model of OCD (Wells, 1997) maintains this terminology but views fusion as a series of interrelated metacognitive beliefs, labeled *thought–event fusion* (TEF), *thought–action fusion* (TAF), and *thought–object fusion* (TOF). With TEF, the person believes that certain thoughts can cause events (e.g., "thinking about an accident will make it happen"). With TAF the belief is that thoughts will cause the commission of unwanted acts (e.g., "thinking about stabbing someone will make me do it"). With TOF, the belief is that thoughts and feelings can be transferred into objects (e.g., "having bad thoughts will contaminate objects I touch").

In depression and PTSD, negative beliefs focus on the uncontrollability of worry and rumination and the meaning of intrusions (e.g., "recurrent thoughts about the trauma mean I'm losing my mind"). In GAD, as we will see later, these beliefs concern the uncontrollability of worry and its dangerous effects on physical and mental functioning.

In the above description of metacognitive beliefs, I have presented them as symbolic and propositional representations, but alternative forms of metacognitive knowledge are important in the S-REF model. Much of the knowledge on which processing draws is not directly verbally expressible and is thought to exist as metacognitive plans or programs for controlling attention, memory, and low-level, emotion-related processing. These can be likened to thinking skills acquired through experiencing executive control. Unfortunately, flexible executive control is often constrained in psychological disorders because of an over-reliance on metacognitions that support the CAS. An implication of this multicomponent view of knowledge is that treatment should aim to enhance flexible control over processing and not simply interrogate the nature of automatic thoughts and more general (nonmetacognitive) schemas.

Understanding GAD

By now it is well established that GAD is responsive to cognitive–behavioral treatments (CBT), but treatment outcomes are variable and modest. Treatment comprised of applied relaxation, anxiety management, and cognitive–behavioral interventions shows a wide range of efficacy rates. At worst, 0% of patients show recovery on the basis of standardized criteria applied to trait–anxiety outcome scores, while at best the rate is 63% at posttreatment (Fisher, 2006). The aggregated recovery rate across studies of CBT is 46% at posttreatment assessed by trait–anxiety and 48% as assessed by the Penn State Worry Questionnaire (Fisher, 2006). These statistics show that there is much ground for improvement.

One of the difficulties facing the clinician in treating GAD is that the content of worry changes which reduces the overall effectiveness of strategies focused primarily on reality testing individual worries. What is required is a model of the factors that give rise to the repeated and difficult-to-control worry process that is a hallmark of GAD, irrespective of the content of that process. The metacognitive approach is an obvious choice.

The metacognitive approach to GAD (Wells, 1995; Wells et al., 2008) makes an important distinction between negative thoughts and sustained processing in the form of worry. Worry is seen as a coping response of sustained thinking in response to negative thoughts. A worry episode is triggered by a negative thought that typically occurs as a "what if?" question and occasionally as a mental image. For example, the person prone to pathological worry may think, on overhearing a conversation about illness, "What if my children become ill?" For most people, a thought of this kind will be dismissed as simply a negative idea; however, those with GAD are less flexible in their choice of thinking strategy and this thought is superseded by chains of negative conceptual activity in the form of worry aimed at assessing a range of negative outcomes and planning ways of dealing with them. The worry sequence might go something like this: "What if my daughter gets ill? It probably won't be serious. But what if it is? I've heard reports of meningitis recently. What if she catches that? It's unlikely to happen, but what if she does? I'd better keep a lookout for any symptoms. What should I look for? She's had a cough recently. What if she has a chest infection? Maybe I shouldn't ignore it. What if it's serious? I should make an appointment with the doctor. What sort of mother will they think I am for leaving it? What if she has spread it to her classmates? ..."

The consequence of worry is that it prolongs and intensifies anxiety. Anxiety and worry persist until displaced by competing goals or distractors, or until the person appraises that the "work of worry" is complete. Typically, internal and inappropriate stop signals exist for worry. For example, some patients worry until they feel confident that they can cope or until they are reassured that there is nothing to worry about. The worry sequence has deleterious consequences for emotional well-being. It prolongs emotional responses and can generate a wider range of negative cognitions that lead to negative beliefs. It diverts attention away from emotional processing and resources away from appropriate control over thinking. It can intensify the person's focus on threat so the environment becomes more subjectively "dangerous."

Sustained worrying emerges from positive and negative metacognitive beliefs. Positive metacognitive beliefs concern the advantages of worry as a means of coping. Typical examples include the following:

- "Worrying helps me cope with threats in the future."
- "If I worry then I'll always be prepared."
- "It's better to anticipate danger than to be taken off-guard."
- "Worrying makes sure I don't miss anything important."
- "I do a better job if I worry about what can go wrong."

Negative metacognitive beliefs are of two broad types that concern uncontrollability and the danger of worry; for example:

- "I have no control over worrying."
- "Worrying just takes over and I cannot stop it."
- "Worrying is harmful and puts my body under stress."
- "Worrying too much could make me lose my mind."
- "I could enter a state of worry and never get my mind to rest."

In this model, the content that counts in determining the development of a disorder is the content of metacognitions rather than the content of negative thoughts (i.e., the content of worry). For example, in MCT the therapist focuses on challenging the belief that worry is uncontrollable and harmful by asking such questions as "Can you stop yourself worrying?" In contrast, the Beckian therapist focuses on reality testing the content of worry by asking such questions as "What kind of distortion does your worry contain?"

The model in action

The model is presented in diagrammatic form in Figure 1.1, and Figure 1.2 provides a case example using the model. A worry episode begins with a negative thought, which is designated as the *trigger*. So, for example, a person hears in the distance the siren of an emergency vehicle and experiences the thought: "What if my partner has had an accident?" Triggers are typically "what if?" questions but sometimes occur in the form of negative inner images.

The trigger activates positive metacognitive beliefs about the value of sustained worrying (e.g., "I need to worry in order to be prepared") and this leads to Type 1 worry, in which catastrophic events are contemplated and ways of coping considered; for example, in Type 1 worry the individual thinks, "What if my partner is injured in an accident? I hope it is not serious, but what if it is serious? What will I do? How can I avoid it?

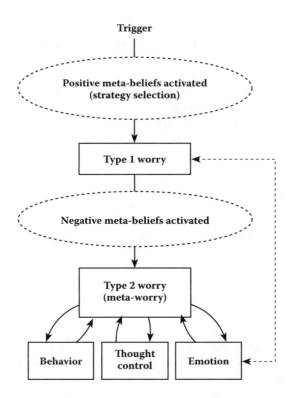

Figure 1.1 The metacognitive model of GAD. (From *Cognitive Therapy of Anxiety Disorders: A Practice Manual and Conceptual Guide,* by A. Wells, 1997, Chichester, U.K.: John Wiley & Sons. Reprinted with permission.)

How will I cope? What if I'm alone? What if I can't manage the children? I'd better make plans. I can ask my parents for help, but what if they're not available? What if I have to go to the hospital?" Type 1 worry content is potentially infinite but it does not concern cognition itself. Type 1 worry leads to an increase in anxiety but a subsequent decrease in anxiety if its goals are met.

Generalized anxiety disorder occurs when negative metacognitive beliefs are activated and develop. During worry episodes—often in response to the experience of anxiety symptoms—negative beliefs are activated concerning loss of control of worrying and its dangerous consequences. At this point, Type 2 worry occurs, which is worry about worrying or negative interpretation of mental processes. In some instances, the interpretation concerns an immediate catastrophe such as "going mad," and then a rapid escalation of anxiety in the form of panic attacks can occur. Some patients

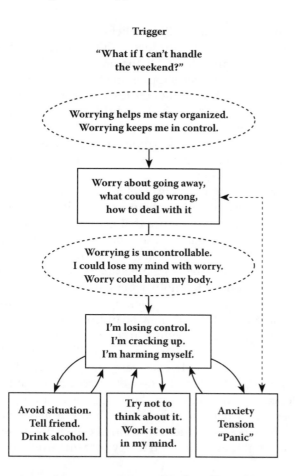

Figure 1.2 A metacognitive case conceptualization. (From *Metacognitive Therapy for Anxiety and Depression*, by A. Wells, 2009, New York: Guilford Press. Reprinted with permission.)

indicate in their narratives that Type 2 worry itself is used as a coping strategy; for example, a patient explained how he would reassure himself when worrying by using self-talk like the following: "It's stupid. Get a grip. If you don't, then you really will lose your mind." In this example, it is of note that the content of worry changes from Type 1 to Type 2, but the process of worrying continues and appropriate control is not executed. As we shall see later, appropriate control would involve suspending the worry process—that is, to discontinue extended thinking and coping.

Once Type 2 worry is activated, a range of unhelpful coping behaviors and thought control strategies can follow. The pattern of metacognitive control strategies is such that individuals often find they are torn between positive and negative metacognitive beliefs. They allow worry to run but are also aware of the threat it presents. This discrepancy is resolved by trying to avoid or suppress thoughts that might act as triggers for worrying (thought control); however, suppression tends to backfire and increase preoccupation with worrying themes (e.g., Wegner, 1997; Wegner et al., 1987). When suppression does work and the person avoids worrying in response to intrusions, this fails to provide evidence that worry is harmless and so metacognitions concerning the danger of worrying remain unchanged and the individual does not develop an alternative way of relating to negative thoughts.

The person suffering from GAD seldom interrupts the worry process once initiated because of beliefs about uncontrollability. This maintains such beliefs. This is another feature that is captured by the thought-control box in the model. In contrast, other behaviors are often implemented (designated by "Behavior" in Figure 1.1), such as seeking reassurance. Reassurance seeking is problematic because essentially it transfers the process of mental control to another person. Thus, beliefs about lack of self-control remain. Reassurance seeking can also backfire because a range of information and advice may be given that increases uncertainty, which acts as a trigger for worrying. In some instances, individuals avoid information such as magazine articles on health or seek information to try to put their mind to rest. In each case, the preoccupation with worry triggers remains, and the person engages in activities that fail to provide direct evidence that worrying can be suspended through self-directed control. Other coping behaviors that maintain the problem include the use of alcohol and drugs and restricted activities, especially those that require breaking of a usual routine and the worry that this would necessitate.

Metacognitive therapy

We have seen that in the metacognitive approach psychological disorder is caused by the extent to which some thoughts are developed and recycled through the processes of the CAS. In the case of GAD, negative automatic thoughts are extended because the person engages in worry in response to them. The approach of metacognitive therapy is a process-focused treatment that aims to modify specific types of extended thinking and enhance flexibility in the way individuals respond to their negative thoughts and beliefs. It does work on content, but on the content of metacognitions and not the content of other thoughts and beliefs. In this section, I describe how these concepts are utilized in treatment.

The MCT model presents the basis of the case formulation, which is used to socialize the patient and direct treatment (see Figure 1.2). The therapist emphasizes the role of beliefs about worry and unhelpful control strategies as central factors giving rise to distressing and out-of-control worrying. The patient is helped to identify how negative beliefs about worry and attempts to suppress thoughts or control thoughts by means of reassurance seeking do not provide effective experiences of self-control. Furthermore, the patient is helped to discover how he or she has not consistently interrupted the worry sequence once started. Typically, socialization incorporates behavioral experiments such as a thought suppression exercise to show how some attempts at self-regulation are not particularly useful. In contrast, the therapist suggests that alternative strategies, that the patient is probably unaware of, may be more effective and can be used to challenge the belief that worry cannot be controlled.

The first target for metacognitive modification is the erroneous belief about the uncontrollability of worry. The metacognitive therapist questions how worry episodes come to an end if they are out of control and helps the patient see how worrying can be displaced by competing demands such as making a telephone call or sleeping. Behavioral experiments involving postponing worry are the main emphasis in this first stage of treatment. First, the therapist helps the patient to make a distinction between initial intrusive thoughts (triggers) and the subsequent worry process. Next, the patient is instructed in and practices *detached mindfulness* (Wells, 2005b; Wells & Matthews, 1994), in which the triggering thought is observed in a detached way without responding to it with extended thinking or trying to push it away or cope. The patient is then instructed that the next time he or she notices a trigger to apply detached mindfulness for homework and postpone any worrying until a specified time at the end of the day. The patient is asked to schedule a worry time, which should last about 15 minutes, and to use this only if absolutely necessary. The therapist explains how most patients do not actually use their worry time, and they tend to forget about the worry topic or it seems less important by the time the worry period arrives. This technique is presented as an experiment to test how controllable worrying really is.

In implementing this strategy, the therapist takes care to differentiate between the suppression of thought content, which is not the aim, and interruption of the Type 1 worry process which is the aim of this procedure. For example, a thought of accidents may remain in consciousness, but the aim is to suspend further conceptual processing of the idea. Normally, the therapist asks the patient for a rating of belief in uncontrollability throughout the use of these verbal and behavioral methods. In addition, the patient is asked to complete measures such as the Generalized Anxiety Disorder Scale–Revised (GADS-R) (Wells, 2009), which provides an index of a range of common negative and positive metacognitive beliefs.

In subsequent treatment sessions, experiments are run in which the patient is asked to try to lose control of a worry sequence to further challenge beliefs about uncontrollability. For instance, the therapist explains that one way to discover that worrying is not uncontrollable and cannot become that way is to try to make it uncontrollable. For homework, the patient is asked to continue with worry postponement and to actually use the postponed worry period on at least two occasions, during which time the patient should recall an earlier worry and engage in intense worry in order to try to lose control of the activity. Later the patient can then be asked to try to lose control of a worry *in situ* when it is spontaneously triggered rather than postponing the activity.

Once beliefs about uncontrollability have been challenged, the next stage in treatment focuses on modifying negative beliefs about the danger of worrying. Verbal reattribution is used to weaken such beliefs. Patients often equate worry with stress and have an oversimplistic view that stress and therefore worry are harmful. One strategy is to decouple the concepts of worry and stress. Moreover, the oversimplistic view of anxiety as a harmful agent should be challenged. For example, the therapist discusses with the patient how stress and anxiety responses are part of the individual's survival program; in fact, humans would not have functioned effectively in evolutionary terms if stress and anxiety had led to death, serious illness, or psychological breakdown. Behavioral experiments are then used in which the patient attempts to produce feared negative outcomes as a result of periodically intensifying the worry process. One patient was fearful that she could induce a mental breakdown through worrying; this was operationalized as losing touch with reality and seeing things that other people could not see (i.e., hallucinations). In the treatment session, the therapist worked with her to try to induce hallucinations by having intense periods of in-session worrying. This led to a reduction in her metacognitive belief, but she had reservations because she had not experienced much anxiety in the treatment session. The therapist asked her to repeat the worry experiment for homework during an actual anxiety-provoking worry episode. This she duly did, and her belief that worrying could lead to mental breakdown was eventually abolished.

Some patients believe that worrying is abnormal and must be a sign of psychological instability. In these instances, the process of worrying can be normalized by asking clients to conduct a mini-survey in which they ask a range of other people if they engage in worry and how frequently and if they are distressed by worrying. Often, patients are surprised to discover that other people who do not have GAD experience frequent worry and find worrying difficult to control. When patients believe that worrying can be physically harmful, the therapist normally questions the mechanism for this proposed effect and explores evidence to the contrary.

Behavioral experiments are also used; for example, a patient believed that worrying would damage her heart. The therapist proposed an experiment in which the effect of worry on heart rate was tested. First, the patient was asked to sit quietly in a chair, and her pulse rate was measured. Next, she was asked to walk briskly up a flight of stairs, and her pulse rate was taken again. Finally, after a brief period of rest she was asked to sit and worry briefly, and her pulse rate was again measured. The patient was surprised to discover, contrary to her predictions, that exercise increased her heart rate more than worry did.

Later in treatment, positive metacognitions about the need to use worrying as a means of preparation and coping are the target of therapeutic modification. Some patients are reluctant to completely abandon worry as a coping strategy; however, the therapist has a range of metacognitive treatment techniques to choose from. First, a review is undertaken of the counter-evidence for positive beliefs, which suggests that worrying does not assist coping. Second, the mechanism by which worrying improves outcomes can be explored and challenged. Next, the therapist introduces the *worry-mismatch* strategy, where the patient is invited to write, in detail, the contents of a recent worry sequence. This is followed by writing out the "reality" script, which is a description of what truly happened in the situation the patient was worried about. The worry script is compared against the reality script, with the aim of emphasizing the discrepancy. Identification of such a discrepancy allows the therapist to question how useful worrying can be when it does not accurately depict reality. *Worry modulation* experiments are also used. Here, the client is asked to increase worry on some days but decrease the frequency of worry on others while observing the effects on coping outcomes. For example, patients can be asked to determine if they cope better or perform more effectively on the days when they worry more.

Treatment normally concludes with reviewing alternative strategies for dealing with intrusions and stresses that trigger worrying. This consists of building up an alternative strategy base (i.e., new knowledge of strategies) so individuals can develop a greater range and flexibility of responses to intrusions and stress that do not necessitate engagement in the CAS. This helps the patient develop an alternative set of plans or subroutines that can be used to direct processing.

Metacognitive therapy for GAD is usually implemented in 6 to 12 sessions, each 45 to 60 minutes in duration. Specific outcome measures are used to track changes in underlying metacognitive variables and the CAS. These include the GADS-R (Wells, 2009), the Metacognitions Questionnaire 30 (MCQ-30) (Wells & Cartwright-Hatton, 2004), or the Meta-Worry Questionnaire (MWQ) (Wells, 2005a). For a comprehensive treatment manual, see Wells (2009).

A case illustration

To illustrate the course and components of treatment, a case example is presented in this section. The client, Sophie, now in her mid-30s, had a history of worry that could be traced back to her teenage years. She reported intermittent intense worry episodes lasting several months and associated with "low mood," which had been a problem for 17 years. Sophie's worry had stopped her making the most of her life, leading to a failure to pursue promotion at work and avoiding moving home or having a large family, which she regretted. She had received psychological treatment in the past consisting of counseling and had been offered drug treatment but had refused this option. Her goals for therapy were to overcome her feelings of tension, eliminate a chronic sense of impending doom, reduce her worrying and nervousness, and improve her mood.

In the first session, the therapist worked with Sophie to develop the case formulation and helped her to discover how she was of "two minds" about worrying by drawing attention to the conflict that existed between her positive beliefs (e.g., "I must worry in order to cope") and negative beliefs (e.g., "My worrying is out of control, and I will lose my mind"). The therapist asked: "How easy is it to stop worrying if you hold both beliefs?" As is often the case, this line of questioning prompted Sophie to explain that she believed that worrying was something that she could not control. This was used to continue socialization by asking the question: "If you believed you could control worry, how much of a problem would you have left?" In this way, Sophie began to see that her problem concerned what she believed about worrying. This process opened the way for shifting work firmly onto a metacognitive footing.

The therapist continued socialization by questioning further: "Where is your evidence that you have no control over your worry?" Sophie responded by stating that proof was the fact that she had a psychological problem. The therapist responded to this by introducing the idea that perhaps Sophie had been using the wrong type of control: "Perhaps the problem is that you have not been using an effective form of control. What do you think?" This was followed by exploring further how having both positive and negative beliefs about worry gave rise to conflicting motivations to engage with but also avoid worrying thoughts. A thought suppression experiment was then used to illustrate how trying not to have thoughts of a green giraffe made such thoughts more likely, and the unhelpful role of thought suppression in the patient's own case formulation was highlighted.

Next, the therapist introduced an alternative way of relating to negative thoughts that normally trigger worrying. The concept of detached mindfulness was introduced, and in-session practice using a range of tasks was implemented; for example, Sophie was asked to passively watch and observe a mental image of a tiger without influencing the behavior of the image in any way. She was then asked to apply the same experience to negative thoughts that triggered worry for homework. The therapist explained how detached mindfulness should be coupled with worry postponement as a means of testing the belief that worry was uncontrollable.

At the second session, examination of scores on the GADS-R showed that Sophie's belief in the uncontrollability of worry had decreased from 80% to 50%. The therapist questioned what the evidence was that maintained the belief at this level. Sophie explained that, although she had been consistently using worry postponement, she had not yet had a "major worry" and so she could not be certain that she had control over major concerns. A discussion followed concerning the evidence that a "major" worry should be any different from the more minor worries she had experienced. By identifying the fact that worries are the same, no matter if they are major or minor, and the only difference is the amount of anxiety associated with them, Sophie was able to weaken her belief further. However, an experiment was conducted in the session in which Sophie was asked to try to deliberately lose control of a worry by activating a recent worry topic. Initially, she believed 40% she would lose control, but by the end of the experiment it was 20%. It was agreed that she should continue with the worry postponement experiment for homework but to use at least two postponement periods, during which time she should actively try to worry and lose control of the activity.

At session four, her belief in uncontrollability was zero, so the therapist turned attention to examining and challenging negative beliefs about the danger of worrying. Two types of danger metacognitions were evident: (1) that worrying could lead to a heart attack, and (2) that it could lead to a "nervous breakdown." By this latter belief, Sophie meant that if she worried excessively she would become depressed and unable to function. The therapist used the earlier discovery that worry was controllable as evidence against the belief that worrying could be dangerous: "You have now discovered that you have always had control over worrying. What does that mean about how dangerous worry really is?" Sophie agreed that this meant that worrying was no longer the threat it used to be, but she was concerned (worried) that perhaps worry had already damaged her body or mind. The therapist took this opportunity to inquire about her physical health, such as her blood pressure, which was normal. A discussion followed of how this was inconsistent with the belief that worrying had damaged her body. However, it is important that the patient does not simply view the problem in terms of applying effective control over worrying. This can act as a form of coping that removes opportunities to discover that worrying is harmless; therefore, the therapist explored further information that worrying is harmless by linking it with the concept of anxiety. Sophie and the therapist discussed how worry can give rise to anxiety and that anxiety is associated with the release of adrenaline in the body. Furthermore, adrenaline has special survival properties. Sophie was asked if she knew what medics did in order to save someone who had suffered a heart attack. It was pointed out that adrenaline was injected into the heart muscle to help restart the heart. This observation conflicted with Sophie's view that worry and anxiety would cause damage. Following this period of verbal reattribution, an experiment was conducted in which Sophie was invited to engage in a period of 2 minutes of worrying and 2 minutes of exercise (walking up a flight of stairs). Her pulse rate was taken after each manipulation to show how exercise had a greater impact on the heart than worrying, and this allowed the therapist to pose the question: "Which one places most strain on the heart?" For homework Sophie was asked to try to lose control of worrying the next time a worry episode occurred rather than postpone the activity to test any remaining beliefs about loss of mental control. She attempted this on one occasion and reported that she had tried to worry as much as possible but this simply ended in her laughing at herself. She no longer believed that it was possible to lose control of worry.

The next couple of sessions focused on other danger-related beliefs and continued with verbal strategies and behavioral experiments. For example, to challenge the belief that worrying could lead to a depressive breakdown, the therapist asked Sophie if she had symptoms of depression (i.e., lack of energy, loss of interest, sadness more days than not, suicidal thoughts, inactivity, slowing down, lethargy) when she was intensely worried. By reviewing her responses, she discovered that rather than feeling slowed down and lethargic, she felt overactive and restless. Sophie was able to identify that her feelings of sadness occurred after she had been worried for some time, and they were associated with thinking she would never recover rather than being the direct effect of worrying. The therapist introduced the idea that it was rumination that contributed to depression rather than worry and showed how ruminations about "never recovering" could be dealt with by using the same process of detached mindfulness and postponement as had been applied to the worry process. For homework, Sophie was asked to worry while taking her usual walk (but more vigorous) to the local shops on two occasions to test whether it led to physical or psychological breakdown. After implementing this experiment on two different occasions she discovered that she became breathless, but rather than having a mental breakdown she found that her mental processes became clearer and more acute. The therapist contrasted this with Sophie's view of mental breakdown which led her to dismiss this erroneous belief about worry.

Entering the final stages of treatment, the therapeutic focus shifted onto testing the remaining positive beliefs about the need to worry. Sophie believed that "worrying helps me cope" and "it means I can avoid harm and mistakes in the future." The therapist explored the evidence supporting these beliefs, and Sophie explained that the fact that she had experienced a reasonably safe life was proof that worrying was helpful. The therapist recognized this as an opportunity to ask whether people who seemed to worry less had more negative or dangerous life events. By following this line of exploration, Sophie concluded that, contrary to her original view, those people who worry less probably do more and as a result have more rewarding lives. The therapist continually reinforced the idea that worry is not beneficial by asking such questions as "How can you know what to worry about in order to remain safe?" This was followed by the *worry-mismatch strategy*, where Sophie was asked to think about a situation that she was worried about (going on vacation for the weekend), and to write out the full worry sequence for this event. This was compared to a description of what actually happened, which was written out at the next session.

In the next session, the worry-mismatch strategy was completed, and it transpired that Sophie had experienced a pleasant and restful visit to the coast. There was a complete discrepancy between the content of the worry script and her reality script. The therapist used this to ask the question: "If your worries and realities do not agree, then how useful do you believe worrying really is?" The *worry modulation experiment* was then introduced as a task for homework. Sophie predicted that if she worried more on one day and not on another then she would make fewer mistakes on the day she worried more. What actually happened was that there was no real difference in the number of mistakes that she made.

In the remaining two sessions of treatment, the therapist worked with Sophie in writing out a therapy blueprint. This consisted of a copy of the case formulation, a list of negative and positive metacognitive beliefs and a summary statement addressing each one. For example, the belief that "My worrying is uncontrollable" was followed by the summary: "I learned that I can readily postpone worrying. I had not used the best strategy before. Even if I try to lose control, I cannot make it happen." In addition to these summaries, the blueprint consisted of a plan for dealing with worries or negative thoughts in the future. The plan consisted of detached mindfulness, worry disengagement, doing rather than thinking, banning reassurance seeking, and increasing exposure to novel situations without planning.

At the end of treatment, Sophie met formal criteria for recovery as measured by the trait–anxiety subscale and the Penn State Worry Questionnaire. She reported that she was no longer distressed by worry, and her positive and negative metacognitive beliefs measured by the Generalized Anxiety Disorder Scale (Wells, 2009) were all at zero. She maintained the treatment gains and her recovery status at 6- and 12-month follow-up.

Empirical status of MCT theory

The metacognitive model of GAD is consistent with preexisting evidence on worry and has been directly tested. Studies of nonpatients who score high in pathological worry and studies of individuals with GAD provide a good level of support for the model. The evidence can be usefully divided into that addressing four sets of theoretically derived predictions:

There should be a positive association between positive metacognitive beliefs and pathological worry. There is strong support for the idea that pathological worry is positively associated with positive metacognitive beliefs. Individuals meeting criteria for GAD give higher ratings for positive reasons for worrying than nonanxious controls (Borkovec & Roemer, 1995). These reasons include the belief that worry is useful for problem solving and superstitious ideas about the effect of worrying.

The Metacognitions Questionnaire (MCQ) has been used to directly test predicted relationships between metacognitive beliefs and pathological worry. In a study of nonpatients, vulnerability to worry was positively associated with positive beliefs about worry and negative beliefs about the uncontrollability and danger of worrying (Cartwright-Hatton & Wells, 1997). Cartwright-Hatton and Wells (1997) compared patients with DSM-III-R GAD, patients with other anxiety disorders, and nonpatient controls. The GAD patients had similar levels of positive worry beliefs as the other groups, despite the fact that worrying is seen as a significant problem by individuals suffering with this disorder.

Wells and Papageorgiou (1998a,b) tested for relationships between metacognitive beliefs and pathological worry while controlling overlaps between these variables and obsessive–compulsive symptoms. Both positive beliefs about worry and negative beliefs concerning uncontrollability and danger were associated with worry, and this relationship was unaffected by overlaps with obsessional symptoms. This study is limited because of some overlap in assessment of uncontrollability by both the worry and negative metacognition measure, but the independent relationship between worry and positive beliefs is supported.

In summary, there is reliable support for the prediction that positive metacognitive beliefs are associated with pathological worry; however, the model assigns greater importance to negative metacognitions in the development of pathological worry and GAD, and it is to data in that area that we turn next.

Negative metacognitive beliefs and meta-worry should be unique predictors of pathological worry and GAD that contribute irrespective of positive beliefs or the nature of worry itself.   The metacognitive model is unique among theoretical approaches to GAD in assigning a crucial and necessary role to negative metacognitions. Negative metacognitions in the model consist of meta-worry (Type 2 worry) and negative metacognitive beliefs about the uncontrollability and danger of worrying.

Wells and Carter (1999) examined the specific contribution to trait pathological worry of Type 2 worry (meta-worry) when Type 1 worry was controlled in a student sample. Type 2 worry was uniquely and positively associated with both pathological worry and a rating of problem level, and the relationship was independent of the frequency of Type 1 worry, trait–anxiety, and the uncontrollability of worry.

Nuevo, Montorio, and Borkovec (2004) replicated the study by Wells and Carter (1999) and extended the findings by examining relationships between meta-worry and worry severity in an elderly Spanish sample. Meta-worry consistently emerged as a positive predictor of both pathological worry and interference from worry. The relationship held even when Type 1 worry frequency, trait–anxiety, and uncontrollability of worry were statistically controlled.

Nassif (1999, study 1) tested the contribution of meta-worry to pathological worry in a Lebanese sample while controlling for Type 1 worry and trait–anxiety. The largest independent contribution to pathological worry was made by meta-worry and trait–anxiety. In a second study (Nassif, 1999), nonpatients were screened for the presence of DSM-III-R GAD. A comparison of the GAD subgroup with a non-anxious group revealed significantly higher meta-worry scores in the participants meeting criteria for GAD.

Cartwright-Hatton and Wells (1997) compared patients with DSM-III-R GAD, patients with OCD, patients with other emotional disorders, and nonpatient controls. Whereas the GAD group endorsed levels of positive beliefs about worry that were similar to the other groups, this group and the OCD group endorsed significantly higher levels of negative beliefs about worry than the mixed emotional disorder group or control group. In a later study, Wells and Carter (2001) compared patients with a DSM-III-R diagnosis of GAD against a group with panic disorder, a social phobia group, a depression group, and a group of nonpatient controls. They found no differences in the endorsement of positive beliefs about worry, but significant differences were found for negative beliefs. Patients with GAD had significantly higher beliefs in the uncontrollability and danger domain than the other groups. In the Wells and Carter study, even when differences in the frequency of Type 1 worry were controlled the group differences remained significant, suggesting that differences in negative metacognitions were not simply a function of differences in worry frequency.

Some of these earlier studies (reviewed above) tested the model in DSM-III-R-diagnosed patients before the introduction of the "uncontrollability" criterion in DSM-IV; however, uncontrollability is now part of the definition of GAD in DSM-IV. Subsequent studies have therefore focused on danger metacognitions rather than uncontrollability in testing the model in order to avoid circularity.

A study by Ruscio and Borkovec (2004) is particularly important in evaluating the specific contribution of metacognitive beliefs to GAD compared with the topological features of Type 1 worry. High worriers with and without GAD were compared on the characteristics of worry and on beliefs about worry, thus addressing the question of whether differences between groups could be attributed to differences in actual worry, in beliefs about worry, or both. The groups showed similar experiences and consequences of worry but differences in the endorsement of negative beliefs about uncontrollability and danger. These differences emerged for both uncontrollability and danger belief dimensions when measured separately.

Wells (2005) examined whether the frequency of meta-worry and strength of conviction in negative beliefs about the danger of worry predicted pathological worry and GAD among nonpatients meeting DSM-IV criteria. This study utilized the meta-worry questionnaire that was designed specifically to assess the danger domain without assessing uncontrollability. Danger-related metacognitions were positively correlated with pathological worry. Furthermore, the frequency of danger-related meta-worry significantly discriminated individuals with GAD from groups with somatic anxiety or nonanxious individuals.

These studies provide strong and reliable support for the predicted relationship between negative metacognitions and pathological worry and GAD. The findings appear to generalize to older age individuals and prove to be consistent across cultural groups. The specific relevance given to negative metacognitions in the form of meta-worry and negative beliefs in GAD is clearly supported.

Worry-based coping should have deleterious consequences, such as blocking emotional processing and self-regulation, leading to greater intrusions and stress.   Early studies of the consequences of brief induced-worry periods are consistent with the idea that worrying can be deleterious. Specifically, Borkovec, Robinson, Pruzinsky, and DePree (1983) examined the effects of 30, 15, and 0 minutes of worry in high and low worriers. During a 5-minute breathing task that followed these worry periods, high worriers reported more anxiety, more depression, less task-focused attention, and more negative thoughts than low worriers. York, Borkovec, Vasey, and Stern (1987) later showed that the induction of worry led to more thought intrusions than a neutral condition. Butler, Wells, and Dewick (1995) examined whether worrying after exposure to a stressful film influenced the frequency of intrusive thoughts about the stressor over a subsequent 3-day period. In contrast to subjects asked to "settle down" and those asked to have images of the film for a brief period afterwards, those asked to engage in a brief period of worry reported more intrusive images than the other groups over the next 3 days. Wells and Papageorgiou (1995) extended this finding by using five post-film mentation conditions: settle down, worry about the film, worry about usual concerns, distraction, and image the film. The result showed that participants who worried reported the most intrusions.

These studies support the idea that worrying can increase the frequency of negative thoughts and may interfere with emotional processing following stress; however, they have induced worry rather than examining more specifically the effects attributed to worry when it is used as a means of coping with negative thoughts. To address this issue, we can turn to studies that have used the Thought Control Questionnaire (TCQ) (Wells & Davies, 1994). The TCQ measures individual differences in the use of a range of metacognitive strategies for controlling unwanted or distressing thoughts, and one of the subscales assesses the use of worry to deal with intrusions.

Warda and Bryant (1998) compared individuals with and without acute stress disorder (ASD) after automobile accidents. Those with ASD endorsed greater use of worry and punishment to control thoughts as assessed by the TCQ. These control strategies were positively correlated with depression, anxiety, intrusive thoughts, and avoidance. Holeva, Tarrier, and Wells (2001) demonstrated that individual differences in the use of worry were positively correlated with severity of ASD symptoms in participants following automobile accidents. A growing number of other studies have found positive relationships between TCQ worry and post-traumatic stress symptoms (Roussis & Wells, 2006), obsessive–compulsive symptoms (Abramowitz, Whiteside, Kalsy, & Tolin, 2003; Amir, Cashman, & Foa, 1997), and, of course, GAD (Coles & Heimberg, 2005). Overall, the data support the hypothesis that the use of worry as a metacognitive coping strategy is associated with psychological disorder and intrusive thoughts.

Metacognitions should prolong distress and cause GAD.   Although some of the above studies, namely those that have manipulated worry, are consistent with a causal role of worry in the exacerbation of subsequent negative thoughts, some studies have sought to directly test the causal role of metacognitions. Nassif (1999, study 2) examined the longitudinal predictors of pathological worry and DSM-III-R GAD. Nonpatient participants completed measures of pathological worry, metacognition, and the presence of GAD on two occasions 12 to 15 weeks apart. Logistic regression predicting the development of GAD over this time demonstrated the following: (1) meta-worry but not frequency of Type 1 worry when both were assessed at time 1 predicted the subsequent development of GAD; and (2) negative beliefs concerning uncontrollability and danger predicted the development of GAD across time. The same effect of negative beliefs was found when outcome was assessed in terms of pathological worry levels.

Prospective data show that using worry as a metacognitive coping strategy to deal with negative thoughts following stress exposure causes trauma symptoms. Holeva, Tarrier, and Wells (2001) tested automobile accident victims on two occasions and found that individual differences in the use of worry to control thoughts were a significant predictor of the later development of posttraumatic stress disorder. Roussis and Wells (2008) examined the predictors of subsequent symptoms of traumatic stress in students who had been exposed to a stressful life event. The use of worry as a thought-control strategy positively predicted the later development of stress symptoms. Furthermore, the relationship was independent of the severity of symptom-related worry, thus presenting evidence of a unique effect of worry when used as a metacognitive coping strategy.

These data combined with the results of studies that have manipulated worry support central predictions of the metacognitive model. Worrying, even for brief periods of time, can increase thought intrusions; using worry to control thoughts may backfire and increase symptoms, particularly following stress; and negative metacognitions (meta-worry and negative beliefs) appear to be causally associated with the development of GAD and the prolongation of stress-related symptoms.

Empirical status of treatment

Our metacognition research program has progressed in a sequential fashion in which model testing has been followed by treatment development and evaluation. Naturally, it is only more recently that we have begun to examine treatment efficacy, so these data are not as abundant as data addressing theoretical predictions.

An initial single case study (Wells, 1995) using an AB design with follow-up provided some preliminary data of the effects associated with MCT. The patient treated was a 25-year-old GAD sufferer who reported a history of chronic worry dating back to early childhood. After a 2-week, no-treatment baseline measurement period, four sessions of MCT were delivered, and the patient was followed up at 3 and 6 months after treatment.

Treatment was associated with large reductions in the frequency and duration of worry and reductions in anxiety and negative metacognitions. The gains were maintained over the follow-up period.

Wells and King (2006) conducted an open trial with 10 consecutively referred patients with GAD. The age of these patients ranged from 25 to 76 years, and the duration of GAD ranged from 2 to 60 years. Half of the patients had a single diagnosis of GAD, and half had additional diagnoses, the most common being a depressive disorder. The number of treatment sessions delivered ranged from 3 to 12, each 45 to 60 minutes in duration, and patients were followed up at 6 and 12 months after treatment. Statistically significant improvements were found in all outcome measures that included anxiety, depression, trait–anxiety, and Type 1 and Type 2 worry. These gains remained significant at follow-up. The effect sizes for all outcome measures were very large. Trait–anxiety after treatment was 2.78; at 12-month follow-up it was 2.58. For meta-worry, the posttreatment effect size was 1.47; at 12-month follow-up it was 1.61. However, effect sizes do not address the clinical significance of the outcomes. The mean improvement in trait–anxiety after treatment was 19.63, and, applying the clinical significance criteria computed by Fisher and Durham (1999) for this measure, 87% of patients met criteria for recovery at posttreatment, and 75% met the criteria at follow up.

In a randomized trial, MCT was compared with applied relaxation (AR) in the treatment of patients suffering from GAD (Wells et al., in preparation). The results showed that MCT was superior to AR in producing improvements in anxiety, worry, and negative metacognitive beliefs. Effect sizes for MCT were very large, and recovery rates for MCT in an independent analysis of efficacy (Fisher, 2006) were 80% at posttreatment and 70% at 6- and 12-month follow-up as assessed by trait–anxiety. Recovery rates were 80% at posttreatment and follow-up as assessed by the Penn State Worry Questionnaire. These rates are higher than the aggregated recovery rates for previous trials of applied relaxation, cognitive therapy, or cognitive–behavioral therapy (Fisher, 2006).

In summary, these initial treatment studies show powerful effects associated with MCT, and the gains are stable and maintained over follow-up. Comparison of MCT with another effective treatment has shown that MCT is superior, and comparison of clinical effectiveness against that computed for other published studies of applied relaxation or cognitive–behavioral therapy show that MCT returns the highest recovery rates. However, further direct comparison of MCT with other effective treatments, particularly the form of CBT developed by Borkovec and colleagues (e.g., Borkovec & Costello, 1993), should be a goal of future studies to assess the consistency of these findings.

MCT *in wider context*

Although this chapter has focused on how the metacognitive theory and treatment have been developed and applied to GAD, the basic underlying MCT theory is universal, meaning that MCT is applicable to most types of disorder. The CAS has been conceptualized and treated in other anxiety and mood disorders; indeed, it is possible to specify the nature of a general treatment that could be applied irrespective of diagnosis (Wells, 2009). Metacognitive theory has been examined in the context of obsessive–compulsive symptoms (e.g., Gwilliam, Wells, & Cartwright-Hatton, 2004; Janeck, Calamari, Riemen, & Heffelfinger, 2003; Myers & Wells, 2005), posttraumatic stress (e.g., Roussis & Wells, 2006, 2008), depression (e.g., Papageorgiou & Wells, 2001, 2003), addictions (e.g., Spada & Wells, 2005; Spada, Moneta, & Wells, 2007), and psychosis (e.g., Morrison & Wells, 2003; Stirling, Barkus, & Lewis, 2007). The concepts have been extended in exploring the important domain of cognitive–affective self-knowledge associated with personality disorder (Leahy, 2002, 2003).

Treatment studies with small samples have begun to emerge that provide support for the efficacy of MCT in obsessive–compulsive disorder (Fisher & Wells, 2008; Simons, Schneider, & Herpertz-Dahlmann, 2006), mood disorder (Papageorgiou & Wells, 2000; Wells et al., 2008), and posttraumatic stress (Wells & Sembi, 2004; Wells et al., 2007).

Experimental investigations of specific metacognitive treatment techniques have shown that attention training (ATT) (Wells, 1990) and metacognitively delivered exposure (Wells, 2009) produce substantial improvements in symptoms. Attention training is associated with improvements in panic and social phobia (Wells, White, & Carter, 1997), with improvements in hypochondriasis (Papageorgiou & Wells, 1998), and with positive neurocognitive changes in depression (Siegle, Ghinassi, & Thase, 2007). Metacognitively delivered exposure has been demonstrated to be more effective than brief exposure delivered with a habituation rationale in social phobia (Wells & Papageorgiou, 1998) and in obsessive–compulsive disorder (Fisher & Wells, 2005). These data are consistent with the idea that psychological change is not simply a function of exposure but can also be rapidly achieved by using or modifying metacognition in the context of brief exposure exercises.

Conclusion

In this chapter, we have seen that metacognitions are a basis of mental control that determine the way an individual responds to negative thoughts and emotions. In the metacognitive (S-REF) theory, psychological disorder is caused by the prolongation of thinking in the form of worry/

rumination, threat monitoring, and coping behaviors that interfere with effective self-regulation and flexible control of processing. Individuals are unable to abandon brooding or conceptual processing because they lack awareness of the activity, have unhelpful metacognitive beliefs about the danger and usefulness of these processes, lack flexible executive control, or have diminished metacognitive knowledge of alternative processing styles. In this chapter, the way in which these factors play out in the pathogenesis and maintenance of GAD was described and the focus of MCT outlined.

Metacognitive theory offers a unique explanation of psychopathology that is expressed in dynamic terms in which thought processes are normally in constant flux but become maladaptively locked onto and recycle and extend certain types of information. The recycling and extension are of a particular type that is damaging for emotional recovery and for the fading of negative ideas. When these ideas relate to danger, threat, and negative self-concept, the unfortunate outcome is a deepening and persistence of negative emotions.

The treatment is one that does not tackle the content of thoughts or of worries or beliefs expressed in ordinary cognition. It modifies metacognitive beliefs, improves flexible control of thinking styles, removes prolonged thinking, and enables patients to develop a transitory relationship with their thoughts in which all ideas can be experienced as separate from the self and decoupled from the cognitive attentional syndrome. The aim of treatment is to help individuals to develop metacognitive control and metacognitive knowledge that act as general-purpose resources for dealing more adaptively with the negative ideas, stress, and challenges that everyday life presents.

References

Abramowitz, J.S., Whiteside, S., Kalsky, S.A., & Tolin, D.A. (2003). Thought control strategies in obsessive–compulsive disorder: a replication and extension. *Behaviour Research and Therapy, 41,* 529–554.

Amir, N., Cashman, L., & Foa, E.B. (1997). Strategies of thought control in obsessive–compulsive disorder. *Behaviour Research and Therapy, 35,* 775–777.

Borkovec, T.D., & Costello, E. (1993). Efficacy of applied relaxation and cognitive–behavioral therapy in the treatment of generalised anxiety disorder. *Journal of Consulting and Clinical Psychology, 61,* 611–619.

Borkovec, T.D., & Roemer, L. (1995). Perceived functions of worry among generalized anxiety subjects: Distraction from more emotional topics? *Journal of Behavior Therapy and Experimental Psychiatry, 26,* 25–30.

Borkovec, T.D., Robinson, E., Pruzinsky, T., & DePree, J.A. (1983). Preliminary exploration of worry: Some characteristics and processes. *Behaviour Research and Therapy, 21,* 9–16.

Brown, R., & McNeill, D. (1966). The "tip-of-the-tongue" phenomenon. *Journal of Verbal Learning and Verbal Behavior, 5,* 325–337.

Butler, G., Wells, A., & Dewick, H. (1995). Differential effects of worry and imagery after exposure to a stressful stimulus: A pilot study. *Behavioural and Cognitive Psychotherapy, 23,* 45–56.

Cartwright-Hatton, S., & Wells, A. (1997). Beliefs about worry and intrusions: The Meta-Cognitions Questionnaire and its correlates. *Journal of Anxiety Disorders, 11,* 279–296.

Coles, M.E., & Heimberg, R.G. (2005). Thought control strategies in generalized anxiety disorder. *Cognitive Therapy and Research, 29,* 47–56.

Fisher, P.L. (2006). The efficacy of psychological treatments for generalised anxiety disorder? In G.C.L. Davey, & A. Wells (Eds.), *Worry and its psychological disorders: Theory, assessment and treatment* (pp. 359–378). Chichester: Wiley.

Fisher, P.L., & Durham, R.C. (1999). Recovery rates in generalized anxiety disorder following psychological therapy: An analysis of clinically significant change in the STAI-T across outcome studies since 1990. *Psychological Medicine, 29,* 1425–1434.

Fisher, P.L., & Wells, A. (2005). Experimental modification of beliefs in obsessive–compulsive disorder: a test of the metacognitive model. *Behaviour Research and Therapy, 43,* 821–829.

Fisher, P.L., & Wells, A. (2008). Metacognitive therapy for obsessive–compulsive disorder: A case series. *Journal of Behavior Therapy and Experimental Psychiatry, 39,* 117–132.

Flavell, J.H. (1979). Metacognition and metacognitive monitoring: A new area of cognitive–developmental inquiry. *American Psychologist, 34,* 906–911.

Gwilliam, P., Wells, A., & Cartwright-Hatton, S. (2004). Does meta-cognition or responsibility predict obsessive–compulsive symptoms: A test of the metacognitive model. *Clinical Psychology & Psychotherapy, 11,* 137–144.

Holeva, V., Tarrier, N., & Wells, A. (2001). Prevalence and predictors of acute PTSD following road traffic accidents: Thought control strategies and social support. *Behavior Therapy, 32,* 65–83.

Janeck, A.S., Calamari, J.E., Riemann, B.C., & Heffelfinger, S.K. (2003). Too much thinking about thinking? Metacognitive differences in obsessive–compulsive disorder. *Journal of Anxiety Disorders, 17,* 181–195.

Leahy, R.L. (2002). A model of emotional schemas. *Cognitive and Behavioral Practice, 9,* 177–190.

Leahy, R.L. (2003). Emotional schemas and resistance. In R. Leahy (Ed.), *Roadblocks in cognitive–behavioral therapy* (pp. 91–115). New York: Guilford Press.

Morrison, A., & Wells, A. (2003). A comparison of metacognitions in patients with hallucinations, delusions, panic disorder, and non-patient controls. *Behaviour Research and Therapy, 41,* 251–256.

Myers, S., & Wells, A. (2005). Obsessive–compulsive symptoms: the contribution of metacognitions and responsibility. *Journal of Anxiety Disorders, 19,* 806–817.

Nassif, Y. (1999, study 1 and 2). *Predictors of pathological worry.* Unpublished M.Phil. thesis, University of Manchester, U.K.

Nelson, T.O., & Narens, L. (1990). Metamemory: A theoretical framework and some new findings. In G.H. Bower (Ed.), *The psychology of learning and motivation* (pp. 125–173). New York: Academic Press.

Nuevo, R., Montorio, I., & Borkovec, T.D. (2004). A test of the role of metaworry in the prediction of worry severity in an elderly sample. *Journal of Behavior Therapy and Experimental Psychiatry, 35,* 209–218.

Papageorgiou, C., & Wells, A. (1998). Effects of attention training in hypochondriasis: An experimental case series. *Psychological Medicine, 28,* 193–200.

Papageorgiou, C., & Wells, A. (2000). Treatment of recurrent major depression with attention training. *Cognitive and Behavioural Practice, 7,* 407–413.

Papageorgiou, C., & Wells, A. (2001). Positive beliefs about depressive rumination: Development and preliminary validation of a self-report scale. *Behavior Therapy, 32,* 13–26.

Papageorgiou, C., & Wells, A. (2003). An empirical test of a clinical metacognitive model of rumination and depression. *Cognitive Therapy and Research, 27,* 261–273.

Rachman, S. (1993). Obsessions, responsibility and guilt. *Behaviour Research and Therapy, 31,* 149–154.

Roussis, P., & Wells, A. (2006). Post-traumatic stress symptoms: Tests of relationships with thought control strategies and beliefs as predicted by the metacognitive model. *Personality and Individual Differences, 40,* 111–122.

Roussis, P., & Wells, A. (2008). Psychological factors predicting stress symptoms: Metacognition, thought control and varieties of worry. *Anxiety, Stress and Coping, 21,* 213–225.

Ruscio, A.M., & Borkovec, T.D. (2004). Experience and appraisal of worry among high worriers with and without generalized anxiety disorder. *Behaviour Research and Therapy, 42,* 1469–1482.

Siegle, G.J., Ghinassi, F., & Thase, M.E. (2007). Neurobehavioral therapies in the 21st century: Summary of an emerging field and an extended example of cognitive control training for depression. *Cognitive Therapy and Research, 31,* 235–262.

Simons, M., Schneider, S., & Herpertz-Dahlmann, B. (2006). Metacognitive therapy versus exposure and response prevention for pediatric obsessive–compulsive disorder. *Psychotherapy and Psychosomatics, 75,* 257–264.

Spada, M.M., & Wells, A. (2005). Metacognitions, emotion and alcohol use. *Clinical Psychology and Psychotherapy, 12,* 150–155.

Spada, M.M., Moneta, G.B., & Wells, A. (2007). The relative contribution of metacognitive beliefs and alcohol expectancies to drinking behaviour. *Alcohol and Alcoholism, 42,* 567–574.

Stirling, J., Barkus, E., & Lewis, S. (2007). Hallucination proneness, schizotypy and meta-cognition. *Behaviour Research and Therapy, 45,* 1401–1408.

Tallis, F., Davey, G.C.L., & Capuzzo, N. (1994). The phenomenology of non-pathological worry: A preliminary investigation. In G.C.L. Davey & F. Tallis (Eds.), *Worrying: Perspectives on theory, assessment and treatment* (pp. 61–89). Chichester: John Wiley & Sons.

Warda, G., & Bryant, R.A. (1998). Cognitive bias in acute stress disorder. *Behaviour Research and Therapy, 36,* 1177–1183.

Wegner, D.M. (1997). When the antidote is the poison: ironic mental control processes. *Psychological Science, 8,* 148–150.

Wegner, D.M., Schneider, D.J., Carter, S.R., & White, T.L. (1987). Paradoxical effects of thought suppression. *Journal of Personality and Social Psychology, 53,* 5–13.

Wells, A. (1990). Panic disorder in association with relaxation induced anxiety: An attention training approach to treatment. *Behaviour Therapy, 21*, 273–280.

Wells, A. (1995). Meta-cognition and worry: A cognitive model of generalised anxiety disorder. *Behavioural and Cognitive Psychotherapy, 23*, 301–320.

Wells, A. (1997). *Cognitive therapy of anxiety disorders: A practice manual and conceptual guide.* Chichester: John Wiley & Sons.

Wells, A. (2000). *Emotional disorders and metacognition: Innovative cognitive therapy.* Chichester: John Wiley & Sons.

Wells, A. (2005a). The metacognitive model of GAD: Assessment of meta-worry and relationship with DSM-IV generalized anxiety disorder. *Cognitive Therapy and Research, 29*, 107–121.

Wells, A. (2005b). Detached mindfulness in cognitive therapy: A metacognitive analysis and ten techniques. *Journal of Rational–Emotive & Cognitive–Behavior Therapy, 23*, 337–355.

Wells, A. (2009). *Metacognitive therapy for anxiety and depression.* New York: Guilford Press.

Wells, A., & Carter, K. (1999). Preliminary tests of a cognitive model of generalised anxiety disorder. *Behaviour Research and Therapy, 37*, 585–594.

Wells, A., & Carter, K. (2001). Further tests of a cognitive model of generalized anxiety disorder: Metacognitions and worry in GAD, panic disorder, social phobia, depression, and nonpatients. *Behavior Therapy, 32*, 85–102.

Wells, A., & Cartwright-Hatton, S. (2004). A short form of the metacognitions questionnaire: properties of the MCQ 30. *Behaviour Research and Therapy, 42*, 385–396.

Wells, A., & Davies, M. (1994). The thought control questionnaire: A measure of individual differences in the control of unwanted thought. *Behaviour Research and Therapy, 32*, 871–878.

Wells, A., & King, P. (2006). Metacognitive therapy for generalized anxiety disorder: An open trial. *Journal of Behavior Therapy and Experimental Psychiatry, 37*, 206–212.

Wells, A., & Matthews, G. (1994). *Attention and emotion: A clinical perspective.* Hove, U.K.: Psychology Press.

Wells, A., & Matthews, G. (1996). Modelling cognition in emotional disorder: The S-REF model. *Behaviour Research and Therapy, 32*, 867–870.

Wells, A., & Papageorgiou, C. (1995). Worry and the incubation of intrusive images following stress. *Behaviour Research and Therapy, 33*, 579–583.

Wells, A., & Papageorgiou, C. (1998a). Social phobia: Effects of external attention focus on anxiety, negative beliefs and perspective taking. *Behavior Therapy, 29*, 357–370.

Wells, A., & Papageorgiou, C. (1998b). Relationships between worry, obsessive–compulsive symptoms, and meta-cognitive beliefs. *Behaviour Research and Therapy, 39*, 899–913.

Wells, A., & Sembi, S. (2004). Metacognitive therapy for PTSD: A preliminary investigation of a new brief treatment. *Journal of Behavior Therapy and Experimental Psychiatry, 35*, 307–318.

Wells, A., Fisher, P.L., Myers, S., Wheatley, J., Patel, T., & Brewin, C. (2008). Metacognitive therapy in recurrent and persistent depression: A multiple-baseline study of a new treatment. *Cognitive Therapy and Research*, doi: 10.1007/s10608-007-9178-2.

chapter two

Specialized cognitive behavior therapy for treatment resistant obsessive compulsive disorder

Debbie Sookman
McGill University
Montreal, Quebec, Canada

Gail Steketee
Boston University
Boston, Massachusetts

Contents

Introduction

Obsessive compulsive disorder (OCD) is a heterogeneous, frequently incapacitating disorder that is distinct from other anxiety disorders in terms
of psychopathology and treatment requirements (Frost & Steketee, 2002).
Cognitive behavior therapy (CBT), with the essential interventions of
exposure and response prevention (ERP), is the empirically established
psychotherapy of choice (American Psychiatric Association, 2007). Several
controlled studies have found that CBT combined with pharmacological
treatment is no more effective than CBT alone for OCD symptoms (Foa
et al., 2005; O'Connor et al., 2006; Rufer, Grothusen, Mab, Peter, & Hand,
2005). Improvement is more sustained with ERP compared with medication, and adding ERP to medication substantially improves response rate
and reduces susceptibility to relapse compared with medication alone
(Kordan et al., 2005; Simpson, Franklin, Cheng, Foa, & Liebowitz, 2005;
Simpson et al., 2008). Indications for combined treatment include presence
of severe comorbid mood disorder or other disorders or symptoms that
require medication (e.g., Hohagen et al., 1998). Thus, it can be concluded
from available empirical evidence that the first-line treatment of choice
for OCD is CBT and that pharmacotherapy, where indicated, should be
administered in combination with CBT for optimal and sustained results.
Unfortunately, many individuals with OCD do not receive CBT (Goodwin,
Koenen, Hellman, Guardino, & Struening, 2002), and fewer still receive
specialized CBT for OCD delivered or supervised by a therapist experienced with this disorder.

An important advance by experts in this field is the development of
specialized approaches for symptom subtypes (for discussion of these
approaches, see Abramowitz, McKay, & Taylor, 2008; Antony, Purdon, &
Summerfeldt, 2007; Sookman, Abramowitz, Calamari, Wilhelm, & McKay,
2005). There is a lag between development of these innovative approaches
and methodologically adequate controlled outcome studies to examine
their efficacy. Based on available controlled studies, approximately 50% of
patients do not respond optimally to CBT even when combined with pharmacotherapy. This includes patients who refuse to participate or drop out
of ERP (20%), do not improve (25%), or have relapsed at follow-up (Baer &
Minichiello, 1998; Cottraux, Bouvard, & Milliery, 2005; Stanley & Turner,
1995). In the few studies where this is reported, only one quarter recover
completely (Eddy, Dutra, Bradley, & Westen, 2004). This is in part due to
many patients being unwilling or unable to collaborate fully with ERP
(Araujo, Ito, & Marks, 1996; Whittal, Thordarson, & McLean, 2005) and to
other patient characteristics, but importantly also to the process and content of CBT administered. Because residual symptoms confer susceptibility to symptom exacerbation and chronic OCD, even at subclinical levels,

is commonly associated with long-term psychosocial impairment and secondary depression, it is important to maximize symptomatic improvement in OCD symptoms.

Given that our aim, whenever possible, is remission at posttreatment and long-term maintenance of improvement, we are far from our goal for many patients. We have proposed the following criteria for CBT resistance in OCD (Sookman & Steketee, 2007, p. 6):

1. The patient does not participate fully in exposure so some avoidance remains.
2. The patient does not engage in and/or sustain complete response prevention during or between sessions.
3. Residual behavioral or cognitive rituals persist.
4. Symptom-related pathology such as beliefs (and/or strategic processing) are not resolved to within normal limits.

Limited response may be due to inadequate administration of empirically based interventions, use of inflexible manualized treatment protocols in research trials that do not allow for individualized CBT delivery, and patient characteristics that complicate treatment, especially in the face of insufficient clinical research to guide the clinician.

This chapter has the following aims: (1) to describe several factors that commonly contribute to resistance during CBT for OCD subtypes; (2) to further describe and illustrate two approaches developed for resistant patients; and (3) to propose an operational definition of intervention and response criteria for CBT resistant OCD. With regard to approaches for resistant patients, we first describe cognitive therapy (CT) modules with promising results that are designed to address specific classes of characteristic dysfunctional beliefs (Wilhelm & Steketee, 2006; Wilhelm et al., 2005). Importantly, this approach may improve participation and response to ERP. We outline and illustrate this approach and discuss available outcome data. Second, we describe the integrative schema-based theoretical model and intervention approach developed by Sookman and colleagues for resistant OCD of different subtypes and present available outcome data. In the final section, intervention and response criteria for CBT resistance are proposed and indications for future research discussed.

In the next section, we briefly discuss selected CBT outcome literature to provide an empirical frame for our discussion of treatment resistance. Key theoretical models that led to empirically validated CBT approaches for OCD developed by Salkovskis, Rachman, Freeston, and the Obsessive Compulsive Cognitions Working Group (OCCWG) have been reviewed extensively elsewhere (e.g., Clark, 2004; Taylor, Abramowitz, & McKay, 2007). Additional review and discussion of recent developments in CBT interventions for OCD subtypes are also available (see Abramowitz, 2006; Abramowitz et al., 2008; Antony et al., 2007; Clark, 2004; Sookman & Pinard, 2007; Sookman & Steketee, 2007).

Outcome literature relevant to treatment resistance

An OCD patient cannot be considered CBT resistant unless an adequate trial of empirically based CBT has been attempted. However, expert consensus regarding criteria for an adequate trial of ERP and cognitive therapy does not currently exist. Review of available outcome literature indicates heterogeneity in procedural variants; for example, exposure sessions range in duration from 30 to 120 minutes at a frequency of 1 to 5 sessions weekly (Abramowitz, 2006). Research provides clinicians with crucial guidelines about optimal administration of CBT, but many findings require replication or extension to additional OCD samples and to specialized subtypes. In a meta-analysis of treatment outcome studies at that time, Abramowitz (1996, 1997) reported that best results with ERP involved prolonged (90-minute) sessions several times weekly, frequent homework, therapist-assisted exposure, and complete response prevention. Although self-directed exposure can be helpful in some cases (e.g., Fritzler, Hecker, & Losee, 1997), Tolin et al. (2007) also reported that patients receiving therapist-assisted ERP showed superior response in terms of OCD symptoms and functional impairment. Fading of therapist involvement is considered important for maintenance and generalization of improvement. Imagined exposure may be helpful for some cases in reducing anxiety and facilitating preparatory coping in combination with *in vivo* ERP (Foa & Franklin, 2003). Like rituals that reduce discomfort and interfere with habituation, reassurance seeking during ERP has been found to interfere with improvement (Abramowitz, Franklin, & Cahill, 2003). Several authors (e.g., Foa et al., 2005) advocate that clinicians expose patients to the most anxiety-provoking stimuli by mid-treatment to allow sufficient practice and generalization. Others have suggested that complete response prevention may be too rigid for some individuals (Abramowitz et al., 2003). Graduated exposure is usually undertaken first as a more tolerable method for confronting feared situations (Abramowitz, 1996); however, intensive exposure, or flooding, may be optimal for some patients (Fontenelle et al., 2000), as described in one of our case illustrations below. Therapist modeling during ERP can be useful in some cases where this does not constitute inappropriate reassurance (Steketee, 1993).

Studies on spacing of ERP sessions have varied in results, based on divergent samples, intervention characteristics, and response criteria. Fifteen 90-minute treatment sessions administered daily for approximately 3 weeks (Franklin, Abramowitz, Kozak, Levitt, & Foa, 2000) were reported to be as effective at 3 months' follow-up as 8 weeks of twice-weekly therapy (Abramowitz et al., 2003); however, neither regimen is sufficient for recovery in many cases. For some patients, the effect of office-based ERP was comparable to ERP administered in patients' naturalistic environments (Rowa, Antony, Summerfeldt, Purdon, & Swinson, 2004). In interpreting these results it is important to underline that efficacy likely depends on the extent to which ERP to salient feared stimuli can be reproduced in the office and on the patient's capacity to engage in ERP homework alone between sessions (Sookman & Steketee, 2007). Benefit in clinical practice settings can be approximately equivalent to outcomes from well-executed clinical trials for some cases (Franklin et al., 2000), but the question of replicability and variability across sites remains.

Several studies have demonstrated the efficacy of both ERP and CT in reducing symptoms and beliefs (e.g., Cottraux et al., 2001; Emmelkamp, van Oppen, & van Balkom, 2002; McLean et al., 2001). Cognitive therapy developed for obsessions (Freeston et al., 1997; Rachman, 2003) involves helping the patient to identify and modify appraisals, emotional responses, and information processing in response to intrusions perceived as threatening (e.g., hypervigilance, selective attention). Some studies found that individual CBT results in greater improvement than group treatment methods (Eddy et al., 2004). Others reported that ERP is equally effective when carried out in an individual versus group format, but that cognitive therapy is more effective when administered individually (McLean et al. 2001; Whittal et al., 2005).

Methodological factors such as overlap of therapeutic ingredients, targets and amount of CT administered, and limited sample size contribute to difficulty in assessing to what extent cognitive therapy significantly adds to the efficacy of ERP (Abramowitz, 2006; Vogel, Stiles, & Götestam, 2004; Wilhelm & Steketee, 2006). Nonetheless, there is considerable support for combining CT with ERP for OCD. Dropout rates have been reported to be lower in CBT that includes cognitive methods (Foa et al., 2005). Individuals with OCD report varied emotional responses in addition to anxiety, and complex metacognitive dysfunction, that may be difficult to ameliorate with exposure alone (Foa & McNally, 1996). Fisher and Wells (2005) reported that explicitly challenging beliefs about the threatening meaning of intrusions with behavioral experiments was more effective in reducing dysfunctional beliefs, urges to ritualize, and anxiety compared with ERP administered with a habituation rationale. OCD patients reported high levels of "cognitive self-consciousness," higher than for generalized anxiety disorder (GAD) patients (Cartwright-Hatton & Wells, 1997). Gwilliam, Wells, and Cartwright-Hatton (2004) found that metacognitive beliefs predicted OC symptoms, while responsibility beliefs did not when their interrelationship was controlled.

The recommended practice by many, if not most, experts is combined CT and ERP from the onset as a first-line treatment (Sookman & Steketee, 2007). More research is needed to clarify which patients benefit most from CT combined with behavioral experiments and/or ERP. As elaborated in the approaches we present in this chapter, in our view cognitive therapy is beneficial for most patients throughout treatment.

Studies on patient characteristics that impact outcome have provided mixed results. In some studies type and severity of OCD symptoms, degree of insight, and comorbid disorders such as severe depression predicted outcome, but in others this was not the case (Foa, Abramowitz, Franklin, & Kozak, 1999; Himle, Van Etten, Janeck, & Fischer, 2006; Mataix-Cols, Marks, Greist, Kobak, & Baer, 2002; Steketee, Chambless, & Tran, 2001). Patients with hoarding tend to report limited distress and recognition of the problem (Steketee & Frost, 2003) and have consistently responded less well to CBT approaches developed for other OCD symptoms (e.g., Abramowitz et al., 2003; Mataix-Cols et al., 2002). A specialized approach developed for this subtype has shown promising results (Steketee, Frost, Wincze, Greene, & Douglass, 2000; Steketee et al., in prep.; Tolin, Frost, & Steketee, 2007). Further research is also required for patients with symptoms of symmetry, exactness, ordering, repeating, counting, and slowness who have been under-represented in treatment trials (Ball, Baer, & Otto, 1996) relative to their estimated prevalence (Calamari et al., 2004). Relevant to family involvement in CBT is the important finding that expressed hostility from family was associated with a greater rate of dropout and poorer response among treatment completers (Chambless & Steketee, 1999). In another study, patients who reported feeling more upset by relatives' criticism reported greater discomfort during exposure and higher daily ratings of anxiety and depression (Steketee, Lam, Chambless, Rodebaugh, & McCullouch, 2007).

Relatively few approaches have been developed for resistant OCD, and, as addressed later in this chapter, a clear definition for CBT resistance in OCD does not currently exist. In describing their St. Louis model, Van Dyke and Pollard (2005) and Pollard (2007) indicated that reasons for nonresponse to CBT include inadequacies of administration of CBT and/ or the presence of treatment-interfering behaviors (TIBs). TIBs are assessed during interview and on their Treatment-Interfering Behavior Checklist (VanDyke & Pollard, 2005). These are defined as "any behavior the therapist believes is incompatible with effective participation in therapy or the pursuit of recovery" (Pollard, 2007). Their "readiness therapy" addresses beliefs, emotional disregulation, skills deficits, and incentive/motivation deficits that may interfere with collaboration in ERP. The St. Louis model involves intensive CBT outpatient treatment that includes 2 hours of daily therapist-assisted ERP and two or three additional individual sessions weekly for other interventions (e.g., cognitive restructuring, pharmaco-therapy). Gradual fading of therapist involvement and relapse prevention are additional components. Meetings with family members are offered for some cases. In a preliminary report, readiness treatment was success-ful in reducing TIBs in 7 of 11 treatment resistant OCD patients (Van Dyke & Pollard, 2005); however, controlled studies have not been done yet.

Stewart, Stack, Farrell, Pauls, and Jenike (2005) reported the efficacy of inpatient residential treatment (IRT) in a sample of 403 patients with severe OCD who had not responded to outpatient treatment. CBT was adminis-tered intensively for 2 to 4 hours daily and combined with pharmacother-apy. Length of hospitalization averaged 66 days, indicating that the typical patients received approximately 200 hours of therapy. Mean Yale–Brown Obsessive Compulsive Scale (Y-BOCS) scores for these severely ill patients reduced from 26.6 to 18.6. A very important recommendation made by these authors, with which we agree, is that up to 3 months of IRT should be administered before considering an OCD patient treatment refractory. Osgood-Hynes, Riemann, and Björgvinsson (2003) reported that follow-ing an average duration of 46 to 65 days of IRTs in two different settings, mean Y-BOCS scores for their inpatients reduced by approximately half (47% to 55%). These results indicate that intensive inpatient CBT can be an effective strategy for some patients whose symptoms have not responded to outpatient therapy. We would expect this to be the case for patients whose rituals do not take place exclusively in their home, although CBT should also be administered in their naturalistic environments.

Compliance with specialized ERP for OCD

A crucial clinical and research question is how to optimize participation in and emotionally meaningful learning during ERP, CT, and behavioral experiments. The heterogeneity of internal and situational stimuli associ-ated with OCD symptoms underlines the need for conceptual and inter-vention models that can be tailored flexibly to the idiosyncratic experience of each patient. As Sookman and Pinard (2007, p. 98) noted:

> Similar OCD symptoms have different functions for different patients (e.g., washing to prevent feared illness as opposed to reduce feelings of disgust). Symptom-related beliefs differ across symptom subtypes. For example, responsibility appraisals (Salkovskis, 1985) are characteristic of checkers with harm-related obsessions but are not charac-teristic of washers who describe "feeling" contami-nated (OCCWG, 2001). Catastrophic misappraisal of

thoughts as dangerous, specifically those viewed
as contrary to one's value system (Rachman, 1998),
with efforts at thought control (Clark, 2004), are central for many patients with obsessions. However,
this aspect of psychopathology is not reported
by other subtypes (e.g., some washers, hoarders).
Thought–action fusion is experienced by some
checkers (e.g., "If I have the thought death, a family member will die"), but not by others (e.g., "If I
don't check my stove properly, my house will burn
down"). Individuals concerned with symmetry or
order may report feeling a need for perfection, or
rather that their symptoms are associated with a
sense of incompleteness or "not just right" experiences (Coles, Frost, Heimberg, & Rhéaume, 2003).

Some patients do not endorse beliefs on available cognitive scales at
dysfunctional levels (Calamari et al., 2006; Taylor et al., 2007). As noted
above, this subgroup may report that their symptoms are related to "not
just right" experiences, feelings of incompleteness, or intolerance of distress without apparent feared consequences except their fear that distress
will not abate (Coles et al., 2005; Summerfeldt, 2004, 2007). Thus, symptom
subtypes should be treated with specialized approaches that target their
diverse cognitive content, themes underlying rituals, feared consequences,
and distressing experience. In fact, complex combinations of symptoms
are a common presentation.

Meanings of and reasons for resistance to cognitive therapy and ERP

Integral to ERP is the basic requirement that each individual experience,
rather than avoid, feared intrusions, emotions, and external stimuli that
provoke distressing inner experience. We summarize below some (over-
lapping) areas or reasons for resistance that in our experience are commonly reported by patients who have difficulty benefiting from cognitive
therapy and participating in ERP. In the sections that follow, we discuss
and illustrate two approaches developed to improve the response of resistant OCD subtypes.

1. The patient is reluctant to disclose content of some obsessions
   (Rachman, 2007) because of fear of being judged or perceived as
   crazy or dangerous. For example: "*If I tell the therapist I have thoughts*

of molesting children (running over bodies, poisoning my dog, forging checks, yelling obscenities in Sunday school, etc.), the therapist might think I am a child molester (or other awful label) and that I might actually do it one day. Maybe it would have to be reported, and my life will be ruined."

2. The patient's model of therapy and process of change includes the belief that talking can sufficiently change thoughts and feelings to the extent that facing feared events without ritualizing would not provoke strong distressing feelings. If this is possible, why face emotional pain perceived as highly distressing or intolerable?

3. The patient fears that intrusions, images, or other experience such as sense of incompleteness or "not just right" will worsen or persist if rituals are not performed. The patient also fears that symptoms will interfere with basic functioning or that these will be experienced as intolerably distressing.

4. The patient fears experiencing, or is unwilling to experience, strong feelings of fear, anxiety, and other emotions (e.g., guilt, disgust) that ERP would provoke, with resultant persistence of risk aversion. These responses may persist despite provision of emotion-management strategies, offer of therapist-assisted ERP, education about the essential role of facing feelings and the high probability distress will subside faster than anticipated, and CT for dysfunctional beliefs associated with distress. For example: *"Strong feelings are dangerous and will never go down. I could go crazy."* (See also Sookman et al., 1994; Sookman & Pinard, 1999; Sookman & Steketee, 2007; Leahy, 2002, 2007; Leahy, this volume.)

5. A strong discrepancy persists between beliefs experienced on "quiet reflection" or reported on cognitive scales and beliefs experienced during exposure to feared situations that interfere with full collaboration during ERP. For example: *"I don't believe it's true, but I feel it's true"* (Sookman & Pinard, 1999).

6. The patient has poor insight or overvalued ideas that are intransigent to disconfirmation in CT. These beliefs are strongly endorsed even when the individual is not in distress and removed from feared situations. In these cases, there is little discrepancy between cognitive and emotional aspects of belief.

7. The patient feels unwilling, or unable, to accept the perceived risks (e.g., *complete loss of control, irreversible spread of contamination, fatal illness, preventable harm to others, future calamity, eternal damnation*) of not engaging in rituals or other safety behaviors. The patient may agree to ritual abbreviation, restriction, or response delay (Schwartz, 1996) but refuses complete ERP.

8. The patient has perceived and/or actual skills deficits with respect to inner and external events. Examples are difficulties with emotional tolerance and regulation, and dysfunctional appraisals of emotional experience. Rituals have become a central cognitive and emotion-relieving strategy with few, if any, perceived alternatives.
9. The patient goes through the motions of engaging partially in ERP without substantial change in emotional responses, dysfunctional beliefs, or strategic processing of internal and external events.
10. The patient is unable to tolerate reduction in therapist time, and treatment gains fail to generalize to other non-treatment settings. There is difficulty with therapist fading and generalization of treatment gains.
11. Intrafamilial and interpersonal problems interfere with treatment.
12. Dysfunctional appraisals and strategic processing, urges to ritualize, and ritualization recur following discontinuation of therapy.
13. The therapist hypothesizes that core schemas may be interfering with emotionally meaningful accommodation to new experience (Piaget, 1960).

Applying CT without formal ERP

Description of CT methods

In their treatment manual, Wilhelm and Steketee (2006) describe a form of Beckian cognitive therapy for OCD that does not include prolonged exposure or restrictions of rituals but uses a variety of cognitive strategies and behavioral experiments to help patients test their (faulty) hypotheses. Treatment is delivered to outpatients via 22 weekly sessions with fading of therapist involvement in the final month to once every 2 weeks. CT begins with an assessment of the patient's OCD symptoms using a variety of measures to help clarify the subtypes (e.g., contamination/washing/cleaning, fears of harm and checking). Beliefs are assessed using an extended version of the 87-item Obsessive Beliefs Questionnaire (OBQ) (OCCWG, 1997, 2007) to identify six theoretically derived subscales and two additional ones on fear of positive experiences and consequences of anxiety; high scores on subscales help identify CT modules needed in treatment. Beliefs are also assessed using a simple five-column thought record form that inquires about situational context, the actual intrusion (obsessive thought), interpretation made and strength of belief, emotion experienced and its strength, and compulsive or avoidance behavior. This recording method was adapted from Beckian CT methods, where it is commonly used.

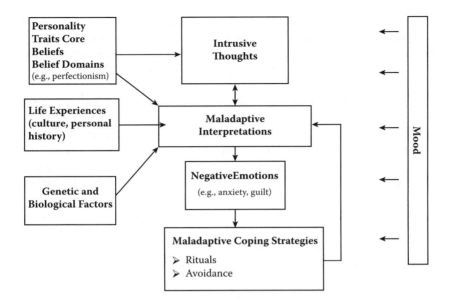

Figure 2.1 Cognitive model of OCD. (From *Cognitive Therapy for Obsessive–Compulsive Disorder: A Guide for Professionals,* by S. Wilhelm and G.S. Steketee, 2006, Oakland, CA: New Harbinger Publications. Reprinted with permission.)

Treatment begins with the therapist interviewing the patient to understand OCD symptoms, related problems, history, and current thinking in obsessive trigger situations. Education follows in which the therapist describes obsessions as ordinary intrusions that are common in the population but have now become triggers for adverse (mis)interpretations. The therapist also provides written material on OCD and the CT model. The therapist and patient develop a shared model for understanding how intrusions are interpreted, their effect on emotional and behavioral responses, and how this sequence negatively reinforces rituals and avoidance behavior. The two also examine how the patient's early experiences, general mood, and core beliefs contribute to misinterpretation (misappraisal) of the meaning of the intrusive thoughts. However, the contribution of core beliefs is not so heavily emphasized in this method as in the schema-based treatment described after this section. A generic model is reproduced in Figure 2.1, and a blank form of this model is used to guide patients to examine specific obsessive situations in light of the CT model for OCD.

The therapist selects CT modules based on the patient's main obsessive concerns as identified from the OBQ, from thought records, and from the therapist's discussions of specific OCD situations during initial sessions and development of the patient's CT model. The treatment modules cover over-importance and control of thoughts, over-estimation of threat or harm, inflated responsibility, perfectionism, and need for certainty, as well as less common concerns of managing high anxiety and fears of positive experiences.

Cognitive strategies within each module are aimed at evaluating and correcting erroneous interpretations and beliefs pertinent to that topic. Patients begin by learning basic techniques such as identifying their own cognitive errors (J. Beck, 1995). Therapists employ the downward arrow method to help patients identify their most feared consequences and possible core beliefs (which are usually addressed later in treatment). Socratic questioning is used throughout treatment to help patients examine the evidence that supports or fails to support their interpretations. As van Oppen et al. (1995) recommended, therapists do not challenge the intrusions themselves (for example, whether or not a stove is on or an item is contaminated) but instead examine only the associated appraisal (such as whether the client is truly careless and the likely effect of carelessness). Therapists commonly employ behavioral experiments to test patients' beliefs and alter their conclusions. These experiments are typically brief and used to test hypotheses rather than habituate anxiety as in ERP methods. In addition to these basic methods, patients who overestimate danger are taught to calculate the probability of harm and those who exaggerate their responsibility learn a pie technique to parcel out all sources of responsibility to the appropriate sources. Mindfulness skills help patients tolerate discomfort and intrusive thoughts; metaphors, stories, and the courtroom technique engage patients in considering perspectives that are different from their own. The therapy manual by Wilhelm and Steketee (2006) provides detailed instructions and forms for conducting this cognitive therapy.

Evidence for success of CT methods

Wilhelm and colleagues (2005) published a case series of their initial pilot findings for CT methods described above with 15 participants; of these patients, 10 had no prior behavioral therapy, and 5 had previous exposure treatment but did not benefit adequately. The full sample of 15 patients showed a 42% decline in OCD symptoms (Y-BOCS, 23.3 at pretest to 13.5 after CT) and 41% reduction in depression. However, the ERP naïve patients' OCD symptoms improved more than the previously treated patients (53% vs. 21%), and the former group also benefited more on beliefs (28% vs. 12%). Certainly the previously treated subgroup had more severe anxiety, depression, and OC beliefs which could account for their poorer outcome, and the findings derive from a very small sample and require cautious interpretation. Nonetheless, it was not clear that previously treatment-refractory patients, at least those receiving ERP, would benefit adequately from CT alone without formal ERP added. A further problem was the relatively brief 14-session treatment delivered in this pilot study. In fact, two of the previously treated sample thought they would have benefited with more sessions. Thus, in a second wait-list controlled study, the CT dosage was increased to 22 sessions which provided more benefit overall.

In a second trial, Wilhelm et al. (2008) compared a wait-list control condition to CT that employed more cognitive techniques and behavioral experiments (but, again, no formal ERP). Findings for 15 patients in each group showed much stronger performance by CT over wait-list in which patients' symptoms did not change. The longer CT in this study produced even better results, with OCD symptoms reduced by an average of 57% across all completers (Y-BOCS, 25.6 pretest to 11.5 after treatment); depressed mood also reduced. Unfortunately, the OCD patients in this study were not considered treatment refractory, so it is impossible to know how well CT would perform for treatment resistant cases.

One concern with regard to treatment resistance that we have raised earlier is that ERP may be rejected by up to 25% of patients as simply too difficult to tolerate (Riggs & Foa, 1993). Interestingly, when we surveyed 15 clinic applicants with OCD who requested psychological treatment from Dr. Wilhelm's OCD clinic, 87% (all but 2) stated that they preferred to enter CT over ERP. Further, dropout rates from our CT studies were low (about 10 to 15%), consistent with other studies that have tested CT for OCD symptoms (e.g., van Oppen et al., 1995). Thus, this CT method may be less stressful to patients, even severe ones, and more acceptable than ERP, leading more patients to choose this method and continue in treatment.

Perhaps the behavioral experiments that test patients' hypotheses make CT less threatening and more acceptable to some patients than the prolonged exposures and ritual blocking from the beginning of therapy. In this CT method, patients draw conclusions about their (mis)interpretations of their intrusive thoughts in light of the evidence and in so doing are encouraged to put these new conclusions into practice. Inevitably, this means stopping avoidance behaviors and rituals, a critical reduction in symptoms that comes about as a logical follow to new understanding of the contexts in which obsessions have occurred in the past. Intrusive thoughts gradually decline as well. Thus, CT with behavioral experiments may accomplish the goal of symptom reduction via an alternative avenue. We also find that CT can be less stressful on the therapist, but it is equally clear that much practice and skill in applying this method are essential as therapists must think on their feet to stay abreast of the patients' obsessive thinking and "yes, but ..." interjections.

It is not yet clear which types of patients may benefit most from the type of CT employed here. Certainly, this will require studies with larger sample sizes than are available currently. Like van Oppen et al. (1995), we suspect that CT will be especially effective for patients whose intrusions trigger concerns about over-importance of thoughts, responsibility, and perfectionism that trigger checking behaviors. We are less sanguine about the benefits of CT over ERP for patients with washing rituals, especially as our research combining outcome data from nine different sites suggested that CT most benefitted patients who did not have contamination or washing fears (Wilhelm, Steketee, & Yovel, 2004).

In examining subtypes, CT may also be beneficial for patients with mental but not behavioral rituals. Having primary obsessive thoughts has usually predicted worse outcomes (e.g., Mataix-Cols et al., 2002), and exposures and ritual blocking methods are harder to design for these patients. In fact, Freeston and colleagues (1997) obtained excellent results using CT and loop-tape exposures in conjunction with ERP methods for these difficult-to-treat patients, suggesting that CT may enhance exposure effects for patients with this subtype. We also find that the CT method works well for patients with religious, sexual, and harming obsessions (Wilhelm et al., 2008). With many studies now conducted (for review, see Antony et al., 2007), CT must be considered an appropriate alternative to ERP for many patients with OCD symptoms and concurrent depressive symptoms. Whether it is a remedy needed for ERP treatment-refractory patients is unclear at this time.

A schema-based model

Sookman and colleagues developed and elaborated a schema-based conceptual model and treatment approach for OCD of different subtypes (Sookman & Pinard, 1999, 2007; Sookman, Pinard, & Beauchemin, 1994; Sookman, Pinard, & A.T. Beck, 2001). Schema-based interventions expand upon standard CT methods described above and are intended to facilitate ERP, improve generalization and maintenance of change, and reduce relapse rates. The methods are combined with Beckian cognitive therapy to change problematic beliefs and reduce anxiety, concurrent ERP and behavioral experiments to reduce rituals, and other techniques to improve learning and train new skills. This approach stems from the hypothesis that dysfunctional schemas may interfere with adaptive learning from potentially disconfirmatory experience (Rosen, 1989). Core beliefs such as "I am a vulnerable or dangerous person" influence appraisals of thoughts and other strategic processing of internal and external events. Such schemas may underlie beliefs about threat (Sookman & Pinard, 2002), render these intransigent, and contribute to difficulty engaging fully in ERP and other

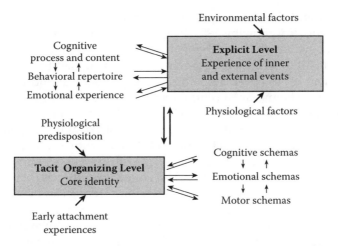

Figure 2.2 Identity structure. (Adapted from "Multidimensional Schematic Restructuring. Treatment for Obsessions: Theory and Practice," by D. Sookman, G. Pinard, and N. Beauchemin, 1994, *Journal of Cognitive Psychotherapy*, *8*, p. 178.)

risk aversion (Sookman & Pinard, 2007; Steketee & Frost, 1994). As contemporary CBT models suggest: (1) dysfunctional responses to inner and external events may indicate dysfunction at the core schema level, and (2) modification of these dysfunctional schemas is critical to prevent symptom recurrence (A.T. Beck, 1996).

The model in theory

The model of OCD proposed by Sookman et al. (1994) is theoretically broad and was developed as a general model for conceptualization and intervention planning given OCD's heterogeneity. The following concepts are proposed as relevant to OCD symptoms: (1) schemas (Beck & Freeman, 1990; Beck, Emery, & Greenberg, 1985); (2) developmental theory (e.g., Piaget, 1960); (3) role of attachment experiences (Bowlby, 1985; Liotti, 1988, 1991); (4) constructivist model of identity structure (Guidano, 1990; Guidano & Liotti, 1985); and (5) metacognitive and appraisal theory (Salkovskis, 1985, 1989; Wells & Mathews, 1994). The figures shown here have been adapted slightly from Sookman et al., 1994.

Figure 2.2 illustrates aspects of the model pertaining to identity structure (adapted from Guidano & Liotti, 1985). In this conceptualization, cognitive, emotional, and motor schemas interact at a tacit level (beyond immediate accessibility to awareness) and influence explicit (experienced) processing of information, emotional retrieval and experience, and behavioral responses. Core schemas are hypothesized to develop during early attachment and developmental formation and to accommodate through life experience (e.g., Bowlby, 1985; Piaget, 1960). Schemas that do not accommodate adequately to new experience may underlie intransigence of dysfunctional patterns (Beck & Freeman, 1990; Rosen, 1989; Safran, 1990a,b).

Sookman et al. (1994) hypothesized that presence and activation of vulnerability schemas are a central mechanism underlying appraisals and emotional experience of danger, characteristic of several subtypes. The Vulnerability Schemata Scale (Sookman et al., 2001) was developed to assess vulnerability schemas characteristic of OCD. Four dimensions are assessed: (1) perceived vulnerability; (2) difficulty with unpredictability, newness, and change; (3) need for control; and (4) view of or response to strong affect. This last subscale assesses beliefs about strong feelings and one's capacity to tolerate and cope with these in oneself and others (e.g., *"Strong feelings are dangerous"* or *"I cannot cope with strong feelings"*). As intended, items on the vulnerability, unpredictability, and control subscales were significantly more strongly endorsed by OCD patients compared with other anxiety disorders and nonpsychiatric controls. Perceived difficulty to cope with strong emotions was found to be more characteristic of both OCD and other anxiety disorders compared with normals. Multidimensional schemas, including emotional, that may underlie psychopathology and impact resistance to change have also been emphasized in recent conceptual models (Beck, Freeman, & Davis, 2004; Leahy, 2002, Leahy, this volume).

Figure 2.3 illustrates the proposed interaction among core schemas and other factors relevant to symptoms. Dysfunctional information processing includes thought–action fusion ("If I think of a bad event, it is more likely to happen") (Shafran, Thordarson, & Rachman, 1996) and emotional reasoning ("I feel scared, so I must be in danger") (Arntz, Rauner, & van den Hout, 1995). Patients' cognitive responses to intrusions illustrated in Figure 2.3 range from appraisals and beliefs to more complex cognitive processes. The delineation "high-level information processing" refers to cognitive phenomena beyond automatic thoughts (Beck, 1976), such as beliefs about appraisals and beliefs about beliefs (metacognition). Metacognition refers to the monitoring, interpreting, and regulating of processes and content of cognition (Wells & Mathews, 1994). Cognitive–emotional processing also involves appraisals of emotion, emotional responses to thoughts, and emotional responses to emotions (e.g., fear of fear) (Goldstein & Chambless, 1978). These phenomena are considered products of activated schemas (Sookman & Pinard, 2007).

Thus, this model offers a general, adaptable frame for individualized case conceptualization and treatment planning based on heterogeneity of symptoms, their function and meaning, related feelings and beliefs, and schemas at a more core level. Factors that may affect resistance to change are operationalized and targeted as precisely as possible for each case.

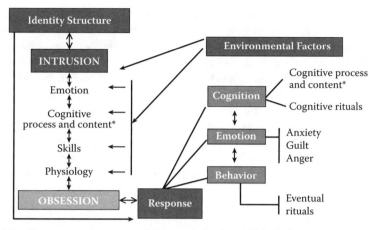

* Cognitive processes and content range from automatic thoughts to high-level information processing.

Figure 2.3 Transformation of an intrusion. (Adapted from "Multidimensional Schematic Restructuring. Treatment for Obsessions: Theory and Practice," by D. Sookman, G. Pinard, and N. Beauchemin, 1994, *Journal of Cognitive Psychotherapy, 8*, p. 179.)

The model in practice: CBT for resistant OCD

Interventions based on this approach are summarized next, with case illustrations. This material is adapted from Sookman and Pinard (1999). First, the therapist collaborates with each patient to develop a profile of emotional, cognitive, interpersonal, and behavioral functioning. Symptom subtype characteristics are assessed, and specifically targeted treatment strategies are tailored to each patient's idiosyncratic experience. Dysfunctional beliefs are assessed using the Interpretation of Intrusions Inventory and the Obsessive Beliefs Questionnaire-87 (OBQ-87) (OCCWG, 2001, 2003, 2005). We prefer the OBQ-87 because of its separate subscales for threat estimation and responsibility, reflecting the clinical picture for many patients. Core beliefs are assessed on the Vulnerability Schemata Scale (Sookman et al., 2001). Other measures are completed on an individualized basis: Personal Significance Scale (PSS) (Rachman, 2003); Thought–Action Fusion Scale (Shafran et al., 1996); Thought Fusion Instrument (Wells, Gwilliam, & Cartwright-Hatton, 2001); Not Just Right Experience Questionnaire–Revised (Coles et al., 2003); and Homework Compliance Form (Promakoff, Epstein, & Covi, 1986). Symptoms, beliefs, and feelings are also assessed ideographically with many cases. Patients rate on a 0 to 100 scale how much they *believe* the idea is true and *feel* it is true (cognitive and emotional aspect of belief) (Sookman & Pinard, 1999).

Beckian (e.g., A.T. Beck, 1995; J. Beck, 1995) cognitive therapy is administered prior to and during ERP and behavioral experiments and as homework assignments for virtually all patients. Therapist-assisted behavioral avoidance tests (BATs) are carried out in patients' naturalistic environments (e.g., Steketee, Chambless, Tran, Worden, & Gillis, 1996). This observational methodology facilitates assessment and modification of information processing, emotional response, rituals, and avoidance that actually occur in feared situations. Strategies to tolerate, decenter, and reappraise intrusions are taught in sessions and during ERP and are given as homework. Imagined and *in vivo* practice of strategies to label, modulate, reappraise, and appropriately express strong feelings precedes and is combined with ERP in situations that provoke these (see Sookman et al., 1994, for illustrations).

Thus, the primary focus of cognitive therapy in this approach is not necessarily cognitive dysfunction. The (hypothesized) inseparable components of schemas: cognitive–emotional–interpersonal–behavioral (Beck, 1996) are targeted. For example, intolerance of distress and "not just right" experience are routinely addressed for washers who "just can't stand the feeling" of contamination without fear of illness and for individuals with symmetry, ordering, and arranging who may not report elevated beliefs on cognitive measures (Taylor et al., 2006). The therapist may elect to use Beckian CT strategies for cognitive and emotional core schemas that seem related to intransigence of symptoms (see below). Schema-based interventions are considered appropriate for about 50% of OCD cases seen in our clinic. These are considered if the patient's participation in ERP is not complete and if avoidance of inner experience or metacognitive dysfunction is not adequately resolved. Use of these strategies is also contingent on attachment and developmental experiences reported.

We generally use graduated exposure with complete RP but may begin with flooding to most feared stimuli when rapid improvement is urgent (e.g., parent whose OCD interferes with child care) or when a graduated approach was previously ineffective. As will be illustrated, an advantage of flooding for some incapacitated patients with pervasive rituals may be speed of habituation, belief change, and self-efficacy. Among the advantages of complete response prevention is that this procedure can preempt the patient's struggle to resist rituals following exposure and thereby reduce distress and suffering. Therapist-assisted *in vivo* ERP is administered in patients' naturalistic environments (home, work) whenever office-based treatment appears suboptimal. Severely ill patients are offered intensive naturalistic CBT or hospitalization. Duration of hospitalization for intensive specialized CBT is approximately 3 months, with 2- to 4-hour sessions 4 times weekly, followed by twice weekly outpatient treatment for at least 6 months. Significant others regularly participate in selected sessions, with the agreement and collaboration of the patient. This involves education, ERP, and adaptive strategies for patients' symptoms such as gradual withdrawal of inappropriate reassurance and fostering of autonomous functioning. Significant others are not included if they are deemed too antagonistic or dysfunctional to participate or if this is not considered appropriate. Other skills strategies such as problem-solving, decision-making, vocational, and social skills are offered to address difficulties or deficits and to help patients "get a life."

Relapse prevention and generalization strategies are integral to CBT methods. These include therapist and family fading, anticipation of triggers, and imagined rehearsal of coping under stress. Guidelines to maintain progress under stress are spelled out. Among the most important are instructions to engage in adaptive strategies for intrusions, self-administered ERP, and corrective cognitive and emotional strategic processing (Sookman & Pinard, 2007) as an immediate response to urges to ritualize. Sookman and colleagues developed the latter strategy[1] to promote change and relapse prevention throughout and following treatment (see illustration below).

Finally, treatment is not time limited and is based on clinical need. Duration of treatment ranges from 6 weeks to 2 years, with booster sessions provided as needed. Severely ill patients who receive schema-based interventions may continue for 2 years or more. Therapy is delivered in a large specialized OCD clinic at the McGill University Health Centre in Montreal that accepts OCD patients of all ages (children to seniors) regardless of comorbidity or illness severity. Psychiatric consultation and pharmacological intervention are available as needed.

Clinical example of CBT without schema-based interventions

This case illustrates the application of complete ERP, using imagined exposure and cognitive therapy, which addressed this patient's specific symptom and belief profile, followed by a flooding paradigm. The thorough case history routinely taken with all patients on intake is not elaborated fully because of space constraints. Her treatment was time limited because she was referred from another country. This case has a long-term (7 years) follow-up outcome.

Michaela was a 47-year-old married woman, with three children, referred from a Middle Eastern country after 10 years of twice weekly psychotherapy (*"to figure out my underlying conflicts"*), a year of twice-weekly

---

[1] In developing this clinical strategy specifically for OCD, we built upon the conceptual and treatment model of OCD proposed by Sookman, Pinard, and Beauchemin (1994); the general information processing model of anxiety proposed by Beck and Clark (1997); and the model of vulnerability schemas in OCD proposed by Sookman, Pinard, and Beck (2001).

outpatient CBT that ended a year prior to the referral, several adequate pharmacotherapy trials that had included augmenting strategies, and a lengthy general hospitalization for severe secondary depression. These treatments had failed to improve her OCD and she had recently made a near-fatal suicide attempt. Certainly, her 100 sessions of previous ERP and CT, combined with pharmacotherapy, qualified her as treatment resistant.

Michaela's symptoms began 17 years earlier when she and her family moved to a different country for a year to accommodate her husband's work. Michaela felt unhappy there because of the restrictive culture, despite her elevated socioeconomic status. Her OCD began when workmen came to her home to do repairs. They had raw beef for lunch, common in this culture. Michaela saw a drop of blood on the floor and recalled thinking: "That is so disgusting; look at the mess they made." She experienced a strong feeling of repulsion and asked her housekeeper to wash the floor. Michaela then scrubbed the floor herself and took a lengthy shower. Over a period of several months her symptoms rapidly generalized to the point that she became housebound, with virtually constant obsessions about the possibility she had touched raw meat. On initial assessment in our clinic, she reported incapacitating cognitive and behavioral rituals with classic patterns of contamination spread from raw meat sources. For example, she felt her car had become contaminated as she thought about the possibility that the wind could blow particles into her car from delivery trucks which might have come into contact with raw meat.

Michaela engaged in extensive washing for about 6 hours daily at home, but she struggled not to require the same behavior from her husband and children. After her children went to bed, she completed extensive washing of all objects that had come from the outside. She was hypervigilant about what her family brought into the house, did ongoing mental reviews of the extent of contamination, and had great difficulty delaying washing her hands for even a few minutes because of "intense urges to get rid of all feelings of contamination." She engaged in lengthy handwashing over 50 times a day, maintained "safe" areas in the home, and made repeated requests for reassurance. To her great sorrow, she had been unable to hug her children for many years except when they were just out of their bath in pajamas. Affection and sexual relations took place with her husband after he had showered. She could not accompany her husband or children to any activities, had withdrawn from friends and relatives, feeling anxious and ashamed. Contributing to her suicidality, she felt that her children and husband "are better off without me." On initial assessment, she said she felt "hopeless" about getting better.

The only symptom-related beliefs Michaela reported were "*Raw meat is disgusting. If I touch it, I feel contaminated. I feel guilty about spreading contamination all over my home. It's not that anything bad will happen to anyone. I just can't face the feeling."* Michaela said she felt she had to wash until she felt better. Obvious information processing distortions were generalization and all-or-nothing thinking: "If one drop of raw meat gets on me, it spreads to everything." At initial assessment, Michaela's total score on the Y-BOCS was 28. Her scores on three cognitive measures (III, OBQ, VSS) were comparable to normals. Idiographic recordkeeping was implemented to assess weekly change in obsessions and rituals, the two symptom-related beliefs she reported, and a variety of feelings.

Michaela was the eldest of three sisters with whom she reported having a good relationship. She described her childhood as happy and privileged and raised by "loving and liberal-minded parents." She felt she had a relatively good relationship with her husband "who sees men and women as equal. We love each other very much," though it was strained because of the severity of her OCD. Michaela reported, and seemed to manifest in sessions, good tolerance for and expression of other strong feelings. She appeared to be highly motivated. Despite thorough exploration of Michaela's attachment and developmental history, cultural and interpersonal experiences, and meaning to her of the perceived precipitating event, ongoing schema-based assessment did not suggest a hypothesis for Michaela's intolerance of this specific experience of disgust. Her developmental and premorbid functioning appeared to have been good, and there were no other identifiable skills deficits.

Michaela reported (and the therapist's written report confirmed) that previous treatment had included education about appraisal models of OCD, and ERP with both habituation and appraisal/belief disconfirmation rationales. Previous cognitive therapy had addressed beliefs about the probability and extent of contamination and self-doubt (e.g., "Did I wash enough? Is the speck of meat that could have been there gone?"). Previous ERP was graduated and therapist assisted. This included looking at pictures of raw meat, walking past raw meat in the supermarket, driving within sight of food trucks, and, finally, touching raw meat "with one finger." Michaela had refused to confront the most contaminated stimuli, and she had been unable to follow response prevention instructions between sessions. She said she sometimes washed at home after sessions, for example, shampooing her hair many times. There was minimal change.

The primary CT interventions in our clinic focused on strategies to help Michaela to tolerate and reappraise dreaded feelings of anxiety and disgust that appeared central to her prior refusal to engage fully in ERP. The therapist told Michaela that avoidance of these feelings perpetuated their intensity and her perceived inability to cope. Although the ultimate goal of therapy, of course, was to diminish her feelings of disgust and related symptoms, the initial goal was conceptualized as helping her to develop more adaptive *responses* to her inner experience. She was advised that if all else failed a recommended strategy was to *"defuse"* or disconnect her thoughts, feelings, and behavior and to follow the ERP "prescription" (see below) regardless of her inner experience. Michaela said intolerance of distress had not been addressed in her previous therapy. She confirmed that she understood the rationale presented, that if she engaged in ERP these feelings were expected to diminish. She agreed she had to face her feelings. Nonetheless, Michaela said: *"I feel I cannot, it's too intense."* She asked the therapist to *"go very slowly so my anxiety is not too bad."*

In view of the failure of previous graduated exposure the therapist recommended the contrary, telling the patient that she would be unlikely to get better unless she faced whatever painful feelings occurred, and proposing that intensive exposure could more rapidly decrease these feelings. Given previous difficulty sustaining ritual prevention, ERP was constructed to prolong response prevention following exposure with the help of a family member. The therapist made it clear that ERP would not be offered until Michaela requested it as recommended.

Treatment began with several sessions of prolonged imagined exposure (90 minutes), in which Michaela was asked to imagine two opposing motivational scenarios. In the first, she faced distressing feelings of disgust for several weeks of intensive therapy by following the therapist's behavioral prescriptions and imagined going home able to physically express her love for her husband and three daughters, hugging them and sharing life experiences she had been missing. In the second scenario, she continued to avoid raw meat and continued to suffer her crippling symptoms. Following three imagined exposure sessions Michaela said: *"I will do anything to have my life back. I want the ERP. I'll do my best to face it."* Michaela stayed locally at her sister's home during treatment. Because of her trusting relationship with her brother-in-law Samuel, a close friend of her husband, she asked him to participate and he agreed.

The schedule and content of ERP were planned collaboratively with the patient and her family. ERP was administered in two 1-hour sessions, 4 times weekly, for 6 weeks—a total of 48 hours of ERP. Samuel attended all sessions and participated in the ERP and assigned homework for the first 2 weeks. Flooding involved the highest step on the hierarchy from the onset. Samuel was asked to bring a package of raw beef to the first ERP session. Each step had been clearly outlined and agreed upon beforehand. The therapist repeated the agreed-upon instructions and asked Michaela to follow these regardless of what she was thinking and feeling, as follows:

T. Okay, Michaela, as we agreed, remove the covering from the meat with your hands.

M. How can I do this? I have not done this for 17 years.

T. You want your life back, there is no way around this.

M. (Opens the package, shaking.)

T. Great. Now, as we agreed, touch the meat completely with both your palms. Put your palms on the piece of raw meat. Think of your daughters while you do it.

M. I'm doing it, but how will I feel afterward? There is blood on my hands now. (She looks at her hands, and looks scared. Samuel tells her she is doing great and he is proud of her. He repeats the same exposure by also touching the meat.)

T. This is going very well. Now, as we discussed, let's do the next steps fast. You can pat your hands for a second on the paper towel once. Good. Now, touch your hair, your face, all your clothes, your shoes. (Michaela does all this, and begins to cry). Now, why don't you and Samuel hug each other so he is also utterly contaminated (said with humor). (They hug, and Samuel says how pleased he feels. Michaela cries and laughs a little at the same time.)

M. I can't believe I just did that. I just can't believe this.

T. How do you feel, Michaela? You did great, you did really great.

M. It's all over me now. I feel a very strong urge to take a shower to get it off me.

T. I know, but you want your life back. Do you feel proud of yourself?

M. I am very scared. Maybe a little bit proud. I have had nothing to feel proud of for 17 years. (She cries, and Samuel puts his arm around her.)

T. Congratulations, Michaela. You have come closer to the life you want back so badly. Okay, now let's review the response prevention that is essential if we want the exposure we just did to work. You go home to your sister's, and as you all agreed, you touch everything so nothing is left untouched. This is very important that there be no exceptions. Everything in the kitchen, every room. Lie in your bed, get under the covers with the clothes you are wearing now, and put your head on your pillow. Touch all of your belongings. Don't wash at all, not your hands or anything else, except to brush your teeth until tomorrow morning before your next session. As we agreed, Samuel will be with you. He will touch everything first, and then you do the same as him. Okay? Any questions?

At the second session the next day, Michaela reported that the RP had been carried out exactly as prescribed. She had difficulty sleeping; her anxiety had dropped from 100% to only around 70%. She had experienced many obsessions about what she had done. The same ERP exercise was repeated four times during the first week, with much encouragement from the therapist and family. Therapist fading was rapidly implemented: At the end of week one, Michaela repeated all the steps in the presence of the therapist and Samuel, but without any instructions from the therapist or modeling by Samuel. At her sister's home, it was recommended she take the initiative in "contaminating" the entire house with Samuel only accompanying her. Week two focused on normalizing a wide range of activities. First with Samuel or her sister and then alone, Michaela bought meat at a supermarket, drove her rental car intentionally behind food trucks, ate at restaurants, and used public washrooms. At end of week two, Michaela was engaging in a wide range of activities in and out of the home. She reported (confirmed by family) that she was ritual free. To her great surprise, she felt that her obsessions and anxiety had dramatically reduced and her feelings of hope and pride had greatly increased.

At week three, the therapist recommended that the patient additionally grill or pan fry hamburgers and steaks daily for her family (treatment took place during the summer). Each step required was reviewed with the therapist beforehand (e.g., how to handle raw beef, use of utensils, serving, cleaning up). Given the duration of dysfunction, essential ingredients to the relearning process involved education about normal meal procedures and rehearsal of resisting inevitable occurrence of urges to engage in "just little rituals." As exposures became easier Michaela asked if she should do the same with raw pork and chicken, although these meats had bothered her less. The therapist recommended against this for realistic health reasons (not one of Michaela's concerns). Further education was provided about normal handling and preparation of these meats and other foods (e.g., brief handwashing after touching) and normal clean-up without rituals.

At Michaela's suggestion, during week three she began to volunteer at a butcher shop cutting meat and serving customers. The therapist said she could not have thought of a better idea. While Michaela still believed about 30 to 40% that raw meat was contaminated, she felt little anxiety and was able to joke with customers as she worked.

In addition to daily exposures described above, the therapist recommended that Michaela agree to see relatives who wished to travel to Montreal from the United States to visit her. Michaela said she had been socially isolated and ashamed of herself for so long, these encounters provoked much initial anxiety and urge to avoid. Social encounters were discussed as behavioral experiments to test whether people would be judgmental as she feared or loving and joyous as she hoped.

The second half of treatment involved detailed discussion of strategies for generalization and maintenance of gains in her home country. The therapist recommended a minimum of 6 weeks of intensive exposure (flooding), replicating the clinic procedures, and jumping into autonomous shopping, cooking, and traveling around the city immediately. This was to be followed by another 6 weeks of ERP 3 times a week, with gradual fading of formal exercises provided there were no rituals or avoidance in her normal daily activities. Michaela gave advance instructions to her housekeeper and family to stop all previous protective and safety behaviors and reassurance. The therapist emphasized the crucial importance of maintaining complete exposure and response prevention regardless of the strength of urges to ritualize. Formal ERP exercises were to be resumed as needed to prevent relapse. Also of crucial importance was resuming varied activities in and outside the home with her husband and daughters, as she had longed for.

An important relapse prevention strategy used was *Corrective Cognitive and Emotional Strategic Processing* (Sookman & Pinard, 2007), referred to above. This was formulated collaboratively, rehearsed during imagined exposure, and given as homework. For example, Michaela proposed the following as helpful to forestall relapse:

1. "I had a strong feeling of disgust touching raw beef for supper tonight (*emotional response to OCD trigger*). What if my OCD comes back? Oh, no, I'm getting anxious. Everything the meat touched is contaminated (*appraisal*). Maybe I should do something to clean up all traces of it (*urge to ritualize*). No, as I learned in therapy, this feeling is a false trigger. These feelings of disgust and contamination are harmless, no matter how strong (*corrective processing*). My husband asked my opinion about an important decision today. This made me feel very happy, but I guess I also feel stressed (*corrective processing— identification of varied emotions, possible precipitant and meaning of symptom exacerbation*). I should try to figure out what's bothering me, talk to him, and deal with it (*problem solving to deal adaptively with emotions and relationship*)."
2. "I have an urge to wash to get rid of this feeling that I am contaminated. But, as I learned in therapy, I can tolerate this feeling without letting it control my behavior. I will not let it affect my behavior because I do not want a recurrence of my OCD (*corrective processing*)."

The last week of treatment, Michaela's husband, Stan, and children came to pick her up, and all went home together. Michaela introduced her daughters to the therapist, laughing and hugging them. During two couple therapy sessions planned from the onset, the procedure for ERP and normalization of activities at home were discussed with her husband with Michaela demonstrating. Her husband was astonished and began to cry. As Michaela had described, he seemed loving and supportive but understandably anxious about her illness and the possibility of relapse. He reported avoiding sharing his feelings or work difficulties with Michaela for fear she was "too fragile" and felt that the strain on him had been "enormous." The couple agreed to try to resume to function as equal partners, as they recalled doing before the onset of OCD. Before she left, Michaela demonstrated her flooding paradigm on videotape and gave consent to show this to other patients who feared ERP.

The therapist offered Michaela weekly phone sessions for 6 weeks, during the implementation of ERP and normalization at home, and then on an as-needed basis. She successfully generalized and maintained her improvement. Michaela reported she continued to feel about 30% *"raw beef is contaminated,"* but this did not usually cause anxiety. Over the months that followed, she reported several stressful periods where the urge to ritualize was very strong but she resisted because *"I never want to get OCD again, and I know ERP is my protection."* Michaela returned to the clinic a year later for 2 weeks, following the death of a close relative. Michaela had not engaged in rituals, but her urges were so strong she felt she was *"in danger of giving in."* Six sessions focused on discussion of her feelings of loss, and the positive evolution of her relationship with her husband and children. At a 7-year follow-up Michaela reported she was completely ritual free and was engaging in varied activities with family and friends, with no avoidance. During this period she spoke with the therapist by phone an additional five times.

Why was Michaela able to engage fully in complete ERP, and in flooding, at our clinic and to maintain her progress at home? She attributed her success to five interventions: (1) emphasis on tolerating and coping with distress; (2) motivational imagined sessions prior to ERP *"helped me get in touch with how strong my feelings are of wanting to share life with my children and husband. I realized these feelings are as strong or stronger than what raw meat made me feel"*; (3) therapist-assisted flooding and complete response prevention, *"we went so fast, the anxiety went down fast, I didn't have to think about rituals because it was not possible to do them if I followed the prescription, I quickly learned I could cope with my feelings"*; (4) imagined practice of corrective strategic processing in sessions, and at home *"Strategies I learned and practiced during therapy, to prepare for going home, that I could use anytime to identify and cope better with what I think and feel"*; and (5) Samuel's collaboration, that was initially indispensable to complete ERP: *"His support and encouragement also made me feel I could do it."* Indeed, in the therapist's experience, Samuel was one of the best significant other co-therapists ever encountered. He was loving, supportive, and he modeled coping. In collaboration with the therapist, Samuel helped Michaela to de-catastrophize her distress, to focus on reality (*"it's just a feeling I can learn to cope with"*) and to envision the future she wanted.

The model in practice: schema-based assessment and treatment interventions for resistant OCD

This section provides a brief summary with a few illustrations of schema-based strategies. Additional information about these methods is provided elsewhere (Sookman & Pinard, 1999, 2007; Sookman & Steketee, 2007; Sookman et al., 1994). In 1994, Sookman et al. proposed that: "The schematic meaning of an obsession encompasses dysfunctional core beliefs, feelings, and memories about the self related to key attachment experiences. …In order to access and modify a schema in treatment, the patient must become able to emotionally experience as well as to cognitively reflect upon its contents" (p. 190). The first step in this process is to start with elements perceived as threatening that are readily accessible to awareness, including *feelings, sensations, images, urges, impulses, intrusions,* and *thoughts*. Some patients readily recognize associations among inner experience and behavior and core aspects such as self-image, but others require intervention. For example, Michael was a 25-year-old orthodox Jewish doctoral student who spent 5 hours checking daily. He had felt unable to participate fully in response prevention in two previous CT and ERP treatments. He stated during an initial session:

> I have many intrusions I will miss a signal that someone else is in danger and I will not act fast enough to save them. Last week I saw that a road sign about a sharp turn ahead had fallen off. The bus was going so fast that by the time I rushed to the front and spoke to the driver he did not know which road I referred to. So I could not report it. I had images all night of someone dying because of me and felt I am basically a bad person who does not care enough about others. I can only feel good about myself if I feel I have done enough checking to make sure others are safe. I'm afraid I will never be able to get over the guilt and these feelings will interfere long-term with my being happy.

Here, the core element of feeling like a bad person unless rituals are performed was readily accessible. The insightful feared consequence was not being able to feel happy due to his own feelings of guilt.

The next step is to identify and to modify aspects that are less accessible to awareness which the patient cannot spontaneously report. This may be crucial in modifying patients' strategic processing of distressing events. As Sookman and Pinard (2007, pp. 101–102) noted:

Patients are typically less aware of: (a) the role of their myriad emotional, cognitive, and behavioral responses to inner and external events in perpetuating symptoms; (b) the influence of core aspects, such as personal values (Rachman, 1998), on their responses to specific events; and (c) the impact of past experience on current functioning. The downward arrow technique (Beck et al., 1985; Burns, 1980) to identify core beliefs in OCD has been described elsewhere (e.g., Freeston et al., 1997; Wilhelm & Steketee, 2006). The aim of the downward arrow in this approach is to reach a level of belief that is relatively undissociated from emotion, that is, at the implicational level (Teasdale & Barnard, 1993). Regardless of content, the therapist assesses and targets dysfunctional emotional beliefs such as *"I don't believe it's true, but I feel it's true."* In the next step, schemas are linked to symptoms, as in the following illustrative sequence of maladaptive information processing, which would be communicated to the patient inserting his or her idiosyncratic content: Pre-existing dysfunctional cognitive and emotional schemas (e.g., vulnerability schemas) influence autonomic and strategic processing of events → specific inner and external events are experienced/appraised as dangerous → strong feelings of anxiety or discomfort, urge to act to restore predictable feelings of safety and comfort, fear of loss of control → hyperattention, vigilance, thoughts about thoughts, thought suppression, cognitive rituals, behavioral rituals, reassurance seeking, and avoidance → appraisals and beliefs about (inevitable) failure of dysfunctional strategies → perceived confirmation of dysfunctional core schemas → escalating anxiety and symptoms.

The therapist explores the effects of past attachment and developmental experiences on current functioning to further understand and reduce intransigent entrenched patterns. Various strategies are employed to help the person tolerate, reappraise, and express core emotional schemas and to risk exposure to situations that activate these. These interventions are combined with ERP and assigned as homework. The patient is helped to identify and engage in adaptive behaviors that are schema inconsistent and to experience "with new eyes" how the outcome differs from child-hood experiences. New skills are taught and practiced. Graduated behav-ioral experiments are designed to disconfirm maladaptive emotional responses and core beliefs (flooding is not recommended here).

Michael's previously intransigent feelings of guilt, and related core beliefs about badness, were addressed by helping him to *emotionally* dif-ferentiate between OCD and normal standards for interpersonal respon-sibility and ethics. He risked disregarding, rather than acting on, urges to repeatedly check. He reconceptualized his feelings of guilt as emanating from his past relationship with his father that he could now disregard in the present. His comments in a schema-based session were:

> My father was more particular even than our ortho-dox rabbi about the way I observed our religion. If I made any mistakes when I would daven (pray) he asked me to repeat sentences over many times. He told me it was not good for my spiritual well-being and happiness to be sloppy. What got to me was the unhappy part, I felt like that when he was around. Frankly, I didn't care then about how per-fectly I recited prayers. But I guess I cared about my father's opinion. ...I swallowed it hook, line, and sinker. Now I am obsessed that if I am sloppy with people I am doomed to unhappiness. Another way to see this is my father was overly rigid ... but I ended up feeling I am basically a bad person. To reassure myself I'm not, I have to check out and act on every imaginable threat to everyone, or else I do not deserve happiness. But maybe my standard of sloppy is a normal person's standard of responsible and my father's standards were unreasonable.

In this approach, schema restructuring becomes a goal within the ther-apeutic relationship as the therapist aims to create a therapeutic experience that fosters *relational affective relearning* (Sookman et al., 1994, p. 90). This process has been described in other theoretical frames (Alexander, 1956; Greenberg & Safran, 1987; Kohut, 1971; Safran, 1990a,b). In this method, the therapist uses spontaneous "hot moments" of emotional opportunity to disconfirm dysfunctional responses and links these to past experience and to current patterns that are now reappraised. The therapist models normal risk taking, anxiety management, and skills as appropriate. To illustrate, we use a few segments from early sessions with a 35-year old-woman with perfectionism and checking rituals related to fear of making mistakes. Sally was recently fired as a legal secretary because of virtually constant symptoms. She had just left her husband of 5 years, though he had said he wanted to stay together. She had quit four previous therapies, during which she was chronically late "due to rituals" and noncompliant with homework (*"I won't do it well enough"*).

> S. You answered the knock on your door instead of ignoring it. I think you should have ignored it.
> T. What did this mean to you?
> S. You really are not concentrating completely on me. I wanted to completely finish the thoughts I was expressing. Now you won't understand me. I know it only took a few minutes … but no reason is okay.
> T. How did this make you feel?
> S. I feel hurt … just like in lots of other situations. I feel you just don't care, like with my husband, as I've already told you. All therapists are pretty much the same. (Her tone is annoyed and devaluing.)
> T. I'm sorry this caused you to feel hurt. I think it's important that you concluded that I don't care about you and that you feel nothing can disconfirm this, that no reason is okay, including an emergency like a burst pipe. (Sally smiles.) I'd like to understand more about why you feel this way. I can tell you this certainly is not accurate about what I am feeling. I feel sorry we had to interrupt. I am genuinely interested in what you are telling me about yourself and in trying to help. (Sally looked surprised and a bit tearful.)

Several sessions then focused on her relationship with her husband. In response to specific questions, Sally was able to talk about experiences with her father, whom she viewed as self-centered and critical, and to reflect on their possible effect on her view of herself and others. She said she had felt "devalued" growing up. Sally expressed a pervasive feeling of emotional isolation, a longstanding core belief that she did not deserve attention or love from others, and a *"constant need to prove myself by not making any mistakes or else nothing I do will be worthy."* The therapist asked: "Is it possible that these core beliefs affect how you feel and think in relationships in the present? If this is the case, you may sometimes be concluding things about others' feelings toward you that are not accurate, as you did with me … and with your husband. I think this is related to your symptoms of perfectionism, feeling of emotional isolation, and quitting relationships so you don't get hurt."

Treatment efficacy for resistant OCD

Sookman and Pinard (1999) and Sookman, Dalfen, Annable, and Pinard (2003) reported outcome data on OCD symptoms, depression, and beliefs using this schema-based approach with two samples (total n = 39) of CBT-resistant OCD patients, including all symptom subtypes. Previous cognitive therapy and ERP had lasted over 2 years. Individual outpatient sessions were administered 1 or 2 times weekly for an average of nearly 10 months. Of the 39 patients, 32 (82%) showed clinically significant improvement in OCD symptoms and depression (Jacobson & Truax, 1991). Mean Y-BOCS scores improved from 23.2 to 11.9 in the second study (n = 32). More importantly, 10 patients were recovered (Y-BOCS score < 7) following treatment. Another 10 reported mild symptoms (Y-BOCS < 16), and 5 remained moderately ill. Dysfunctional beliefs assessed on the OBQ-87 and core beliefs on the Vulnerability Schemata Scale reliably improved for responders and did not change for nonresponders. Symptomatically recovered patients showed reductions in dysfunctional beliefs to within normal range at posttreatment. We attribute these strong results for previously resistant samples to the specificity of this CBT approach, such as attention to subtype characteristics and other factors that seemed relevant to patients' resistance to change. Some patients who previously did not participate in ERP did so in these trials. The important question of long-term maintenance of change is currently under study in a 5-year follow-up.

Implications for future research of CBT resistance in OCD

As evident from the above review and illustrations of treatment, cognitive therapy methods produce positive results for OCD symptoms and may be especially potent when combined with behavioral ERP strategies. Expanded interventions that focus on schema-level features that appear to be common in patients who have not benefited from previous therapy, even well-executed ERP, seem very promising. Certainly, more clinical trials are needed to further examine the efficacy of these methods for a range of patients with various OCD subtypes and personality characteristics. However, before commencing such trials there is a need for consensus on intervention and response criteria for CBT-resistant OCD (Pallanti et al., 2002; Simpson, Huppert, & Petkova, 2005; Sookman et al., 2006). Available studies have considerable heterogeneity in samples, interventions, and assessment of response (Moher, Schulz, & Altman, 2001; Tolin, Abramowitz, & Diefenbach, 2005). What combination of ERP and CT interventions, with respect to content, duration, speed, location, and degree of

therapist and family assistance, constitutes an adequate trial of specialized CBT for various OCD subtypes? As several experts have pointed out,
criteria are needed to further define resistance to CBT, to identify contributing factors, and to develop strategies for addressing these (e.g., Cottraux
et al., 2005). The intervention and response criteria proposed below for
CBT-resistant OCD are based on current available empirical literature and
our own clinical experience.

Intervention criteria for CBT resistance in OCD

We propose the following criteria for determining whether an adequate
trial of specialized CBT has been provided:

1. Specialized CBT is administered by a therapist, or under the
   supervision of a therapist, experienced in treating OCD. As a general guideline, the therapist should have engaged in supervised
   CBT with at least 10 and preferably 20 OCD patients of varying subtypes. Considerably more supervised experience may be required
   for some therapists to successfully treat patients with the schema-
   based approaches described earlier and for patients who have not
   responded well to an initial trial of CBT. Multidimensional assessment of symptoms, comorbid conditions, medical status, skills repertoire, resources, and intrafamilial and psychosocial functioning
   has been adequate to formulate an empirically based individualized
   CBT case conceptualization and treatment plan, which evolves with
   the patient's active collaboration during treatment. Assessment strategies include standardized scales to assess subtypes and severity of
   OCD symptoms, comorbid conditions, beliefs, emotional distress,
   quality of life, and other relevant variables (e.g., degree of insight),
   and direct behavioral observation and interviews with significant
   others when possible. Idiographic recordkeeping during treatment is
   important unless contraindicated for cases of severe perfectionism.
2. Delivery of empirically based CBT and/or CT with behavioral experiments. ERP includes planned prolonged exposures and prevention
   of rituals and avoidance behaviors triggered by these exposures. CT
   addresses appraisals of intrusions, beliefs, emotional responses, and
   metacognitive dysfunction characteristic of OCD. These treatments
   are directed at all subtypes of OCD symptoms present.
3. At least 40 hours of therapy are delivered in intensive or spaced for-
   mats with therapist assistance unless the patient recovers sooner. If
   clear progress is evident but the patient is not scoring in the subclinical range on OCD symptoms, additional treatment should be

provided. If spaced sessions (e.g., once weekly) do not produce clear evidence of improvement after 10 hours, treatment should be intensified (2 or 3 times weekly or even daily), and session duration should be lengthened (90 minutes or more). ERP and CT methods should be employed by the patient in relevant naturalistic environments; if needed to complete assigned tasks, assistance from family members or the therapist should be added.

4. Relevant daily ERP and CT homework is assigned, monitored, and adjusted regularly during sessions.
5. Skills limitations have been identified and addressed with skills acquisition interventions (e.g., emotion tolerance and modulation, interpersonal skills, decision making).
6. Family/significant other difficulties that may impede improvement are addressed in meetings with significant others. Unless this is deemed inappropriate, significant others receive education about OCD, recommendations for adaptive responses to the patient's symptoms, and strategies to foster healthy functioning. These recommendations are provided with the patient's knowledge and prior consent (except in emergencies) and are congruent with the patient's progress in treatment (e.g., degree/level of ritual prevention following ERP).
7. Referral for prior or concurrent pharmacological treatment is empirically based (i.e., comorbid disorders or symptoms that require medication). When adequate CBT produces limited response by mid-treatment, medications may be added when hypothesized reasons for poor outcome suggest a need for medication rather than change in psychological strategy. Pharmacotherapy dosage and adherence are optimal, and empirically based augmenting strategies are employed.
8. Therapy fading, generalization, and relapse prevention strategies are provided. Fading requires that therapists and family members assisting in office or home-based sessions reduce the frequency and intensity of their involvement over time. Hospitalized patients should receive regular outpatient sessions following discharge for at least 6 months with a graduated reduction schedule. Generalization refers to the need to apply exposures and CT methods across a broad range of situations in which symptoms occur to ensure learning across relevant contexts. Methods to sustain gains include stress management strategies and anticipation and planning for likely future triggers of symptoms.
9. Treatment-interfering behaviors (Pollard, 2007) have been identified and addressed.
10. Booster sessions are provided as needed.

Criteria for remission or recovery following CBT for OCD

We propose the following response criteria for remission/recovery following specialized CBT for OCD (see also Sookman & Steketee, 2007):

1. The patient no longer meets diagnostic criteria for OCD.
2. Y-BOCS total score is 7 or lower.[2]
3. No subjective distress due to OCD symptoms.
4. No rituals are performed (minimal obsessions and urges to ritualize may occur).
5. No avoidance of previously feared situations and OCD triggers.
6. Dysfunctional appraisals and beliefs, and other OCD-linked symptoms such as secondary depression, are resolved to within normal limits (see scores for normal controls on cognitive measures; OCCWG, 2003).
7. Absence of functional impairment, or return to premorbid level of function, in multiple quality of life spheres including work, activity level, and interpersonal relationships.
8. The patient cooperated fully in ERP or CT with behavioral experiments.
9. Improvement is maintained for at least 6 months.

Thus, *optimal treatment response* refers to remission rather than merely clinically significant improvement; this goal is also shared by other experts (e.g., Hollander & Zohar, 2004). Although patients with a Y-BOCS score below 16 at posttreatment would not meet the criteria for a clinical trial, they still suffer noticeable symptoms which can adversely impact their quality of life. Further, continuing dysfunctional beliefs and negative mood can also impair functioning and contribute to relapse.

Criteria for CBT resistance in OCD

Following from the above-listed criteria for adequate treatment and for recovery, we also propose that a patient be considered resistant to CBT if the following response criteria are met after an adequate trial of CBT has been delivered or attempted:

1. The patient continues to meet diagnostic criteria for OCD.
2. Y-BOCS total score 14 or higher and/or less than 50% improvement in OCD symptoms from pretreatment.[3]

---

[2] Within normal range, ≤1 standard deviation above the mean for normal controls reported by the OCCWG (2003); 2.5 (mean) + 4.3 (standard deviation) = 6.8; $n = 87$.

[3] Within mild range of OCD symptom severity, ≥1 standard deviation below the mean for clinical OCD samples reported by the OCCWG (2003); 20.5 (mean) – 6.9 (standard deviation) = 13.6; $n = 248$.

3. Mild or greater subjective distress due to OCD symptoms.
4. Continued rituals are performed in response to obsessions and urges to ritualize.
5. Continued avoidance of feared situations and OCD triggers.
6. Dysfunctional beliefs and other OCD-linked symptoms, such as secondary depression, remain within dysfunctional limits (see scores for OCD clinical samples on cognitive measures; OCCWG, 2003).
7. Mild or greater functional impairment due to OCD symptoms in one or more quality of life spheres including work, activity level, and interpersonal relationships.
8. Refusal to cooperate fully in ERP or CT with behavioral experiments. Reasons for refusal have been directly addressed without success and consultation with an expert in OCD has been undertaken.
9. Improvement is not maintained at a short-term follow-up of 6 months, with a sustained worsening of OCD symptoms by 25% or more since end of treatment.

Further controlled research is required to examine specific therapeutic ingredients and mediators of sustained change. Although the statistical significance of mean change scores and pre–post effect sizes are important, they are of limited value in examining treatment resistance. We recommend that published reporting of group results include clinical categorization according to the number of patients who recover, who achieve clinically meaningful improvement (i.e., into mild range), and who do not achieve such benefits, as well as long-term outcomes in each of these categories. To date, results have been reported this way in relatively few studies (Eddy et al., 2004; Hollander et al., 2003; Rufer et al. 2005; Simpson et al., 2005; Sookman et al., 2003), and in some of our own research we are equally at fault. Investigation of characteristics (predictors) among recovered patients, and those on the continuum of recovery, can facilitate further development and refinement of interventions. For example, neurobiological correlates of change may help us to understand differences among patients on the continuum from CBT resistant to recovered. Further, an essential issue in addressing CBT resistance is treatment delivery and how to best disseminate expertise available at specialized OCD clinics.

On an individual basis, there are different degrees of resistance to treatment that require further examination. Theoretically, individuals are susceptible to relapse if they continue to ritualize in response to feared events. The extent of change in cognitive, emotional, and behavioral responses to inner and external events, especially if these return to within normal limits, may mediate long-term maintenance of change. Continued practice of adaptive skills taught in therapy would be important to operationalize and assess. *Corrective Strategic Processing* (cognitive and emotional processing and regulation) may be a particularly sensitive predictor of outcome. Susceptibility to maladaptive reactions to intrusions may persist, or reappear under stress, without instigating relapse if the patient's cognitive and emotional strategic processing is corrective (Sookman & Pinard, 2007). How to achieve the goals outlined in this chapter for more OCD patients is a challenge for the future.

References

Abramowitz, J.S. (1996). Variants of exposure and response prevention in the treatment of obsessive–compulsive disorder: A meta-analysis. *Behaviour Therapy, 27,* 583–600.

Abramowitz, J.S. (1997). Effectiveness of psychological and pharmacological treatment for obsessive–compulsive disorder: A quantitative review. *Journal of Consulting and Clinical Psychology, 65,* 44–52.

Abramowitz, J.S. (2006). *Understanding and treating obsessive–compulsive disorder: A cognitive behavioral approach.* Mahwah, NJ: Lawrence Erlbaum.

Abramowitz, J.S., Foa, E.B., & Franklin, M.E. (2003). Exposure and ritual prevention for obsessive–compulsive disorder: Effects of intensive versus twice-weekly sessions. *Journal of Consulting and Clinical psychology, 71,* 394–398.

Abramowitz, J.S., Franklin, M.E., & Cahill, S.P. (2003). Approaches to common obstacles in the exposure-based treatment of obsessive–compulsive disorder. *Cognitive and Behavioral Practice, 10,* 14–22.

Abramowitz, J.S., McKay, D., & Taylor, S. (2008). *Clinical handbook of obsessive–compulsive disorder and related problems.* Baltimore, MD: The Johns Hopkins University Press.

Alexander, F. (1956). *Psychoanalysis and psychotherapy: Development in theory, technique, & training.* New York: W.W. Norton.

American Psychiatric Association. (2007). Practice guideline for the treatment of patients with obsessive–compulsive disorder. *American Journal of Psychiatry, 164,* 1–56.

Antony, M.M., Purdon, C., & Summerfeldt, L.J. (2007). *Psychological treatment of obsessive–compulsive disorder: Fundamentals and beyond.* Washington, D.C.: American Psychological Association.

Araujo, L.A., Ito, L.M., & Marks, I. (1996). Early compliance and other factors predicting outcomes of exposure for obsessive–compulsive disorder. *British Journal of Psychiatry, 169,* 747–752.

Arntz, A., Rauner, M., & van den Hout, M. (1995). "If I feel anxious, there must be danger": *Ex consequentia* reasoning in inferring danger in anxiety disorder. *Behaviour Research and Therapy, 33,* 917–925.

Baer, L., & Minichiello, W.E. (1998). Behavior therapy for obsessive–compulsive disorder. In M.A. Jenike, L. Baer, & W.E. Minichiello (Eds.), *Obsessive–compulsive disorder: Practical management* (pp. 337–367). St. Louis, MO: Mosby.

Ball, S.G., Baer, L., & Otto, M.W. (1996). Symptom subtypes of obsessive–compulsive disorder in behavioral treatment studies: A quantitative review. *Behaviour Research and Therapy, 47,* 47–51.

Beck, A.T. (1976). *Cognitive therapy and the emotional disorders.* New York: International University Press.

Beck, A.T. (1995). Cognitive therapy: Past, present, and future. In M.J. Mahoney (Ed.), *Cognitive and constructive psychotherapies: Theory, research, and practice* (pp. 29–40). New York: Springer.

Beck, A.T. (1996). Beyond belief: A theory of modes, personality, and psychopathology. In P.M. Slakovskis (Ed.). *Frontiers of cognitive therapy* (pp. 1–25). New York: Guilford Press.

Beck, A.T., & Clark, D.A. (1997). An information processing model of anxiety: Autonomic and strategic processes. *Behaviour Research and Therapy, 35,* 49–58.

Beck, A.T., & Freeman, A. (1990). *Cognitive therapy of personality disorders.* New York: Guilford Press.

Beck, A.T., Emery, G., & Greenberg, R.L. (1985). *Anxiety disorder and phobias: A cognitive perspective.* New York: Basic Books.

Beck, A. T., Freeman, A., & Davis, D. (2004). *Cognitive therapy of personality disorders.* New York: Guilford Press.

Beck, J. (1995). *Cognitive therapy: Basics and beyond.* New York: Guilford Press.

Beck, J. (2005). *Cognitive therapy for challenging problems: What to do when the basics don't work.* New York: Guilford Press.

Bowlby, J. (1985). The role of childhood experience in cognitive disturbance. In M.J. Mahoney, & A. Freeman (Eds.), *Cognition and psychotherapy* (pp. 181–200). New York: Plenum Press.

Burns, D. (1980). *Feeling good.* New York: Avon.

Calamari, J.E., Cohen, R.J., Rector, N.A., Szacun-Shimizu, K., Riemann, B.C., & Norberg, M.M. (2006). Dysfunctional belief-based obsessive–compulsive disorder subgroups. *Behavior Research and Therapy, 44*(9), 1347–1360.

Calamari, J.E., Wiegartz, P.S., Riemann, R.C., Jones, R.M., Greer, A., Jacobi, D.M., Jahn, S.C., & Carmin, C. (2004). Obsessive–compulsive disorder subtypes: An attempted replication of a symptom-based taxonomy. *Behaviour Research and Therapy, 42,* 647–670.

Carthwright-Hatton, S., & Wells, A. (1997). Beliefs about worry and instructions: The metacognitions questionnaire and its correlates. *Journal of Anxiety Disorders, 11,* 279–296.

Chambless, D.L., & Steketee, G. (1999). Expressed emotion and behavior therapy outcome: A prospective study with obsessive–compulsive and agoraphobic outpatients. *Journal of Consulting and Clinical Psychology, 67,* 658–665.

Clark, D.A. (2004). *Cognitive–behavioral therapy for OCD.* New York: Guilford Press.

Coles, M.E., Frost, R.O., Heimberg, R.G., & Rhéaume, J. (2003). "Not just right experiences": Perfectionism, obsessive–compulsive features and general psychopathology. *Behavior Research and Therapy, 41,* 681–700.

Coles, M.E., Heimburg, R.G., Frost, R.O., & Steketee, G. (2005). Not just right experiences and obsessive–compulsive features: Experimental and self-monitoring perspectives. *Behaviour Research and Therapy, 43*(2), 153–167.

Cottraux, J., Bouvard, M.A., & Milliery, M. (2005). Combining pharmacotherapy with cognitive–behavioral interventions for obsessive–compulsive disorder. *Cognitive Behavior Therapy, 34,* 185–192.

Cottraux, J., Note, I., Yao, S.N., Lafont, S., Note, B., Mollard, E., Bourvard, M., Sauteraud, A., Bourgeois, M., & Dartigues, J.F. (2001). A randomized controlled trial of cognitive therapy versus intensive behavior therapy in obsessive–compulsive disorder. *Psychotherapy and Psychosomatics, 70,* 288–297.

Eddy, K.T., Dutra, L., Bradley, R., & Western, D. (2004). A multidimensional meta-analysis of psychotherapy and pharmacotherapy for obsessive–compulsive disorder. *Clinical Psychology Review, 24,* 1011–1030.

Emmelkamp, P.M.G., van Oppen, P., & van Balkom A.J. (2002). Cognitive changes in patients with obsessive–compulsive rituals treated with exposure *in vivo* and response prevention. In R.O. Frost & G.S. Steketee (Eds.), *Cognitive approaches to obsessions and compulsions: Theory, assessment and treatment* (pp. 391–401). Amsterdam: Elsevier.

Fisher, P.L., & Wells, A. (2005). Experimental modification of beliefs in obsessive–compulsive disorder: A test of the metacognitive model. *Behaviour Research and Therapy, 43,* 821–829.

Foa, E.B., & Franklin, M.E. (2003). Cognitive-behavioral therapy: Efficacy and applications. *CNS Spectrums, 8,* 339.

Foa, E.B., & McNally, R.J. (1996). Mechanisms of change in exposure therapy. In R.M. Rapee (Ed.), *Current controversies in the anxiety disorders* (pp. 329–343). New York: Guilford Press.

Foa, E.B., Abramowitz, J.S., Franklin, M.E., & Kozak, M.J. (1999). Feared consequences, fixity of belief, and treatment outcome in patients with obsessive–compulsive disorder. *Behavior Therapy, 30,* 717–724.

Foa, E.B., Liebowithz, M.R., Kozak, M.J., Davies, S., Campeas, R., Franklin, M.E., Huppert, J.D., Kjernisted, K., Rowan, V., Schmidt, A.B., Simpson, H.B., & Tu, X. (2005). Treatment of obsessive–compulsive disorder by exposure and ritual prevention, clomipramine, and their combination: A randomized, placebo controlled trial. *American Journal of Psychiatry, 162,* 151–161.

Fontenelle, L., Soares, I.D., Marques, C., Rangé, B., Mendolowicz, M.V., & Versiani, M. (2000). Sudden remission of obsessive–compulsive disorder by involuntary, massive exposure. *Canadian Journal of Psychiatry, 45,* 666–667.

Franklin, M.E., Abramowitz, J.S., Kozak, M.J., Levitt, J.T., & Foa, E.B. (2000). Effectiveness of exposure and ritual prevention for obsessive–compulsive disorder: Randomized compared with non randomized samples. *Journal of Consulting and Clinical Psychology, 68,* 594–602.

Freeston, M.H., Ladouceur, R., Gagnon, F., Thibodeau, N., Rheaume, J., Letarte, H., & Bujold, A. (1997). Cognitive–behavioral treatment of obsessive thoughts: A controlled study. *Journal of Consulting and Clinical Psychology, 65,* 405–413.

Fritzler, R.O., Hecker, J.E., & Losee, M.C. (1997). Self-directed treatment with minimal therapist contact: Preliminary findings for obsessive–compulsive disorder. *Behaviour Research and Therapy, 35*(7), 627–631.

Frost, R.O., & Steketee, G. (Eds.). (2002). *Cognitive approaches to obsessions and compulsions: Theory, assessment, and treatment.* Amsterdam: Elsevier.

Goldstein, A.J., & Chambless, D.L. (1978). A reanalysis of agoraphobia. *Behavior Therapy, 9,* 47–59.

Goodman, W.K., Price, L.H., Rasmussen, S.A., Mazure, C., Delgado, P., Heninger, G.R. et al. (1989). The Yale–Brown Obsessive Compulsive Scale. II. Validity. *Archives of General Psychiatry, 46*(11), 1012–1016.

Goodman, W.K., Price, L.H., Rasmussen, S.A., Mazure, C., Fleischmann, R.L., Hill, C.L. et al. (1989). The Yale–Brown Obsessive Compulsive Scale. I. Development, use, and reliability. *Archives of General Psychiatry, 46*(11), 1006–1011.

Goodwin, R., Koenen, K.C., Hellman, F., Guardino, M., & Struening. E. (2002). Help seeking and access to mental health treatment for obsessive–compulsive disorder. *Acta Psychiatrica Scandinavica, 106*(2), 143–149.

Greenberg, L.S., & Safran, J.D. (1987). *Emotion in psychotherapy: Affect, cognition and the process of change.* New York: Guilford Press.

Guidano, V.F. (1990). *The self in process: Towards a post-rationalist cognitive therapy.* New York: Guilford Press.

Guidano, V.F., & Liotti, G. (1985). A constructivist foundation for cognitive therapy. In M.J. Mahoney and A. Freeman (Eds.), *Cognitive and psychotherapy* (pp. 101–142). New York: Plenum Press.

Gwilliam, P., Wells, A., & Carthwright-Hatton, S. (2004). Does metacognition or responsibility predict obsessive–compulsive symptoms: A test of the metacognitive model. *Clinical Psychology and Psychotherapy, 11,* 137–144.

Himle, J.A., Van Etten, M.L., Janeck, A.S., & Fischer, D.J. (2006). Insight as a predictor of treatment outcome in behavioural group treatment for obsessive–compulsive disorder. *Cognitive Therapy and Research, 30*(5), 661– 666.

Hohagen, F., Winklemann, G., Rasche-Rauchle, H., Hand, I., Konig, A., Munchau, N., Hiss, H., Geiger-Kabisch, C., Kappler, C., Schramm, P. et al. (1998). Combination of behaviour therapy with fluvoxamine in comparison with behaviour therapy and placebo. *British Journal of Psychiatry, 173,* 71–78.

Hollander, E., &, Zohar, J. (2004). Beyond refractory obsessions and anxiety states: Towards remission. *Journal of Clinical Psychiatry, 65,* 2–5.

Hollander, E., Koran, L.M., Goodman, W.K., Greist, J.H., Ninan, P.T., Yang, H., Li, D., & Barbato, L.M. (2003). A double-blind, placebo-controlled study of the efficacy and safety of controlled-release fluvoxamine in patients with obsessive–compulsive disorder. *Journal of Clinical Psychiatry, 64,* 640–647.

Jacobson, N.S., & Truax, P. (1991). Clinical significance: A statistical approach to defining meaningful change in psychotherapy research. *Journal of Consulting and Clinical Psychology, 59,* 12–19.

Kohut, H. (1971). *The analysis of the self.* New York: International Universities Press.

Kordan, A., Kahl, G., Brooks, A., Voderholzer, U., Rasche-Räuchle, H., & Hohagen. F. (2005). Clinical outcome in patients with obsessive–compulsive disorder after discontinuation of SRI treatment: Results from a two-year follow-up. *European Archives of Psychiatry and Clinical Neuroscience, 5*(1), 48–50.

Leahy, R.L. (2002). A model of emotional schemas. *Cognitive and Behavioral Practice, 9,* 177–190.

Liotti, G. (1988). Attachment and cognition: A guideline for the reconstruction of the early pathogenic experiences in cognitive psychotherapy. In C. Perris, I.M. Blackburn, & H. Perris (Eds.), *Cognitive psychotherapy: Theory and practice* (pp. 62–79). New York: Springer-Verlag.

Liotti, G. (1991). Patterns of attachment and the assessment of interpersonal schemata: Understanding and changing difficult patient–therapist relationships in cognitive psychotherapy. *Journal of Cognitive Psychotherapy, 5,* 105–114.

Mataix-Cols, D., Marks, I.M., Greist, J.H., Kobak, K.A., & Baer, L. (2002). Obsessive–compulsive symptom dimensions as predictors of compliance with and response to behaviour therapy: Results from a controlled trial. *Psychotherapy and Psychosomatics, 71,* 255–262.

Mataix-Cols, D., Rauch, S.L., Manzo, P.A., Jenike, M.A., & Baer, L. (1999). Use of factor-analyzed symptom dimensions to predict outcomes with serotonin reuptake inhibitors and placebo in the treatment of obsessive–compulsive disorder. *American Journal of Psychiatry, 156,* 1409–1416.

McLean, P.D., Whittal, M.L., Thordarson, D.S., Taylor, S., Sochting, I., Koch, W.J., Paterson, R., & Anderson, K.W. (2001). Cognitive versus behavior therapy in the group treatment of obsessive–compulsive disorder. *Journal of Consulting and Clinical Psychology, 69,* 205–214.

Moher, D., Schulz, K.F., Altman, D.G., & CONSORT. (2001). The CONSORT statement: Revised recommendations for improving the quality of reports of parallel group randomized trials. *Lancet, 357*(9263), 1191–1194.

Obsessive Compulsive Cognitions Work Group. (1997). Cognitive assessment of obsessive–compulsive disorder. *Behaviour Research and Therapy, 35,* 667–681.

Obsessive Compulsive Cognitions Working Group. (2001). Development and initial validation of the Obsessive Beliefs Questionnaire and the Interpretation of Intrusions Inventory. *Behaviour and Research Therapy, 39,* 987–1005.

Obsessive Compulsive Cognitions Working Group. (2003). Psychometric validation of the Obsessive Beliefs Questionnaire and the Interpretation of Intrusions Inventory: Part 1. *Behaviour Research and Therapy, 41,* 863–878.

Obsessive Compulsive Cognitions Working Group. (2005). Psychometric validation of the Obsessive Beliefs Questionnaire and the Interpretation of Intrusions Inventory: Part 2. *Behaviour and Research Therapy, 43,* 1527–1542.

O'Connor, K.P., Aardema, F., Robillard, S., Guay. S., Pélisser, M.C., Todorov, C., Borgeat, F., Leblanc, V., Grenier, S., & Doucet, P. (2006). Cognitive behaviour therapy and medication in the treatment of obsessive–compulsive disorder. *Acta Psychiatrica Scandinavica, 113, 5,* 408–419.

Osgood-Hynes, D., Riemann, B., & Björgvinsson, T. (2003). Short-term residential treatment for obsessive–compulsive disorder. *Brief Treatment and Crisis Intervention, 3*(4), 413–435.

Pallanti, S., Hollander, E., Bienstock, C., Koran, L., Leckman, J., Marazziti, D. Pato, M., Stein, D., & Zohar, J. (2002). Treatment non-response in OCD: Methodological issues and operational definitions. *International Journal of Neuropsychopharmacology, 5,* 181–191.

Piaget, J. (1960). *The child's conception of the world* (J. & A. Tomilson, Trans.). Totowa, NJ: Littlefield, Adams. (Original work published in 1926.)

Pollard, C.A. (2007). Treatment readiness, ambivalence, and resistance. In M.M. Antony, C. Purdon, & L. Summerfeldt (Eds.), *Psychological treatment of OCD: Fundamentals and beyond.* Washington, D.C.: APA Books.

Promakoff, L., Epstein, N., & Covi, L. (1986). Homework compliance: an uncontrolled variable in cognitive therapy outcome research. *Behavior Therapy, 17,* 433–446.

Rachman, S. (1998). A cognitive theory of obsessions: Elaborations. *Behaviour Research and Therapy, 36,* 385–401.

Rachman, S. (2007). Self-constructs in obsessive–compulsive disorder. *Journal of Cognitive Psychotherapy, 21*(2), 257–261.

Rachman, S. (2003). *The treatment of obsessions.* Oxford: Oxford University Press.

Riggs, D.S., & Foa, E.B. (1993). Obsessive compulsive disorder. In D.H. Barlow (Ed.), *Clinical handbook of psychological disorders: A step-by-step treatment manual* (2nd ed.) (pp. 189–239). New York: Guilford Press.

Rosen, H. (1989). Piagetian theory and cognitive therapy. In A. Freeman, K.M. Simon, L.E. Beutler, & H. Arkowitz (Eds.), *Comprehensive handbook of cognitive therapy* (pp. 189–212). New York: Plenum Press.

Rowa, K., Antony, M.M., Summerfeldt, L.J., Purdon, C., & Swinson, R.P. (2004). *The effectiveness of office-based versus home-based exposure with response prevention for obsessive compulsive disorder.* Poster presented at the meeting of the Association for Advancement of Behavior Therapy, New Orleans, LA.

Rufer, M., Grothusen, A., Mab, R., Peter, H., & Hand. I. (2005). Temporal stability of symptom dimensions in adult patients with obsessive–compulsive disorder. *Journal of Affective Disorders, 88,* 99–102.

Safran, J.D. (1990a). Towards a refinement of cognitive therapy in light of interpersonal therapy: I. Theory. *Clinical Psychology Review, 10,* 87–105.

Safran, J.D. (1990b). Towards a refinement of cognitive therapy in light of interpersonal therapy: II. *Clinical Psychology Review, 10,* 107–121.

Salkovskis, P.M. (1985). Obsessional–compulsive problems: A cognitive–behavioural analysis. *Behaviour Research and Therapy, 23,* 571–583.

Salkovskis, P.M. (1989). Cognitive–behavioural factors and the persistence of intrusive thoughts in obsessional problems. *Behaviour and Research Therapy, 27,* 677–682.

Schwartz, J.M. (1996). *Brain lock: Free yourself from obsessive–compulsive behaviour.* New York: Harper Collins.

Shafran, R., Thordarson, D.S., & Rachman, S. (1996). Thought–action fusion in obsessive–compulsive disorder. *Journal of Anxiety Disorders, 10,* 379–391.

Simpson, H.B., Foa, E.B., Liebowitz, M.R., Ledley, D.R., Huppert, J.D., Cahill, S., Vermes, D., Schmidt, A.B., Hembree, E., Franklin, M., Campeas, R., Hahn, C.G., & Petkova, E. (2008). A randomized, controlled trial of cognitive–behavioral therapy for augmenting pharmacotherapy in obsessive–compulsive disorder. *American Journal of Psychiatry, 165*(5), 621–630.

Simpson H.B., Franklin, M.E., Cheng J., Foa, E.G., & Liebowitz, M.R. (2005). Standard criteria for relapse are needed in obsessive–compulsive disorder. *Depression and Anxiety, 21,* 1–8.

Simpson, H.B., Huppert, J.D., & Petkova, E. (2005). Response versus remission in obsessive–compulsive disorder. *Journal of Clinical Psychiatry, 67*(2), 269–276.

Sookman, D., & Pinard, G. (1999). Integrative cognitive therapy for obsessive–compulsive disorder: A focus on multiple schemas. *Cognitive and Behavioral Practice, 6,* 351–361.

Sookman, D., & Pinard, G. (2002). Overestimation of threat and intolerance of uncertainty in obsessive compulsive disorder. In R.O. Frost & G. Steketee (Eds.), *Cognitive approaches to obsessions and compulsions: Theory, assessment and treatment* (pp. 63–89). Oxford: Elsevier.

Sookman, D., & Pinard, G. (2007). Specialized cognitive behavior therapy for resistant obsessive–compulsive disorder: Elaboration of a schema-based model. In L.P. Riso, P.L. du Toit, D.J. Stein, & J.E. Young (Eds.), *Cognitive schemas and core beliefs in psychological problems: a scientist-practitioner guide* (pp. 93–109). Washington, D.C.: American Psychological Association.

Sookman, D., & Steketee, G. S. (2007). Directions in specialized cognitive behaviour therapy for resistant obsessive–compulsive disorder: Theory and practice of two approaches. *Cognitive and Behavioural Practice, 14*(1), 1–17.

Sookman, D., Abramowitz, J.S., Calamari, J.E., Wilhelm, S., & McKay, D. (2005). Subtypes of obsessive–compulsive disorder: Implications for specialized cognitive behavior therapy. *Behavior Therapy, 36,* 393–400.

Sookman, D., Calamari, J., Abramowitz, J., Wilhelm, S., Rector, N., & Clark, D. (2006). *Directions in specialized cognitive behavior therapy for resistant obsessive–compulsive disorder: A multi-site study.* Paper presented at the 40th annual convention of Association for Behavioral and Cognitive Therapies, November 16–19, Chicago, IL.

Sookman, D., Dalfen, S., Annable, L., & Pinard, G. (2003). *Role of dysfunctional beliefs on efficacy of CBT for resistant OCD.* Paper presented at the 37th annual convention of Association for Advancement of Behavior Therapy, November 20–23, Boston, MA.

Sookman, D., Pinard, G., & Beauchemin, N. (1994). Multidimensional schematic restructuring. Treatment for obsessions: theory and practice. *Journal of Cognitive Psychotherapy, 8,* 175–194.

Sookman, D., Pinard, G., & Beck, A.T. (2001). Vulnerability schemas in obsessive–compulsive disorder. *Journal of Cognitive Psychotherapy: An International Quarterly, 15,* 109–130.

Stanley, M.A., & Turner, S.M. (1995). Current status of pharmacological behavioral treatment obsessive–compulsive disorder. *Behavior Therapy, 26,* 163–186.

Steketee, G.S. (1993). *Treatment of obsessive compulsive disorder.* New York: Guilford Press.

Steketee, G.S., & Frost, R.O. (1994). Measurement of risk-taking in obsessive–compulsive disorder. *Behavioural and Cognitive Psychotherapy, 22,* 287–298.

Steketee, G.S., & Frost, R.O. (2003). Compulsive hoarding: Current status of the research. *Clinical Psychology Review, 23,* 905–927.

Steketee, G.S., Chambless, D.L., & Tran, G.Q. (2001). Effects of axis I and II comorbidity on behavior therapy outcome for obsessive–compulsive disorder and agoraphobia. *Comprehensive Psychiatry, 42,* 76–86.

Steketee, G.S., Chambless, D.L., Tran, G.Q., Worden, H., & Gillis, M.A. (1996). Behavioral avoidance test for obsessive compulsive disorder. *Behaviour Research and Therapy, 34,* 73–83.

Steketee, G.S., Frost, R.O., & Bogart, K. (1996). The Yale–Brown Obsessive Compulsive Scale: Interview versus self-report. *Behavior Research and Therapy, 34,* 675–684.

Steketee, G.S, Frost, R.O., Tolin, D.F. et al. *A waitlist controlled trial of treatment for compulsive hoarding.* Paper in preparation.

Steketee, G.S., Frost, R.O., Wincze, J., Greene, K., & Douglas, H. (2000). Group and individual treatment of compulsive hoarding: A pilot study. *Behaviour and Cognitive Psychotherapy, 28,* 259–268.

Steketee, G.S., Lam, J.N., Chambless, D.L., Rodebaugh, T.L., & McCullouch, C.E. (2007). Effects of perceived criticism on anxiety and depression during behavioural treatment of anxiety disorders. *Behavioural Research and Therapy, 45,* 11–19.

Stewart. S.E., Stack, D.E., Farell, C., Pauls, D.L., & Jenike, M.A. (2005). Effectiveness of intensive residential treatment (IRT) for severe, refractory obsessive–compulsive disorder. *Journal of Psychiatric Research, 39,* 603–609.

Summerfeldt, L.J. (2004). Understanding and treating incompleteness in obsessive–compulsive disorder. *Journal of Clinical Psychology/In Session, 60,* 1155–1168.

Summerfeldt, L.J. (2007). Symmetry, incompleteness, and ordering. In J. Abramowitz, D. McKay, & S. Taylor (Eds.), *Obsessive–compulsive disorder: Subtypes and spectrum conditions.* Baltimore, MD: The Johns Hopkins University Press.

Taylor, S., Abramowitz, J.S., & McKay, D. (2007). Cognitive–behavioral models of obsessive–compulsive disorder. In M.M. Antony, C. Purdon, & L. Summerfeldt (Eds.), *Psychological treatment of obsessive–compulsive disorder: Fundamentals and beyond.* Washington, D.C.: APA Books.

Taylor, S., Abramowitz, J.S., McKay, D., Calarari, J.E., Sookman, D., Kyrios, M., Wilhelm, S., & Carmin, C. (2006). Do dysfunctional beliefs play a role in all types of obsessive–compulsive disorder? *Journal of Anxiety Disorder, 20,* 85–97.

Teasdale, J.D., & Barnard, P.J. (1993). *Affect, cognition, and change: Re-modeling depressive thought.* Hillsdale, NJ: Lawrence Erlbaum.

Tolin, D.F., Abramowitz, J.S., & Diefenbach, G.J. (2005). Defining "response" in clinical trials for OCD: A signal detection analysis of the Yale–Brown Obsessive Compulsive Scale, *Journal of Clinical Psychiatry, 66,* 1549–1557.

Tolin, D.F., Frost, R.O., & Steketee, G.S. (2007). *Buried in treasures: Help for compulsive acquiring, saving, and hoarding.* Oxford: Oxford University Press.

Van Dyke, M.M., & Pollard, C.A. (2005). Treatment of refractory obsessive–compulsive disorder: The St. Louis Model. *Cognitive and Behavioural Practice, 12,* 30–39.

Van Oppen, P., De Haan, E., Van Balkom, A.J.L.M., Spinhoven, P., Hoogduin, K., & Van Dyck, R. (1995). Cognitive therapy and exposure *in vivo* in the treatment of obsessive–compulsive disorder. *Behaviour Research and Therapy, 33*(4), 379–390.

Vogel, P., Stiles, T.C., & Götestam, K.G. (2004). Adding cognitive therapy elements to exposure therapy for obsessive compulsive disorder: A controlled study. *Behavioural and Cognitive Psychotherapy, 32,* 275–290.

Wells, A., & Matthews, G. (1994). *Attention and emotion: A clinical perspective.* Hove, U.K.: Lawrence Erlbaum.

Wells, A., Gwilliam, P., & Carthwright-Hatton, S. (2001). *The thought fusion instrument.* Unpublished self-report scale. University of Manchester, U.K.

Whittal, M.L., Thordarson, D.S., & McLean, P.D. (2005). Treatment of obsessive–compulsive disorder: Cognitive behavior therapy vs. exposure and response prevention. *Behavior Research and Therapy, 43,* 1559–1576.

Wilhelm, S. (2004). Cognitive treatment of obsessions. *Brief Treatment and Crisis Intervention, 60*(3), 187–199.

Wilhelm, S., & Steketee, G. (2006). *Cognitive therapy of obsessive–compulsive disorder: A guide for professionals.* Oakland, CA: New Harbinger.

Wilhelm, S., Steketee, G., & Yovel, I. (2004). *Multi-site study of predictors of treatment outcome for OCD.* Paper presented at the 11th annual OC Foundation, July 23–25, Chicago, IL.

Wilhelm, S., Steketee, G., Fama, J.M., Buhlmann, U., Teachman, B.A., & Golan, E. (submitted). Modular cognitive therapy for obsessive–compulsive disorder: A waitlist-controlled trial. *Journal of Cognitive Psychology.*

Wilhelm, S., Steketee, G., Reilly-Harrington, N., Deckersbach, T., Buhlmann, U., & Baer, L. (2005). Effectiveness of cognitive therapy for obsessive–compulsive disorder: An open trial. *Journal of Cognitive Psychotherapy, 19*, 173–179.

chapter three

Treatment for complex PTSD

Christie Jackson
New York University School of Medicine
New York, New York

Kore Nissenson
Montefiore Medical Center
Bronx, New York

Marylene Cloitre
New York University School of Medicine
New York, New York

Contents

Treatments for posttraumatic stress disorder (PTSD) were originally proposed to address the consequences of a specific traumatic event, such as a rape or an automobile accident. It is now acknowledged that single incidents of trauma are rare, and among those who are exposed to trauma multiple traumatic exposures are the norm rather than the exception (Kessler, 2000). PTSD related to chronic and repeated forms of trauma (e.g., childhood abuse, domestic violence, being a witness to genocide) is associated with a more complex constellation of symptoms that can be especially resistant to treatment. In this chapter, we describe PTSD in its more complex forms and introduce a modular sequential treatment approach that has been successful in addressing complex PTSD symptoms and in resolving some of the difficulties that have been identified in using traditional PTSD treatments. We provide an overview of the treatment, its evidence base, and clinical case vignettes illustrating the application of these interventions.

Overview of PTSD

Posttraumatic stress disorder is characterized by three symptom clusters: (1) reexperiencing the traumatic event, (2) avoidance of reminders of the event or feeling emotionally numb, and (3) hyperarousal, such as exaggerated startle response and hypervigilance. Estimates of the lifetime prevalence of PTSD in the general population range from 7 to 12% (Breslau, 2002; Keane, Marshall, & Taft, 2006; Kessler, Sonnega, Bromet, & Hughes, 1995; Sareen et al., 2007). Epidemiological studies indicate that approximately 80% of individuals with PTSD have a comorbid psychiatric diagnosis (Kessler et al., 1995). Brady and colleagues (1997) reported that PTSD is likely to co-occur with affective disorders, other anxiety disorders, somatization, substance abuse, and dissociative disorders. There is also significant overlap between PTSD and personality disorders (e.g., Dunn et al., 2004; Jones, Burrell-Hodgson, Tate, & Fowler, 2006; Shea, Zlotnick, & Weisberg, 1999), and the presence of Axis II pathology often results in poorer PTSD treatment outcomes (e.g., Cloitre & Koenen, 2001; Heffernan

& Cloitre, 2000; Hembree, Cahill, & Foa, 2004). Epidemiological, community, and clinical sample studies suggest that PTSD is among the most disabling and costly of psychiatric disorders (e.g., Kessler, 2000; Schoenfeld
et al., 1997).

Reviews and meta-analyses of treatments for PTSD indicate that various forms of cognitive–behavioral therapy (CBT) are effective for PTSD
(e.g., Bradley, Greene, Russ, Dutra, & Westen, 2005; Sherman, 1998; Van
Etten & Taylor, 1998). Indeed, effect size analyses indicate that approximately 50% of clients who complete a CBT experience significant reduction
in PTSD symptoms, making them among the most successful psychosocial interventions to date (Bradley et al., 2005). CBT interventions include
prolonged exposure (PE), cognitive processing therapy (CPT), and stress
inoculation training (SIT), all of which are recommended in the Practice
Guidelines for PTSD (Foa, Davidson, & Frances, 2000). However, there are
few interventions that have been designed to address the full spectrum
of difficulties that are often seen in chronic PTSD, such as anger management problems, tendency to use substances to cope, and problematic
interpersonal and social relationships, which have been well documented,
particularly among combat veterans (Creamer, Morris, Biddle, & Elliott,
1999; Jordan et al., 1992; Kulka et al., 1990; Zatzick et al., 1997). Accordingly,
there has been a recent call for treatment research to address and evaluate
the efficacy of treatments in resolving such difficulties (Foa, Friedman,
Keane, & Cohen, 2008).

Defining complex PTSD and its treatment

Complex PTSD or "PTSD and its associated features," as it is designated
in the DSM-IV (APA, 2000), identifies the presence of problems such as
impaired affect modulation and impaired relationships with others, and
as such can incorporate the symptoms described above. However, complex PTSD was intended to describe a set of symptoms associated with
particular kinds of traumatic events, such as childhood abuse or being
a prisoner of war (Herman, 1992), where symptoms such as substance
abuse or anger problems were not viewed as *secondary* or reactive to PTSD
(e.g., using substances to cope with hyperarousal) but rather as impairments that were directly the result of prolonged trauma, equal in salience
to those of the symptoms clusters of PTSD (reexperiencing, avoidance/
numbing, and hyperarousal) and conceptually viewed as impairments
in affective and interpersonal self-regulatory functions (e.g., van der
Kolk, 1996). Under this conceptualization, the classic symptoms of PTSD
themselves are viewed as a form of a chronic dysregulated emotional
response as reflected in contrasting and often co-occurring symptoms of

hyperarousal/emotional numbing, hypervigilance/poor concentration, and reexperiencing/avoidance (e.g., Frewen & Lanius, 2006; Litz, Orsillo, Kaloupek, & Weathers, 2000).

Complex PTSD has also been particularly identified as arising from childhood abuse, perhaps due to its prevalence (e.g., Finkelhor & Dziuba-Leatherman, 1994), its prototypically recurring nature (e.g., Stewart, Livingston, & Dennison, 2008), and its well-documented status as a risk factor for exposure to other types of childhood and adulthood traumas (e.g., Coid et al., 2001; Dong et al., 2004). The study of complex PTSD in the context of childhood abuse has highlighted and reinforced a view of the disorder as related to emotion dysregulation and related interpersonal problems. Several developmental studies have found that abused children show rigid and situationally inappropriate affective displays, diminished emotional self-awareness, difficulty modulating excitement in emotionally arousing situations, difficulty recovering from frustration or distress, and mood lability (Shields, Cicchetti, & Ryan, 1994; Shipman, Edwards, Brown, Swisher, & Jennings, 2005; Shipman, Zeman, Penza, & Champion, 2000). They also show impaired interpersonal and social functioning, particularly in stressful or high affect situations; have problems in management of conflictual situations and reactive aggression (e.g., Sroufe, Fox, & Pancake, 1983); and have a tendency to expect little support in times of distress or need (Shipman et al., 2000, 2005; Suess, Grossmann, & Sroufe, 1992). Similar symptoms are seen in adults with childhood histories (Cloitre, Stovall-McClough, Zorbas, & Charuvastra, 2008). All of above are instances of the symptoms described in complex PTSD.

The presence of these symptoms indicates the need to revise and expand current PTSD treatment to address and resolve such difficulties. They are reported as troubling to PTSD patients and have been found to contribute to overall functional impairment. A recent evaluation of factors contributing to functional impairment as measured by problems in work, home, social, and family relationships found that difficulties with emotion regulation (managing negative moods) and interpersonal problems account for as much functional impairment as PTSD symptoms themselves, even after controlling for the latter (Cloitre, Miranda, Stovall-McClough, & Han, 2005). Moreover, in a review of 98 consecutive initial evaluations at our trauma clinic, the symptom or problem most frequently identified as the reason for seeking treatment was interpersonal problems (67%), followed by PTSD symptoms (59%) and mood problems (31%) (Levitt & Cloitre, 2005).

Finally, these difficulties have been identified as related to limited success in traditional PTSD treatments. Problems with emotion regulation have been associated with reduced PTSD symptom resolution in CBT treatments (Blanchard & Hickling, 1997; Foa, Riggs, Massie & Yarczower, 1995; Tarrier, Sommerfield, Pilgrim, & Faragher, 2000; Taylor et al., 2001). In particular, problems with anger, difficulty managing anxious arousal, and a tendency to dissociate have been identified as predictors of less successful outcome in exposure-based treatment (Jaycox & Foa, 1996). Poor compliance (Burnstein, 1986; Scott & Stradling, 1997) and high dropout rates (McDonagh-Coyle et al., 2005; Schnurr et al., 2007) have been associated with this emotionally intensive form of treatment among those who have experienced multiple traumatization and/or a history of abuse or difficulty with anger (Chemtob, Novaco, Hamada, Gross, & Smith, 1997).

Nevertheless, the emotional processing of traumatic material, via some form of exposure to the memories, is largely agreed to be a critical ingredient to the resolution of PTSD symptoms. In addition, there is evidence that, when a client has successfully engaged in exposure therapy, the long-term benefits are superior to those found in other treatments (Foa, Rothbaum, Riggs, & Murdock, 1991; McDonagh-Coyle et al., 2005) and include continued reduction in PTSD symptoms at 6-month follow-up.

Rather than reject the use of exposure and its potential long-term benefits, we have followed the recommendation of several experts in the study of complex PTSD who have long advocated phase-based treatments, in which the first phase serves as an orienting or stabilizing stage of treatment and the second phase focuses on trauma processing (e.g., Herman, 1992). We have developed and tested a phase-based treatment for complex PTSD in which the organization, content, and goals of each phase have been informed by the empirical literature (Cloitre, Cohen, & Koenan, 2006). The first phase of treatment, skills training in affective and interpersonal regulation (STAIR), is comprised of interventions that address difficulties typical of PTSD patients related to emotion regulation and interpersonal functioning. The second phase of treatment focuses primarily on the working through and meaningful reorganization of traumatic memories, which we propose is supported by and reinforces the emotion regulation skills work completed in the first phase.

The often-stated mechanism of action attributed to the success of trauma memory processing in reducing PTSD symptoms is the extinction of the fear response associated with the traumatic memory which in turn allows access to and reorganization of the memory. An alternative and complementary proposal is that trauma memory processing is an activity that recruits, reinforces, and consolidates emotion regulation capacities and allows exploration and meaningful reworking of highly charged emotional memories. This interpretation provides an explanation for the sometimes observed effective resolution of trauma-related emotional disturbances in single sessions or single life experiences ("catharsis").

The evidence base for STAIR/modified prolonged exposure (MPE) is comprised of four studies, three among adults and one among adolescents. A randomized controlled trial enrolling women ($n = 58$) with PTSD related to childhood abuse found that compared to a wait-list control ($n = 31$), STAIR/MPE ($n = 27$) produced significant improvement not only in PTSD symptoms but also in several affect regulation problems, including dissociation, anger, anxiety, and negative mood regulation beliefs, as well as improvement in interpersonal problems and social adjustment (Cloitre, Koenen, Cohen, & Han, 2002). Moreover, Phase 1 therapeutic alliance and improved negative mood regulation predicted Phase 2 exposure success in reducing PTSD, suggesting the value of establishing a strong therapeutic relationship and emotion regulation skills before exposure work.

A second follow-up randomized controlled trial study ($n = 104$) compared STAIR/MPE to each of its treatment component parts, where supportive counseling (SC) was introduced into each of the comparison treatments to control for number of sessions, length of treatment, and time with therapist: STAIR/MPE ($n = 33$) versus SC/MPE ($n = 38$) versus STAIR/SC ($n = 33$). The combination treatment (STAIR/MPE) was superior to the other two treatments in PTSD remission and in the reduction of emotion regulation and interpersonal problems (Cloitre, 2007a). Importantly, drop-out rates were significantly lower in the combination treatment (16%) as compared to the exposure alone condition (48%) and similar to the non-exposure treatment (27%), suggesting better engagement in the therapy. We also observed less session-to-session distress during exposure when it was preceded by the skills training as compared to when it was not (i.e., when the patient received only supportive counseling before exposure).

In a third study, the treatment was implemented in a sample ($n = 59$) of treatment-seeking clients with posttraumatic stress and other symptoms related to exposure to the terrorist attacks at the World Trade Center on 9/11. The treatment was administered in a flexible manner, where the number of sessions on each major component of the treatment (emotion regulation skills, interpersonal skills, and exposure) was guided by the client's needs. Using a benchmarking approach, the treatment was found to be as effective for this population (using an effect size metric) as for those with PTSD related to childhood abuse (Levitt, Malta, Martin, Davis, & Cloitre, 2007). In particular, the treatment was effective in reducing use of alcohol to cope and in increasing the use of social support, both well-identified problems in disaster populations. Thus, the intervention appears successful in treating the range of symptoms it was intended to target in multiply traumatized populations and also appears to address problems that tend to get ignored in less troubled populations.

Finally, a study comparing the treatment in its adolescent adaptation (called *life skills/life story*) for multiply traumatized inner-city girls ($n = 53$)

found that, relative to an assessment-only comparison ($n = 30$), girls who participated in the treatment ($n = 23$) reported better emotion regulation and social skills and showed improved conduct in the classroom as rated by the teacher (Cloitre, 2007b).

Structure and content of treatment

STAIR is a hybrid treatment that blends together elements from several stress and emotion management interventions, including those from stress inoculation training (SIT), which addresses anger management difficulties (Chemtob et al., 1997), and dialectical behavior therapy (DBT) (Linehan, 1993). The DBT interventions included are those that focus on emotion regulation and on effective interpersonal functioning and have been tailored for the complex trauma population. In STAIR, each session incorporates psychoeducation, skills acquisition, skills application and practice, and assignment of between-session work to generalize the application of skills. During the exposure phase, the memory processing is followed by an exploration of the meaning of the trauma, particularly as related to views of self and self in relation to others. In the research setting, we have typically implemented the treatment in 16 sessions with 8 sessions of skills training followed by 8 sessions of exposure work. In private practice, we have used this sequenced treatment over a much lengthier period and have found that an iterative process of cycling through the skills and memory work several times can be effective in strengthening skills and the client's clarity that the memory of the trauma is truly "in the past." The structure of the treatment and a session-by-session summary of its focus are presented in Figure 3.1.

STAIR treatment goals and associated interventions include: (1) enhancing emotional awareness through directed attention and description of feelings as they emerge in daily activities; (2) improving emotion regulation through training in sustained online emotional awareness and affective expression through actions, words, and thoughts; (3) learning the adaptive use of emotions to achieve social goals; (4) learning to identify adaptive and achievable social goals in different kinds of relationships (i.e., flexibility); and (5) attaining a sense of emotional and social self-efficacy and self-acceptance that facilitates living in the world with compassion and empathy (agency and compassion).

Emotional awareness

In the first few sessions, clients are taught how to become aware of and validate their own emotions. We provide psychoeducation about the impact of trauma on emotional functioning, including tendencies to numb

Review of Phase I Sessions

Session 1   *Introduction to Treatment.* Treatment overview and goals; introduction to focused breathing

Session 2   *Emotional Awareness.* Psychoeducation on impact of childhood abuse on emotion regulation; importance of recognizing feelings; exploration and guidance in feeling identification; practice of self-monitoring

Session 3   *Emotion Regulation.* Psychoeducation on connections among feelings, thoughts, and behaviors; identification of strengths and weaknesses in emotion regulation; tailoring and practicing emotion coping skills; identification of pleasurable activities

Session 4   *Emotionally Engaged Living.* Psychoeducation on acceptance of feelings/distress tolerance; assessment of pros and cons of tolerating distress; awareness of positive feelings as a guide to goal identification

Session 5   *Understanding Relationship Patterns.* Psychoeducation on interpersonal schemas and relationship between feelings and interpersonal goals; introduction to Interpersonal Schemas Worksheet I

Session 6   *Changing Relationship Patterns.* Psychoeducation on role plays; identification of relevant interpersonal situations; role plays; generation of alternative schemas; introduction to Interpersonal Schemas Worksheet II

Session 7   *Agency in Relationships.* Psychoeducation on assertiveness; discussion of alternative schemas and behavioral responses; role plays requiring assertiveness; generation of alternative schemas

Session 8   *Flexibility in Relationships.* Psychoeducation on flexibility in interpersonal relationships; discussion of alternative schemas and behavioral responses; role plays requiring flexibility; generation of alternative schemas; discuss transition form Phase I to Phase II of treatment

Figure 3.1 Building emotional and social resources: summary of Phase I (STAIR) sessions.

feelings and experiencing feelings as either extreme or nonexistent, and discuss that in some traumatic circumstances (childhood abuse, being a prisoner of war) emotions can be more of a liability than an asset. Clients are taught that emotions serve important functions in everyday life and are vital in decision making and effective interpersonal functioning. We utilize a self-monitoring form (see Appendix A) in the session and assign it for between session tasks to help clients begin to label their feelings, triggers, cognitions, and typical coping responses.

Review of Phase II

Session 9   *Motivating and Planning for Memory Work.* Rationale for narrative
                 work and creation of memory hierarchy

Session 10   *Introduction to Exposure.* Review rationale for narrative work; practice
                 with neutral memory; conduct first narrative; therapist and client listen
                 to first tape together; explore beliefs about self and other in the narrative

Session 11   *Deepening Exploration of Memories and Contrasting with the Present.*
                 Begin with emotional check in; review analysis of last memory; conduct
                 narrative (same or new memory); review and revise narrative-based
                 interpersonal schemas; practice role plays relevant to new schemas

Session 12+   *Exploration of Other Affective Themes.* Continue selection of memories;
                 explore affective themes other than fear, such as shame and loss;
                 identify and revise schemas related to shame and loss

Figure 3.1 (cont.) Modified prolonged exposure: summary of Phase II (MPE)
sessions.

Emotion regulation

Emotion regulation skills are built and capitalize on whatever healthy
coping strategies the client brings to the treatment. Clients are introduced to the traditional "three channels of distress" in a visual format.
We explain that emotional reactions involve each of these three channels
(physiological/somatic, cognitive, and behavioral), which are interrelated.
Many clients immediately conclude (correctly) that negative or maladaptive emotions can be exacerbated as they cycle through the three channels.
The therapist points out that the interrelatedness of the three channels can
be beneficial in that adaptive modification or regulation of any one of the
three channels can influence the others. For example, the therapist will
propose that (and suggest that the client explore whether) reciting a list of
positive self statements can ameliorate feelings of sadness or worthless-
ness or that taking a time-out can help reduce an angry reaction. Clients
are encouraged to expand their repertoire of coping skills so they can
experiment with various ones for goodness of personal fit and continue to
refine their emotional coping strategies.

Emotionally engaged living

Emotion regulation skills training incorporates strategies not only to
reduce or manage negative feelings but also to increase exposure to positive ones through assigned pleasant events scheduling and self-soothing

tasks. For clients with complex trauma, the notion of feeling happy or allowing pleasurable events to occur can be fraught with guilt and shame because they feel they do not deserve it and it is inconsistent with whom they believe themselves to be (e.g., a victim who let bad things happen and now deserves no better than a bad life). Moreover, clients sometimes describe that feeling miserable and "living in the negative" have the value of familiarity and can be comforting in their predictability. The predictability of events and emotional experiences, even if they are negative, can be particularly appealing to those who have experienced trauma. Unpredictability and uncontrollability are the defining characteristics of a traumatic event (e.g., terrorist attack, repeated attacks in warfare or domestic violence), so these characteristics, even in nontraumatic circumstances (e.g., a novel or surprising event), can be experienced as threatening. The therapist validates the fear and uncertainty in the new and unknown but encourages the client to consider "building a life worth living" (Linehan, 1993). This ideally opens up conversation, exploration, and motivation for clients to consider their wishes, desires, and goals which in turn supports them in imagining a life other than the traumatized life in which they tend to feel stuck or "frozen."

Changing relationship patterns

We provide psychoeducation about the development of interpersonal capacities using the concept of interpersonal schemas. The concept of interpersonal schemas is derived from John Bowlby and other attachment theorists who consider these beliefs "working models of relating" (Bowlby, 1969). The construct of interpersonal schemas was further developed by Safran and Segal (1990) who adapted Bowlby's model for cognitive therapy. Interpersonal schemas are core beliefs about the self and others that identify expectations about how others will respond, based on early life experiences. For those who have experienced childhood abuse, other early life adversity (e.g., neglect) or chronic exposure to violence, these schemas reflect negative and often very vivid life circumstances along with the individual's adaptive response to the circumstance. These perceptions, which often facilitated effective living at the time of the trauma, are often maladaptive in "ordinary," nontraumatic environments. Examples of schemas that have emerged in our work with complex PTSD clients include: "If I make my needs known, others will not care" or "If I show my feelings, then people will think I'm overreacting or selfish." Clients are given an Interpersonal Schema Sheet (see Appendix B) to begin exploring their expectations about themselves and others. These schemas reflect feelings and beliefs that are often associated with interpersonal trauma, and they reflect chronic experiences of abuse, invalidation, abandonment, rejection,

specific treatment-interfering scenarios. We also include case vignettes to demonstrate the therapeutic strategies we have found to be most helpful.

Resistance toward experiencing feelings at all

Clients might come into treatment wanting to get rid of their emotions, as feelings have only caused them distress and conflict. They may carry beliefs that having feelings is a weakness and that not having feelings at all is the only way they can be successful. After clarifying and validating the etiology of these beliefs, we provide psychoeducation about the value and necessity of emotional experiences. We provide boundaries around the emotional experience, so it is not perceived as overwhelming and incapacitating.

C. I don't want to have feelings! They just cause me trouble! When I was growing up, the only emotion anyone showed was extreme anger. I never saw love, happiness, or even sadness or fear. When I cried, my dad told me to just shut up or he would give me something to cry about.

T. Well, I know that, growing up, if you showed your feelings you were punished. So I can see why you have grown up believing that emotions are nothing but destructive, so you wish that you didn't even have them.

C. Exactly, so I hope by "emotion regulation," you mean not feeling anything.

T. Actually, emotion regulation means having awareness of your emotions and having choice over how you respond. It also means using the power of your emotions to help you. Emotions always serve some function, always communicate something to us; for example, being scared tells us not to walk down that dark alley, and being angry tells us our rights have been violated. Imagine for a moment that you truly have no emotions—like Spock on *Star Trek*. Now imagine that the world is a place with no emotions.

C. Hmmm ... it would be a cold and dreary place, and I would be bored out of my mind. I guess I don't want to get rid of emotions entirely. But, if I allow myself to start crying, I'm afraid I just won't stop!

T. Yes, I can understand how you could feel that way given that you've closed off your emotions for some time. You may be afraid if you get in touch with your emotions that you'll be opening up a Pandora's box. The difference is that now I am here with you, and I will help you see that emotions have a beginning *and* an end. Emotions naturally come and go, like a wave. If you let yourself experience them, you will see that. Moreover, I will be here to track the experience with you and help identify them. Being aware of what you are feeling and giving recognition and a name to your feelings are likely to make the experience manageable. What are you feeling right now?

C. I have no idea, but I know my heart is racing.

T. Good, often times checking in with what your body is doing is a great way to start. Let's keep going with this and see if we can figure out what you're feeling. I'm noticing your foot is bouncing up and down. Does that feel like anxiety or fear—or excitement?

Resistance toward implementing alternative emotion regulation skills

It is fairly common for clients to face hurdles as they try to implement alternative coping skills from each of the three channels of distress— physiological, behavioral, and cognitive. For example, working with the physiological channel can present challenges that are unique to the complex PTSD patient. Individuals who have histories of interpersonal violence (e.g., rape, combat, childhood sexual abuse) may have trouble with body-based strategies such as focused breathing because directing attention to their body can be incredibly frightening.

T. Let's begin today by reviewing your homework. Your assignment was to practice the diaphragmatic breathing exercise every day that you learned last session.

C. I didn't do it. When I was alone, I just couldn't bring myself to do the breathing.

T. What happened? What got in the way?

C. Even thinking about it made me anxious. I'm sorry to tell you this, but I don't think this breathing is going to help me. It makes me more scared, not less scared.

T. Tuning in to your body sensations can be a scary thing at first. Let's work on this together. Put one hand on your stomach and one on your chest. You don't need to close your eyes if that helps. Now, what are you noticing?

C. I'm realizing that my outbreaths are warmer than my inbreaths, and my stomach feels a little queasy.

T. Okay, good. You're noticing now that your stomach feels a little queasy; maybe it was feeling that way all along and now you're just aware of it. Becoming aware of these body sensations will not make them worse. In fact, developing an awareness of pain in an area of the body and gently sending the breath to that area can even help to alleviate the pain. Often, people who have experienced trauma only feel things from the neck up and subsequently do not take care of their physical or medical needs appropriately.

Resistance toward experiencing positive feelings

What may be less evident than intolerance to negative affect on the part of PTSD clients is discomfort with positive affect. Clients who have experienced complex trauma may believe that feeling positive emotions or being happy is invalidating to their trauma. Bereaved individuals sometimes worry that if they stop mourning they are disrespecting the memory of their loved one. Similarly, clients with complex PTSD may feel that recovery from traumatic events invalidates the person they were when they experienced it, or the person they could have been had the trauma not occurred.

In addition, clients sometimes report they are always "waiting for the other shoe to drop" when pleasure is experienced or when anything good happens to them. If their trauma occurred during a happy period in life, they may develop the illusory belief that if they are never happy again they will not get hurt. Further complicating matters is that PTSD is usually associated with excessive guilt. Survivors of various types of traumas often develop extraordinarily negative views about themselves, their competence and worth as humans, and their right to experience pleasure.

T. Today in our session I would like to discuss the other part of emotion regulation—increasing exposure to positive emotions. Look at this list of pleasurable activities, and tell me which ones you enjoy or would be willing to try.

C. I really don't feel comfortable trying any of these. Isn't it kind of selfish to go around doing pleasurable events all the time?

T. Increasing your exposure to positive feelings is just as important as learning to deal with negative ones. It sounds like you feel that you don't deserve to feel happy.

C. I guess you are right—it feels weird to be happy. It is also scary. Remember, my mother died in a car crash the same day I was full of excitement and happiness, after I got that promotion at work.

T. Yes, I do remember that, and it makes sense that you have associated being happy with bad things happening. Do you think that getting that promotion and feeling happy *caused* your mother's death?

C. Well, no, of course not. I know it was a freak accident and that, if anything, the drunk driver in the other car was to blame. Let me look at this list again. I really don't know what I like. I have spent a lot of time avoiding feelings. I have just gone along with what other people told me to do or with what they wanted to do and tried to feel as little as possible.

T. Then what we will do now is give you a chance to learn what you enjoy and what you do not. In addition, over time you will have some evidence that being happy does not always lead to disastrous outcomes. Which item on the list would you be willing to try before the next session?

Resistance toward working with anger

Experiencing problems with anger and irritability is one of the symptoms of PTSD, and issues related to anger have been shown to be associated with poor treatment outcome in PTSD clients (e.g., Foa et al., 1995). For individuals with complex PTSD, anger often serves certain important, but sometimes maladaptive, functions. First, anger is an emotion that can rapidly replace other emotions such as fear, sadness, or even shame. This makes sense given the protective function of anger; for example, it may sometimes be an emotion that quickly replaces the emotion of fear as a way to protect an individual from feeling vulnerable or getting hurt. Second, anger can be an over-learned behavior resulting from exposure to traumatic environments (e.g., a physically abusive parent or family system) and adopted as a general response to any distressing situation. Third, anger can occur as a way of titrating intimacy within relationships, including the relationship with the therapist. Fourth, "righteous anger" is another problem that can significantly hinder interpersonal relationships. Clients may say that they feel injustice has been done to them and therefore behave in a hostile or aggressive manner to people, including therapists.

T. I am noticing on your self-monitoring sheet that you mention feeling angry several times a day. A variety of triggers seem to elicit feelings of anger—the interaction with your boss, waiting in line at the grocery store, talking to your sister on the phone.

C. Yes, people tell me I'm always angry. Actually, I have lost a lot of friends because of arguing with them.

T. I would like to focus on this example of talking to your sister on the phone. You wrote that she told you she would not be able to attend your birthday party, and you felt anger at a level of "9" on a 0 to 10 scale. Let's slow down this reaction just a bit. Your thought was, "She is never there when I want her to be." Right in that moment, what else were you feeling?

C. Sad.

T. Were there any thoughts that went along with feeling sad?

C. Yeah, I was thinking, "No one ever does anything for me. I am always disappointed. I don't deserve to be happy anyway."

T. Okay, and when you were thinking that you do not deserve to be happy, I wonder if perhaps you may have been feeling a bit of guilt or shame?

C. Shame? Oh, no, the emotion of shame is not on my radar. Shame does not exist for me.

T. I see. Well, let me throw out another possibility. Anger serves a protective function, and, for individuals who have experienced trauma, feeling angry can seem safer than feeling ashamed or feeling scared or sad. Anger can become the "go-to" emotion. In addition, anger is really effective at putting up barriers between you and other people, so I wonder if when you start to become close to someone you feel the urge to push them away, and one way to do that is to get angry at them. Let's go back to the self-monitoring form and see if we can generate some alternative coping strategies.

Resistance toward more skillful interpersonal functioning

As noted previously, maladaptive patterns in relationships are common for clients with complex PTSD. Clients may be reliving their past relational patterns in current interactions with others, leading to difficulties (Cloitre, Cohen, & Scarvalone, 2002; van der Kolk, 1996). Often, the client's commitment to these interpersonal behaviors is rooted in their adaptive function and effectiveness in a traumatic environment. The therapist attempts to validate the important function of these behaviors in the trauma context but also to indicate that the trauma is over and that old behaviors may not suit current needs. Interpersonal behaviors that may be maladaptive to current circumstances are often related to issues with power and control, with assertiveness, and with flexibility in relationships.

C. My boyfriend got angry at me last night because I hadn't called him for a couple of days.

T. Why didn't you call?

C. I don't think he wants me to call. I feel stupid when I call him, even though he told me I should call him whenever I want to talk or whenever I want to see him. But, I like it better when he calls, because then I know he definitely wants to see me and he's thinking about me. But, a lot of times I get mad when we go several days without talking.

T. Sounds like you're having a difficult time being an equal partner in this relationship.

C. Oh, I didn't think of it that way. I just never felt comfortable being totally honest with people. As a kid it was very bad news to say what you felt. Anyway, doesn't he know me by now?

T. You have to educate people in your life. Part of his getting to know you is through your communication with him about your needs and preferences. Often people with a history of trauma have a hard time feeling like they deserve to have their feelings known and have difficulty making requests. And, I know that you may keep quiet a long time about what you want to do and then get very angry at him later for something irrelevant. The other thing is that educating people about your needs does involve taking a risk and being vulnerable. This is really hard, especially since whenever you expressed your needs growing up you've said you were told to "shut up." Instead, let's practice expressing yourself and being assertive, rather than being passive or aggressive. Why don't we practice that by doing a role play where you initiate a call to your boyfriend?

Resistance toward exposure work

The process of doing exposure and addressing the memories and feelings associated with trauma can seem frightening and overwhelming for clients who generally avoid strong emotions. Doing exposure work or the fear of doing it can cause an exacerbation of PTSD symptoms, attrition, inconsistent attendance or tardiness, and dissociation (McDonagh-Coyle et al., 2005; Pittman, Altman, Greenwald, & Longpre, 1991; Scott & Stradling, 1997; Tarrier et al., 1999). It often helps to point out that the anticipatory anxiety is often worse than the actual experience of recounting the trauma-related memories. Therapists can remind clients which emotion regulation strategies have been helpful so far and help them continue to use these during the second phase of treatment. In addition, emphasizing that the client is not alone and that this is the client's chance to tell his or her story can often be comforting.

In STAIR/MPE, we audiotape the client's telling of the traumatic memory and ask the client to listen to the tape for homework. We have found that if the therapist and client listen to the first tape together in session it prepares for continuing the work at home. We also discuss balancing the distress of listening to the tapes with self-care behaviors and pleasurable activities after the task is done. Therapists may wish to encourage clients to discuss with significant others that they are doing intense work in therapy and explain that they may be more irritable, less affectionate, etc. Significant others can be provided with psychoeducation regarding PTSD and the rationale for exposure and may be valuable sources of support. In some cases, therapists may opt to have a couple or partner session. Finally, safety is always the top priority in any psychotherapy; therefore, it may be necessary to establish a safety agreement (e.g., no self-harm, no substance use) with certain clients and discuss the therapist's availability and limits regarding crisis management.

The Subjective Units of Distress Scale (SUDS) is used both while recording the narrative in the session and while listening to the tapes at home. If clients report consistently low numbers during these exercises, it is important to distinguish whether the clients are truly feeling low levels of emotion or are distancing themselves from their real feelings. Therapists should validate concerns and worries related to memory processing but also remind clients that they are safe and supported and have the skills to help them navigate this experience.

> C. I have my exposure homework sheet for you. I listened to the tape every day since I saw you last, like you asked me. (Client hands the therapist her homework sheet, and the therapist sees that the client has listed a 30 for every SUDS rating.)
> T. Great job listening to the tape every day. I know doing this can be frightening. Coping with the intense feelings that are brought up can be so difficult. I see here that you were experiencing a consistently low level of distress each time you listened to your trauma memory. This is a lot different from what you felt during the exposure work last session. Tell me, what did the 30 feel like in your body?
> C. Um, my heart was beating kind of fast and, really, that's all I remember. I think I wasn't really listening. (Client starts to cry.)
> T. That is okay. We are going to listen to this together now, and I am going to help you feel your feelings so the exposure exercises will work, and I will help you implement all the emotion regulation skills you have been working so hard to learn up to now.

Resistance toward adhering to the structure of the therapy: ongoing crises/chaos

Crises are common for this population and can occur for a variety of reasons. Crises can be related to the chaos and burdens of daily living, to low socioeconomic status, or to maladaptive interpersonal habits (e.g., tendency to engage in conflictual relationships). Crises may also be related to avoidance of the therapy process. For example, clients may spend time in the session discussing the problem of global warming instead of focusing on their own more immediate struggles. In any case, whatever issues clients bring in can serve as "grist for the mill" in teaching the skills that are the focus of the session, be it emotional awareness or assertiveness training. CBT techniques such as consistently setting the agenda at the beginning of the session, reviewing between session work, and beginning and ending on time also help create structure and teach clients organizational skills.

The following example illustrates how a therapist used the "crisis de jour" as material to teach the topic of the session—assertiveness in relationships:

> C. (Client arrives 20 minutes late, in an obvious state of distress.) You won't believe what happened today! I'm so angry! My son's teacher had the nerve to say he is always acting out in class! Well, I really put her in her place! She is so stupid and has no idea what she's talking about. I guess they'll let anyone be a teacher these days.
> T. Sounds like this was a very tough situation. What happened next?
> C. They had to call security because they said *I* was making a big scene. The nerve!
> T. What an intense interpersonal interaction! I can see that you are still angry. Actually, this is related to what we are going to talk about in our session today, being assertive with others.

The therapist then elicits expectations the client has about herself and others, revealing that the client believes the teacher thinks she is a horrible mother, so she lashed out in anger to protect herself from feelings of vulnerability and fears of being attacked. After providing psychoeducation about assertive behavior, the therapist role plays assertive reactions with the client.

Resistance toward change

In addition to invalidating their trauma histories, the notion of change may provoke the feeling that "the devil that I know is better than the devil that I don't" for clients with complex PTSD. Therapists may employ several techniques to help motivate change, beginning with talking openly about the frightening aspects of change as well as why change is necessary in relation to achieving life goals. This discussion should include weighing the pros and cons of change and tolerating the distress that will be an inherent part of this process (Linehan, 1993). For some clients, just acknowledging the cons of change, including any losses that may be associated with it, is so validating that clients feel empowered to try the alternative. For example, the client described above expressed her sense of loss and grieving at giving up anger as her "go-to" emotion. She then felt ready to experiment with other strategies. It is important to take an idiographic approach and elicit specific barriers to change, because they can vary from one client to another. For some, the barrier is fear of the unknown; for others, it is invalidating their trauma histories, or it may be fear of failure. Here the therapist allows the client to explain his fear of really living life:

C. I just live my life in fear, and I don't know any other way.

T. What do you mean exactly?

C. Well, you know that kid at the ice skating rink who clings to the side for hours because he's afraid of letting go? Afraid to go flying across the ice, afraid of falling down, afraid of getting hurt? That's me. I'm constantly afraid of living my life. Ever since the Twin Towers collapsed, I've been that way. I thought I had gotten away from my childhood with all its violence and hatred, and now I feel like you can never get away from it. I have just given up.

In another example, the therapist uses pros and cons to address ambivalence:

T. You have missed two sessions in a row. I am wondering how you might be feeling about coming to therapy.

C. Well, I'm not so sure about this therapy, to be honest with you.

T. I know you have mentioned to me before that you have dropped out of therapy every time you've tried in the past. Yet, here you are, sitting in that chair across from me. There is a part of you that keeps fighting to change. Let's list the pros and cons of your continuing in therapy together.

C. Cons of therapy: feeling overwhelmed and spiraling out of control, being scared of the hard work, learning things that I don't want to know about myself, becoming more angry at my mother and not being able to control it, disappointing the therapist, and feeling vulnerable and weak regarding reaching out for help. Pros: having a chance to tell my story, improving my relationships, decreasing or eliminating negative coping such as bingeing, having a sense of accomplishment, and living life more fully by feeling emotions and not being afraid of them.

Additional considerations

The therapeutic alliance

Psychopathology in the family history as well as the impaired interpersonal functioning that is a hallmark of complex PTSD often hinder clients' ability to successfully establish a therapeutic relationship, a necessary ingredient for any effective treatment. Not surprisingly, establishing a strong therapeutic alliance is related to the successful implementation of exposure therapy and positive treatment outcome (Cloitre, Stovall-McClough, Miranda, & Chemtob, 2004). Therefore, we encourage therapists to view each session as an opportunity to enhance the alliance between themselves and their clients. This may be accomplished in a variety of ways, including adopting a warm and supportive stance, modeling healthy interpersonal functioning, acknowledging one's competence and experience working with trauma and also one's limitations, striving to be honest and genuine, validating clients' emotional experiences and trauma histories, guiding them through treatment successes, predicting therapeutic ruptures before they occur, and apologizing for one's mistakes.

Due to the interpersonal nature of complex trauma, the therapeutic relationship itself can be a stimulus that elicits fear and anxiety. Just sitting in the room with a therapist can be exposure work for some clients, and this important bond between client and therapist can provide the opportunity for a corrective emotional experience, serving as a template for healthy relationships. However, because the therapist–patient relationship contains a power differential, it is also exploitable (Yalom, 2002). Additionally, the intensity of therapy, especially trauma-focused therapy, increases the potential of mismanagement (Chu, 1988).

Fear of navigating through this relationship may lead some clients to ask provocative questions of the therapist. On the other hand, a strong desire to rescue individuals from their traumatic experiences or their sequellae can lead to therapists taking on the role of savior in the relationship (Chu, 1988). Individuals with PTSD seem to be particularly adept at eliciting our own needs to care-take. Both of these predicaments are related to the issue of boundaries in therapy. Therapists should refrain from detailing their own traumatic experiences or lack thereof. We have found that the need for strong, clear boundaries in treatment is directly and inversely related to the client's capacity for healthy interpersonal functioning. In other words, the more compromised a person's skills are, the stronger the boundaries should be (e.g., where the therapist lives, what the therapist's political beliefs are). That being said, it is important to always maintain an honest and open dialog regarding the therapeutic relationship itself. A good rule of thumb is to utilize self-disclosure only when it can benefit the client or the therapy. Finally, just as we advise our clients to focus on what they can control and practice acceptance with the rest, we would do well to examine our own expectations regarding helping clients.

Therapist self-care

As practitioners of CBT, our job is to teach clients how to be their own therapists. We espouse the importance of behaviors that reduce emotional vulnerability, such as healthy eating, getting adequate sleep, and pleasant events scheduling. Taking our own advice is another matter. It is advisable for any therapist to maintain healthy self-care behaviors, but the trauma therapist in particular should be attuned to healthy ways of coping. Working with survivors of trauma necessarily involves exposure to the horrific details of the many ways human beings can be cruel to each other and the often devastating sequellae of catastrophic events. It can be normal for therapists to feel angry, depressed, scared, confused, and alienated. These feelings, as well as adopting some of the symptoms of PTSD such as hypervigilance and anxiety, have been described as vicarious traumatization, secondary traumatic stress, or compassion fatigue (Figley, 2002; Jenkins & Baird, 2002; McCann & Pearlman, 1990).

Although a review of self-care strategies is beyond the scope of this chapter, we recommend that therapists routinely assess and balance the acuity of their caseload. We also suggest that therapists limit the number of clients simultaneously receiving exposure therapy. Support from and consultation with other therapists working with issues related to trauma are critical. We believe that observing one's own limits (Linehan, 1993) and balancing work with other activities can maximize therapeutic efficacy while minimizing therapeutic burnout. A helpful and concise list of additional therapist self-care strategies can be found in Norcross (2000).

Conclusion

Posttraumatic stress disorder is a disorder of avoidance. Add on the associated features of complex PTSD, including emotion dysregulation, dissociation, impulsive behaviors, and interpersonal dysfunction, and the result is a population of individuals who are often less amenable to CBT. We have presented a phase-based treatment protocol that has been shown to be effective in improving emotional and interpersonal dysregulation, the primary barriers to successful CBT treatment among clients with complex trauma. Our research suggests that a complex interplay of skills training and a strong therapeutic alliance allow some of these otherwise treatment-resistant individuals to participate in exposure-based therapy, allowing them to experience significant reductions in their PTSD symptoms and improve their quality of life (Cloitre et al., 2004). We have emphasized the importance of the therapeutic relationship as not only a vehicle for change among a group of individuals who have traditionally been abused and mistreated by others, but also as a critical component of effective CBT.

References

American Psychiatric Association. (2000). *Diagnostic and statistical manual of mental disorders* (4th ed., rev.). Arlington, VA: American Psychiatric Association.

Blanchard, E.B., & Hickling, E.J. (1997). *After the crash: Assessment and treatment for motor vehicle accident survivors.* Washington, D.C.: American Psychological Association.

Bowlby, J. (1969). *Attachment and loss.* Vol. 1. *Attachment.* New York: Basic Books.

Bradley, R., Greene, J., Russ, E., Dutra, L., & Westen, D. (2005). A multidimensional meta-analysis of psychotherapy for PTSD. *American Journal of Psychiatry, 162,* 214–227.

Brady, K. (1997). Posttraumatic stress disorder and comorbidity: Recognizing the many faces of PTSD. *Journal of Clinical Psychiatry, 58*(9), 12–15.

Breslau, N. (2002). Epidemiologic studies of trauma, posttraumatic stress disorder, and other psychiatric disorders. *The Canadian Journal of Psychiatry (La Revue canadienne de psychiatrie), 47*(10), 923–929.

Burnstein, A. (1986). Treatment noncompliance in patients with posttraumatic stress disorder. *Psychometrics, 27,* 37–40.

Chemtob, C.M., Novaco, R.W., Hamada, R.S., Gross, D.M., & Smith, G. (1997). Anger regulation deficits in combat-related posttraumatic stress disorder. *Journal of Traumatic Stress, 10,* 17–35.

Chu, J.A. (1988). Ten traps for therapists in the treatment of trauma survivors. *Dissociation, 1*(4), 24–32.

Cloitre, M. (2007a). *Treating complex trauma: Psychotherapy for the interrupted life-researching and implementing an attachment-based treatment for complex trauma.* Paper presented at the 18th Annual International Trauma Conference, June 20–23, Boston, MA.

Cloitre, M. (2007b). *Trauma and resiliency: The assessment and treatment of inner-city children and adolescents.* Paper presented at the New York City Health and Hospital Corporation Annual Behavioral Health Conference, June 14–15, Bronx, New York.

Cloitre, M., & Koenen, K.C. (2001). The impact of borderline personality disorder on process group outcome among women with posttraumatic stress disorder related to childhood abuse. *International Journal of Group Psychotherapy, 51*(3), 379–398.

Cloitre, M., Cohen, L.R., & Koenen, K.C. (2006). *Treating survivors of childhood abuse: psychotherapy for the interrupted life.* New York: Guilford Press.

Cloitre, M., Cohen, L.R., & Scarvalone, P. (2002). Understanding revictimization among childhood sexual abuse survivors: An interpersonal schema approach. *Journal of Cognitive Psychotherapy: An International Quarterly, 16*(1), 91–111.

Cloitre, M., Koenen, K.C., Cohen, L.R., & Han, H. (2002). Skills training in affective and interpersonal regulation followed by exposure: a phase-based treatment for PTSD related to childhood abuse. *Journal of Consulting and Clinical Psychology, 70*(5), 1067–1074.

Cloitre, M., Miranda, R., Stovall-McClough, K.C., & Han, H. (2005). Beyond PTSD: Emotion regulation and interpersonal problems as predictors of functional impairment in survivors of childhood abuse. *Behavior Therapy, 36*(2), 119–124.

Cloitre, M., Stovall-McClough, K.C., Miranda, R., & Chemtob, C.M. (2004). Therapeutic alliance, negative mood regulation, and treatment outcome in child abuse related posttraumatic stress disorder, *Journal of Consulting and Clinical Psychology, 72*(3), 411–416.

Cloitre, M., Stovall-McClough, K.C., Zorbas, P., & Charuvastra, A. (2008). Adult attachment, emotion regulation and expectations of support among treatment seeking adults with childhood maltreatment. *Journal of Traumatic Stress, 21,* 282–289.

Coid, J., Petruckevitch, A., Feder, G., Chung, W., Richardson, J., & Moorey, S. (2001). Relation between childhood sexual and physical abuse and risk of revictimization in women: A cross-sectional survey. *Lancet, 358*(9280), 450–454.

Creamer, M., Morris, P., Biddle, D., & Elliott, P. (1999). Treatment outcome in Australian veterans with combat-related posttraumatic stress disorder: A cause for cautious optimism? *Journal of Traumatic Stress, 12*(4), 545–558.

Dong, M., Anda, R.F., Felitti, V.J., Dube, S.R., Williamson, D.F., Thompson, T.J. et al. (2004). The interrelatedness of multiple forms of childhood abuse, neglect, and household dysfunction. *Child Abuse & Neglect, 28*(7), 771–784.

Dunn, N.J., Yanasak, E., Schillaci, J., Simotas, S., Rehm, L.P., Souchek, J. et al. (2004). Personality disorders in veterans with posttraumatic stress disorder and depression. *Journal of Traumatic Stress, 17*(1), 75–82.

Figley, C.R. (2002). Compassion fatigue: psychotherapists' chronic lack of self-care. *Journal of Clinical Psychology, 58*, 1433–1441.

Finkelhor, D., & Dziuba-Leatherman, J. (1994). *Victimization of children.* Malden, MA: Blackwell Publishing.

Foa, E.B., & Rothbaum, B.O. (1998). *Treating the trauma of rape: cognitive–behavioral therapy for PTSD.* New York: Guilford Press.

Foa, E.B., Davidson, J.R.T., & Frances, A. (2000).The expert consensus guideline series: Treatment of posttraumatic stress disorder. *Journal of Clinical Psychiatry, 61*(10), 784–785.

Foa, E.B., Friedman, M.J., Keane, T.M., & Cohen, J.A. (2008). *ISTSS guidelines: Effective treatments for PTSD* (2nd ed.). New York: Guilford Press.

Foa, E.B., Riggs, D.S., Massie, E.D., & Yarczower, M. (1995). The impact of fear activation and anger on the efficacy of exposure treatment for PTSD. *Behavior Therapy, 26*, 487–499.

Foa, E.B., Rothbaum, B.O., Riggs, D.S., & Murdock, T.B. (1991). Treatment of posttraumatic stress disorder in rape victims: a comparison between cognitive–behavioral procedures and counseling. *Journal of Consulting and Clinical Psychology, 59*, 715–723.

Frewen, P.A., & Lanius, R.A. (2006). Toward a psychobiology of posttraumatic self-dysregulation: Reexperiencing, hyperarousal, dissociation, and emotional numbing. In R. Yehuda (Ed.), *The psychobiology of post-traumatic stress disorders: A decade of progress* (pp. 110–124). Malden, MA: Blackwell Publishing.

Heffernan, K., & Cloitre, M. (2000). A comparison of posttraumatic stress disorder with and without borderline personality disorder among women with a history of childhood sexual abuse: etiological and clinical characteristics. *Journal of Nervous and Mental Disease, 188*(9), 589–595.

Hembree, E.A., Cahill, S.P., & Foa, E.B. (2004). Impact of personality disorders on treatment outcome for female assault survivors with chronic posttraumatic stress disorder. *Journal of Personality Disorders, 18*(1), 117–127.

Herman, J.L. (1992). Complex PTSD: A syndrome in survivors of prolonged and repeated trauma. *Journal of Traumatic Stress, 5*(3), 377–391.

Jaycox, L.H., & Foa, E.B. (1996). Obstacles in implementing exposure therapy for PTSD: case discussions and practical solutions. *Clinical Psychology and Psychotherapy, 3*, 176–184.

Jenkins, S.R., & Baird, S. (2002). Secondary traumatic stress and vicarious trauma: A validation study. *Journal of Traumatic Stress, 15*, 423–432.

Jones, S., Burrell-Hodgson, G., Tate, G., & Fowler, B. (2006). Personality disorder in primary care: Factors associated with therapist views of process and outcome. *Behavioural and Cognitive Psychotherapy, 34*(4), 453–466.

Jordan, B.K., Marmar, C.R., Fairbank, J.A., Schlenger, W.E., Kulka, R.A., Hough, R.L. et al. (1992). Problems in families of male Vietnam veterans with posttraumatic stress disorder. *Journal of Consulting and Clinical Psychology, 60*(6), 916–926.

Keane, T.M., Marshall, A.D., & Taft, C.T. (2006). Posttraumatic stress disorder: etiology, epidemiology, and treatment outcome. *Annual Review of Clinical Psychology, 2,* 161–197.

Kessler, R.C. (2000). Posttraumatic stress disorder: The burden to the individual and to society. *Journal of Clinical Psychiatry, Special Issue: Focus on Posttraumatic Stress Disorder, 61*(5), 4–14.

Kessler, R.C., Sonnega, A., Bromet, E., & Hughes, M. (1995). Posttraumatic stress disorder in the national comorbidity survey. *Archives of General Psychiatry, 52*(12), 1048–1060.

Kulka, R.A., Schlenger, W.E., Fairbank, J.A., Hough, R.I., Jordan, B.K., Marmar, C.R., & Weiss, D.S. (1990). *Trauma and the Vietnam war generation: Report of findings from the National Vietnam Veterans Readjustment Study.* New York: Brunner/Mazel.

Levitt, J.T., & Cloitre, M. (2005). A clinician's guide to STAIR/MPE: Treatment for PTSD related to childhood abuse. *Cognitive and Behavioral Practice, 12,* 40–52.

Levitt, J.T., Malta, L.S., Martin, A., Davis, L., & Cloitre, M. (2007). The flexible application of a manualized treatment for PTSD symptoms and functional impairment related to the 9/11 World Trade Center attack. *Behaviour Research and Therapy, 45,* 1419–1433.

Linehan, M. (1993). *Cognitive–behavioral treatment of borderline personality disorder.* New York: Guilford Press.

Litz, B.T., Orsillo, S.M., Kaloupek, D., & Weathers, F. (2000). Emotional processing in posttraumatic stress disorder. *Journal of Abnormal Psychology, 109*(1), 26–26.

McCann, L., & Pearlman, L.A. (1990). Vicarious traumatization: a framework for understanding the psychological effects of working with victims. *Journal of Traumatic Stress, 3*(1), 131–149.

McDonagh-Coyle, A., Friedman, M., McHugo, G., Ford, J., Sengupta, A., Mueser, K. et al. (2005). Randomized trial of cognitive–behavioral therapy for chronic posttraumatic stress disorder in adult female survivors of childhood sexual abuse. *Journal of Consulting and Clinical Psychology, 73*(3), 515–524.

Norcross, J.C. (2000). Psychotherapist self-care: practitioner-tested, research-informed strategies. *Professional Psychology: Research and Practice, 31,* 710–713.

Pitman, R.K., Altman, B., Greenwald, E., & Longpre, R.E. (1991). Psychiatric complications during flooding therapy for posttraumatic stress disorder. *Journal of Clinical Psychiatry, 52*(1), 17–20.

Safran, J.D., & Segal, Z.V. (1990). *Interpersonal process in cognitive therapy.* New York: Basic Books.

Sareen, J., Cox, B.J., Stein, M.B., Afifi, T.O., Fleet, C., & Asmundson, G.J. (2007). Physical and mental comorbidity, disability, and suicidal behavior associated with posttraumatic stress disorder in a large community sample. *Psychosomatic Medicine, 69*(3), 242–248.

Schnurr, P.P., Friedman, M.J., Engel, C.C., Foa, E.B., Shea, M.T., Chow, B.K., Resick, P.A., Thurston, V., Orsillo, S.M., Haug, R., Turner, C., & Bernardy, N. (2007). Cognitive behavioral therapy for posttraumatic stress disorder in women: A randomized controlled trial. *JAMA, 297,* 820–830.

Schoenfeld, W.H., Verboncoeur, C.J., Fifer, S.K., Lipschutz, R.C., Lubeck, D.P., & Buesching, D.P. (1997). The functioning and well-being of patients with unrecognized anxiety disorders and major depressive disorder. *Journal of Affective Disorders, 43,* 105–119.

Scott, M.J., & Stradling, S.G. (1997). Client compliance with exposure treatments for posttraumatic stress disorder. *Journal of Traumatic Stress, 10*(3), 523–526.

Shea, M.T., Zlotnick, C., & Weisberg, R.B. (1999). Commonality and specificity of personality disorder profiles in subjects with trauma histories. *Journal of Personality Disorders, 13*(3), 199–210.

Sherman, J.J. (1998). Effects of psychotherapeutic treatments for PTSD: A meta-analysis of controlled clinical trials. *Journal of Traumatic Stress, 11,* 413–435.

Shields, A., Cicchetti, D., & Ryan, R.M. (1994). The development of emotional and behavioral regulation and social competence among maltreated school-age children. *Development and Psychopathology, 63,* 57–75.

Shipman, K., Edwards, A., Brown, A., Swisher, L., & Jennings, E. (2005). Managing emotion in a maltreating context: A pilot study examining child neglect. *Child Abuse & Neglect, 29*(9), 1015–1029.

Shipman, K., Zeman, J., Penza, S., & Champion, K. (2000). Emotion management skills in sexually maltreated and nonmaltreated girls: a developmental psychopathology perspective. *Development and Psychopathology, 12*(1), 47–62.

Sroufe, L.A., Fox, N.E., & Pancake, V.R. (1983). Attachment and dependency in developmental perspective. *Child Development, 54*(6), 1615–1627.

Stewart, A., Livingston, M., & Dennison, S. (2008). Transitions and turning points: examining the links between child maltreatment and juvenile offending. *Child Abuse & Neglect, 32*(1), 51–66.

Suess, G.J., Grossmann, K.E., & Sroufe, L.A. (1992). Effects of infant attachment to mother and father on quality of adaptation in preschool: From dyadic to individual organization of self. *International Journal of Behavioral Development, 15,* 43–65.

Tarrier, N., Pilgrim, H., Sommerfield, C., Faragher, B., Reynolds, M., Graham, E., & Barrowclough, C. (1999). A randomized trial of cognitive therapy and imaginal exposure in the treatment of chronic posttraumatic stress disorder. *Journal of Consulting and Clinical Psychology, 67,* 13–18.

Tarrier, N., Sommerfield, C., Pilgrim, H., & Faragher, B. (2000). Factors associated with outcome of cognitive–behavioural treatment of chronic post-traumatic stress disorder. *Behaviour Research and Therapy, 38,* 191–202.

Taylor, S., Fedoroff, I.C., Koch, W.J., Thordarson, D.S., Fecteau, G., & Nicki, R.M. (2001). Posttraumatic stress disorder arising after road traffic collisions: Patterns of response to cognitive-behavior therapy. *Journal of Consulting and Clinical Psychology, 69,* 541–551.

van der Kolk, B.A. (1996). *The complexity of adaptation to trauma: Self-regulation, stimulus discrimination, and characterological development.* New York: Guilford Press.

van der Kolk, B.A., Roth, S., & Pelcovitz, D. (1993). *Complex PTSD: Results of the PTSD field trials for DSM-IV.* Washington, D.C.: American Psychiatric Association.

van der Kolk, B.A., Roth, S., Pelcovitz, D., Sunday, S., & Spinazzola, J. (2005). Disorders of extreme stress: The empirical foundation of a complex adaptation to trauma. *Journal of Traumatic Stress, 18*(5), 389–399.

Van Etten, M.L., & Taylor, S. (1998). Comparative efficacy of treatments for posttraumatic stress disorder: A meta-analysis. *Clinical Psychology & Psychotherapy, 5,* 126–144.

Yalom, I.D. (2002). *The gift of therapy: An open letter to a new generation of therapists and their patients.* New York: HarperCollins.

Zatzick, D., Marmar, C.R., Weiss, D.S., Browner, W.S., Metzler, T.J., Golding, J.M., Stewart, A., Schlenger, W.E., & Wells, K.B. (1997). Posttraumatic stress disorder and functioning and quality of life outcomes in a nationally representative sample of male Vietnam veterans. *American Journal of Psychiatry, 154,* 1690–1695.

Appendix A. Self-monitoring and alternative coping strategies

Feeling	Intensity (0–10)	Trigger	Thoughts	Response/ coping strategy	Alternative coping strategies (feelings, thoughts, behaviors)

Appendix B. Interpersonal schema sheet

Interpersonal situation	Feelings/beliefs about self	Other's feelings/ beliefs about self	Resulting action
What happened?	*What did I feel and believe about myself?*	*What did I believe the other person felt and believed about me?*	*What did I do?*
Interpersonal goals	Alternative feelings/beliefs about self	Other's alternative feelings/beliefs about self	Alternative action
What are my goals in this situation?	*What else could I feel and believe about myself?*	*What else could the other person feel and believe about me?*	*What else could I do?*

chapter four

Understanding and managing treatment-resistant panic disorder

Perspectives from the clinical experience of several expert therapists

Timothy J. Bruce
University of Illinois College of Medicine
Peoria, Illinois

William C. Sanderson
Hofstra University
Hempstead, New York

Contents

Introduction

Panic disorder (PD) is a distressing and disabling anxiety disorder characterized by an onset of recurrent unexpected panic attacks (American Psychiatric Association, 2000). Panic attacks involve a sudden rush of intense fear accompanied by any of several physical symptoms (e.g., palpitations, dizziness, sweating) and cognitive attributions (e.g., fear of dying, losing control, or going crazy). Sufferers of PD fear subsequent attacks and become preoccupied with potential "catastrophic" or otherwise unwanted consequences they believe could result from an attack (e.g., suffering serious medical or mental harm). Many individuals experiencing PD develop agoraphobia. Agoraphobia in this sense refers to fear and/or avoidance of activities or situations that the sufferer believes could provoke another panic attack, where immediate escape may be difficult (e.g., public transportation, elevators), or where help may be unavailable should the sufferer feel he or she needs it (e.g., being at home alone, far from home, or where medical help is not readily available). The severity of panic attacks and agoraphobia can range from multiple daily attacks and house-boundness to infrequent attacks and endurance of feared situations with discomfort, respectively.

Cognitive–behavioral therapy (CBT) has distinguished itself as the psychological treatment of choice for PD (Roy-Byrne, Craske, & Stein, 2006). Although there have been different applications of CBT for PD (Margraf, Barlow, Clark, & Telch, 1993), most have included the following emphases:

1. Psychoeducation
2. Cognitive restructuring of fear-relevant thought content and processes
3. Exposure to feared bodily sensations (interoceptive or sensation exposure)
4. Exposure to feared situations (exteroceptive or situational exposure)
5. Panic and anxiety coping strategies

Psychoeducation is a prominent emphasis throughout CBT. Its purpose in general is to educate clients in ways that facilitate their therapeutic gains and maintenance of gains. Much of early-therapy psychoeducation involves providing clients with accurate information about PD while dispelling myths and misinformation that may be fueling their fears. A cognitive–behavioral model of the development and maintenance of PD is also conveyed. Its essential message is that avoidance in response to biased fearful beliefs about panic or its consequences maintains a cycle of fear and avoidance that distresses and disables. The rationale for treatment, which highlights challenging and overcoming these fears through activities that disprove them, follows accordingly. Other emphases, designed to facilitate the client's understanding, adaptation, and engagement in therapy, include the goal-directed nature of the therapy, the collaborative nature of the therapeutic relationship, the role of homework, and the importance of compliance.

Cognitive restructuring helps clients identify, challenge, and change the biased, fearful beliefs that maintain their fear and avoidance. This aspect of treatment derives from an application of Beck's cognitive therapy (Beck, 1976; Beck, Rush, Shaw, & Emery, 1979) to PD, as described by Clark (1986), and has demonstrated efficacy (e.g., Clark et al., 1994). In cognitive restructuring, the client initially is oriented to the importance of thoughts as potential triggers of emotions, including anxiety and panic (e.g., "An increase in my heart rate is a sign that I'm having a heart attack!"). Fearful thoughts are then carefully examined, questioned, and empirically challenged in light of any evidence that supports or does not support them. Common biases are identified, such as overestimating the risk posed by panic or its consequences. Alternative evidence-based hypotheses that correct for the biases are then generated and tested through exercises termed *behavioral experiments.* In behavioral experiments, fearful and alternative hypotheses, often couched as predictions, are tested through an activity designed to eventually produce one or the other outcome. For example, a common fear in PD is that one will panic, become immobilized, and lose control if he or she drives past a certain "safe" boundary. This fearful prediction overestimates the client's vulnerability to incapacitation and may be overestimating the likelihood that panic will indeed occur. It can be tested against an alternative prediction (e.g., anxiety may be experienced, but it will be managed successfully until it resolves) through exercises, gradated or not, that ultimately have the client drive past the boundary. The exercises are often recorded by the client and reviewed with the therapist in subsequent sessions. The eventual goal of this process is to disconfirm biased predictions in favor of the alternatives using the accumulating evidence from the exercises.

The exposure aspect of CBT for PD derives from the four-decades-long history of the use of exposure of various forms to successfully treat fear-based problems (for a review, see McNally, 1994). Examples of exposure-based therapies include systematic desensitization, exposure *in vivo*, flooding, social reinforcement, and guided mastery. Its current application to PD is most notably exemplified by Barlow and Craske's panic control therapy (Barlow & Craske, 2008; Craske & Barlow, 2006), which uses exposure within a multimodal approach. Panic control therapy has also demonstrated efficacy in major trials (e.g., Barlow, Craske, Cerny, & Klosko, 1989; Barlow, Gorman, Shear, & Woods, 2000). The most recent version of this kind of CBT uses two primary types of exposure: interoceptive (exposure to feared bodily sensations associated with panic) and exteroceptive (exposure to feared, external situations). In interoceptive exposure, clients are systematically exposed to feared bodily sensations that resemble or are associated with past panic attacks and, as a result, have come to be feared and avoided. Fear and avoidance hierarchies are typically constructed and guide the client through a series of physical exercises that expose the client to an increasing intensity and duration of sensations. For example, the starting exercise may involve walking up stairs at a distance and pace that increase heart rate to 100 beats per minute for 2 minutes. Subsequent exercises would gradually increase the demand, working eventually to an exercise that produces 150 beats per minute for 5 minutes. From a behavioral model, interoceptive exposure is designed to extinguish fear conditioned to changes in sensations. From a cognitive model, it allows the client to learn through direct experience that, although uncomfortable, the physical sensations are not dangerous and can be tolerated.

In exteroceptive exposure, clients systematically confront feared external situations, particularly those associated with agoraphobic avoidance. Hierarchies are often used here, as well, beginning with situations least feared and working up to those most feared (e.g., driving 1 mile on a highway up to driving 20 miles on a highway). Patients are asked to work toward the goal of engaging and completing the exposure tasks, without escaping or avoiding, and while tolerating any discomfort engendered by them. Although exercises are often gradated to allow the client to accomplish successive approximations of the final task, the success of flooding (for a review, see McNally, 1994) and recent initial success of intensive (nongraduated) exposure for PD (Bitran, Morissette, Spiegel, & Barlow, 2008) suggest that intensive exposure is a viable option for some clients, as well.

Anxiety management skills, such as breathing retraining and muscle relaxation, have conventionally been taught to clients to help them manage anxiety experienced before or during exposure. Although formal relaxation training as a stand-alone treatment has been shown to reduce unexpected panic attacks, it has been found that relaxation and breathing are used by some clients as a way to avoid (counter-therapeutically) feared sensations (Barlow & Craske, 2008). That risk, as well as evidence suggesting that breathing retraining is not necessary for a successful treatment outcome (de Beurs, Lange, van Dyck, & Koele, 1995), has led some to advise caution in the use of anxiety management skills training for PD (e.g., Barlow & Craske, 2008).

Roy-Byrne and colleagues (2006) recently noted that "CBT is the most widely studied and validated psychotherapeutic treatment for PD." Two major meta-analyses across multiple studies have reported large effect sizes for CBT (Mitte, 2005; Westen & Morrison, 2001). CBT has proven effective for PD occurring within comorbid conditions, showing an ability to improve the associated condition as well (e.g., Tsao, Mystkowski, Zucker, & Craske, 2002). For most clients completing it, CBT has been shown to reduce panic attacks, generalized anxiety, agoraphobic avoidance, and depression (e.g., Barlow et al., 2000). Although results across studies vary slightly, most show that CBT results in a posttreatment panic-free rate of approximately 75 to 90% (Barlow, Allen, & Basden, 2007). In longer term follow-up studies across 2 to 10 years posttreatment, CBT has been associated with maintenance of therapeutic gains in approximately two-thirds to three-fourths of recipients (e.g., Brown & Barlow, 1995; Bruce, Spiegel, & Hegel, 1999; Fava et al., 2001). CBT meets the highest level criteria (i.e., "well established") for the treatment for PD as defined by American Psychological Association's Society of Clinical Psychology Task Force on Promotion and Dissemination of Psychological Procedures (Chambless & Ollendick, 2001; Chambless et al., 1998). It is also a first-line treatment option for PD in psychiatric best-practice guidelines (e.g., American Psychiatric Association, 1998, 2006).

Despite robust evidence for the effectiveness of CBT for PD, some clients show a suboptimal response to it in that they either do not respond or respond only partially (Brown & Barlow, 1995; Rosenbaum, Pollack, & Pollack, 1996). The empirical literature on the prediction, prevention, and psychotherapeutic management of suboptimal PD treatment response is not advanced. A recent review of studies exploring pretreatment factors associated with poor outcome (McCabe & Antony, 2005) identified three factors with consistent support for poorer outcome: symptom severity, comorbid depression, and comorbid personality disorder. Although information of this type is useful to practicing clinicians in anticipating potential challenges in treatment, empirical guidance on the types of problems commonly encountered in clinical practice that lead to suboptimal response and how best to prevent or manage them is lacking. In light of this absence of empirical guidance, we recently conducted a study in which several therapists, experienced in CBT for PD, were asked what they have found to contribute to poor treatment outcome and what strategies they have found useful in the prevention and management of treatment resistant PD (Sanderson & Bruce, 2007).

Participants in the Sanderson and Bruce (2007) study were members of the Association for Behavioral and Cognitive Therapies (ABCT) who were selected and invited to complete an online survey. Invited participants were those who had made significant contributions to the study and application of CBT for PD (for a list of the participants, see Sanderson & Bruce, 2007). The survey asked these therapists in open-ended format what, in their experience, have been the primary reasons why some clients have had incomplete responses to conventional CBT for panic disorder, as well as how they believe each of the problems they identified is best approached therapeutically. Verbatim responses were categorized by independent reviewers and then ranked. Recommendations for addressing each identified cause were categorized and summarized, yielding a set of core recommendations for each identified cause.

Table 4.1 Rank Order of Reasons
Cited for Treatment Resistance

Rank	Cause of treatment resistance (total ranking points)
1	Lack of engagement in behavioral experiments (35 points)
2	Noncompliance (20 points)
3	Comorbidity (11 points)
4	Inadequate case formulation or misdiagnosis (10 points)
4	External support of PD behavior (secondary gain, fear of disruption) (10 points)
4	Problems with cognitive restructuring (10 points)
7	Presence of other negative life events (3 points)
8	Medication complications (2 points)
8	Poor delivery of CBT (2 points)
10	Therapeutic relationship barriers (1 point)

Table 4.1 shows the factors identified as being responsible for treatment resistance in the order in which survey respondents ranked them. Also shown are the summed ranks for each factor which show the spread of the rankings. These data suggest that the first factor, "lack of engagement in behavioral experiments," was the top-rated cause of suboptimal treatment response. "Noncompliance" finished a distant second and removed from a third group of similarly ranked factors: "comorbidity," "inadequate case formulation or misdiagnosis," "external support of PD behavior (secondary gain, fear of disruption)," and "problems with cognitive restructuring."

For this chapter, we will expand our discussion of the results of this study to offer a practical set of recommendations for addressing common causes of treatment resistant PD.

Causes and recommended strategies for treatment-resistant panic disorder

Lack of engagement in behavioral experiments or exposures

As noted previously, CBT for PD asks clients to face and challenge their fears. This is done primarily through behavioral experiments or exposures in which clients encounter feared sensations and situations in ways that test whether their fears will be realized (Craske & Barlow, 2006). The unwillingness of clients, intentional or not, to engage themselves fully in these exercises and risk the feared consequences was the most frequently cited cause of a suboptimal response to PD treatment. Most therapists interpret this unwillingness to fully engage as a form of avoidance, albeit sometimes subtle. Examples included persistently doing only part of an exposure exercise, provoking only less-feared sensations as opposed to pushing oneself further, using breathing or relaxation to prevent feared sensations from becoming too strong, or using various forms of distraction. From the point of view of the CBT model, this avoidance precludes valid testing, restructuring, and eventual reduction of fears. Losing control, suffering an adverse medical event, and embarrassing oneself were commonly cited examples of fears that clients were reluctant to challenge. Some simply did not want to experience again the negative affect engendered by exposure.

Participants in our study who cited this factor described how they approach it therapeutically. From those descriptions, the following recommendations are offered.

Educate
Through initial and ongoing psychoeducation, emphasize the importance of engagement in therapeutic exercises as a crucial goal of therapy. In discussing exposure, for example, emphasize to clients that testing their fears in a way that is valid to the client is one of its primary purposes. The therapist and client then work collaboratively to identify these fears and create those valid tests through some form of behavioral experiment, typically involving exposure. One method for creating behavioral experiments is to frame each of the client's fears as a prediction, generate an alternative prediction for each that corrects for the biases implicit in the client's prediction, and then construct an activity that will test the two sets of predictions. For example, a client may avoid driving outside a certain boundary for fear that he or she will panic and be unable to get help. Biases in this predication include overestimating the likelihood of panic and incapacitation and underestimating the likelihood that the client will be able to cope with whatever demands the situation presents.

Accordingly, the alternative prediction would correct for the over- and underestimation and paint a scenario in which the client copes successfully without incapacitation, perhaps with some anxiety or panic. The behavioral experiment could then involve a trip in which the client would drive outside the boundary of some agreed-upon distance sufficient to test the predictions. Prior to the trip, the task would be broken down into manageable units and rehearsed imaginally. Possible obstacles (e.g., experiencing symptoms of panic) would be identified and methods for coping (e.g., thought stopping, using calming breathing, and refocusing on the behavioral task) would be identified and rehearsed. The exposure would be conducted and reviewed at the soonest opportunity. That review would explicitly include an evaluation to test these predictions. To the degree that clients understand the rationale and goals of these exposures, they may be more likely to engage in them. Accomplishing full engagement may take time.

Graduated exposure

Consider using individualized graduated exposure tasks as a way to ease wary clients toward full engagement. The notion here is to build up to full engagement by building a history of successfully accomplishing less feared tasks first and gradually making them more challenging. In sensation exposure, for example, some clients are asked to generate and then manage lightheadedness by breathing rapidly for a short time, then stopping and coping with the consequences toward building self-efficacy in managing sensations and reducing fears of the sensations. This type of exposure commonly tests fears that these types of symptoms will lead to fainting or some other unmanageable or intolerable feelings. Testing these fears usually requires the client to generate and cope with relatively strong lightheadedness (e.g., intensity ratings of 7 to 10 on a 10-point scale) that may last for minutes. This ultimate goal may deter some clients from engaging in this exercise. Allowing clients to start very gradually (e.g., a few breaths, stop, then a few more, and so forth), building success upon success, may help them develop the confidence to engage eventually in the more demanding task that will be a more valid test of their fears and more likely to advance their therapeutic gains.

Directly observe and assess possible avoidance

The therapist can observe the client's fearful and avoidant behavior, as opposed to relying solely on self-report, during initial assessment (e.g., through a behavioral avoidance test) and during initial and other critical behavioral experiments. The therapist can use these observations to identify and problem-solve obstacles to engagement. Participant modeling, in which the therapist first demonstrates the successful completion of an exercise before the client tries it, can be an excellent tool for teaching as well as assessing and encouraging a client's progress.

Consider using motivational enhancement techniques

Motivational enhancement techniques (e.g., Arkowitz, Miller, Rollnick, & Westra, 2007; also, see chapter by Westra and Arkowitz, this volume) are derived in part from work on the transtheoretical model of behavior change described by Prochaska, DiClemente, and Norcross (1992). These techniques are designed to encourage movement toward behavior change by tailoring interventions to a client's current level of motivation to change. The levels have been described as stages: precontemplation, contemplation, preparation, action, and maintenance. The therapist needs to assess which stage the client is in and then use motivational enhancement techniques to move him or her toward action and engagement. Examples of motivational enhancement techniques as they apply to PD and agoraphobia include the following: validating the client's particular stage of change through the expression of empathy, identifying discrepancies between the client's goals and problem behaviors (e.g., avoidance precludes goal attainment), "rolling with resistance" (e.g., reframing treatment as an experiment that is under the client's personal control), and encouraging self-efficacy through a focus on the client's personal strengths and positive movement. A fuller description of this approach is provided by Westra and Arkowitz in Chapter 7.

Encourage acceptance of negative feelings

The aversiveness of experiencing panic, particularly the first novel few times, leaves some clients strongly intolerant and avoidant of experiencing it again. Unfortunately, therapeutic gains require the client to risk feeling uncomfortable at times. Reframing panic sensations and other aversive feelings as not dangerous, manageable, and, although unpleasant, tolerable as well as a necessary as part of the therapeutic process is recommended when intolerance of negative affect seems responsible for lack of engagement. The therapist can use education and support to help clients better learn about and accept the experience of negative affect. Normalize the experience by describing how common the panic is in the human condition and how it is a natural expression of our nervous system. To help clients resist becoming passive victims of their feelings, suggest that they take a monitor's (observer's) perspective during uncomfortable emotional experiences, and use that perspective as an opportunity to learn what triggers these experiences, what they involve, and what works best to tolerate them. Practicing these skills using sensation exposure exercises may be useful.

Avoid labeling and concluding that the client is "resistant"

Ironically, the label "treatment resistant" can be its own obstacle when clients who are not engaging in therapy are dismissed as nonresponders. Therapists may not be as motivated to work with clients they have classified this way and, by believing that their therapeutic efforts will be futile, may actually create a self-fulfilling prophecy. Although it is possible that some clients may ultimately be resistant to treatment, they should not be ruled out as responders until strategies, such as those detailed above, have failed to help them overcome problems with engagement.

Noncompliance

The second most cited reason for treatment resistance in our survey was noncompliance. With clients suffering from anxiety disorders, noncompliance is often an expression of avoidance due to fear. Yet, it can also be due to lack of motivation, resource limitations, scheduling problems, forgetfulness, or a poor understanding of the purpose of a task or exercise (Meichebaum & Turk, 1987). The previously discussed factor, lack of engagement, could justifiably be characterized as noncompliance due to fear and avoidance. We are distinguishing engagement from noncompliance here primarily because our survey respondents did. Indeed, most instances of noncompliance cited by respondents referred to noncompliance with therapeutic "homework." Examples included not doing self-monitoring tasks, failure to read psychoeducational materials, not completing an assigned exposure exercise, not practicing coping strategies, and not engaging in tasks related to identifying or challenging cognitive biases. Ideally, noncompliance is prevented, as opposed to managed after it occurs. Recommended strategies are listed below.

Establish realistic expectations of the therapy

The therapist can ensure that clients understand what CBT, as a psychotherapeutic approach, involves and asks of them; for example, CBT requires active participation and work outside of the session. It asks clients to be willing to risk feeling uncomfortable at times, but this discomfort may help them achieve their goal of overcoming their fears. Helping clients understand these and other realistic expectations of CBT can help prevent unrealistic assumptions from causing noncompliance. For example, it is important for a client to understand that he or she is supposed to feel uncomfortable during exposure exercises, rather than believing that this is a sign that the therapy is not working (thus leading to noncompliance).

Educate

Adjunctive educational material can be used to expand and reinforce the client's new knowledge. Educational materials such as books and websites can facilitate clients' understanding of the condition (e.g., facts, symptoms, prognosis) and begin the process of correcting misinformation that may be contributing to it (e.g., belief that panic can lead to psychosis). Information about the various emphases in treatment can also be conveyed. Regarding cognitive restructuring, for example, clients could be asked to read about the link between thought and feeling and why management of thinking is emphasized in CBT.

Using time in session to review what the client has read can be useful, especially if the therapist can make it relevant to the client's personal experience. This can increase understanding and encourage further educational initiative on the client's part. The following is an example in which the therapist follows up on a reading task to place an emphasis on the point about the misappraisal of symptoms that often characterizes panic attack sufferers during initial panic attacks:

C. I read that some people also think they are going crazy during a panic attack.
T. Yes, that's a very common thing to think during panic. Often it depends on what you are feeling at the moment and whether you think it is dangerous or not. Like, some people feel very short of breath. Others feel chest pressure or pain.
C. I bet they think they're having a heart attack. I saw where some people think that.
T. That's exactly what I mean. Can you remember what you were feeling when you thought you were going crazy?
C. It was like the outside world suddenly changed, like things were slowed down or something.

From there, the therapist can follow up to determine if the client is experiencing derealization and discuss it accordingly.

Explain the rationale for interventions

One of the most effective ways to prevent noncompliance is to help clients understand why they are being asked to do something. Noncompliance may result from the client's difficulty understanding the therapeutic rationale for a task or how the particular task is related to overall therapeutic goals. Of course, often the rationale for a task seems obvious, as when a client who fears driving in a car is assigned driving as an exercise. Sometimes, however, the connection is not as clear. A therapist may use situations that are not directly relevant to the client's functioning in targeting agoraphobic avoidance. A client who fears traveling on an airplane because of feelings of being trapped may be asked, for practical purposes, to use a train as a way to approximate the airplane setting. The client who does not understand the relevance of these tasks may, consequently, not comply with them. As Meichenbaum and Turk (1987) suggested, providing a therapeutic rationale for every recommendation made to a client and confirming that it has been understood can help prevent a number of problems with noncompliance.

Record sessions

One way to increase treatment adherence is to audiotape, or otherwise record, a session and ask the client to revisit it at least once prior to the next session. Some clients are willing to do this and benefit from the repeated presentation. Some find themselves better able to listen and think about a session later than when trying to do so while having to interact with the therapist. Of course, some will find this burdensome.

Increase accountability

Connecting completion of a therapeutic task to a more immediate contingency (reporting progress to the therapist), particularly early in therapy, can build compliance through accountability. Some clients may feel more compelled to engage in treatment outside of the session if they are asked to be more accountable. For some, simply coming in to the next session and reporting what they did or did not do is sufficient. For others, however, asking them to complete some type of monitoring form (e.g., a record of relaxation practice sessions, thought records) or asking them to phone or e-mail when they complete an exercise is necessary to improve compliance.

Be clear and specific when assigning a task

When assigning a homework exercise to be carried out between sessions, give the client a "behavioral prescription." Write down exactly what the client is expected to do. Include the specific task (e.g., "drive from Exit 17 to 20 on the highway"), as well as the days and times (e.g., "daily at 9 a.m." or "Monday, Wednesday, and Friday at lunchtime."). It is important to do this in a collaborative way. The prescription should be developed with input and agreement from the client rather than simply being told to them. Collaboration itself facilitates compliance, in that it ensures that the client and therapist have the same goals in mind. Immediately after agreeing on a task is a good time to review the rationale and potential benefit for each assignment.

Anticipate obstacles with each assignment

Preparing the client to anticipate and problem-solve obstacles to completing a task is an effective way to prevent noncompliance. Ask clients what they see as possibly preventing them from completing a given task. Consider what is necessary to do the task (e.g., a car, time to drive, a babysitter) and assess whether the client has these resources available. Ask about how the task could be interrupted (e.g., someone using power tools in another room during the relaxation exercise) and plan around this. Anticipating obstacles allows the therapist and client to obtain solutions that facilitate compliance.

Reduce "hassle factors"

Sometimes tasks can be structured in ways that unnecessarily introduce burdens to clients and increase the chances that they will not do them. To minimize this risk, make homework tasks as easy to carry out as possible; for example, if a client prefers to use a blank piece of paper to record her thoughts, as opposed to an "official" thought record, encourage her to do so. Similarly, take advantage of changes in technology. Sometimes relaxation instructions or a recording from a previous session can be put onto a computer audio file or iPod, which clients may prefer.

Reward positive behavior

Therapists should be sensitive to reinforcing the completion of any assigned task, especially near the beginning of treatment when the behavior may be new and developing. Praise can be very uplifting and motivating, especially keeping in mind that the tasks being done by the client represent an ongoing struggle. Examples include saying: "That's great that you were able to [complete the task]. I know how hard it is for you" or "You're doing a great job with your effort. This type of effort is associated with significant improvement over time."

Review homework at each session

Knowing the therapist will follow up on homework communicates that the expectation is that it will be completed. Therapists should therefore be mindful of reviewing all assigned homework at some point during the next available session. The review communicates to the client that the homework is an important part of the therapeutic process and establishes an expectation that it should be done. Even following up on a small reading assignment is recommended. For example, the therapist can say, "We agreed last week that you were going to read the NIMH panic disorder brochure. Have you had a chance to do so? ... What did you find useful about it?"

Problem-solve existing noncompliance

When addressing existing noncompliance in the context of therapy, it is best to deal with it immediately and openly and to take a problem-solving approach to resolving it. The therapist does not want to come across as critical but instead concerned about the noncompliance. The therapist should also convey the belief that solutions to resolve the noncompliance can be generated. For example, the therapist can say something such as: "I know these exercises can be hard to remember to do, but I'm concerned that if things keep going this way you will not get very much out of the treatment. Let's try to figure out what the problem is and how we can try to solve it." The therapist should encourage the client to express any reservations about completing the exercise: "Do you have any concerns about doing this exercise? Is it too involved, or do you think it really won't help that much?" Identified obstacles should then be brainstormed for solutions. Possible solutions are then evaluated, and the most feasible is put into play. Reevaluating the effectiveness of the plan is done next and leads either to more problem solving or the conclusion that the problem is resolved satisfactorily. For example, the client may say, "I don't believe that if I do this repeatedly the anxiety will eventually subside." The therapist can help the client generate options for resolving the problem, such as asking others who have dealt with a similar problem and treatment, examining the client's life to see if there are any examples to support that anxiety subsides over repeated exposure, or even suggesting that the client try it for a period of time and report on the (behavioral) experiment.

Comorbidity

The presence of comorbid mental disorders or other clinically significant difficulties was one of four cited causes of poor treatment response that ranked within a third tier of cited causes in our survey. Although some respondents cited examples of difficult comorbid anxiety disorders (e.g., OCD), the majority discussed comorbid depression. Interestingly, existing data on the impact of comorbidity on treatment outcome for clients with a principal diagnosis of PD suggests that in many cases the presence of another anxiety disorder does not necessarily diminish the efficacy of CBT focused on the panic disorder (Brown, Antony, & Barlow, 1995). Of course, factors such as the type and severity of the comorbid anxiety disorder may mediate that relationship in individual clients. Studies of comorbid depression suggest that its presence can clearly interfere with successful outcome (Brown, Antony, & Barlow, 1995; McLean, Woody, Taylor, & Koch, 1998). Recommendations for dealing with comorbidity were stepwise and included the following.

Treat severe, interfering comorbidity

If the comorbid syndromes, symptoms, or problems are judged severe enough to prevent the initiation or completion of CBT for PD, then the recommendation is to address the comorbid condition first. Examples range from severe symptoms that need to be stabilized to allow participation in CBT (e.g., danger to self or others; extreme anhedonia and withdrawal) to symptoms that interfere with the desired level of engagement in the treatment (e.g., hopelessness and fatigue that result in little motivation to come to therapy or do therapeutic homework; depressive rumination that interferes with a client's ability to focus or entertain alternatives).

Target panic disorder in cases of lesser comorbidity

In the more subtle case of secondary conditions or symptoms that are coexistent but not as severe nor interfering with CBT, the recommendation is to target the panic disorder for treatment. The therapist should monitor the panic disorder and comorbidity throughout treatment and follow up by targeting for further treatment any residual syndromes or symptoms. This clinical consensus recommendation is also supported empirically by studies that suggest comorbid disorders and symptoms can remit with successful treatment of a primary panic disorder (Brown et al., 1995). For example, a client who is depressed, particularly if the depression seems related to setbacks due to the panic disorder, is likely to feel less depressed as the panic disorder responds to therapy. It can be useful to ask the client something to the effect of, "If you were guaranteed that you would have no more panic attacks, do you think you would still feel depressed?" The answer can help assess to what degree the depression may be resulting from the distress or disability imposed by the panic as well as the likelihood that it will respond to treatment of the panic. Some therapists may elect to treat the panic and related symptoms concurrently, as opposed to successively, unifying them into a single case formulation. Of course, which approach is better, sequential or concurrent, remains a clinical judgment yet to be evaluated empirically. The recommendation to follow up and address residual symptoms or problems is supported by studies showing that their presence places clients at risk for continued or emergent problems (Fava et al., 2001; McLean et al., 1998).

Inadequate case formulation or misdiagnosis

As recommended by nearly every treatment guideline (American Psychiatric Association, 1998), if a client does not respond to a reasonable course of conventional treatment, the clinician should reconsider the diagnosis or case formulation. The following are specific considerations.

Rule out possible medical and substance-related causes

The decision tree for diagnosing PD requires first ruling out symptoms that are due to the direct physiological effects of a general medical condition (e.g., hyperthyroidism) or a substance-induced syndrome (e.g., CNS depressant withdrawal, stimulant intoxication) before making the diagnosis of panic disorder (American Psychiatric Association, 2000). This ruling out should be done at initial evaluation, but if treatment is ineffective consider revisiting it in a more thorough reevaluation. Some of the respondents to our survey cited examples in which symptoms of panic that did not respond to CBT were found subsequently to be products of medical conditions such as pheochromocytoma or hyperthyroidism.

Reconsider the principal psychiatric diagnosis or case formulation
Unexpected panic attacks, the diagnostic hallmark of panic disorder, may occur in the context of other mental disorders as well, especially other anxiety disorders. It is possible, for example, that another mental disorder may better characterize the observed symptomatology and change the intervention sufficiently to improve the client's response. One survey respondent shared the following example: The focus of exposure therapy for a particular female client being treated for PD was on exercises designed to increase her ability to be alone outside of her home. Initially, as is common, her fear of being alone was seen as reflecting agoraphobic safety concerns in the event she had a panic attack (e.g., "If I have a panic attack, I may need someone to take me to get help!"). During the course of exposures, her fear did not subside as expected. Upon reassessment, it became clear that the fear of being alone was related to a feeling first generated after a sexual assault she had experienced earlier in her life that she had heretofore been too embarrassed to disclose. When treatment was reoriented within this context, her phobic response improved. Thus, reevaluating a diagnosis or case formulation may improve treatment effectiveness.

External support of PD behavior (secondary gain, fear of disruption)

Situations in which the fear and avoidance of PD are being positively or negatively reinforced (e.g., they result in a disability check or not having to work) or where overcoming them would cost the client something personally important (e.g., spousal attention, sympathy from others) were cited by some respondents as barriers to improvement. No respondent cited malingering for gain (e.g., faking the panic disorder for workers' compensation). Rather, factors cited here were seen as obstacles to improvement of a real panic disorder. Examples included the loss of social attention, social pressure to remain dependent, and loss of disability payments, all creating an incentive to remain "ill." In some cases, clients were described as losing their confidence in being able to be return to their premorbid roles and responsibilities. In some cases, premorbid functioning may have been impaired. Recommendations to address apparent secondary gain issues were as follows.

Conduct a functional analysis
Identify the functional relationship between improvement and its consequences. Assess what the client believes will change (positive and negative) as the panic disorder improves. Does the client fear, or otherwise not want, any of these changes? As discussed previously, factors related to lack of improvement often involve fears and avoidance. Develop a list of the foreseeable positive and negative consequences to process with the client.

Problem-solve obstacles to improvement

As noted with noncompliance, problem solving can be useful in preventing or managing possible secondary gain, as well. Begin by identifying obstacles to improvement through a functional analysis, as just described. Generate options for addressing them, evaluate these options, and develop a plan based on the options judged most likely to be effective. Consider graduating the implementation of any plans involving fear on the client's part, as you would with any challenging exposure; for example, graduated goals may be to return to work less than half-time, then half-time, and then full-time.

Directly address secondary gain with the client

Regardless of whether the client's lack of improvement is due to fear and avoidance or some reward for remaining ill, a unanimous recommendation by the respondents to our survey was to discuss the issue directly with the client, without shying away from the topic of whether continued therapy is desired by the client. The question being asked is, "Does the client really want what comes along with successful treatment?" This type of direct evaluation of the client's motives can help reinvigorate his or her commitment to therapy and change or lead to the realization that now is not the time.

Problems with cognitive restructuring

As noted previously, cognitive restructuring is a principle component of CBT for PD. It involves elucidating what the client finds threatening, the biases in the appraisal of threat, and the generation of alternative appraisals that aim to correct for those biases (i.e., rational responses). These identified fears and alternative appraisals serve as hypotheses that are tested through behavioral experiments, typically involving some form of exposure to what is feared. Repeated disconfirmation of biased, fear-based predictions helps the client shift from fearful appraisals to ones more in line with the actual threat posed by the feared stimulus (Beck, 1995). Problems with cognitive restructuring were one of three causes of treatment resistance ranking within the third tier of responses by participants in our survey. Those causes and suggested treatment options are as follows.

Acceptance of rational responses

As one may imagine, accepting or believing the alternative rational response described above is crucial to reducing fear. A common problem that arises in cognitive restructuring is that the client may unrealistically expect to believe the rational response before completing the behavioral experiment; for example, the client does not want to test whether he will faint in a phobic situation when anxious until he believes that he, in fact, will not faint. Of course, it is the behavioral experiment that will facilitate the change in belief, in that the patient's change in experience is likely to lead to a change of cognition; therefore, clients must begin these experiments before they are convinced that it is okay to begin. A desire to avoid usually emerges in those who feel that they are being asked to do something before they are ready. In this case, the unrealistic expectation sets up that situation and ultimately precludes engagement.

The recommendation involves providing the client with an explanation of how the repeated exposure process typically works. Although it makes sense that individuals do not want to engage in an activity that they believe is threatening unless they are sure it is not, at some point, to change cognitions, they do have to take a chance and test the belief. To assist with this process, the therapist can break down the behavioral experiments into smaller steps that allow for partial disconfirmation leading up to the ultimate task. For example, initially clients could go into the situation with a safe person who could assist them "in case they faint." Next, clients could go alone into the situation but sit in a place where they feel it would be safe if fainting actually occurred. They would then work toward eventually eliminating all of these safety signals, allowing them to ultimately test their fearful belief.

It is also helpful to supplement the information provided during the therapy session with information from self-help books, websites, etc., to reinforce the content of the rational response. In this instance, for example, reading that fainting is not associated with panic may facilitate the eventual acceptance of this response.

Elucidating fear-provoking cognitions

A poor response to cognitive restructuring may occur if key and often subtle fears are not elucidated and targeted. This may occur when assessment is rushed, not allowing for full exploration of the individual's cognitions. Therapists' expectations of what they are likely to hear can sometimes lead them to cut off the assessment prematurely, missing some important information. Therapists are advised to take the time to conduct a comprehensive initial assessment of fearful cognitions, using guided discovery and possibly a psychometric tool as an adjunct to the assessment (e.g., Agoraphobic Cognitions Questionnaire, Anxiety Sensitivity Index). Periodically revisiting this assessment throughout therapy will help fine-tune further assessment and determination of treatment response.

Presence of negative life events/circumstances

Although the diagnosis of panic disorder may be the reason an individual comes to treatment, other negative life events may coexist and require therapeutic attention, particularly if, as with comorbidity, they are creating clinically significant distress or disability or otherwise interfering with the client's ability to commit to the CBT. Commonly cited negative life events included relationship distress (e.g., marital problems), job stress, and financial problems. The recommendations for addressing other life circumstances can be summarized as follows.

Assess the relationship between the circumstances and the PD and intervene accordingly

Respondents who highlighted this problem in our survey indicated that they assess the functional relationship of the negative life circumstances to the PD before deciding how to proceed. One of the critical questions asked in this assessment is whether or not the PD is the primary cause of the negative life circumstance. Marital distress, for example, can be independent of panic disorder (e.g., present before panic onset, focused on issues unrelated to the panic) or a result of the stresses that panic disorder can impose on a relationship (e.g., clients needing their partner to accompany them frequently). If marital problems are independent of the PD but are interfering with the client's ability to engage in treatment, then addressing them, including consideration of marital therapy, before starting or continuing CBT for PD is suggested. When the distress seems due primarily to the PD, the stressor may be addressed in the context of the CBT for PD, particularly if the couple will participate together in the treatment. The stresses that the PD are imposing on the relationship and how to minimize and manage them would become an additional set of therapeutic goals. Examples of common emphases include teaching the couple the primary goals of the therapy, explaining each participant's therapeutic role, teaching the couple how to communicate and resolve conflicts that arise, and teaching them how to gradually remove the partner as a safety cue over the course of the therapy. Research supports the positive role that participating spouses can have on the outcome of PD treatment (e.g., Cerny, Barlow, Craske, & Himadi, 1987). If the couple cannot attend together, however, one can work with the individual client toward similar goals. To summarize, when external stressors begin interfering with the client's ability to engage in the therapy, they should be evaluated and, if necessary, targeted for improvement either before or concurrent to the treatment of the PD, depending on the therapist's judgment regarding the functional relationship between them and the panic.

Medication complications

Many clients who begin CBT for PD are also on psychotropic medication, often antidepressants such as selective serotonin reuptake inhibitors (SSRIs), benzodiazepines (BZDs), or both. The presence of medication during CBT can interfere with response to the treatment through several potential means (for a review, see Otto, Smits, & Reese, 2005). Changes in dose or in medication type can produce symptoms or side effects that can interfere with the client's response to CBT. For example, antidepressants can cause an increase in arousal and agitation, and these symptoms can interfere with a client's ability to engage in CBT. Decreasing or discontinuing some medications may result in withdrawal or other symptoms that can similarly complicate CBT.

Somewhat counterintuitively, successful symptom control can impede some of the goals of CBT. For example, many clients using medication enter CBT with the goal of learning skills through the therapy that will eventually allow them to discontinue medication. The symptom attenuation or suppression that results from medication use, however, may actually reduce the client's motivation to learn the needed skills. More subtly, in CBT sensations of anxiety and panic are treated as phobic cues and targeted for exposure toward the goal of reducing fear of sensations. Symptom suppression through medication use can preclude or attenuate the benefits of sensation exposure procedures.

Despite its intuitive appeal, combining medication with CBT does not necessarily produce a positive additive benefit. Certain combination treatments have actually proven less effective than CBT alone. For example, the use of benzodiazepines during exposure therapy has resulted in higher relapse rates after treatment discontinuation relative to use of exposure only (e.g., Marks et al., 1993). Studies on the topic suggest that if medication is going to be used concurrently with CBT and possibly discontinued at some point, it must be managed in particular ways (e.g., tapered during the exposure phase of treatment) to avoid increasing the risk of relapse (for a review, see Spiegel & Bruce, 1997). The following are recommendations made by survey respondents for preventing and managing medication complications.

Coordinate with the prescribing physician

Consider contacting the prescribing physician at the beginning of treatment to discuss the client's goals, for the CBT and the pharmacotherapy. The therapist and physician can then make a plan to address both sets of goals. For example, if a patient is on a benzodiazepine and wants to discontinue, the therapist can work with the physician to develop a discontinuation plan that integrates those aspects of CBT that maximize the client's chances of successfully discontinuing (e.g., integrating the taper with sensation and situational exposure). Along the same lines, if the physician is planning to increase the dose of medication, he or she can educate the therapist about potential side effects so they can be factored into the therapist's ongoing evaluation.

Discuss medication complication issues with the client

Most clients are unaware of the research examining the combined treatment of PD. Informed therapists can provide this information to their clients to help them make an informed decision. In addition to the negative impact benzodiazepines seem to have on outcome (as discussed above), attribution of treatment success to a pill as opposed to the client's own efforts during therapy has predicted relapse after combined treatment when the medication has been discontinued (e.g., Basoglu, Marks, Kilic, Brewin, & Swinson, 1994). Discussing the roles and rationales of each treatment modality can clarify the goals of each and may help to prevent predictable obstacles.

Employ empirically supported discontinuation protocols

When discontinuation of medication becomes a goal within CBT, consider using a protocol that has been empirically supported (for a review, see Spiegel & Bruce, 1997). For a treatment manual describing these methods, see Otto, Pollack, and Barlow (2004).

Poor delivery of treatment

Of course, before determining whether or not a client is responding to treatment, it is necessary to confirm that the treatment is being delivered and received. Poor delivery of CBT was not a highly cited obstacle to a good treatment response by respondents to our survey but was mentioned by some participants. The common theme of examples cited was that therapists do not always persevere to get the most from each phase of treatment. For example, it was noted that therapists are sometimes reluctant to have clients challenge themselves strongly during exposure, thus weakening the intervention. Recommendations were as follows.

Do high-fidelity treatment

Attend to delivering each of the primary emphases of CBT for PD (i.e., psychoeducation, somatic skills, cognitive restructuring, and exposure) in ways that maximize the gain a client can potentially receive from them. Rather than simply explaining how a particular therapeutic task is done, consider demonstrating it; observe the client doing it and then use corrective feedback to help develop the skill to its fullest. As has been suggested previously for other issues, supplement educational interventions with readings or other media that reinforce the primary messages. Periodically assess whether the client is learning and consolidating the knowledge and skills conveyed in the therapy.

Expose the exposer

One recommendation for therapists who find themselves hesitant to encourage clients to challenge themselves is to expose themselves to asking clients to do just that. Being a participant model, as has been suggested several times previously, may make this easier to do. The bottom line of this recommendation is that, if therapists' fears (e.g., of having a client experience an aversive emotion, of having a client becoming angry) are preventing them from encouraging their clients to do difficult but therapeutic tasks, then these therapists should "practice what they preach" and expose themselves to their own fears to overcome them.

Consult with colleagues

Consulting with a colleague may result in suggestions that improve one's own treatment delivery. Consider calling a colleague or posting a question on a clinically oriented List Serve (e.g., the ABCT member list at abct-members@lists.abct.org).

Continuing education

Observing experts, personally, through workshops or videotapes offers opportunities to learn tried and tested methods.

Therapeutic trust

Therapists who use exposure-based therapies ask clients to overcome fears by facing them. This is a frightening prospect for clients and requires that they trust their therapists' assurances that the process will be safe and therapeutic, albeit challenging. Although finishing last in our survey, lack of trust was cited by some respondents and can be a critical obstacle to client engagement when it is present. Recommendations for building therapeutic trust were as follows.

Convey previous success of others

One suggestion for building trust is to allow clients to confirm that what they are being asked to do has been tried before by others and has been successful. As has been recommended across the survey, psychoeducation may facilitate this. Consider providing resources (e.g., websites, books) that describe CBT and its track record of effectiveness for PD.

Build trust through success experiences

Within the therapeutic process, another suggestion for building clients' trust and confidence is to prescribe therapeutic exercises, particularly initially, that are highly likely to be success experiences for the client. This can lend experiential support to the client's belief that what the therapist is prescribing is safe and helpful.

Validate

When clients feel invalidated (e.g., that the therapist does not understand how difficult it is to confront the anxiety) they may be reluctant to follow therapeutic advice. In addition to making statements that validate the client's fear, it can be helpful to use appropriate self-disclosure in demonstrating understanding. For example, a therapist who teaches might say, "I understand how hard it is to confront anxiety. When I first started teaching, I felt like avoiding it each week." What is particularly important about the self-disclosure is to demonstrate the teacher's ultimate decision to face the fear or otherwise do what is being asked of the client in the therapy (e.g., "By repeatedly doing it and working with my thoughts, it became easier each week").

Integration and summary

In some branches of medicine (e.g., infectious disease), the term *treatment resistance* has traditionally been defined more narrowly than we have here. This narrower definition refers to instances in which a treatment is delivered as intended (i.e., with good treatment fidelity) and received by the client (i.e., compliance is confirmed) but nonetheless results in a poorer than expected response. In the Sanderson and Bruce (2007) study, we intentionally broadened the definition to include any factor that the therapist respondents thought accounted for a poorer then expected response. We did this to get a sense of what factors therapists commonly encounter in their day-to-day practices across the range of possible factors.

In discussing factors that could lead to treatment resistance, it is helpful for us to think first about what an optimal treatment response would look like. In this perhaps hypothetical scenario, the client's problems directly related to his or her distress and disability are accurately identified. A treatment plan that targets those problems is formulated and delivered as intended. And, the client engages and complies with the therapy. It seems that problems at any of these steps could potentially lead to a suboptimal response.

Results from our survey suggest that problems with engagement (in behavioral experiments) and compliance are the most frequently encountered reasons for a poor treatment response. Problems with the case formulation were also a commonly cited factor responsible for a less than desirable treatment response. This factor appeared in several forms: missed primary diagnosis, missed comorbid diagnoses, other life circumstances not taken into consideration, or inaccuracies in behavioral analysis of fear triggers. Although not cited as strongly as engagement and compliance, formulation problems were endorsed by nearly half of respondents to the survey. This suggests that when treatment response is poorer than expected, and fidelity and compliance appear good, revisiting the case formulation may be helpful. Interestingly, poor treatment delivery appeared rarely in survey results. This may be a partial product of sampling bias, in that we might expect to see fewer of these problems in a sample of experienced therapists like the ones surveyed. Of course, regardless of experience, every therapist should consider his or her role in the client's lack of response among the other considerations.

From the results of our survey, guidelines for preventing or managing treatment resistance in PD can be constructed (see Table 4.2). They ring familiar as the kinds of practices advocated by every good clinical training program. They also overlap with other work that has attempted to provide further information to clinicians regarding improving treatment outcome of those who struggle with panic disorder and agoraphobia (e.g., Huppert & Baker-Morissette, 2003; McCabe & Antony, 2005; Otto & Gould, 1996).

Table 4.2 Guidelines for Preventing or
Managing Treatment Resistance of Panic Disorder

Do a thorough initial evaluation.

Rule out general medical and substance conditions the direct physiological effects of which are accounting for symptoms.

Assess for comorbid psychiatric disorders, particularly depression, substance use, and other anxiety disorders, as well as clinically significant symptoms that may not be sufficient to warrant a diagnosis but are nonetheless distressing or disabling.

Do a comprehensive review of psychosocial systems and life circumstances that could influence the clinical picture, interfere with engagement in treatment, serve as a gain to remain ill, or that otherwise may have to be addressed by the treatment plan.

Do a thorough functional assessment of fears, triggers, and avoidance strategies, facilitated when possible by guided discovery, direct observation, and/or psychometric measurement.

Deliver CBT with integrity to the model and with sensitivity toward its difficulty.

Build the trust of the client.

Collaborate, clarify, and emphasize the goals for each phase of therapy.

Explain rationales for prescribed practices.

Emphasize continuing education of key concepts.

Explain, model, and shape the development of the therapeutic skills being taught.

Emphasize and facilitate engagement in valid behavioral experiments.

Model and graduate therapeutic tasks, as needed.

Assess barriers and facilitators of therapeutic progress; functionally analyze and problem-solve barriers; reinforce facilitators.

Facilitate treatment adherence.

Make homework specific, clear, and relevant to clearly stated goals.

Explain, model, and shape the development of the homework task being assigned.

Prompt desired behavior in the natural environment (e.g., by making a phone call or tying it to another high-frequency activity), and reinforce it when it has been completed.

Gradate or simplify tasks that are likely or proving to be difficult.

Reevaluate poor response. When progress is less than expected:

Ensure fidelity.

Ensure compliance.

Reevaluate diagnostic accuracy.

Reevaluate the functional assessment of fears and triggers.

References

American Psychiatric Association. (1998). Practice guideline for the treatment of patients with panic disorder. *American Journal of Psychiatry, 144*(5), 1–34.

American Psychiatric Association. (2000). *Diagnostic and statistical manual of mental disorders* (4th ed., text revised). Arlington, VA: American Psychiatric Association.

American Psychiatric Association. (2006). *American Psychiatric Association practice guidelines for the treatment of psychiatric disorders: Compendium 2006.* Washington, D.C.: American Psychiatric Publishing.

Arkowitz, H., Miller, W.R., Rollnick, S., & Westra, H.A. (2007*). Motivational interviewing in the treatment of psychological problems.* New York: Guilford Press.

Barlow, D.H., & Craske, M.G. (2008). Panic disorder and agoraphobia. In D.H. Barlow (Ed.), *Clinical handbook of psychological disorders: A step-by-step treatment manual* (pp. 1–64). New York: Guilford Press.

Barlow, D.H., Allen, L.B., & Basden, S.L. (2007). Psychological treatments for panic disorders, phobias, and generalized anxiety disorder. In P.E. Nathan & J.M. Gorman (Eds.), *A guide to treatments that work* (3rd ed.) (pp. 351–394). New York: Oxford University Press.

Barlow, D.H., Craske, M.G., Cerny, J.A., & Klosko, J.S. (1989). Behavioral treatment of panic disorder. *Behavior Therapy, 20,* 261–282.

Barlow, D.H., Gorman, J.M., Shear, M.K., & Woods, S.W. (2000). Cognitive–behavioral therapy, imipramine, or their combination for panic disorder: A randomized controlled study. *Journal of the American Medical Association, 283,* 2529–2536.

Basoglu, M., Marks, I.M., Kilic, C., Brewin, C.R., & Swinson, R.P. (1994). Alprazolam and exposure for panic disorder with agoraphobia: attribution of improvement to medication predicts subsequent relapse. *British Journal of Psychiatry, 164*(5), 652–659.

Beck, A.T. (1976). *Cognitive therapy and the emotional disorders.* New York: International Universities Press.

Beck, A.T., Rush, A.J., Shaw, B.F., & Emery, G. (1979). *Cognitive therapy of depression.* New York: Guilford Press.

Beck, J. (1995). *Cognitive therapy: Basics and beyond.* New York: Guilford Press.

Bitran, S., Morissette, S., Spiegel, D., & Barlow, D. (2008). A pilot study of sensation focused intensive treatment for panic disorder with moderate to severe agoraphobia: Preliminary outcome and benchmarking data. *Behavior Modification, 32,* 196–214.

Brown, T.A., & Barlow, D.H. (1995). Long-term outcome of cognitive–behavioral treatment of panic disorder: clinical predictors and alternative strategies for assessment. *Journal of Consulting and Clinical Psychology, 63,* 754–765.

Brown, T.A., Antony, M.M., & Barlow, D.H. (1995). Diagnostic comorbidity in panic disorder: Effect on treatment outcome and course of comorbid diagnoses following treatment. *Journal of Consulting and Clinical Psychology, 63,* 408–418.

Bruce, T.J., Spiegel, D.A., & Hegel, M.T. (1999). Cognitive–behavioral therapy helps prevent relapse and recurrence of panic disorder following alprazolam discontinuation: A long-term follow-up of the Peoria and Dartmouth studies. *Journal of Consulting and Clinical Psychology, 67*(1), 151–156.

Cerny, J.A., Barlow, D.H., Craske, M., & Himadi, W.G. (1987). Couples treatment of agoraphobia: a two-year follow-up. *Behaviour Research and Therapy, 18,* 401–405.

Chambless, D.L., & Ollendick, T.H. (2001). Empirically supported psychological interventions: Controversies and evidence. *Annual Review of Psychology, 52,* 685–716.

Chambless, D.L, Baker, M.J., Baucom, D., Beutler, L.E., Calhoun, K.S., Crits-Christoph, P., Daiuto, A., DeRubeis, R., Detweiler, J., Haaga, D.A.F., Johnson, S.B., McCurry, S., Mueser, K.T., Pope, K.S., Sanderson, W.C., Shoham, V., Stickle, T., Williams, D.A., & Woody, S.R. (1998). Update on empirically validated therapies, II. *The Clinical Psychologist, 51*(1), 3–16.

Clark, D.M. (1986). A cognitive approach to panic. *Behaviour Research and Therapy, 24,* 461–471.

Clark, D.M., Salkovskis, P.M., Hackmann, A., Middleton, H., Anastasiades, P., & Gelder, M.G. (1994). A comparison of cognitive therapy, applied relaxation and imipramine in the treatment of panic disorder. *British Journal of Psychiatry, 164,* 759–769.

Craske, M.G., & Barlow, D.H. (2006). *Mastery of your anxiety and panic (therapist guide).* New York: Oxford University Press.

de Beurs, E., Lange, A., van Dyck, R., & Koele, P. (1995). Respiratory training prior to exposure *in vivo* in the treatment of panic disorder with agoraphobia: Efficacy and predictors of outcome. *Australian and New Zealand Journal of Psychiatry, 29,* 104–113.

Fava, G.A., Rafanelli, C., Grandi, S., Contis, S., Ruini, C., Mangelli, L., & Belluardo, P. (2001). Long-term outcome of panic disorder treated by exposure. *Psychological Medicine, 31,* 891–898.

Huppert, J.D., & Baker-Morissette, S.L. (2003). Beyond the manual: The insider's guide to panic control treatment. *Cognitive and Behavioral Practice, 10*(1), 2–13.

Margraf, J., Barlow, D.H., Clark, D.M., & Telch, M.J. (1993). Psychological treatment of panic: Work in progress on outcome, active ingredients, and follow-up. *Behaviour Research and Therapy, 31,* 1–8.

Marks, I.M., Swinson, R.P., Basoglu, M., Kuch, K., Noshirvani, H., O'Sullivan, G.O., Lelliott, P.T., Kirby, M., McNamee, G., & Sengun, S. (1993). Alprazolam and exposure alone and combined in panic disorder with agoraphobia: A controlled study in London and Toronto. *British Journal of Psychiatry, 162,* 776–787.

McCabe, R.E., & Antony, M.M. (2005). Panic disorder and agoraphobia. In M. Antony, D.R. Ledley, and R. Heimberg (Eds.), *Improving outcomes and preventing relapse in cognitive behavioral therapy* (pp. 1–37). New York: Guilford Press.

McLean, P.D., Woody, S., Taylor, S., & Koch, W.J. (1998). Comorbid panic disorder and major depression: Implications for cognitive–behavioral therapy. *Journal of Consulting and Clinical Psychology, 66,* 240–247.

McNally, R.J. (1994). *Panic disorder: A critical analysis.* New York: Guilford Press.

Meichenbaum, D., & Turk, D.C. (1987). *Facilitating treatment adherence: A practitioner's guidebook.* New York: Plenum Press.

Mitte, K. (2005). A meta-analysis of the efficacy of psycho- and pharmacotherapy in panic disorder with and without agoraphobia. *Journal of Affective Disorders, 88,* 27–45.

Otto, M.W., & Gould, R.A. (1996). Maximizing treatment outcome for panic disorder: Cognitive–behavioral strategies. In M.H. Pollack, M.W. Otto, & J.F. Rosenbaum (Eds.), *Challenges in clinical practice: Pharmacologic and psychosocial strategies* (pp. 113–140). New York: Guilford Press.

Otto, M.W., Pollack, M.H., & Barlow, D.H. (2004). *Stopping anxiety medication (SAM): Panic control therapy for benzodiazepine discontinuation (patient workbook)*. New York: Oxford University Press.

Otto, M. W., Smits, J. A. J., & Reese, H. E. (2005). Combined psychotherapy and pharmacotherapy for mood and anxiety disorders in adults: Review and analysis. *Clinical Psychology: Science & Practice, 12*(1), 72–86.

Prochaska, J.O., DiClemente, C.C., & Norcross, J. (1992). In search of how people change. *American Psychologist, 47*, 1102–1114.

Rosenbaum, J.F., Pollack, M.H., & Pollack, R.A. (1996). Clinical issues in the long-term treatment of panic disorder. *Journal of Clinical Psychiatry, 57*, 44–48.

Roy-Byrne, P.P., Craske, M.G., & Stein, M.B. (2006). Panic disorder. *The Lancet, 368*, 1023–1032.

Sanderson, W.C., & Bruce, T.J. (2007). Causes and management of treatment-resistant panic disorder and agoraphobia: A survey of expert therapists. *Cognitive and Behavioral Practice, 14*(1), 26–35.

Spiegel, D.A., & Bruce, T.J. (1997). Benzodiazepines and exposure-based cognitive behavior therapies for panic disorder: Conclusions from combined treatment trials. *American Journal of Psychiatry, 154*, 773–781.

Tsao, J.C.I., Mystkowski, J., Zucker, B., & Craske, M.G. (2002). Effects of cognitive–behavioral therapy for panic disorder on comorbid conditions: Replication and extension. *Behavior Therapy, 33*, 493–509.

Westen D., & Morrison K. (2001). A multidimensional meta-analysis of treatments for depression, panic, and generalized anxiety disorder: An empirical examination of the status of empirically supported therapies. *Journal of Consulting and Clinical Psychology, 69*, 875–899.

chapter five

Emotional schemas in treatment-resistant anxiety

Robert L. Leahy
The American Institute for Cognitive Therapy
New York, New York

Contents

Emotional schemas and resistance to change in anxiety disorders

Although there is considerable evidence that cognitive–behavioral therapy (CBT) is highly effective in the treatment of anxiety disorders, many prospective patients do not complete the recommended course of treatment (Leung & Heimberg, 1996; van Minnen, Arntz, & Keijsers, 2002; Vogel, Stiles, & Gotestam, 2004). *Treatment resistance* can be defined in a variety of ways, including unwillingness to enter treatment, premature dropout, difficulty in completing exposure and response prevention, falling back into noncompliance after some improvement, and becoming discouraged even though there is significant progress. In this chapter, I will describe how the patient's conceptualization of emotional experience and anxiety affects the problematic strategies that are used to maintain the patient's anxiety disorder and to interfere with effective treatment. In addition, I will outline therapeutic interventions, based on emotional schema therapy (EST), that can help overcome obstacles in treatment.

Problems with compliance and demoralization in treatment may be related to the patient's expectations about what treatment can or should accomplish. Does the patient hope to improve daily functioning and to achieve important life goals? For example, would the patient be satisfied if he were able to function more effectively at work or in interpersonal relationships? Or, does the patient expect to *eliminate* urges, thoughts, feelings, and all other symptoms? How does the patient see it, and how is this unrealistic? The view advanced in this chapter is that treatment resistance can be understood as a combination of unrealistic expectations about progress and outcome, problematic ideas about the nature of emotion and discomfort, and reliance on self-fulfilling negative strategies of emotional control and avoidance.

Because CBT requires continued exposure with response prevention for anxiety-provoking behavior, patients understandably may be reluctant to continue in treatment—or, if they do continue, they may be reluctant to comply with direct exposure. Indeed, effective exposure necessitates the activation of sufficient fear (Foa & Kozak, 1986). Some patients may believe that activation of fear will result in an overwhelming, long-lasting, and impairing experience that may have serious, if not dangerous, consequences. These beliefs about "what happens when emotion is dysregulated" can affect the willingness to enter into CBT or to engage in even the first level of exposure.

Each anxiety disorder reflects the patient's theory of emotional dysregulation that underpins resistance to engage in exposure; for example, panic disorder is characterized by the belief that one's sensations will escalate out of control into a panic attack that will be devastating (Barlow,

2002; Clark, 1986). Obsessive–compulsive disorder (OCD) results from the belief that one's intrusive thoughts confer responsibility and require monitoring and control (Purdon, 1999; Purdon, Rowa, & Antony, 2005; Salkovskis, Forrester, & Richards, 1998). Social anxiety disorder is based on the underlying belief that anxiety symptoms and behaviors are personally reprehensible, humiliating, and must be controlled or hidden from others (Rapee & Heimberg, 1997; Wells & Papageorgiou, 1998).

All of us experience uncomfortable or unpleasant emotions, such as sadness, anxiety, fear, or anger, but not everyone develops a diagnosable psychiatric disorder. Most, if not all, of us have intrusive thoughts or "strange ideas," but we do not all develop obsessive–compulsive disorder. It is proposed here that noncompliance in cognitive–behavioral therapy for anxiety disorders is partly related to the role of emotional avoidance and fear of anxiety. Further, this emotional avoidance and fear of anxiety can be viewed as a consequence of the *emotional schemas* endorsed by the patient that underlie the anxiety disorder and resistance to change.

Emotional schemas

The role of emotional processing in anxiety disorders has been the focus of a number of studies. Of specific interest has been the construct of *alexithymia*—that is, the difficulty in labeling or identifying one's own emotions. Alexithymia has been viewed as a "meta-emotional" deficit reflecting difficulties recalling emotions or identifying the situations that give rise to emotions (Taylor, Bagby, & Parker, 1997). Overall levels of anxiety are positively related to alexithymia (Culhane & Watson, 2003; Eizaguirre, Saenz de Cabezon, Alda, Olariaga, & Juaniz, 2004). In a study of 85 combat veterans, alexithymia was predictive of posttraumatic stress disorder (PTSD) (Monson, Price, Rodriguez, Ripley, & Warner, 2004), while in another study alexithymia was found to be essentially a *symptom* (that is, emotional numbing) characteristic of PTSD (Bandura, 2003). Alexithymia is related to maladaptive coping with anxiety, such as drinking (Stewart, Zvolensky, & Eifert, 2002) and the search for perfectionism (Lundh, Johnsson, Sundqvist, & Olsson, 2002).

In addition to the role of alexithymia in anxiety disorders, emotional avoidance has also been implicated as a vulnerability factor (Borkovec, Alcaine, & Behar, 2004; Hayes, Wilson, Gifford, Follette, & Strosahl, 1996; Mennin & Farach, 2007). It has been argued that "experiential avoidance" interferes with effective habituation or desensitization and only serves to maintain the anxiety disorder (Hayes, Luoma, Bond, Masuda, & Lillis, 2006). Of course, Mowrer's two-factor theory of anxiety proposed over 50 years ago that anxiety is "conserved" through avoidance or escape because it is reinforced (Mowrer, 1956). Consequently, exposure—especially with the activation of anxiety—is viewed as a necessary condition for reducing this conservation of anxiety (Foa & Kozak, 1986; Hayes et al., 1996).

Although recognizing, labeling, and differentiating emotions are part of an essential first step in emotional processing, individuals also differ in their interpretations of and strategies employed in response to their own emotions (Leahy, 2001b, 2003a). Once an emotion is activated, the first step is to *attend* to the emotion. This first step can include both noticing the emotion and labeling the emotion—a process underlying alexithymia. Of course, more than one emotion may be activated, thus adding further to the complexity of this first step. The next step can involve emotional and cognitive avoidance of the emotion, as reflected by dissociation, binge-ing, or alcohol consumption. For example, individuals with social anxiety disorder rely on alcohol or drugs to manage their emotions so their emotional arousal will be diminished, thereby decreasing the likelihood that they will be humiliated because they might appear anxious. Similarly, individuals with PTSD also rely on alcohol and drugs to reduce the emotional impact of their intrusive images or they dissociate, thereby lessening the impact of their anxious experiences. Indeed, they may dissociate in therapy, especially when disturbing memories or problematic relationships are the topic of discussion (see Chapter 3 by Jackson, Nissenson, and Cloitre, this volume).

Each of the anxiety disorders entails emotional schemas (interpretations and strategies) of the sensations, emotions, or intrusive thoughts and images that are experienced. Negative emotional strategies and interpretations include validation ("Other people understand the way I feel"), comprehensibility ("My emotions don't make sense to me"), guilt and shame ("I shouldn't have these feelings" or "I don't want anyone to know I feel this way"), simplistic thoughts ("I should not have mixed feelings"), higher values ("My feelings reflect my higher values"), control ("I am afraid my feelings will go out of control"), rationality ("I should be logical and rational, not emotional"), duration ("My feelings will last a long time"), consensus ("Other people have the same feelings"), acceptance ("I can accept the feelings I have"), rumination ("I sit and dwell about how bad I feel"), expression ("I can allow myself to cry"), and blame ("Other people cause me to feel this way"). The emotional schema model is shown in Figure 5.1.

We have found that these negative emotional schemas are related to depression, anxiety, PTSD, metacognitive aspects of worry, alcohol abuse, marital discord, and personality disorders (Leahy, 2001a, 2002a,b, 2003b; Leahy & Kaplan, 2004). Of interest in this chapter is the relation between emotional schemas and specific anxiety disorders; for example, individuals with panic disorder are expected to believe that their sensations and emotions are not comprehensible, they will go out of control, they will

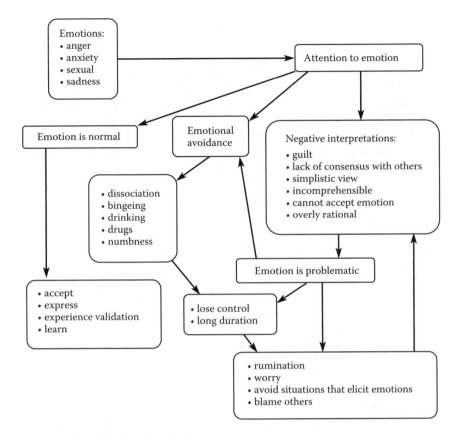

Figure 5.1 A model of emotional schemas.

last a long time, other people would not have these experiences, these sensations cannot be accepted, and they cannot be expressed. Indeed, cognitive–behavioral therapy addresses many of these interpretations by using bibliotherapy, explanation of the nature of panic disorder, setting up experiments, and testing specific predictions. Similarly, the treatment of obsessive–compulsive disorder entails addressing the patient's beliefs in thought–action fusion (loss of control), responsibility for neutralizing intrusions (control and guilt), and the personal implication of intrusions (guilt and shame) (Clark, 2005). These cognitive elements of OCD are also emotional schemas in that they constitute a rulebook that these individuals use for handling unwanted thoughts, images, and emotions. Wells' metacognitive model also suggests that OCD can be viewed as the interpretation of intrusive thoughts and the use of strategies of thought control (Wells, 1997).

Each anxiety disorder is based on the individual's *theory of mind*—specifically, a theory about the meaning, danger, and control of anxiety and the thoughts, images, and sensations related to anxiety. The meta-emotional and metacognitive model outlined here attempts to directly address these theories of anxiety in a manner consistent with other metacognitive models of treatment (Papageorgiou & Wells, 2001; Wells & Carter, 2001). These dimensions include beliefs about control, duration, shame, uniqueness, personal implication, validation, expression, and the role of rumination and other strategies. Specific interventions based on the emotional schema model are described below.

The solution is the problem

Each anxiety disorder may be characterized as a set of rules that are employed to avoid the negative effects of anxious arousal, thoughts, or sensations. These strategies include hypervigilance for emotion, attempts to suppress emotion, escape or avoidance, and the use of safety behaviors. These interpretations and strategies are viewed by the patient as solutions to the "problem." Individuals with social anxiety disorder, for example, are hypervigilant for any signs of their own arousal or signs of negative evaluation from others. They attempt to suppress or hide their arousal from others, they often escape from or avoid situations that elicit their anxiety, and they rely on safety behaviors (overpreparing, clutching furniture, lowering their eyes, misusing alcohol) to prevent others from detecting their anxiety (Rodebaugh, Holaway, & Heimberg, 2004). Each of these "solutions" constitutes social anxiety, thereby making the solution the problem.

Similarly, individuals with generalized anxiety disorder (GAD) are hypervigilant for any thoughts about potential mistakes or bad outcomes. They engage in safety behaviors (such as overpreparing, or "what-iffing"), they attempt to eliminate their worries by searching for perfect solutions in order to eliminate uncertainty, and they may procrastinate or avoid situations that might trigger their worry. Again, these solutions actually constitute GAD.

Each anxiety disorder is an attempt to eliminate anxiety because of the individual's negative interpretation of anxious thoughts, sensations, or arousal. These interpretations and strategies—which I call *emotional schemas*—are impediments to cognitive–behavioral therapy, since prolonged exposure to anxiety is in conflict with the individual's theory of how anxiety should be handled (Leahy, 2003a). Indeed, the therapist is asking the patient to abandon the solutions to discover that the problem will disappear once the solutions are relinquished. Thus, cognitive–behavioral therapy may seem counterintuitive to the anxious patient.

Emotion control strategies and resistance

Anxiety theories held by patients follow a Catch-22 logic: First, if there are breakthrough high escalations of anxiety, the patient concludes that one should implement the emotion control strategies even more forcefully. Second, in the more likely case that emotions do not escalate to catastrophic levels, the patient will conclude that the strategies are working. An emotional schema approach to these "anxiety theories" allows the therapist to identify the patient's idiosyncratic beliefs about the disorder, consider how these beliefs will interfere with compliance to exposure with response prevention, and modify these beliefs using cognitive, behavioral, and experiential techniques.

Anticipating noncompliance

Identifying the patient's theory of anxiety

Cognitive–behavioral therapy addresses a number of the components of the emotional schema model in the treatment of each of the anxiety disorders; for example, CBT emphasizes psychoeducation (comprehensibility, consensus, guilt/shame), exposure (expression), and prevention of neutralization, escape, or the use of safety behaviors (acceptance, duration, control). Directly addressing the emotional schema dimensions prior to exposure may enhance compliance with treatment. For example, in the treatment of panic disorder and agoraphobia, patients can be given information and rational perspectives on the issues of "comprehensibility" (i.e., panic disorder is a genetically predisposed condition that was adaptive in the evolutionary primitive environment to enhance avoidance of situations that conferred danger such as open spaces, heights, closed spaces). Similarly, their guilt or shame can be reduced by indicating that panic is an automatic and adaptive response that means that their ancestors were more likely to survive but now it is the *right* response at the *wrong* time. Many patients with anxiety disorders believe that the intense experience of their anxiety will continue to rise with continued exposure—a question that can be directly addressed prior to exposure: "What do you think will happen with your anxiety if you do this? How long will it be at these high levels?" Abandoning safety behaviors or escape can also be addressed: "You may believe that your anxiety will continue to rise unless you control it—have you ever given up trying to control it to see what happens?" From the perspective advanced here, anxiety disorders are less about anxiety arousal and are more a reflection of the interpretation of that arousal and the strategies activated to control it.

Strategies for intervention

Treatment of each of the anxiety disorders will involve some degree of exposure, which requires the activation of emotional schemas. I review below a number of dimensions of emotional schemas that are relevant to noncompliance and fear of treatment.

Validation and self-reward

Many patients with anxiety disorders have been encouraged to "snap out of it," "get your mind off of it," and "look at things realistically." These dismissive and potentially demoralizing statements only add to the problem, as not only do they not work but they also give the patient the view that they are seen as not doing the "simple things you need to do." Emotional schema therapy encourages the patient and therapist to partner in validating the difficulty in both having the problem and solving it. The therapist can acknowledge that having the problem is difficult, recognize that solving it seems even more challenging, and encourage patients to validate their own suffering, develop a compassionate self toward anxiety, and always remember to reward themselves for doing what is hard to do.

When will relief come?

Anxiety is myopic. The goal for many patients is to feel better in the short term, thus leading to reliance on avoidance, escape, and neutralization. Moreover, the patient may quit if relief is not *immediate*. This is related to the fear that anxiety will unravel and escalate to levels that are intolerable or even dangerous. Avoidance and neutralization often reduce anxiety very rapidly, reinforcing the idea that the only way to get relief is to rely on rituals, neutralization, and avoidance. In EST, the therapist can ask, "Is your goal to get better for the next 5 years or only for the next 5 minutes? To get better over the long term, it is important to do hard things now so they will be easier in the future. This requires *investing in discomfort* and in *persisting with practice*. The costs are upfront."

Emotional processing and personal effectiveness are the goals

Exposure and response prevention (ERP) requires the experience of anxiety to be effective. The goal in EST is not simply disconfirmation of a belief (e.g., "My house will be burglarized if I don't check the locks"). Rather, the goal is to decrease the struggle against emotion—that is, to allow the anxious feeling to occur and to tolerate this feeling. It is not simply habituation of anxiety; rather, the goal is tolerance of distress, the ability to do what is uncomfortable. As one patient commented after doing many exposures, "I learned I was able to do things I didn't think I was capable of doing." Similar to the concept of self-efficacy (Bandura, 2000), the ability to *tolerate discomfort* is a goal about self-efficacy and competence, not about feeling less anxious. When the patient is able to temporarily give up the goal of reducing anxiety and to adopt the goal of self-efficacy, then discomfort, anxiety, and exposure become a *means to an end*. The endpoint is *efficacy*, not comfort.

Constructive discomfort: investing in anxiety

Emotional schema therapy recognizes that discomfort is inevitable in the treatment of anxiety. Arguments that one must "feel ready," "be motivated," or "want to do it" are interpreted as *functioning to prolong avoidance*. When a patient with OCD complains that "I don't feel ready" when confronted with an exposure trial, the therapist responds, "The consequence of relying on 'being ready' is that you can avoid doing what needs to be done." Similarly, the consequence of relying on the rule that "I have to want to do it" is that avoidance is prolonged. The patient is encouraged to recognize that comfort is hopeless but not necessary. Because the patient will be uncomfortable with his anxiety disorder and uncomfortable in overcoming it, the real choice is whether their discomfort will be *useful*: "You do not have the luxury of an option that is comfortable." We use the term *constructive discomfort* to capture the intentional use of discomfort as a tool or as a means to an end (Leahy, 2005): "If you can be uncomfortable enough to do what it takes, you can make progress on your OCD." The therapist encourages the patient to view discomfort as a choice and as a tool—even as a goal: "If you are not doing something every day that is uncomfortable, then you are not making progress." One patient found it helpful to think of this as building "mental muscle."

Emotional schema therapy helps the patient focus on beliefs about discomfort, including beliefs about sensations, arousal, intrusive thoughts, or impairment. Thus, the therapist will elicit predictions about discomfort (duration, intensity, impairment, need for control) for the hours or entire day after exposure and collect information about what actually happened to the discomfort. In addition, the therapist can take a discomfort history ("What have you done before that was uncomfortable?"), pride in discomfort tolerance ("Have you felt proud of doing things that were unpleasant to do?"), and tracking discomfort tolerance ("Keep track of your ability to tolerate discomfort facing your anxiety"). Rather than focus on reducing anxiety, the therapist reframes discomfort as a motivator ("Tell me how much discomfort and anxiety you have sought out over the week"). The goal is discomfort as a means to an end.

Comprehensibility and consensus

A distinctive feature of CBT is socialization and the psychoeducation of patients. The patient is viewed as part of a collaborative alliance in addressing the problems that are presented. To reduce noncompliance, the therapist

can validate the difficulty of the anxiety disorder: "It must be very difficult
to feel awkward and anxious around people" (for social anxiety disorder),
or "Your OCD has interfered in your daily life so much that you often have
felt hopeless about ever getting better." It is important to recognize that not
only do many patients wish to have their problems solved but they also want
to have their emotional struggle recognized and appreciated—they want
to feel cared for. Validation is the first step in effective CBT. Understanding
the nature of the problem—and the solution—will help the patient gain a
sense of control. Indeed, if the patient does not understand why the problem exists, it is difficult to imagine how he or she will believe that the solution is worth the discomfort of exposure. Bibliotherapy or the use of patient
information handouts helps the patient make sense of the problem and, in
fact, can help the patient recognize that millions of other people have similar problems (Leahy & Holland, 2000). Patient interest groups, such as the
OCD Foundation or the National Alliance for the Mentally Ill, also reduce
the sense that one is alone with the problem.

Acceptance

Accepting that one has anxiety symptoms (rather than struggling, ruminating, or feeling ashamed of them) is an important starting point for
changing them. The individual who does not accept the symptom adds
to the sense of danger, personal implication, shame, guilt, and loss of control. Acceptance is a core strategy of emotional processing in dialectical
behavior therapy, acceptance, and commitment therapy and mindfulness training (Blackledge & Hayes, 2001; Linehan, 1993). Acceptance of
an intrusion would eliminate the hypervigilance and suppression of the
intrusion which can allow the patient to test the belief that one must be on
guard for internal states of anxiety. Similarly, acceptance of uncertainty
can reduce the need to worry to find perfect solutions, dramatically reducing the symptoms of GAD (Dugas, Buhr, & Ladouceur, 2004).

In EST, acceptance of urges, intrusions, and sensations is enhanced by
helping the patient examine the costs and benefits of acceptance versus
anger or attempts to control the intrusion. In addition, the therapist can
encourage the patient to use imagery of surrendering rather than controlling or "obeying" the intrusions.

> T. Rather than fight against your intrusive thought, perhaps you can
> imagine that you are floating on the water and the thought is float-
> ing alongside of you.
> C. But, I want to get rid of the thoughts. They bother me.
> T. Yes, you have been trying to get rid of the thought, but that hasn't
> worked. Imagine you were in deep water and you fought against the
> water, slapping it because you were angry. What would happen?

C. I'd drown.

T. Rather than fight against the water, surrender and float on it, and imagine doing the same with your obsessive thoughts. Let them be and float alongside of them.

Expression

Expression of emotion—allowing oneself to have an emotion—can allow the patient to test the beliefs that having anxiety will lead to escalation, loss of control, mental collapse, or physical danger. The patient's predictions about the consequences of expression can be elicited and set up as an experimental test of a theory of anxiety. It is essential that the exposure to having the emotion is extended, as short exposure without habituation runs the risk of sensitizing the patient to emotional experience. For example, the OCD patient's belief that the expression or experience of anxiety will rise and remain high cannot be disconfirmed without extensive and repeated exposure. Indeed, the short exposures that the patient may have experienced may have continued to confirm the belief that expression or acceptance simply makes things worse. Expression of an intrusive thought also serves the purpose of testing out the belief that continuing to have an "unwanted" experience will make matters worse. We encourage patients with intrusions to repeat them slowly, methodically, like a "zombie," in a manner similar to a mindful observation of the thought. Expressing the thought that "I might get contaminated no matter what I do" allows the patient to observe that the anxiety associated with the thought increases and then abates, further disconfirming the view that control of thoughts and sensations is necessary.

Duration and variability

A common misconception that anxious individuals have is that their intense anxiety will rise uncontrollably unless they escape or neutralize. The obsessive–compulsive individual believes that the intense anxiety will escalate and last indefinitely, requiring immediate neutralization, and the patient with panic disorder believes that the intense panic attacks will also last indefinitely. This belief can be addressed directly prior to exposure: "Many people with anxiety problems believe that their anxious arousal will escalate beyond control and will last indefinitely unless they escape from the situation. This belief has maintained and reinforced your anxiety—since you seldom stay long enough to find out that your anxiety will naturally decline on its own—even if you do absolutely nothing to make it decline." The question of duration of anxiety can be addressed by asking the patient what has happened after every increase in anxiety—has the anxiety decreased? This is similar to the dialectical behavior therapy view that reality (including emotions) is *impermanent*. Activity scheduling can allow the patient to track the variability of anxiety (and other emotions), thereby disconfirming the belief that emotions are stable or permanent. If emotions or arousal are impermanent, then there is less to fear.

Control

Anxious individuals believe that their sensations, intrusive thoughts or images, or anxious arousal must be controlled or dire consequences will ensue. Because control is often immediately implemented (in panic, by escaping; in OCD, by neutralizing; in social anxiety disorder, by hiding, avoiding, or escaping), the individual does not have the opportunity to disconfirm the belief that control needs to be taken. Control beliefs underlie the reliance on safety behaviors that serve to neutralize or protect the anxious individual from losing control (Salkovskis, Clark, Hackmann, Wells, & Gelder, 1999). If the patient continues to believe that the safety behaviors are necessary, then exposure is compromised (Wells, 1997). The purpose of exposure is to disconfirm the patient's belief that giving up control (neutralization, avoidance, or escape) will result in catastrophe. Indeed, practicing the symptom (anxiety or physical sensations) without struggling to gain control confirms the belief that anxiety can be tolerated and, therefore, does not need to be controlled.

These beliefs about controllability increase the *sense of lack of control*, because intrusive thoughts and images cannot be eliminated and anxious arousal is not amenable to willful affirmations (Wegner, 1989; Wegner & Zanakos, 1994). Simply, the more the patient tries to control intrusive thoughts and unpleasant emotions, the more uncontrollable and frightening they appear. The therapist can point out that illusions of needing and manifesting control have maintained the anxiety disorder by requiring the impossible (control of the uncontrollable) (Hayes et al., 2006). In fact, uncontrollability can be viewed as a phobic problem in itself—that is, the fear of losing control. This can be addressed directly through experiments in losing control ("Try going crazy") or mindfulness exercises that refocus to being an observer rather than someone who controls and judges anxious arousal (Roemer & Orsillo, 2002; Wells, 2008). Similarly, relinquishing control can also be manifested by attentional training and reduced vigilance (Bogels & Mansell, 2004; Wells, 1997), setting up the experiment of intentionally redirecting attention elsewhere to see what happens with the anxiety ("If I don't control it, does it escalate?"). The use of mindfulness may engage a metacognitive mode of processing and increase flexibility in response to threat (Toneatto, 2002; Wells, 2002) that allows the patient to detach from the experience while observing it. In this sense, metacognitive, acceptance, and mindfulness models of emotional avoidance complement one another.

Globalization beliefs

Related to the sense of control is the degree of helplessness and hopelessness about the symptoms that reoccur. In addition, beliefs about the self ("I am a neurotic") that are global and stable may also demoralize anxious individuals who consider treatment. Dunmore, Clark, and Ehlers (1999) found that longer term outcome for patients with PTSD was affected by appraisal of symptoms, perceived negative responses of others, and beliefs in permanent change. Thus, the interpretation of controllability, global personal inference, and shame are important components of the maintenance of symptoms (Ehlers & Clark, 2000; Ehlers et al., 1998). The belief that one's symptoms are part of a larger pattern of incompetence or insanity also undermines effective outcome (Steil & Ehlers, 2000). The therapist can address these global beliefs by asking the patient to consider the anxiety disorder as a "limited and specific vulnerability." For example, the patient can list all of the behaviors, thoughts, feelings, and relationships where the anxiety disorder is not disabling. Compartmentalizing the problem allows the patient to feel less overwhelmed and more hopeful of change.

Shame

The sense of humiliation that accompanies many anxiety disorders makes it difficult for some patients to pursue treatment. For example, a male patient believed that his continued PTSD was a sign of weakness and failure and delayed seeking treatment, as treatment was further evidence that he was not a man—an example consistent with the predictors of poor outcome for traumatized patients (Clohessy & Ehlers, 1999). Individuals with OCD may feel guilt about their intrusive images and thoughts, making them reluctant to engage in exposure. Indeed, the shame that accompanies these intrusive thoughts and urges may inhibit the patient from either disclosing these thoughts or continuing treatment (Gilbert & Andrews, 1998). Patients with OCD or PTSD who experience shame about their intrusive thoughts, images, and avoidance may be encouraged to know that shame is a common core feature of the disorder. We have found it useful to tell patients directly that intrusive thoughts and images often evoke shame in patients because of their perfectionistic standards for their emotions and thoughts. Indeed, the shame that accompanies these intrusions makes them more disturbing and thus adds to their personal significance and to the attention given them. If the individual were not ashamed of these mental and emotional phenomena—and recognized that a vast majority of nonclinical individuals have similar thoughts and images—then the shame could be reduced.

Shame, of course, is a central component of social anxiety disorder, because the individual attempts to hide the anxiety symptoms from other people. The patient can be asked exactly what is predicted should someone know that he or she is anxious and then to test these predictions by disclosing the anxiety to several friends. Further, the shame can be reduced by having the patient canvas other people about their psychological problems. We have found that this often reduces the shame—and increases the consensus and validation—because many friends or family members will acknowledge specific phobias, obsessions, or other problems.

Guilt

A sense of responsibility to do something about an intrusive thought or image is a central feature of both OCD and GAD (Clark, 2004; Purdon & Clark, 1993, 1994; Wells, 2000). The individual believes that the occurrence of the intrusion and the possibility that one can take action to neutralize constitute an absolute responsibility to do something. Accordingly, anxious patients are driven by an impossible standard of responsibility that they believe will help avoid future regret. Acceptance of lack of control and the "reasonable person" criteria for responsibility are important antidotes to the perfectionistic standards used by individuals with OCD or GAD: "Would a reasonable person think that they had to get rid of every intrusive thought?" Moreover, the belief that one should never regret anything also constitutes a demand for absolute certainty that drives patients toward anticipating every possible way that things can go badly (Dugas et al., 2004). The therapist can point out that responsibility is based on *reasonable* ability to know and control—and that "moral standards" are those that we would apply universally to enhance human dignity (Leahy, 2001b).

Rumination

Rumination leads to increased self-focus on negative feelings that increase access to negative cognitions, thereby maintaining these negative emotions (Nolen-Hoeksema, 2000). Rumination also reduces the opportunity to experience pleasurable activities. Individuals ruminate because they view this process as a problem-solving strategy (Nolen-Hoeksema, 2000; Papageorgiou & Wells, 2001). When we apply this to emotions, we can see that the individual who has a simplistic view of feelings ("I should have only one emotion") would be perplexed and would be more likely to ruminate. Similarly, a belief that emotions are problematic and that one should always emphasize rationality and logic would lead someone to ruminate to get rid of the emotion. Rumination is reduced when the individual experiences validation and finds that others share similar feelings, thereby making his feelings comprehensible and therefore not requiring further rumination. Furthermore, by making feelings comprehensible and finding consensus, the individual is less likely to feel guilty and less likely to believe that he or she will lose control.

A woman who is angry with her mother, for example, and who is ruminating about this can find validation from friends or her therapist and can learn that others would respond to the mother in a similar way. Thus, her feelings make sense for her; she is not alone. This reduces her guilt. She may also learn that she can love her mother and be angry at her—learning to tolerate ambivalent feelings—and that she does not always have to be rational and logical. The tolerance of ambivalence and the recognition that her feelings make sense may help her recognize that her angry feelings or her confusion will not last indefinitely.

I have outlined in Table 5.1 a variety of questions, interventions, and behavioral experiments that might be used to address the patient's underlying theory of anxiety regulation and the emotional schemas that may be an impediment to effective treatment. The section that follows gives a brief description of how some of these techniques were useful in the treatment of a patient with obsessive–compulsive disorder.

Case example

The patient was a man with a 30-year history of OCD focused on fears of becoming contaminated and contaminating others. When he first consulted the author, the patient was seeing a very experienced behavior therapist who "assisted" him in exposure in the patient's home. The patient reported relying on the behavior therapist, his psychiatrist, and his friends for ongoing reassurance. These safety behaviors became a target of our work—that is, the goal was to eliminate safety behaviors and reassurance. In assessing his motivation to change, the patient indicated that his OCD interfered with all aspects of his life. Because of fears of contamination, he could not enjoy his apartment, his work space, sexual intimacy, and relationships, and his recreational life was limited. The costs of getting better were outlined: taking risks, the possibility of regrets, continual discomfort, and the possibility of "falling apart."

The goals of therapy—from the patient's point of view—were to feel comfortable doing exposure and to be rid of intrusive thoughts about contamination. These targets were viewed by the therapist as hopeless goals that would only impede progress in doing exposure. The therapist suggested different goals: (1) be able to do what you don't want to do, (2) tolerate discomfort, and (3) feel effective in overcoming obstacles. These newer goals were contrasted with the problematic emotional schema goals that the patient had insisted on. Because he viewed his emotions as intolerable,

Table 5.1 Emotional Schemas: Interventions

Dimensions	Interventions
Validation	Are there some people who accept and understand your feelings? Do you have arbitrary rules for validation? Do people have to agree with everything you say? Are you sharing your emotions with people who are critical? Do you accept and support other people who have these emotions? Do you have a double standard? Why?
Comprehensibility	Do the emotions make sense to you? What could be some good reasons why you are sad, anxious, angry, etc.? What are you thinking (what images do you have) when you are sad, etc.? What situations trigger these feelings? If someone else experienced this, what kinds of different feelings could that person have? If you think your feelings don't make sense right now, what does this make you think? Are you afraid that you are going crazy, losing control? Are there things that happened to you as a child (or at other times) that might account for why you feel this way?
Guilt and shame versus legitimacy	What are the reasons that you think your emotions are not legitimate? Why shouldn't you have the feelings that you have? What are some reasons that your feelings make sense? Is it possible that others could have the same feelings in this situation? Can you see that having a feeling (like anger) is not the same as acting on it (for example, being hostile)? Why are certain emotions good and others are bad? If someone else had this feeling, would you think less of him? How do you know if an emotion is bad? What if you looked at feelings and emotions as experiences that tell you that something is bothering you—like a caution sign, a stop sign, or a flashing red light? How is anyone harmed by your emotions?
Simplicity versus complexity	Do you think that having mixed feelings is normal or abnormal? What does it mean to have mixed feelings about someone? Aren't people complicated, and so you could have different, even conflicting, feelings? What is the disadvantage of demanding that you have only one feeling?

Relationship to higher values	Sometimes we feel sad, anxious, or angry because we are missing something that is important to us. Let's say you feel sad about a breakup in a relationship. Doesn't this mean that you have a higher value that's important to you—for example, closeness and intimacy? Doesn't this say something good about you? If you aspire to higher values, doesn't this mean that you will have to be disappointed at times? Would you want to be a cynic who values nothing? Are there other people who share your higher values? What advice would you give them if they were going through what you are going through?
Controllable/ tolerable versus chaotic/ overwhelming	Do you think that you have to control your feelings and get rid of the negative feelings? What do you think would happen if you couldn't get rid of that feeling entirely? Is it possible that trying to get rid of a feeling completely makes that feeling too important to you? Are you afraid that having a strong feeling is a sign of something worse? Going crazy? Losing complete control? Isn't there a difference between controlling your actions and controlling your feelings?
Numbness	Are there situations that trigger spacing out? No feelings? Are there situations that bother most people that don't bother you? Do people think that you are blunted or empty in your feeling? What kinds of strong feelings do you have? Do you ever notice having a strong feeling and then you try not to have it? Do you ever have the feeling like you are going to cry but you stop it? What do you fear would happen if you let go and let yourself have those feelings? What kinds of thoughts do you have when you have strong feelings? Do you ever drink or use drugs or binge on food to get rid of those strong feelings?
Rationality, anti-emotional	Do you think you should always be logical and rational? What would you be concerned about if you were not rational or logical? Do you think that people who are rational or logical are "better" people? What's happened in the past when you haven't been rational or logical? Is it possible that some experiences are not rational or logical but simply emotional? Is there a rational painting? Rational song? Can your emotions tell you about what is hurting? What needs to be changed? Are emotions an important source of need, desire, neglect, and rights? Do you know other people who are less rational than you, but who have a happier or fuller life?

(continued)

Table 5.1 (continued) Emotional Schemas: Interventions

Dimensions	Interventions
Duration of strong feelings	Do you have fears that a strong feeling will last too long? Have you had strong feelings before? What happened? Did they end? Why did they end? Do strong feelings go up and down? If you had a strong feeling in our meeting, what do you think would happen? If you cried or felt really bad for few minutes, what would you think would happen? What would you gain by finding out that your strong feelings can be expressed and can go away?
Consensus with others	Exactly what feelings do you have that you think other people don't have? If someone else had these feelings, what would you think of them? When you see very emotional plays or movies or read emotional novels or stories, why do you think they appeal to people? Do you think that people like to find out that other people have the same feelings? Are there other people who are sad, angry, or anxious? Is it normal to be upset, have fantasies, etc.? If you are ashamed of your feelings and don't tell people, do you think that this keeps you from finding out that others have the same feelings?
Acceptance or inhibition	What will happen if you allow yourself to accept an emotion? Will you act on it (feeling–action fusion)? Do you fear that if you accept an emotion it won't go away? Or, do you think that not accepting your emotions will motivate you to change? What are the negative consequences of inhibiting a feeling? Excessive use of attention and energy? Rebound effect? Does the emotion conflict with a belief about good–bad feelings? If you deny that something bothers you, how could you fix the problem?

Rumination versus instrumental style	What are the advantages and disadvantages of focusing on how bad you feel? When you are focusing on how bad you feel, what kinds of things are you thinking and feeling? Do you sit and think, "What's wrong with me?" or "Why is this happening to me?" Do you focus on sadness, replaying in your mind the same things over and over? Do you sometimes think that if you keep thinking about it you will come up with a solution? Does your rumination (worry) make you worry that you can't control your worries? Try setting aside 30 minutes each day when you will intensely worry and set aside your worries until that time. Rephrase your worries into behaviors that you can carry out, problems that you can solve. Distract yourself by taking action or calling a friend and talking about something other than your worries. Exactly what do you predict will happen? Have your predictions proved false? When you are ruminating, you are chewing things over. Is there some "truth" or "reality" that you just refuse to accept?
Expression	If you expressed a feeling, would you lose control? Feel worse? How long would you feel worse? Can expressing a feeling help you clarify your thoughts and feelings? Conversely, if you only focus on expressing a feeling, will you over-focus on these feelings? Will you become self-absorbed? Are there things that you can do to distract yourself or solve problems?
Blaming others	What did other people say or do that made you feel the way you do? What thoughts did you have that made you feel sad, angry, anxious, etc.? If you thought about this differently, what would you feel or think? Are your feelings dependent on what others think of you? Are you focused on getting approval, respect, appreciation, or fairness? What would be the advantage and disadvantage of not needing approval, etc.? What rewards does the other person currently control? Can you have rewarding experiences despite what they said, did, etc.? Is it possible that your feelings are a combination of what is happening to you and what you are thinking? What would you like to feel? Angry? Sad? Curious? Indifferent? Accepting? Challenged? What are the costs and benefits of these different feelings? What would you have to think in order to have each of these feelings, given the situation? What would you like to have happen? How can you be more assertive? Solve problems? What thoughts would you have to change?

dangerous, interminable, and incomprehensible—and as a sign of a fundamental flaw of being defective—his avoidance made sense to him. In contrast, an emotional schema model would allow him to test out whether he could tolerate discomfort and whether discomfort in doing exposure ruined his day (or made it better).

His emotional schemas about compulsive feelings were that, unless he neutralized these feelings, they would escalate and ruin his day and that, on future occasions, he would be even more compulsive. His beliefs about these emotions (or desires) were then set up as emotional hypotheses: "Let's test out your prediction that your compulsive desire increases over the next 24 hours if you do not neutralize after exposure." Invariably, these predictions led to the recognition that compulsive urges decreased substantially after 30 minutes and that the days in which he engaged in ERP were usually better than the days during which he avoided doing so.

A variety of safety behaviors and thoughts were identified. These included wearing gloves when touching certain objects, relying on reassurance, using the behavior therapist to make decisions as to exposure, engaging in exposure in a frenzied manner, insisting on the need to be ready, and claiming that he was too fragile to do certain exposures. The patient's claim that the he was *too fragile* served the function of allowing him to avoid exposure or, in some cases, hedge his exposure by immediately neutralizing. This, too, was a safety behavior. It was helpful to him to recognize that his self-label of fragility was part of an underlying strategy to stay safe, but the goal of therapy now was to tolerate risk and discomfort. Moreover, the patient was urged to test predictions about how fragile his self would be if he did exposure by collecting data as to his functioning for the day after exposure and response prevention. The functional consequences of self-labels ("I am too fragile" or "I am too neurotic") were evaluated—less in terms of their factual basis and more in terms of how they allowed him to continue avoidance. These self-labels were part of his problematic emotional schemas.

The therapist focused on three new emotional schema goals that were related to the overall goal of personal efficacy:

1. *Constructive discomfort*—"Being able to use discomfort to make progress"
2. *Successful imperfection*—"Being able to do things imperfectly every day in order to get better daily"
3. *Pride in overcoming obstacles*—"Looking for obstacles to overcome so I will have a legitimate basis for self-esteem"

Contrary to the emotional goals of comfort and relaxation, the new goals were mental toughness and resilience. Constructive discomfort

Table 5.2 Challenging Negative
Beliefs about Emotions

Negative	Adaptive
Anxiety is a sign that it is dangerous.	Anxiety is a sign that you are facing your fears and making progress.
My anxiety will escalate and become unbearable.	If I tolerate the anxiety and stay with it, the anxiety may decrease. Let's find out.
I need to feel ready before I do it.	I can do it even if I don't feel ready. Doing it will make me more ready in the future.

involved seeking out discomfort as a goal every day: "If you are not doing something every day that is uncomfortable, then you are not making progress." Thus, when the patient would contemplate exposure, his first response often was "This is very unpleasant" or "I don't want to do this." The therapist's response was "The goal is to be uncomfortable and to do what you don't want to do." Similarly, *successful imperfection* was invoked as a strategy that would allow him to do ERP imperfectly. Although he would sometimes neutralize after exposure, the imperfect progress of the exposure was reinforced as a step forward with successful imperfection. It was better than no exposure.

Like many people with chronic anxiety, there is often a lack of self-reward. Here, self-validation and self-reward in overcoming the obstacles of anxiety were emphasized: "Let's look at all the obstacles that you have overcome this past week." These obstacles included his intrusive thoughts, his desire to avoid or to neutralize, and his past habits of OCD. The model that was suggested was that self-esteem is better built on overcoming obstacles than on simply telling yourself how good you are. This new model of self-esteem (and efficacy) seemed far more plausible. It further reinforced the need to find obstacles to overcome as a means of building and maintaining self-esteem. This naturally contributed to the willingness to engage in ERP (see Table 5.2).

Because his fears were based on the consequences of contamination, these consequences could not be invalidated either through rational restructuring or through collecting the information. After all, contamination might lead to consequences in the distant future that could not be determined. The goal of therapy could not be to test out the contamination fears; instead, it was changed to *tolerate the discomfort of having those fears.* The new goals of therapy were summarized as follows:

1. Accept the risks that reasonable people accept.
2. Do what you do not want to do.
3. Seek out discomfort as a goal.

4. Give yourself credit for overcoming obstacles.
5. Aim for feeling effective in your life.

The patient endorsed several global beliefs about himself—as defective, flawed, and as a "pariah." These labels further added to his sense of hopelessness: "Even if I get better, who would want me?" The therapist helped the patient evaluate the OCD behaviors as a limited and *compartmentalized* vulnerability. Using the pie technique, the patient could identify a number of non-OCD behaviors and qualities that placed his OCD in the context of a more differentiated self-concept. In addition, the patient reported a great deal of shame about his symptoms, viewing them as totally unacceptable to other people. In fact, on closer examination of the evidence, his OCD was not the problem in prior relationships; it was his reassurance seeking, rumination, and complaining about OCD. These could now be seen as problematic ways of relating even if there were no OCD. Furthermore, the patient was able to acknowledge that OCD was not equivalent to some moral deficit but only to a problematic way of handling his own intrusive thoughts and impulses. In utilizing the emotional schema model to enhance exposure and response prevention, the patient acknowledged that he was doing so much exposure on his own that he was running out of feared objects.

Conclusions

Noncompliance—early dropout, unwillingness to engage in exposure, and low compliance with self-help homework—poses significant problems in the treatment of anxiety disorders. This is especially true with cognitive–behavioral treatments that require exposure and response prevention. I have suggested that the clinician might benefit by identifying the patient's theory of anxiety—and how anxiety is regulated—using a meta-emotional and metacognitive framework. The model described here is consistent with other models that target experiential avoidance and emotional processing as key factors in the efficacy of exposure and the treatment of anxiety (Blackledge & Hayes, 2001; Foa & Kozak, 1986; Mennin, Heimberg, Turk, & Fresco, 2002). A specific value of the emotional schema model is that it directly addresses the patient's conceptualization and strategy for difficult emotions, providing the clinician with potentially helpful interventions.

The clinician needs to be mindful that not only may exposure treatment appear counterintuitive to the emotionally avoidant patient, but it may also activate strategies of escape and avoidance, such as noncompliance or premature dropout. The emotional schema model acknowledges that the patient's "motivational" problem may reflect more pervasive problematic views of difficult emotions. This model allows both clinician and patient to anticipate and address these roadblocks that can interfere with successful treatment. Indeed, these roadblocks, which constitute the solutions to the problem of anxiety, are themselves the anxiety disorder.

References

Bandura, A. (2000). Self-efficacy: The foundation of agency. In W.J. Perrig & A. Grob (Eds.), *Control of human behaviour, mental processes and consciousness* (pp. 17–33). Mahwah, NJ: Lawrence Erlbaum.

Bandura, A. (2003). Theoretical and empirical exploration of the similarities between emotional numbing in posttraumatic stress disorder and alexithymia. *Journal of Anxiety Disorders, 17*(3), 349–360.

Barlow, D.H. (2002). *Anxiety and its disorders: The nature and treatment of anxiety and panic* (2nd ed.). New York: Guilford Press.

Blackledge, J.T., & Hayes, S.C. (2001). Emotion regulation in acceptance and commitment therapy. *Journal of Clinical Psychology, 57*(2), 243–255.

Bogels, S.M., & Mansell, W. (2004). Attention processes in the maintenance and treatment of social phobia: Hypervigilance, avoidance and self-focused attention. *Clinical Psychology Review, 24*(7), 827–856.

Borkovec, T.D., Alcaine, O.M., & Behar, E. (2004). Avoidance theory of worry and generalized anxiety disorder. In R.G. Heimberg, C.L. Turk, & D.S. Mennin (Eds.), *Generalized anxiety disorder: Advances in research and practice* (pp. 77–108). New York: Guilford Press.

Clark, D.A. (Ed.). (2005). *Intrusive thoughts in clinical disorders: Theory, research, and treatment*. New York: Guilford Press.

Clark, D.M. (1986). A cognitive approach to panic. *Behaviour Research & Therapy, 24*(4), 461–470.

Clohessy, S., & Ehlers, A. (1999). PTSD symptoms, response to intrusive memories and coping in ambulance service workers. *British Journal of Clinical Psychology, 38*(3), 251–265.

Culhane, S.E., & Watson, P.J. (2003). Alexithymia, irrational beliefs, and the rational–emotive explanation of emotional disturbance. *Journal of Rational–Emotive & Cognitive Behavior Therapy, 21*(1), 57–72.

Dugas, M.J., Buhr, K., & Ladouceur, R. (2004). The role of intolerance of uncertainty in the etiology and maintenance of generalized anxiety disorder. In R.G. Heimberg, C.L. Turk, & D.S. Mennin (Eds.), *Generalized anxiety disorder: Advances in research and practice* (pp. 143–163). New York: Guilford Press.

Dunmore, E., Clark, D.M., & Ehlers, A. (1999). Cognitive factors involved in the onset and maintenance of posttraumatic stress disorder (PTSD) after physical or sexual assault. *Behaviour Research and Therapy, 37*, 809–829.

Ehlers, A., & Clark, D.M. (2000). A cognitive model of posttraumatic stress disorder. *Behaviour Research and Therapy, 38*, 319–345.

Ehlers, A., Clark, D.M., Dunmore, E., Jaycox, L., Meadows, E., & Foa, E.B. (1998). Predicting response to exposure treatment in PTSD: The role of mental defeat and alienation. *Journal of Traumatic Stress, 11*(3), 457–471.

Eizaguirre, A.E., Saenz de Cabezon, A.O., Alda, I.O.d., Olariaga, L.J., & Juaniz, M. (2004). Alexithymia and its relationships with anxiety and depression in eating disorders. *Personality & Individual Differences, 36*(2), 321–331.

Foa, E.B., & Kozak, M.J. (1986). Emotional processing of fear: Exposure to corrective information. *Psychological Bulletin, 99*, 20–35.

Gilbert, P., & Andrews, B. (Eds.). (1998). *Shame: Interpersonal behavior, psychopathology, and culture.* London: Oxford University Press.

Hayes, S.C., Luoma, J.B., Bond, F.W., Masuda, A., & Lillis, J. (2006). Acceptance and commitment therapy: Model, processes and outcomes. *Behaviour Research and Therapy, 44*(1), 1–25.

Hayes, S.C., Wilson, K.G., Gifford, E.V., Follette, V.M., & Strosahl, K. (1996). Experiential avoidance and behavioral disorders: A functional dimensional approach to diagnosis and treatment. *Journal of Consulting and Clinical Psychology, 64*, 1152–1168.

Leahy, R.L. (2001a). *Emotional schemas in cognitive therapy.* Paper presented at the Association for the Advancement of Behavior Therapy, November 15, Philadelphia, PA.

Leahy, R.L. (2001b). *Overcoming resistance in cognitive therapy.* New York: Guilford Press.

Leahy, R.L. (2002a). A model of emotional schemas. *Cognitive and Behavioral Practice, 9*(3), 177–190.

Leahy, R.L. (2002b). *A model of emotional schemas.* Paper presented at the Association for the Advancement of Behavior Therapy, November 14, Reno, NV.

Leahy, R.L. (2003a). Emotional schemas and resistance in cognitive therapy. In R.L. Leahy (Ed.), *Roadblocks in cognitive–behavioral therapy: Transforming challenges into opportunities for change* (pp. 91–115). New York: Guilford Press.

Leahy, R.L. (2003b). *Metacognition, emotional schemas, and personality disorders.* Paper presented at the European Association of Cognitive and Behavioral Psychotherapy, Prague, September 9–12, Czech Republic.

Leahy, R.L. (2005). *The worry cure: Seven steps to stop worry from stopping you.* New York: Harmony/Random House.

Leahy, R.L., & Holland, S.J. (2000). *Treatment plans and interventions for depression and anxiety disorders.* New York: Guilford Press.

Leahy, R.L., & Kaplan, D. (2004). *Emotional schemas and relationship adjustment.* Paper presented at the Association for the Advancement of Behavior Therapy, November 18–21, New Orleans, LA.

Leung, A.W., & Heimberg, R.G. (1996). Homework compliance, perceptions of control, and outcome of cognitive–behavioral treatment of social phobia. *Behaviour Research & Therapy, 34*(5–6), 423–432.

Linehan, M.M. (1993). *Cognitive–behavioral treatment of borderline personality disorder.* New York: Guilford Press.

Lundh, L.-G., Johnsson, A., Sundqvist, K., & Olsson, H. (2002). Alexithymia, memory of emotion, emotional awareness, and perfectionism. *Emotion, 2*(4), 361–379.

Mennin, D.S., & Farach, F.J. (2007). Emotion and evolving treatments for adult psychopathology. *Clinical Psychology: Science & Practice, 14*(4), 329–352.

Mennin, D.S., Heimberg, R.G., Turk, C.L., & Fresco, D.M. (2002). Applying an emotion regulation framework to integrative approaches to generalized anxiety disorder. *Clinical Psychology: Science & Practice, 9*(1), 85–90.

Monson, C.M., Price, J.L., Rodriguez, B.F., Ripley, M.P., & Warner, R.A. (2004). Emotional deficits in military-related PTSD: An investigation of content and process disturbances. *Journal of Traumatic Stress, 17*(3), 275–279.

Mowrer, O.H. (1956). Two-factor learning theory reconsidered, with special reference to secondary reinforcement and the concept of habit. *Psychological Review, 63*(2), 114–128.

Nolen-Hoeksema, S. (2000). The role of rumination in depressive disorders and mixed anxiety/depressive symptoms. *Journal of Abnormal Psychology, 109*, 504–511.

Papageorgiou, C., & Wells, A. (2001). Metacognitive beliefs about rumination in major depression. *Cognitive and Behavioral Practice, 8*, 160–163.

Purdon, C. (1999). Thought suppression and psychopathology. *Behaviour Research and Therapy, 37*, 1029–1054.

Purdon, C., & Clark, D.A. (1993). Obsessive intrusive thoughts in nonclinical subjects. I. Content and relation with depressive, anxious, and obsessional symptoms. *Behaviour Research & Therapy, 31*(8), 713–720.

Purdon, C., & Clark, D.A. (1994). Obsessive intrusive thoughts in nonclinical subjects. II. Cognitive appraisal, emotional response, and thought control strategies. *Behaviour Research and Therapy, 32*, 403–410.

Purdon, C., Rowa, K., & Antony, M.M. (2005). Thought suppression and its effects on thought frequency, appraisal and mood state in individuals with obsessive–compulsive disorder. *Behaviour Research and Therapy, 43*(1), 93–108.

Rapee, R.M., & Heimberg, R.G. (1997). A cognitive–behavioral model of anxiety in social phobia. *Behaviour Research & Therapy, 35*(8), 741–756.

Rodebaugh, T.L., Holaway, R.M., & Heimberg, R.G. (2004). The treatment of social anxiety disorder. *Clinical Psychology Review, 24*(7), 883–908.

Roemer, L., & Orsillo, S.M. (2002). Expanding our conceptualization of and treatment for generalized anxiety disorder: Integrating mindfulness/acceptance-based approaches with existing cognitive–behavioral models. *Clinical Psychology: Science & Practice, 9*(1), 54–68.

Salkovskis, P.M., Clark, D.M., Hackmann, A., Wells, A., & Gelder, M.G. (1999). An experimental investigation of the role of safety-seeking behaviours in the maintenance of panic disorder with agoraphobia. *Behaviour Research and Therapy, 37*, 559–574.

Salkovskis, P.M., Forrester, E., & Richards, C. (1998). Cognitive–behavioural approach to understanding obsessional thinking. *British Journal of Psychiatry, 173*(Suppl. 35), 53–63.

Steil, R., & Ehlers, A. (2000). Dysfunctional meaning of posttraumatic intrusions in chronic PTSD. *Behaviour Research & Therapy, 38*(6), 537–558.

Stewart, S.H., Zvolensky, M.J., & Eifert, G.H. (2002). The relations of anxiety sensitivity, experiential avoidance, and alexithymic coping to young adults' motivations for drinking. *Behavior Modification, 26*(2), 274–296.

Taylor, G.J., Bagby, R., & Parker, J.D.A. (1997). *Disorders of affect regulation: Alexithymia in medical and psychiatric illness.* New York: Cambridge University Press.

Toneatto, T. (2002). A metacognitive therapy for anxiety disorders: Buddhist psychology applied. *Cognitive & Behavioral Practice, 9*(1), 72–78.

van Minnen, A., Arntz, A., & Keijsers, G.P.J. (2002). Prolonged exposure in patients with chronic PTSD: Predictors of treatment outcome and dropout. *Behaviour Research & Therapy, 40*(4), 439–457.

Vogel, P.A., Stiles, T.C., & Gotestam, K. (2004). Adding cognitive therapy elements to exposure therapy for obsessive–compulsive disorder: A controlled study. *Behavioural & Cognitive Psychotherapy, 32*(3), 275–290.

Wegner, D.M. (1989). *White bears and other unwanted thoughts: Suppression, obsession, and the psychology of mental control.* New York: Penguin.

Wegner, D.M., & Zanakos, S. (1994). Chronic thought suppression. *Journal of Personality, 62,* 615–640.

Wells, A. (1997). *Cognitive therapy of anxiety disorders: A practice manual and conceptual guide.* New York: John Wiley & Sons.

Wells, A. (2000). *Emotional disorders and metacognition: Innovative cognitive therapy.* New York: John Wiley & Sons.

Wells, A. (2002). GAD, metacognition, and mindfulness: An information processing analysis. *Clinical Psychology: Science & Practice, 9*(1), 95–100.

Wells, A. (2008). *Metacognitive therapy for anxiety and depression.* New York: Guilford Press.

Wells, A., & Carter, K. (2001). Further tests of a cognitive model of generalized anxiety disorder: Metacognitions and worry in GAD, panic disorder, social phobia, depression, and nonpatients. *Behavior Therapy, 32*(1), 85–102.

Wells, A., & Papageorgiou, C. (1998). Social phobia: Effects of external attention on anxiety, negative beliefs, and perspective taking. *Behavior Therapy, 29,* 357–370.

chapter six

Augmenting exposure-based treatment for anxiety disorders with principles and skills from dialectical behavior therapy

Stacy Shaw Welch
Anxiety and Stress Reduction Center of Seattle (ASRC)
  and University of Washington
Seattle, Washington

Travis L. Osborne
Anxiety and Stress Reduction Center of Seattle (ASRC)
  and University of Washington
Seattle, Washington

Jayde Pryzgoda
Anxiety and Stress Reduction Center of Seattle (ASRC)
  and University of Washington
Seattle, Washington

Contents

Substantial advancements have been made in the treatment of anxiety disorders during the past several decades. Effective psychosocial and pharmacological treatments are now available for each of the primary anxiety disorders (Barlow, 2002). Cognitive–behavioral therapy (CBT), in particular, has been found to be quite effective across the range of anxiety disorders, in both efficacy (randomized controlled trials) and effectiveness studies (Barlow, 2002; Hoffman & Smits, 2008; Roy-Byrne et al., 2005). Despite these advances, a sizeable proportion of clients who receive evidence-based, "gold standard" treatments for anxiety-related problems do not benefit sufficiently for a variety of reasons, including inability or unwillingness to engage or remain in treatment, treatment nonresponse, partial treatment response with residual symptoms, and relapse of symptoms following effective treatment. Consequently, many clinicians are faced with the challenge of needing to augment standard anxiety treatments, although limited data and resources are available to guide these decisions.

The anxiety disorders as a group share many clinical features, including increased physiological reactivity in response to phobic cues, faulty cognitions often involving overestimations of threat, avoidance of phobic cues, and the use of a range of "safety" behaviors that are designed to neutralize feelings of anxiety or facilitate behavioral, cognitive, or emotional avoidance and escape. Although CBT treatment protocols for anxiety disorders differ based on the unique features of each disorder, as well as differences in emphasis on the causal mechanisms for change, many also share a number of common components. These include psychoeducation about anxiety and the disorder, relaxation training (e.g., diaphragmatic breathing, progressive muscle relaxation), identification and modification of faulty thinking patterns (i.e., thought records, behavioral experiments to test the accuracy of cognitions), exposure to feared stimuli, and decreasing safety/escape behaviors (Barlow, 2002).

Although these strategies are usually effective, there are several major sets of challenges that occur in clinical practice that can undermine the efficacy of these interventions. Frequently, diagnostic complexity is the rule rather than the exception, making focused treatment on anxiety difficult or impossible. Many clients present with a complex set of symptoms, comorbid conditions, or severe behavioral dyscontrol that make it difficult to work in a linear manner through a manualized treatment protocol. Clients may also have other coping skills deficits that hinder treatment progress, such as difficulties coping with other life stressors. As a result, these stressors often take center stage in treatment, precluding focused treatment of the anxiety symptoms. Another major challenge involves the demands of the treatment itself. CBT requires that clients be active and engages participants in treatments that typically involve directly confronting difficult emotion states (e.g., anxiety, sadness, guilt). Many clients experience ambivalence about change, particularly when the treatments emphasize approaching feared stimuli and necessitate some degree of discomfort. This can lead to a range of therapy-interfering behaviors (e.g., homework noncompliance, treatment dropout) that must be successfully addressed in order for therapy to be implemented effectively (Pollard, 2007).

Problems with *emotion regulation* may be one factor at the core of many of the problems that can arise in therapy with clients with treatment-resistant anxiety. Recently, there has been a significant increase in awareness of and interest in the role of maladaptive efforts to regulate emotion in the anxiety disorders (Amstadter, 2008; Hannesdottir & Ollendick, 2007). For example, several theorists have modified current conceptualizations of anxiety disorders by placing a greater emphasis on emotion (as opposed to cognition and behavior) and the array of ineffective emotion regulation strategies (e.g., situational avoidance, use of safety signals, thought suppression, distraction, worry) that anxious individuals engage in that reduce short-term distress but perpetuate symptoms over time (Campbell-Sills & Barlow, 2007; Menin, Heimberg, Turk, & Fresco, 2005). New treatment protocols for anxiety-related problems that are based on these theoretical frameworks are currently being developed and tested (e.g., Barlow, Allen, & Choate, 2004; Mennin, 2004, 2006). Related to work on emotion regulation is the concept of *experiential avoidance*, or the use of mental and behavioral strategies that function to change one's internal experience, such as emotions, thoughts, and body sensations. This style of coping may represent one emotion regulation strategy that is quite relevant to the anxiety disorders (Orsillo, Roemer, & Holowka, 2005). Treatments that conceptualize clinical problems as stemming from experiential avoidance specifically, such as acceptance and commitment therapy (ACT) (Hayes, Strosahl, & Wilson, 1999), are discussed separately in this volume and are being increasingly used to treat anxiety-related problems.

Although controlled trial data are not yet available for interventions emphasizing emotion regulation as a central feature of anxiety, this emerging direction in the anxiety disorders field suggests a possible role for dialectical behavior therapy (DBT) (Linehan, 1993a,b), an established treatment for significant emotion regulation difficulties in clinical problems other than anxiety disorders. Indeed, Mennin (2005) has suggested that DBT "will likely be quite relevant to improving treatments for the anxiety disorders," given its emphasis on emotion regulation skills and its basis in current emotion research. DBT offers a therapeutic structure, a set of underlying treatment principles, and a format for teaching a range of specific coping skills that may be useful for augmenting standard CBT protocols for anxiety disorders when problems related to emotion regulation are present. Our aim is to describe specific ways that DBT can be applied to such cases to enhance treatment effectiveness. Our specific objectives are to:

1. Provide a brief summary of the theory, principles, and skills that comprise DBT, emphasizing their relevance to anxiety disorders.
2. Propose a levels-of-care approach (based on stepped-care principles) to applying DBT to address various problems that can arise in the treatment of anxiety, as well as recommendations for when to consider each level of care.
3. Provide clinical examples of how we have integrated DBT into the treatment of anxiety disorders in difficult-to-treat cases.
4. Review the emerging body of literature describing ways in which aspects of DBT have been incorporated into anxiety treatments.

We want to emphasize that we advocate that clients first receive the indicated evidence-based treatment protocols that are available for their specific anxiety symptoms and that minimal data on the use of DBT principles and strategies for anxiety disorders are available at this time. However, in cases where standard approaches have been applied competently and are not effective or sufficient, we encourage clinicians to consider whether DBT and the strategies described here might be a useful augmentation approach. In some cases, the strategies described are unique to DBT. In others, the strategies used in DBT borrow from traditional cognitive–behavioral approaches and have substantial overlap with standard treatments for anxiety. However, we believe that DBT may offer a useful structure for both conceptualization and intervention in treatment-resistant cases.

Brief overview of DBT

Dialectical behavior therapy is first a behavioral therapy, employing principles and strategies that are used across cognitive–behavioral treatments. The emphasis on emotion regulation, as well as the addition of particular strategies that are not part of traditional CBT interventions (i.e., mindfulness, acceptance, dialectics) came out of attempts to develop an effective treatment for chronically suicidal and self-injurious individuals meeting criteria for borderline personality disorder (BPD) (Linehan, 1993a). DBT was developed in part from the observation that standard behavior therapy approaches were not effective with this population. Thus, from its inception, one underlying focus of DBT has been on engaging and helping individuals who have traditionally been considered treatment resistant. A fundamental assumption of the theory underlying DBT is that the core of treatment resistance is not resistance on the part of the client in a willful or manipulative manner. Instead, the emphasis is on the profound difficulties these individuals have with regulating emotion and how these difficulties can prevent optimal engagement in treatment.

Over time, DBT has come to be viewed as a treatment that is effective with clients who have complex and multiple problems, at the core of which are emotion regulation difficulties. Consequently, the treatment has garnered considerable interest and has been applied to a number of complex clinical problems that seemingly stem, at least in part, from significant problems with emotion regulation. Research indicates that in addition to being an efficacious treatment for suicide attempts and self-injurious behaviors (Koons et al., 2001; Linehan, Armstrong, Suarez, Allmon, & Heard, 1991; Verheul et al., 2003), DBT is also an effective treatment for binge eating disorder (Telch, Agras, & Linehan, 2001), bulimia (Safer, Telch, & Agras, 2001), substance dependence comorbid with BPD (Linehan et al., 1999, 2002), and depression in older adults (Lynch, Morse, Mendelson, & Robins, 2003). Although the findings from these studies suggest that DBT has useful applications to a range of clinical problems, it is important to note that, to date, randomized controlled trials have not been conducted evaluating the efficacy of DBT for anxiety disorders.

Standard DBT is delivered through weekly individual therapy and a weekly skills group. This structure was designed to ensure that skills to improve the ability to regulate emotions across a number of domains were taught effectively and not usurped by crises or other pressing matters that arise during individual therapy sessions. Four skills modules are taught as part of DBT, including mindfulness, distress tolerance, and emotion regulation; interpersonal effectiveness skills are also taught, although they have not been included in all adaptations of DBT (see Telch et al., 2001, for binge eating disorder). In individual DBT therapy sessions, therapists are guided by a prioritized list of treatment targets, including life-threatening behaviors, therapy-interfering behaviors, and quality-of-life interfering behaviors, which are addressed in that order if any of these issues have been present in a given week. The treatment is structured according to four stages of treatment (Linehan, 1993a). In Stage 1 DBT, clients are considered to have poor behavioral control, and life-threatening and therapy-interfering behaviors are expected. All published randomized control trials to date have been on Stage 1 DBT. By Stage 2, clients would have developed good behavioral control, and in this stage other complex issues (e.g., trauma) would be addressed. In Stage 3, the focus would be on "ordinary problems in living," and Stage 4 includes a focus on increasing one's capacity for joy. DBT includes many standard elements of CBT, including structured sessions, self-monitoring of symptoms, behavioral analysis, cognitive restructuring, exposure, and other behavioral techniques that will not be reviewed here. We will, however, review several principles and strategies which, although present in some CBT and non-CBT treatments, are emphasized and used in DBT in ways that may prove helpful to clinicians working with difficult-to-treat clients with anxiety problems. These include dialectics, validation, targeting, and emphasis on contingency management, particularly with regard to the therapeutic relationship.

A levels-of-care approach to integrating DBT for treatment-resistant anxiety

Based on our experiences of integrating DBT and evidence-based treatments for anxiety disorders in treatment-resistant cases (i.e., competently delivered first-line treatment did not work or there were significant problems with implementing first-line treatments), we have developed a decision-making framework that outlines three primary ways in which this integration can be implemented (Table 6.1). We conceptualize this as a *levels-of-care* approach that is based on principles of stepped care, with each level representing a greater degree of integration of DBT into treatment. These levels of care include: (1) integration of specific DBT skills only, (2) integration of both DBT skills and treatment principles, and (3) treatment of anxiety symptoms within the full DBT model. Before providing a rationale and case examples for each level of care (below), we believe it is important to clarify why a model analogous to stepped care is appropriate.

Stepped care models of psychotherapy emphasize the provision of the least restrictive level of care that will still provide significant gain (Bower & Gilbody, 2005). Traditionally, this approach has focused on providing less intensive interventions (e.g., bibliotherapy, computer-assisted therapy, brief interventions) than standard practice (e.g., a full course of individual

CBT) that still lead to significant improvement for at least some clients. Ideally, criteria are also delineated for how to decide when to step up care if a less intensive intervention is not effective (Bower & Gilbody, 2005). When working with clients with treatment-resistant anxiety, there is an assumption, by definition, that prior intervention has already failed to achieve the desired outcome; consequently, considering a less intensive form of treatment would typically not be appropriate. More likely, it will be important in such cases to step up the level of care, either by increasing the duration or frequency of sessions (e.g., intensive outpatient treatment, inpatient treatment) or augmenting with other treatment strategies, such as DBT.

The degree to which DBT is integrated into anxiety treatments should be carefully weighed for several reasons. First, standard DBT, as it was initially developed and researched, involves 1 hour of individual therapy, 2 hours of group skills training, and telephone consultation on a weekly basis for 12 months (Linehan, 1993a). Thus, this level of care is more intensive for clients (in terms of time and money) than standard outpatient treatment for anxiety disorders, which in the community would frequently involve weekly individual therapy. Second, this level of care is also more intensive for clinicians and the mental health system in that it requires a high level of specialized training, therapists to participate in a DBT consultation team (Linehan, 1993a), and a system to provide an intensive level of services (i.e., individual therapy, group skills training, and telephone consultation). When considering whether DBT would be a useful augmentation strategy for clients with treatment-resistant anxiety, we are careful to weigh whether clients truly need the full DBT treatment package, or whether less intensive (and thereby less restrictive), DBT-informed approaches might be more efficient. We encourage clinicians to make this decision on a case-by-case basis in response to the unique needs of individual clients and hope that our discussion of specific ways in which we implement each of three levels of DBT integration can serve as a guide for making decisions about where to begin and when to step up care if needed.

Level 1: supplement standard treatment with select DBT skills

This approach likely represents the most common application of DBT to the treatment of anxiety disorders to date. DBT skills are presented in a concrete, easy-to-remember format and lend themselves well to integration into ongoing treatment. If a clinician wishes to augment treatment using DBT skills, we recommend the following considerations (Table 6.1). DBT skills should be considered when: (1) a first-line, evidence-based treatment has already been tried and treatment response was insufficient;

Table 6.1 Recommendations for Levels of Integration of DBT for Treatment-Resistant Anxiety

Level	Recommended use	Examples	Contraindications
Level 1 Supplement standard treatment with select DBT skills. *Suggested level of training:* familiarity with CBT-based coping skills and the DBT skills training manual.	A first-line, evidence-based treatment has been competently delivered and was not effective. Client is not responding to specific strategies in first-line, evidence-based treatment, and specific DBT skills would increase ability to benefit from treatment (e.g., mindfulness). Client refuses to engage in some treatment strategies (e.g., specific exposures that are recommended) because of skills deficits, and specific DBT skills might increase compliance (e.g., emotion regulation and distress tolerance skills).	Mindfulness strategies are taught to increase the client's experiential awareness and ability to observe and let go of thoughts, sensations, and emotions and to attend during exposures. Distress tolerance skills (particularly radical acceptance skills) are taught to increase the client's ability to tolerate exposure. Emotion regulation and distress tolerance (crisis management) skills are taught to help the client successfully cope with and resolve ongoing life stressors and crises.	A first-line, evidence-based treatment has not been delivered or was not implemented well. *Recommendation:* Consider implementing first-line treatment before augmenting with DBT. A client presents with significant, ongoing life-threatening or therapy-interfering behaviors. *Recommendation:* Consider a higher level of DBT integration (Levels 2 and 3).

Level 2 Supplement standard treatment with DBT principles and skills. *Suggested level of training:* some formal training, solid familiarity with DBT treatment principles and skills.	When conditions in Level 1 are present, plus: Client exhibits ongoing, serious therapy-interfering behavior (e.g., refusal to engage in an entire treatment strategy, such as exposure). Despite intermittent suicidality, suicidal ideation, or nonsuicidal self-injury, the client is engaged and willing to comply with treatment recommendations. Comorbid diagnosis of BPD with related behaviors interfere with Level 1 interventions (i.e., augmenting with DBT skills only). Ongoing, serious emotion regulation difficulties or life crises interfere with Level 1 interventions.	Purposeful use of validation engages the client in treatment, particularly during difficult, change-oriented interventions. Use targeting strategies to help organize and structure treatment targets. Use dialectical strategies to increase movement and change in treatment. Add contingency management strategies to increase the client's use of skills and participation in treatment interventions, such as exposure. This could include an emphasis on contingencies operating in the therapeutic relationship.	Chronic and/or serious life-threatening behaviors are present and require focused treatment. Client presents with life crises that preclude focus on the anxiety disorder and cannot be successfully resolved. Multiple diagnoses and problems are present, such that there is no clear focus of treatment, focus of treatment shifts quickly, or anxiety disorder is not the top priority. Client presents with a primary diagnosis of BPD. *Recommendations for all:* Consider a higher level of DBT integration (Level 3).

(continued)

Table 6.1 (continued) Recommendations for Levels of Integration of DBT for Treatment-Resistant Anxiety

Level	Recommended use	Examples	Contraindications
Level 3 Treat anxiety within the full DBT treatment approach. *Suggested level of training:* formal training in DBT. Supervision may also be needed, depending on the degree of experience with DBT. Participation with a DBT consultation team is ideal to be adherent to the treatment model.	When conditions in Level 1 and 2 are present, plus: Contraindications listed in Level 2 include chronic and/or serious life-threatening behaviors, frequent life crises, multiple problems and diagnoses, or a primary BPD diagnosis.	Weekly individual DBT, weekly DBT skills group, and, as needed, telephone coaching are used for skills generalization. Client's anxiety disorder is treated according to DBT targets or after Stage 1 DBT is complete.	There is a clear rationale for use of another evidence-based approach (e.g., medication, inpatient treatment, substance use treatment, treatment for a psychotic disorder). *Recommendation:* Consider augmenting with, or referring to, the appropriate treatment. Client presents with difficulties with emotion regulation, suicidality, or multiple life problems but does not need the level of intense care provided by standard DBT. *Recommendations:* Consider a lower level of DBT integration first (see Level 2) and then increase to full DBT if needed.

(2) the client is not responding to certain strategies in ongoing treatment and DBT skills might increase his or her ability to benefit from these strategies (i.e., by improving other coping skills); or (3) the client refuses to engage in important treatment strategies (e.g., exposure), and DBT skills might increase his or her willingness and compliance. Extensive training in DBT on the part of the therapist is unlikely to be necessary to incorporate the skills in the treatment of anxiety disorders. However, facility with behavioral theory and mindfulness-based approaches is likely very helpful. The skills could augment a first-line treatment for anxiety in many ways, from informal integration into therapy sessions, to a more formal focus on skills training in additional sessions.

Specific DBT skills

See Table 6.2 for examples of applications of DBT skills to treating anxiety.

Mindfulness

As stated above, DBT emphasizes the acquisition of four sets of behavioral skills (Linehan, 1993b). Mindfulness skills teach clients to attend to the present moment with an accepting, nonjudgmental stance. Mindfulness practice is a centuries-old tradition that has recently received a great deal of attention from Western scientists, and mindfulness-based treatments are the subject of increasing interest and study for multiple psychological problems, including anxiety (Hayes, Follette, & Linehan, 2004; Orsillo & Roemer, 2005). Mindfulness practice likely has many implications for treating anxiety disorders; for example, Gratz, Tull, and Wagner (2005) described a variety of features of anxiety that can be addressed via the DBT mindfulness skills, including attentional biases toward threat-related information, threat interpretation biases in response to benign cues, future-oriented/catastrophic thinking, reacting to thoughts as fact, experiential and behavioral avoidance, judging one's own emotional reactions, and inflexible responding when faced with perceived threat. Although several mindfulness protocols are available, Linehan's presentation of mindfulness skills in DBT is structured and concrete, which lends them particularly well to augmenting standard evidence-based treatments. The skills are also designed to be practiced in a time-limited manner that can build over time. The DBT mindfulness skills are therefore structured differently than many other mindfulness-based treatment models—such as mindfulness-based cognitive therapy (MBCT) (Segal, Williams, & Teasdale, 2002) and mindfulness-based stress reduction (MBSR) (Kabat-Zinn, 1990)—which require much more time and practice with mindfulness as *the* core component of treatment, as opposed to an adjunct for other interventions.

Table 6.2 Examples of DBT Skills and Their Application to Specific Symptoms and Problems in Treating Anxiety[a]

DBT skill module	Target symptom/behavior to decrease using the skill	Desired ability/behavior to increase using the skill
Mindfulness[b]	1. Limited or unclear understanding of anxiety cues; faulty assumptions of threat about anxiety cues 2. Avoidance of anxiety-producing stimuli 3. Distracted attention and/or cognitive avoidance during exposure 4. Distracted attention in daily life due to future focused thoughts (i.e., worry) 5. Vacillation in commitment to treatment; noncompliance with exposure-related tasks	1. Accurately observe and interpret internal and external stimuli. 2. Observe internal and external stimuli without acting to avoid them. 3. Focus and sustain attention on a desired cue to facilitate exposure and new learning. 4. Attend to the current moment in daily life to increase positive reinforcement and engagement in valued action. 5. Act effectively and focus on long-term goals even when confronted with emotionally distressing cues.
Emotion regulation	1. Emotional distress or dysregulation that interferes with participation in treatment 2. Limited understanding of emotional reactions or the function of emotions 3. Self-invalidation and judging of anxiety-related experiences and responses (e.g., physical sensations, cognitions, emotions, avoidance behaviors), often leading to unhelpful secondary emotions (e.g., shame, guilt)	1. Self-regulate emotions to facilitate participation in treatment tasks (e.g., exposure, cognitive restructuring). 2. Accurately identify emotions and understand the important functions of emotions. 3. Validate one's experiences and responses.

Distress tolerance	1. Fluctuating willingness to engage in anxiety-producing tasks; noncompliance with exposure-related tasks; refusal to engage in treatment 2. Engagement in harmful behaviors (e.g., self-harm, substance use) in response to heightened anxiety or distress 3. Intermittent denial or judgment of symptoms, leading to periods of unwillingness to follow treatment recommendations 4. Use of suppression strategies designed to control or fight anxiety	1. Weigh long-term benefits of participating in treatment against short-term benefits of avoidance behaviors and act in ways consistent with long-term goals. 2. Tolerate distress and ride out difficult emotion states without engaging in harmful behaviors. 3. Accept reality as it is in the current moment and be consistent and proactive in following treatment recommendations. 4. View and accept anxiety as a natural part of life.
Interpersonal effectiveness[c]	1. Passivity in response to demands from others; not asserting one's wants/needs to others 2. Poor interpersonal skills that interfere with developing or maintaining effective relationships	1. Ask for what one wants/needs and decline unwanted requests. 2. Initiate and maintain relationships using a range of effective interpersonal skills (e.g., validating others, having an easy manner, being truthful, balancing one's needs with the needs of others).

[a] See Linehan (1993b) for comprehensive descriptions of the DBT skills and acronyms. The examples provided here are by no means comprehensive and are limited to specific applications for anxiety disorders.

[b] Many of the recommended applications for mindfulness skills are taken from Gratz et al. (2005).

[c] The interpersonal effective skills may be useful for clients with social anxiety or comorbid interpersonal difficulties that require focused attention.

Mindfulness in DBT is comprised of several main skills, including three "what" skills that describe what one does to be mindful and three "how" skills that describe the quality of the attitude brought to mindfulness practice. The "what" skills include *observe* (just noticing experience without labeling or judging), *describe* (putting words/constructs on experience, again without judgment), and *participate* (fully engaging with an experience, ideally with full attention and without self-consciousness). The "how" skills include *nonjudgmental* (describing the facts of a situation or experience without evaluation), *one-mindful* (paying attention to one thing at a time and bringing full attention to a current task), and *effective* (being aware of long-term consequences and choosing actions wisely to achieve valued goals). Clients are taught a range of exercises to help them practice these skills and increase mindful awareness and participation in daily life.

The overarching mindfulness concept taught in DBT is that of *wise mind*, which emphasizes internal awareness and attention as a means to wisdom. In teaching the concept, the therapist differentiates between "reasonable mind" (responding based purely on logic and analytical reasoning) and "emotional mind" (responding based purely on emotional experiencing). The pros and cons of each are discussed, and it is highlighted that making decisions based solely on logic or emotion alone leaves out critical information needed to make wise choices. A *wise choice* is defined as one that moves one closer to effective, long-term goals; thus, wise mind is the integration of reasonable mind and emotional mind. Because the representation of wise mind in any given situation differs depending on the context, it is difficult to provide a concise behavioral definition. However, wise mind can be thought of as a "meta-skill" that involves being able to do the following: (1) observe and describe emotion; (2) be aware, in the moment, of one's long-term goals and the possible impact of current behaviors on reaching those goals; (3) and choose a course of action that balances one's emotional experiences with one's reasoned goals. Practice of the "what" and "how" mindfulness skills provides one way for clients to increase their awareness of, and access to, wise mind. Given that, for many clients, the practice of accessing wise mind through intentional focus on internal experience is quite challenging, DBT also offers many concrete exercises and metaphors to encourage consistent practice.

Distress tolerance

Distress tolerance skills are a set of strategies intended for use when a painful situation cannot be immediately ameliorated. The objective is to provide clients with the skills to tolerate difficult emotions and situations without escaping or avoiding. The distress tolerance skills fall into two main categories: (1) *crisis survival*, and (2) *reality acceptance*. Crisis survival skills are meant to assist in coping with the current moment without adding any additional distress (i.e., getting through a crisis without making it worse). They include basic coping skills such as evaluating the pros and cons of engaging in a particular behavior, self-soothing, and brief and well-chosen distraction (not meant to be a long-term strategy). Reality acceptance skills refer to the process of fully, and without judgment, observing the facts of the current situation (rather than avoiding) and learning to tolerate painful situations that cannot be changed immediately and must be accommodated into one's life. The reality acceptance skills include, like the mindfulness skills, concrete ideas for practice that can be built upon over time.

Distress tolerance skills may be particularly useful to incorporate into treatment for anxiety if a client has difficulty (1) managing or tolerating exposure, or (2) accepting his or her symptoms or the work needed to engage in treatment. The application of DBT distress tolerance skills to treatments for anxiety disorders likely necessitates more focus on the reality acceptance portion of the module. Though crisis survival skills may be very useful at times, some of these skills emphasize avoidance of painful emotions, including anxiety, and as a result might be problematic. However, the reality acceptance skills seem clearly useful as an adjunct to standard treatment for anxiety disorders. Most manualized anxiety treatment protocols include well-crafted rationales and models for exposure, although they typically do not include any detailed suggestions for how clients who balk at these ideas can work on accepting and tolerating the anxiety they must endure as part of treatment. Strategies for intolerance of distress have been described in several specialized cognitive therapy approaches (Leahy, 2003; Leahy, this volume; Sookman & Pinard, 1999, 2007; Sookman & Steketee, this volume; Wilhelm & Steketee, 2006). The concrete skills presented in DBT could be also be useful to clinicians struggling to engage clients in exposure-based treatments that require a high level of commitment and homework outside of sessions. This may be particularly true for clients who do not have sufficient coping skills to tolerate engaging in behavioral experiments, often used in cognitive therapy, to test out the beliefs they may have about how difficult or intolerable exposure tasks will be.

Emotion regulation

The emotion regulation skills teach methods for understanding the function of one's emotions, observing one's emotional experience, reducing vulnerability to negative emotion, reducing the intensity of negative emotion, and increasing possibilities for positive emotion. They include specific skills for understanding and regulating feelings of anxiety and fear, as well as a set of frequently experienced emotions (sadness, anger, disgust, shame, guilt, jealousy, envy, joy, and love). To reduce vulnerabilities, clients are taught to be mindful of maintaining physical self-care (sleeping, eating, exercising, avoiding mood-altering substances, and treating physical illness) and to *cope ahead*, or develop an effective coping plan in advance of stressful situations. This skill includes some imaginal rehearsal of the situation, which may also function as a form of imaginal exposure. To increase positive emotions, clients are encouraged to intentionally plan pleasant events and to build mastery by challenging themselves with new or necessary tasks, as well as to examine and create long-term goals that are in line with their values. Exposure is built into the emotion regulation skills in the form of a skill called *opposite action*, in which clients are taught to intentionally choose to act in opposition to unhelpful action urges associated with specific emotions. For instance, they might approach situations that make them anxious instead of avoiding them, get active when depressed instead of withdrawing, or gently avoid a person with whom they are angry instead of attacking. Brief cognitive restructuring strategies, called *checking the facts*, are also taught. This skill involves examining whether available evidence supports a specific cognition or interpretation of events but does not involve the use of a formal thought record as in other cognitive therapy protocols.

Clearly, the emotion regulation skills include coping strategies common to many CBT protocols. For instance, one emotion regulation skill teaches clients to manage emotions through healthy exercise and other basic self-management skills. As with the above-mentioned DBT skills, their strength is likely in the concrete, teaching-friendly format. These skills have accompanying acronyms and handouts (Linehan, 1993b) that many clinicians may find to be a useful means of presenting information. They may also be useful for clients when (1) a concise model of general emotion or emotion regulation is needed, (2) self-management skills (e.g., maintaining physical self-care) are of use to help manage anxiety symptoms, or (3) they have significant problems with emotion regulation and these problems interfere with treating the anxiety disorder (e.g., a client cannot adequately regulate his emotions following a difficult exposure and then refuses to do additional exposures).

Interpersonal effectiveness

Of the four sets of DBT skills, the set that has perhaps been the least applied to the treatment of anxiety is the interpersonal effectiveness skills set, which focuses on assertiveness skills for making or declining requests, as well as basic social skills (e.g., validating others, acting interested) and self-respect skills (e.g., behaving in a manner that is consistent with one's values). These might at times be useful for clients with interpersonal deficits or social anxiety disorder, where assertiveness is often a problem; however, a number of CBT protocols are readily available to address these same issues. Although the format for teaching these skills may be somewhat different in DBT, the basic components of the interpersonal effectiveness skills will be familiar to anyone experienced in using a CBT framework for teaching social skills.

Case example[1]

"Katie" was a 22-year-old woman treated by the first author who presented for treatment and met criteria for generalized anxiety disorder, social anxiety, and panic disorder with agoraphobia. She had not responded well to several trials of selective serotonin reuptake inhibitors (SSRIs) and refused to try other medications. She had dropped out of two prior courses of CBT-oriented psychotherapy, because she was unwilling to engage in exposure. Panic disorder was the initial focus of the current treatment and proceeded using an evidence-based treatment protocol (Barlow & Craske, 2000). Treatment progressed well through the initial stages of the protocol, including psychoeducation, breathing retraining, cognitive restructuring, and an initial session focused on interoceptive exposure to the sensations Katie feared during panic attacks. As she began to do *in vivo* exposure to places she avoided due to fear of having a panic attack, however, treatment began to stall.

Katie's main fears included having a panic attack in a public place and then choking, suffocating, or looking "crazy" (i.e., behaving in extreme ways) and feeling humiliated. On the lower end of her hierarchy were fears such as a using her debit card in public because she worried that others would notice her hands shaking. On the higher end included items such as shopping at smaller, specialty stores during peak hours in areas where she knew people. Katie reported that, despite practicing some exposures, she was not experiencing a decrease in her anxiety. She also refused to let the therapist accompany her during exposures to coach her, because that increased her sense of being watched and her anxiety. She became increasingly discouraged with her lack of progress, her homework compliance declined, and she began talking about dropping out of treatment. Careful assessment indicated that Katie had difficulty observing her experience when her anxiety increased and, despite effort on her part, had trouble identifying her thoughts and feelings during exposure. She had difficulty accurately predicting her anxiety level before engaging in exposures and often replied that she "just couldn't rate" how anxious she had been during exposures. She would typically report that she was either "terribly anxious" or "fine" and would become so distressed by her

---

[1] All identifying information for case examples has been changed to protect confidentiality.

experience of anxiety during exposures that she would end them prematurely. She commented frequently that she felt she was not strong enough to do a "difficult treatment like CBT."

The decision was made to augment her treatment with mindfulness training, using a DBT format, to help her develop more skills to accurately observe her anxiety symptoms. It was hoped that this would facilitate a greater sense of predictability and control during anxious moments and help the therapist work with her to solve problems occurring in exposure therapy. Because the therapist was not coaching directly in the *in vivo* situations, it seemed essential for Katie to increase her ability to observe and record her own experiences. Emphasis was placed on the *observe, describe,* and *one-mindful* DBT mindfulness skills, and she engaged in mindfulness exercises in session, such as sitting mindfully and observing thoughts, emotions, and physical sensations distinctly as they arose. Initially, this was done for nonemotionally evocative thoughts, sensations, and images. Over time, the transition was made to practicing in situations that evoked panic-like images and sensations. For a week, active exposure was halted, and she practiced these mindfulness skills on thoughts and emotions as they arose during her daily life. When she resumed exposure practice with an item that was relatively low on her hierarchy, she was instructed to use these skills to notice her thoughts, emotions, etc. Katie noted that she had several cognitions that interfered with the exposure and also focused her attention internally as opposed to externally. This prevented her from perceiving corrective information. Katie reported feeling that practice of mindfulness skills greatly facilitated her ability to address these obstacles during the exposures.

As she increased her awareness of her thoughts, emotions, and physiological sensations as distinct phenomenon, Katie was able to employ cognitive restructuring and attention focus strategies as needed. For example, she learned to focus on people's faces and test out whether they seemed to be staring at her judgmentally as her anxiety increased. She also noticed that she had been engaging in some subtle avoidance strategies she had previously not been aware of, including avoiding looking up from the floor as she shopped and gripping the shopping cart as she walked so she would not fall (one of her fears was that she would faint in the store if she had a panic attack and thereby draw attention to herself). Katie's engagement in treatment improved significantly and exposures began to proceed in a much more standard fashion. As Katie's fear continued to decrease, she commented that as she reread some of her CBT materials, she could see that what she had done in her mindfulness training (such as focusing her attention externally) was "in there already ... I just needed a little more practice learning how to do those things, or I couldn't have done them when I was scared."

Level 2: supplement standard treatment with DBT principles and skills

The second approach to incorporating DBT in the treatment of treatment-resistant anxiety disorders includes using DBT treatment principles in addition to specific skills. A Level 2 approach would be considered when, in addition to the problems present in Level 1, there are more serious indicators of: (1) emotion regulation difficulties, including BPD traits or diagnosis; (2) ongoing, therapy-interfering behaviors (e.g., refusal to engage in an entire treatment strategy, such as exposure); or (3) intermittent suicidality or nonsuicidal self-injury, but the client is engaged in treatment and willing to comply with recommendations (Table 6.1). If these behaviors are so serious that focused treatment on the anxiety disorder cannot continue, a Level 3 approach would be indicated (see below). As with many of the DBT skills, some of these principles are not necessarily found only in DBT; however, they are organized and presented in a way that may be quite transportable, even with cases that do not necessitate the full DBT model. These principles, although not exhaustive, include the following: targeting, validation, strategic use of the therapeutic relationship, and dialectical strategies (all discussed below). Therapists using this approach should be familiar with all DBT principles. Some training or familiarity with the Linehan text (1993a) and skills manual (1993b) is highly recommended, and external training or supervision may be useful.

Targeting

As noted above, standard DBT was designed to help the therapist prioritize and structure individual therapy with chronically emotionally "dysregulated" clients who have high levels of suicidal behaviors (suicide attempts or ideation, nonsuicidal self-injury), therapy-interfering behaviors (e.g., missing sessions, homework noncompliance), and other quality-of-life-interfering behaviors (e.g., any ongoing problem, such as an Axis I disorder, housing problems, relationship difficulties). In standard DBT, these set categories of problems (life-threatening, therapy-interfering, and quality-of-life-interfering) are referred to as *treatment targets*. Therapy proceeds through these targets hierarchically, starting with addressing immediately life-threatening behaviors, then any relevant therapy-interfering behaviors, and, finally, problems that interfere with quality of life. Within the standard DBT model, the treatment of anxiety disorders would be considered a quality-of-life target and would not be targeted until life-threatening and therapy-interfering behaviors had been successfully addressed. If all three of these problems are present in the case of a client with an anxiety disorder, or if chronic life-threatening behaviors are present, it may be most prudent to consider full DBT (Level 3, below).

We recognize that many clinicians would address life-threatening and therapy-interfering behaviors before anxiety-related problems, even when working outside of a DBT model; however, we find the explicit targeting structure of DBT particularly useful when working with multiple-problem, difficult-to-treat clients, as the extent and complexity of problems in these clients' lives can make it challenging for the therapist to keep treatment on track.

In our experience, what occur most frequently in clients with anxiety disorders are behaviors that interfere with the progression of therapy. These behaviors most often interfere with effective exposure, but could also interfere with other elements of treatment. As described by Pollard and colleagues (Pollard, 2007; VanDyke & Pollard, 2005), these behaviors can include not showing up for or being tardy for sessions, not identifying clear goals for treatment, not following the treatment plan, not doing homework, and excessive arguing with the therapist about aspects of treatment, such as exposure. As suggested by Linehan in the case of DBT (Linehan, 1993a) and Pollard in the case of anxiety disorders (Pollard, 2007), we suggest that therapy-interfering behaviors be targeted before beginning exposure. For example, the first author recently treated a client who met criteria for obsessive–compulsive disorder (OCD) (scrupulosity subtype) who refused to engage in exposure if there was any risk that he would be offensive to God. He wished to engage in response prevention only or exposure done with excessive reassurance. Rather than begin exposure and response prevention (ERP), this therapy-interfering behavior was addressed first through extensive discussion of the behavior and a combination of acceptance (e.g., validation, warm engagement) and change techniques (e.g., dialectics, problem solving, contingency management). In this manner, there is a chance to address the behaviors that will likely interfere with successful treatment so therapy has a better chance of succeeding later. Furthermore, this approach helps make it clear to clients that they have not yet engaged in an effective treatment before they have truly done so. This can reduce the likelihood that clients will leave therapy with the sense that they have done the treatment and it did not work, when in fact they never fully engaged.

Validation

A second key component of DBT is validation of the client's experience and emotion. Indeed, the primary "dialectic" in DBT is the emphasis on both acceptance and change simultaneously, based on Linehan's (1993a) experience that clients with emotion regulation difficulties generally have a very difficult time with, or refuse to engage in, change-oriented treatments. Therapists, therefore, use validation of painful emotion and the difficulty of treatment tasks to help clients regulate their emotions and increase willingness to change. Because many treatments for anxiety emphasize exposure to highly feared stimuli, some clients are understandably reluctant to engage in treatment. In the case of clients who retreat when pushed toward change, use of validation strategies as outlined in DBT may be quite useful. While this may be key to any good therapy, it has been particularly emphasized in DBT with very specific skills and levels of validation for the clinician to draw upon.

Six levels of validation are outlined in DBT, including: (1) listening and observing, (2) accurate reflection (similar to active listening), (3) articulating the unverbalized, (4) sufficient causes (validates clients' responses as expected given their life experiences or recent events), (5) reasonable in the moment (validates clients' responses as normative given the current situation), and (6) radical genuineness (therapist is authentic self in response to the client; see Linehan, 1993a). Linehan also highlights that validation can be verbal or functional. Functional validation of a client's need could involve taking action to help (e.g., scheduling an extra session or phone call to provide extra support following a particularly stressful life event or offering a home visit if it appears that doing so will provide needed information about why the client is getting stuck in therapy). Validation is always balanced with requests for change and is often used as a way of soothing clients through difficult periods of change. In relation to the treatment of anxiety disorders, validation can be a soothing alternative to reassurance. Whereas it would be counter-therapeutic in an exposure-based framework to provide an anxious client with reassurance when confronting a feared stimulus, validating the difficulty of the treatment and the client's strength in proceeding may provide the necessary care and support for successful completion of an exposure task.

Case example

"Jamie," a 46-year-old woman, was referred to the clinic for "treatment-refractory" OCD from another CBT-oriented therapist in the community who reported having some experience with OCD. Jamie's primary symptom was having thoughts of harming small children, and she had been in treatment with several therapists who had all begun ERP. She had dropped out of therapy each time, feeling that the exposures were too difficult for her. As treatment began, this same process began to occur as she moved up her exposure hierarchy. She would become very tearful and upset as a new exposure was presented and insist that she was unable and unwilling to engage in treatment. Each time this occurred, the therapist would emphasize validation strategies. This was very successful with this client, who said later (after successful treatment) that the validation made her feel for the first time that the therapist "really got it ... how hard all of this was ... in a way that the other ones just didn't," and because of that she felt that she could take a risk to trust the therapist and engage in the exposure. The client also worked on validating for herself the difficulty of maintaining her gains in treatment, which she felt proved invaluable. Rather than saying, "I can't do this; it's too hard" and either assuming that her OCD was too severe to treat or she was too weak to do the treatment, she focused instead on validating and accepting her emotions, which motivated her to continue moving toward change. It is also important to note that Jamie may not have received adequate trial(s) of previous empirically based CBT, as cognitive therapy was not administered prior to and during attempts at ERP (see Chapter 2 by Sookman and Steketee).

Contingency management/strategic use of the therapeutic relationship

Dialectical behavior therapy places a strong emphasis on contingency management. These principles will not be reviewed here, as they are part of most behavioral protocols. Although all good therapies include an emphasis on the therapeutic relationship, there is a particular emphasis in DBT on using the relationship strategically and employing principles of contingency management where appropriate within the relationship. For example, "John," a 62-year-old male, was very engaged with his therapist, primarily due to the use of validation strategies. He had chronic symptoms of panic disorder, as well as several other anxiety disorders and possible Axis II features, and he had not responded well to other CBT treatments. This may have been partially due to poor homework compliance. Although John wanted to remain in therapy, he did not want to engage in exposure-based treatment and was quite avoidant of other change-focused strategies. Rather than remove the focus on the therapeutic relationship entirely, a shorter, 30-minute session that focused more on the therapeutic relationship was scheduled on a day following a longer exposure session each week. Focusing on the relationship in treatment was therefore contingent upon the client engaging in exposure. John was fully oriented to the reason for this and accepted the need for change-focused procedures as long as he could retain the focus on "just understanding and supporting me" in a shorter session.

We realize that to some clinicians this approach might seem somewhat manipulative on the part of therapists; however, contingency management is routinely used in behavior therapies (and daily life) and is frequently effective in shaping behavior (e.g., providing rewards to children who complete household chores, teaching adult clients to positively reinforce themselves for engaging in difficult exposure tasks). In DBT, there is a particular emphasis on building a strong therapeutic relationship via increased use of validation and commitment strategies, in part so the therapist will be able to leverage this relationship later in treatment in an effort to help facilitate client participation in the often difficult tasks of treatment. Indeed, for some clients, particularly those who are difficult to treat, this relationship may be the only meaningful contingency that the therapist can apply. Thus, the relationship is used strategically to help overcome obstacles that might otherwise lead to an unsuccessful treatment outcome.

Dialectical strategies

A key component of DBT is the philosophy of dialectics, which includes the theory that natural change occurs as the result of the interaction of two opposing worldviews and that there is truth found on both sides of an argument that can be synthesized to form an entirely new worldview. In DBT, the primary dialectical tension is between the therapeutic stances of acceptance and change; for example, a client may have the belief that it is too difficult for her to change and that she cannot engage in treatment (acceptance). At the same time, she may be aware that she must change in order for her life to improve (change). In this case, both are true: Change is currently too difficult and change must occur if the client's quality of life is to improve. Working toward a synthesis of acceptance and change in this situation would involve helping the client (and therapist) find a new view of the struggle that allows for accepting the truth of her experience (e.g., "My anxiety is so bad I cannot stand in front of a room full of people and make a presentation") and leaves room for the possibility of change (e.g., "Even if I can't give an entire speech right now, I can learn how to take some small steps").

Dialectical strategies in DBT always emphasize at least one of the poles of acceptance and change and are designed to maximize movement on the part of the client. Linehan (1993a) described a number of specific examples of dialectical techniques that can be extremely useful for clinicians to learn and implement in their clinical work with difficult-to-treat clients (e.g., the use of metaphor, irreverence, balancing acceptance and change). In the therapy, the concept of dialectics is taught to clients as a skill to reduce all-or-nothing thinking and is also used to observe any interpersonal polarization that may occur between client and therapist. This concept is one that may be useful to apply in any therapy situation where the therapist and client feel stuck and see little progress being made. The question "What is being left out of our understanding/conceptualization?" may lead to new perspectives and the possibility of getting unstuck.

Consider a client being treated for anxiety who understands the rationale and model of exposure but does not believe it applies to his situation or that it will be useful for him, and he wishes to continue with other aspects of therapy (e.g., general coping skills, cognitive restructuring). The therapist may believe that exposure is the best course of treatment and that the client will not progress if he does not engage in exposure. In this situation, there is the potential for both the therapist and client to become rigid in their positions and for therapy to end prematurely and without maximal benefit on the part of the client. A dialectical approach would suggest that each party look for the truth in the other's position and search for a synthesis of their views. The therapist might seek to do this by highlighting the dialectical polarization: "You don't see a benefit in doing exposure, but based on my experience and work with you I feel it is essential for you to get better." The therapist would then provide a synthesis that captures what is true in both positions: "Although we have different ideas about what will help you get better, we both seem to have the same underlying goals: reduce your anxiety and improve your quality of life. Let's make sure we both understand each other's viewpoints. How about if I list all the valid reasons you have for not wanting to do exposure? You tell me if I've got it right, and then I'll have you list all the reasons you think I want you to try exposure." The reduction in polarization that may result from such a synthesis could allow both the client and therapist to consider alternative solutions to the problem: "I wonder if you would be willing to do an experiment with me to test out which approach is most helpful for you. Would you be willing to try working on other coping strategies for a period of time and then work on exposure for a period of time so we could assess what is most helpful for you?" Addressing this impasse in a dialectical manner may reduce polarization between the client and therapist that could lead to the client leaving treatment. However, it requires a willingness on the part of the therapist to look for what is true in the client's position, even if the therapist disagrees with this position.

Case example from the literature

A published case study by Becker (2002) provides an excellent description of the effective integration of DBT principles and skills (what we have referred to as Level 2) into evidence-based treatment for comorbid OCD, posttraumatic stress disosrder (PTSD), and features of BPD. Exposure and response prevention (ERP) and exposure therapy protocols were used to target symptoms of OCD and PTSD, respectively. As the client had been unable to tolerate such interventions during prior courses of therapy, a number of elements of DBT were used to address problems that had previously interfered with treatment. Validation strategies were deliberately used in an effort to increase rapport and engagement early in treatment, based on the client's report that she felt invalidated in prior treatments and that this is what led in part to prior treatment dropout. The theory of the development of BPD that informs DBT was also presented given the presence of features of BPD. The client reportedly experienced this as further validation of her experiences and agreed to a plan of including some of the DBT skills in the treatment for her anxiety disorders. Various DBT skills were taught during the course of treatment to address specific problems that arose during exposure treatment for her OCD and PTSD symptoms, including dissociation and difficulties attending to a single stimulus during exposure (the "what" mindfulness skills), unhelpful secondary emotions (anger) following exposure (distraction–distress tolerance skill), and urges to engage in self-harm following both planned exposures (self-soothe–distress tolerance skill; opposite action–emotion regulation skill) and encountering unexpected triggers (wise mind–mindfulness skill).

At termination, the client's symptoms of OCD, as measured by the self-report version of the Yale–Brown Obsessive Compulsive Scale (Y-BOCS) (Goodman et al., 1989), and depression, as measured by the Beck Depression Inventory (BDI) (Beck, Rush, Shaw, & Emery, 1979), were markedly reduced as compared to pretreatment assessments, and these gains were maintained at 1-year follow-up: Y-BOCS total scores were 31, 15, and 12 at pretreatment, posttreatment, and 1-year follow-up, respectively. BDI scores were 25 and 24, 6, and 2 at two assessments prior to treatment, posttreatment, and 1-year follow-up, respectively. Unfortunately, PTSD symptom severity was not assessed at pretreatment, although assessments at posttreatment and 1-year follow-up using the PTSD Checklist (PCL) (Blanchard et al., 1996) indicated scores of 34 and 27, respectively, both of which were below the recommended cut-off score of 50. Becker reported that the integration of DBT principles and skills into treatment was a key factor in the successful treatment outcome with a previously treatment-resistant client.

Although it is not clear why the client was not referred to full DBT given her difficulties with emotion regulation, self-harm, and suicidality, this may have been due in part to the fact that an official diagnosis of BPD was not given at intake. Regardless of the reasoning for this decision, this case illustrates why a levels-of-care approach to using DBT to augment other anxiety treatment protocols is important. This client was treated in 49 sessions of individual therapy over the span of 10 months. The first 20 treatment sessions were each 1.5 hours and occurred twice weekly. After this, the remaining 29 sessions were each 1 hour; they initially were weekly but then tapered to monthly toward the end of treatment. Thus, the client participated in a total of 59 hours of therapy, and her symptoms were effectively treated. This level of care, although somewhat greater than indicated by standardized anxiety treatment protocols, is still significantly less that a standard course of DBT, which would involve 52 hours of individual therapy and 104 hours of group skills training classes over the course of 1 year. In this case, it appears that effective integration of

DBT into existing treatment protocols for the client's anxiety disorders was more parsimonious and less restrictive (for the client and the mental health system) than treatment within the full DBT model. This highlights the importance of careful decision making when selecting the level of integration of DBT that might be useful in a specific case.

Level 3: treating anxiety within the full DBT treatment approach

The final method of integrating DBT with the treatment of anxiety is to treat the client's anxiety disorder within the full, standard DBT model (Table 6.1). This approach is recommended when there is sufficient comorbidity or complexity of circumstance that a consistent, focused approach with a standard CBT protocol is not possible. This might occur if there is high suicidality or ongoing self-injury, a BPD diagnosis with significant dysfunction due to BPD symptoms (such as severe difficulty with emotion regulation), or one or more comorbid conditions that would make it difficult to focus on the anxiety disorder. Though comorbidity is the rule for many individuals with anxiety disorders, this may not interfere with treatment if the patient has sufficient behavioral control to focus on one problem at a time. DBT is designed to treat highly complex problems, where a consistent, week-by-week focus on any one problem may not be possible, at least in the beginning of treatment. It provides a structure that assists the individual therapist in targeting while ensuring that consistent skills acquisition occurs through weekly, adjunct skills groups. Full, standard DBT might be considered either at the outset of treatment or when standard individual CBT has not been sufficient and it has become clear that full DBT might provide a structure that would address this problem. We have made both types of recommendations in our clinical work based on the unique presentation and needs of different clients. One difficulty encountered by many treatment providers, however, is the lack of an available DBT skills group or full DBT treatment program. In such cases, it might be possible to refer a client for individual DBT skills training (as opposed to skills training done in a group format) if available, although this option has pros and cons. Ideally, this would be done by a separate therapist to ensure that the focus is exclusively on skills acquisition. When treating anxiety within the full DBT model, we recommend that all therapists involved be well trained in DBT and that referrals to a DBT therapist or program be made as appropriate.

Case example

"Anna," a 27-year-old female treated by the third author, was referred for nonsuicidal self-injury (NSSI), suicidal ideation, and previous serious suicide attempts. She experienced intense anger, which was intermittently expressed toward her family and led to ongoing distress in these relationships. In addition to meeting full criteria for BPD, she was also diagnosed with moderately severe OCD. At the start of treatment, Anna was not working and had dropped out of school due to her OCD symptoms. Her OCD involved a number of rituals that reduced her extreme anxiety about offending God or that harm would come to her family. She previously participated in outpatient treatment for her OCD, during which she showed some success but had numerous relapses of her OCD symptoms, as well as suicide attempts. At one point during her prior treatment, she was hospitalized due to severe OCD-related anxiety.

Following the standard DBT model, Anna attended both weekly individual sessions and a weekly 2-hour skills training group. Following DBT target guidelines, the initial treatment targets were Anna's NSSI and suicidal ideation. Although teaching both distress tolerance and emotion regulation skills was an initial important intervention, it soon became apparent that long-term reductions in suicidal behaviors would require effectively treating her OCD. Over the course of repeated behavioral chain analyses[2] of her suicidal ideation and NSSI, it became clear that a primary cue for these behaviors was her inability to tolerate OCD-related anxiety. At this point, an ERP protocol was designed, and time was dedicated each week to ERP. For a period of time, individual meetings had to be increased to twice weekly to focus on ERP as well as to target ongoing life-threatening urges and behaviors.

Over time, as Anna's suicide and self-harm urges and behaviors decreased, ERP became more central. Despite this, it appeared to be extremely useful to keep the therapy rooted in the larger DBT model. Issues repeatedly arose that are common in treating clients with BPD (e.g., suicidality, emotion regulation problems), and the inclusion of ERP within the larger DBT context helped the therapist and client quickly address these issues, resolve them, and continue to focus on the OCD. For example, therapy-interfering behavior often arose in the form of her repeatedly deciding to quit treatment, typically in response to serious and pervasive emotion regulation difficulties. Solving this problem and ultimately keeping Anna in treatment required both the willingness and ability to validate her frustration and careful assessment of what led to her urges

---

[2] A behavioral chain analysis is a moment-by-moment assessment of all behaviors, thoughts, feelings, body sensations, events, and environmental circumstances that occur within a particular time period. It is a primary assessment tool in behavior therapy. Usually, a particular behavior is identified to be analyzed (e.g., avoidance behavior, compulsive ritual), and all aspects of the behavior and its antecedents and consequences are examined. Each behavior, thought, feeling, etc., is considered a link in the chain of behavior. This careful assessment is then used to identify possible interventions for changing the specified behavior.

to quit. With time, it became clear to both Anna and the therapist that urges to quit were the result of experiencing intense guilt that she was not working or in school because of her OCD and that her parents were paying for her treatment. Her experience of guilt would lead to "emotional mind" behavior (i.e., acting to eliminate the immediate sensations of guilt rather than to meet her long-term goals; see above). This type of response often took the form of self-invalidation or attempting to convince herself that she did not really have OCD and that she was just being lazy; if she simply pushed herself hard enough, she could "will away" her anxiety and return to work and school without finishing treatment. In addition to feelings of guilt, she also reported making many judgments about herself for having OCD and struggling with thoughts that having OCD meant her brain was damaged and that she therefore could not be as perfect as she wanted to be. Such thoughts would often lead to increased shame, anxiety, and sadness, as well as increased thoughts of suicide and NSSI.

At this point in treatment, four key concepts from DBT became central to treatment: validation, wise mind, radical acceptance, and emotion regulation. Consistent validation of Anna's emotional and cognitive experience of having OCD was important for both teaching *self-validation* and countering previous messages she had received that her OCD was just an act to get attention. Validation was achieved though a combination of education about OCD, attendance at an OCD support group, and consistent messages from the therapist highlighting both the difficulty of ERP and the examples of how it had been effective for her. Anna's experience of guilt was addressed through a combination of validating that many people would feel some negative emotions if they felt there was an imbalance in the give and take of their family relationships and encouraging *opposite action* (an emotion regulation skill) to guilt because it was ineffective in obtaining her long-term goal of decreasing OCD symptoms to the point that she would be able to return to work and school.

The practice of accessing wise mind was essential for Anna to be able to make choices in line with her long-term goals, even in the face of intense guilt, sadness, or anxiety. Later in treatment, she reported that wise mind was her favorite DBT skill; she became so proficient at finding this centered and balanced part of herself that when thoughts of quitting treatment would arise she would immediately think "wise mind" and then either reach out for help from others or use other distress tolerance skills to avoid taking any hasty action. Finally, *radical acceptance*, or the practice of willingly and nonjudgmentally looking at the facts of the situation, was an ongoing discussion in therapy sessions. Anna's feelings of guilt, which led to behavioral avoidance, also led to internal avoidance and unwillingness to observe the facts and patterns of her anxiety. Patient encouragement was required to repeatedly ask her to observe her OCD experiences nonjudgmentally and to observe which responses seemed to help her (ignoring and avoiding them or ERP). Though ERP progress was slow, this client ultimately completed her exposure hierarchy and experienced enough relief from her OCD symptoms to resume taking college-level courses again.

Emerging treatments for anxiety disorders that integrate DBT

In recent years, elements of DBT have begun to be incorporated into newly developed treatment protocols for several of the anxiety disorders, suggesting that the DBT skills and principles address possible gaps in extant CBT interventions. We briefly describe several of these treatment approaches, focusing primarily on protocols for treating PTSD, OCD, and GAD. We also indicate instances in which an intervention is consistent with one of the levels of care that we have described regarding degree of DBT integration into the protocol. Finally, when available, we review any empirical data supporting the efficacy of these interventions.

Posttraumatic stress disorder

There is growing interest in the application of DBT skills to the treatment of posttraumatic stress disorder (PTSD) (for more comprehensive reviews, see Becker & Zayfert, 2001; Welch & Rothbaum, 2007). A small body of empirical data suggests that augmenting more traditional PTSD treatment programs with DBT may be beneficial. Two studies have been published that represent examples of what we have referred to as Level 1 integration of DBT. In both studies, participants were randomly assigned to either the treatment condition or a control condition (wait-list or no-contact conditions). In the first study, Cloitre and colleagues (Cloitre, Koenen, Cohen, & Han, 2002) developed the skills training in affective and interpersonal regulation (STAIR)/modified prolonged exposure (MPE) treatment protocol for the treatment of clients with histories of PTSD and child sexual abuse (CSA). The treatment consists of two phases: (1) Phase I, which involves 8 sessions of psychoeducation, skills acquisition, skills application/practice, and between session homework; and (2) Phase II, which consists of a modified version of prolonged exposure (PE) in which the *in vivo* exposure component was removed (imaginal exposure was retained) and several components were added, including postexposure coping, emotion regulation, cognitive restructuring, and skills review (for a more detailed description of the protocol, see Levitt & Cloitre, 2005). The treatment was informed in part by DBT emotion regulation and interpersonal effectiveness skills. Compared with a minimal attention control group (12 weekly

15-minute phone calls with an assessor), participants in the STAIR/MPE treatment demonstrated significant improvement in affect regulation and interpersonal problems during Phase I and PTSD symptoms in Phase II. Treatment gains were maintained at 3- and 9-month follow-up. In the second study, a different two-phase treatment for PTSD was developed by Bradley and Follingstad (2003) that also incorporated DBT skills. The first nine sessions of the treatment emphasize psychoeducation and emotion regulation, and the second nine sessions involve structured writing assignments about life experiences, including interpersonal victimization. Comparisons to a no-contact control condition indicated significant reductions in PTSD symptoms, as well as mood and interpersonal problems. Although such studies have been criticized (Cahill, Zoellner, Feeny, & Riggs, 2004) and more methodologically rigorous studies are needed before definitive conclusions about efficacy can be drawn, they offer preliminary support for the integration of DBT into PTSD treatments.

Obsessive–compulsive disorder

Several DBT-related concepts have recently been integrated into CBT treatment approaches for obsessive–compulsive disorder (OCD). In a recent cognitive therapy manual for OCD, Wilhelm and Steketee (2006) adapted Linehan's (1993a) concept of *wise mind* for use with clients who have problems with overestimating the importance of their intrusive or obsessive thoughts. Clients are oriented to the concept of states of mind (i.e., emotional mind, rational mind, and wise mind; these are described above in the section on DBT mindfulness skills) and are then asked to identify examples of their own rational-based and emotion-based thoughts. Wilhelm and Steketee noted that clients with OCD often experience both types of thoughts in response to an obsession; clients can simultaneously believe that there is a high level of danger or threat present when experiencing an obsessive thought and also recognize that their thoughts about danger or threat are unreasonable. However, much of the time, behavior in response to an obsession is dictated more by emotion-based thoughts (avoidance/neutralizing behaviors in response to perceived threat and associated feelings of fear) than rationally based thoughts (resisting avoidance/neutralizing behavior due to awareness that the perceived threat is unfounded).

Clients are encouraged to evaluate their own reactions to obsessive thoughts and to then work toward synthesizing emotional and rational information so they can respond with wise mind. With regard to OCD, the aim of responding from wise mind is to acknowledge feared responses and at the same time be aware of logical and factual information to help decrease the importance that is given to a particular intrusive thought. It is important to note that wise mind is one of many (non-DBT) skills in the treatment protocol and, as such, illustrates the level of integration of DBT that we have referred to as Level 1. A similar example is Sookman and Pinard's (1999) differentiation between "cognitive" and "emotional" aspects of dysfunctional beliefs which are addressed in their specialized CBT approach for treatment-resistant OCD to reduce overestimation of threat and risk aversion that interfere with a client's full participation in ERP.

Pollard and colleagues (Pollard, 2007; VanDyke & Pollard, 2005) have developed an approach for addressing treatment resistance in clients with treatment-refractory OCD that they term *readiness treatment* and which is in many ways consistent with what we have referred to as Level 2. This approach integrates elements from a variety of CBT treatments, including DBT. The aspect of the protocol that is most closely aligned with DBT principles is the direct targeting of treatment-interfering behavior (TIB). The spirit in which TIB is addressed in the model is also highly consistent with the style of DBT. Pollard (2007) describes the importance of orienting clients to the concept of TIB, emphasizing the function of the behavior (instead of the intention of the behavior), and adopting a nonjudgmental stance when addressing these behaviors to decrease client defensiveness. As is the case in DBT, persistent TIB is targeted before moving on to other treatment targets and interventions—in this case, ERP. Although the practice of addressing treatment-inferring behavior is not unique to DBT, the structure and frame of the treatment provide a clear roadmap for when and how to address these issues, and the readiness treatment described by Pollard is a useful example of how these concepts can be incorporated into the treatment of anxiety-based problems. There is some evidence supporting the approach; a preliminary evaluation of the readiness treatment intervention significantly reduced TIB in 7 out of 11 clients with treatment-resistant OCD (VanDyke & Pollard, 2005).

Generalized anxiety disorder

Roemer and Orsillo (2005) have developed an acceptance-based behavior therapy for generalized anxiety disorder (GAD) that draws primarily from acceptance and commitment therapy but also from other acceptance-based treatments, including MBCT, MBSR, and DBT. DBT reportedly influenced the development of the treatment in several ways. First, the concept of dialectics and, more specifically, the dialectical balance between acceptance and change is similar to the fundamental assumptions of the treatment model. The concept of dialectics is not taught to clients directly, as is the case in DBT, but the balance between acceptance and change informs the therapist's frame and stance during treatment. Second, the protocol involves teaching about the function of emotions early in treatment, using concepts similar to those emphasized in DBT (Roemer & Orsillo, 2005); this is not often the focus of therapy in existing CBT treatments for GAD. Finally, the treatment involves considerable instruction in and practice of various mindfulness exercises, some of which are included formally or informally in DBT.

Roemer and Orsillo have recently reported on data from both an uncontrolled open trial and a small randomized controlled trial (RCT) evaluating their acceptance-based behavior therapy for GAD (Roemer & Orsillo, 2007). Results from the open trial (n = 16) showed that participants displayed significant reductions on measures of GAD severity, worry, and depression from pre- to posttreatment. Effect sizes were large and generally maintained at 3-month follow-up (follow-up data were available for 12 of the 16 participants). Importantly, significant decreases were also observed on measures that assessed some of the proposed mechanisms of change that underlie the treatment: experiential avoidance, as measured by the Acceptance and Action Questionnaire (AAQ) (Hayes et al., 2004), and fear of emotional responses, as measured by the Affective Control Scale (ACS) (Williams, Chambless, & Ahrens, 1997). In the follow-up RCT, participants were randomly assigned to either immediate treatment (n = 15) or delayed treatment following a 14-week wait-list period (n = 16) (Roemer, Orsillo, & Salters-Pedneault, 2008). The findings from the RCT support the results of the prior open trial; acceptance-based behavior therapy resulted in significant decreases in GAD severity, worry, and depression, and these gains were maintained at 3- and 9- month follow-up. The study also found additional support for some of the treatment's proposed mechanisms of action; significant *decreases* in experiential avoidance, as measured by the AAQ, and significant *increases* in present-moment mindful awareness, as measured by the Mindful Attention Awareness Scale (MAAS) (Brown & Ryan, 2003), were observed from pre- to posttreatment, and these improvements were maintained at both follow-up periods. A new study is currently underway comparing acceptance-based behavior therapy for GAD and applied relaxation. More data are needed to establish the efficacy of this treatment approach, although the preliminary findings are quite promising. It is important to reiterate that DBT is just one of several acceptance-based treatments that influenced the development of this intervention. Nonetheless, this innovative approach speaks to the possible utility of using elements of DBT to enhance anxiety treatments.

Summary and future directions

In this chapter, we have described a model to guide clinicians in the use of elements of DBT for treatment-resistant anxiety disorders. Although there is very limited empirical research on this approach, two main factors provide a compelling rationale for considering DBT as a potential treatment augmentation strategy in this population: (1) the growing emphasis on emotion regulation in the anxiety disorders literature and the corresponding focus on emotion regulation in DBT, and (2) the myriad of techniques emphasized in DBT to engage individuals who have traditionally been considered treatment resistant (or, in some cases, impossible to treat). Despite this strong justification for the use of DBT, caution is warranted when considering the degree to which DBT might be integrated into treatment for a particular client. As we have described, standard DBT is an intensive outpatient treatment, and not all clients with treatment-resistant anxiety who might benefit from elements of DBT will require this level of care.

Based on our own experiences of integrating DBT and standard treatments for anxiety disorders, as well as examples in the literature of how others have approached this issue, we have outlined a decision-making framework that describes three levels of integration of DBT into standard anxiety treatment protocols (see Table 6.1). Level 1 involves augmenting standard treatments with select DBT skills only. Level 2 involves a greater level of integration of DBT by including both underlying treatment principles, in addition to specific skills. Finally, Level 3 involves treatment of the anxiety disorder within the full, standard DBT model. The levels-of-care approach that we have described is based on principles of stepped care, with the goal being to offer the least restrictive (or intensive) treatment that will still be effective for the client. We hope that our recommendations about when to consider each level, or degree, of integration of DBT will be useful to clinicians as they consider these issues.

Considerable empirical research on these augmentation approaches is also clearly needed to help guide these decisions. For example, it is unknown whether the components of DBT that have been integrated into the emerging anxiety treatments discussed above contribute to treatment outcome above and beyond the other interventions that comprise these treatments. It is also unknown whether these integrated approaches are any more effective than standard treatments for anxiety problems. The few published studies that are available have not included active treatment comparison groups and therefore cannot answer these important questions. Controlled trials including active treatment comparison groups are greatly needed in order to determine whether DBT skills and principles provide any additive benefit to clients. Preliminary data, although encouraging, need to be further substantiated. In the absence of further data, we encourage clinicians to critically evaluate when and how DBT might be of benefit to specific clients with treatment-resistant anxiety.

References

Amstadter, A. (2008). Emotion regulation and anxiety disorders. *Anxiety Disorders, 22*, 211–221.

Barlow, D.H. (Ed.). (2002). *Anxiety and its disorders: The nature and treatment of anxiety and panic* (2nd ed.). New York: Guilford Press.

Barlow, D.H., & Craske, M.G. (2000). *Mastery of your anxiety and panic* (3rd ed., client workbook). San Antonio, TX: Psychological Corporation.

Barlow, D.H., Allen, L.B., & Choate, M.L. (2004). Toward a unified treatment for emotional disorders. *Behavior Therapy, 35*, 205–230.

Beck, A.T., Rush, A.J., Shaw, B.F., & Emery, G. (1979). *Cognitive therapy of depression: A treatment manual.* New York: Guilford Press.

Becker, C.B. (2002). Integrated behavioral treatment of comorbid OCD, PTSD, and borderline personality disorder. *Cognitive and Behavioral Practice, 9*, 100–110.

Becker, C.B., & Zayfert, C. (2001). Integrating DBT-based techniques and concepts to facilitate exposure treatment for PTSD. *Cognitive and Behavioral Practice, 8*, 107–122

Blanchard, E.B., Jones-Alexander, J., Buckley, T.C., & Forneris, C.A. (1996). Psychometric properties of the PTSD checklist (PCL). *Behaviour Research and Therapy, 34*, 669–673.

Bower, P., & Gilbody, S. (2005). Stepped care in psychological therapies: Access, effectiveness, and efficiency. A narrative review. *British Journal of Psychiatry, 186*, 11–17.

Bradley, R.G., & Follingstad, D.R. (2003). Group therapy for incarcerated women who experienced interpersonal violence: A pilot study. *Journal of Traumatic Stress, 16*, 337–340.

Brown, K.W., & Ryan, R.M. (2003). The benefits of being present: mindfulness and its role in psychological well-being. *Journal of Personality and Social Psychology, 84*, 822–848.

Cahill, S.P., Zoellner, L.A., Feeny, N.C., & Riggs, D.S. (2004). Sequential treatment for child abuse-related posttraumatic stress disorder: methodological comment on Cloitre, Koenen, Cohen, and Han (2002). *Journal of Consulting and Clinical Psychology, 72*, 543–548.

Campbell-Sills, L., & Barlow, D.H. (2007). Incorporating emotion regulation into conceptualizations and treatment of anxiety and mood disorders. In J.J. Gross (Ed.), *Handbook of emotion regulation* (pp. 542–559). New York: Guilford Press.

Cloitre, M., Koenen, K.C., Cohen, L.R., & Han, H. (2002). Skills training in affective and interpersonal regulation followed by exposure: A phase-based treatment for PTSD related to childhood abuse. *Journal of Consulting and Clinical Psychology, 70*, 1067–1074.

Goodman, W.K., Price, L.H., Rasmussen, S.A., Mazure, C., Fleichmann, R.L., Hill, C.L., & Charney, D.S. (1989). The Yale–Brown Obsessive Compulsive Scale I: Development, use, and reliability, *Archives of General Psychiatry, 46*, 1006–1011.

Gratz, K.L., Tull, M.T., & Wagner, A.W. (2005). Applying DBT mindfulness skills to the treatment of clients with anxiety disorders. In S.M. Orsillo & L. Roemer (Eds.), *Acceptance and mindfulness-based approaches to anxiety: Conceptualization and treatment* (pp. 147–161). New York: Springer.

Hannesdottir, D.K., & Ollendick, T.H. (2007). The role of emotion regulation in the treatment of child anxiety disorders. *Clinical Child and Family Psychology Review, 10,* 275–293.

Hayes, S.C., Follette, V.M., & Linehan, M.M. (Eds.). (2004). *Mindfulness and acceptance: Expanding the cognitive–behavioral tradition.* New York: Guilford Press.

Hayes, S.C., Strosahl, K.D., & Wilson, K.G. (1999). *Acceptance and commitment therapy: An experiential approach to behavior change.* New York: Guilford Press.

Hayes, S.C., Strosahl, K.D., Wilson, K.G., Bissett, R.T., Pistorello, J., Toarmino, D. et al. (2004). Measuring experiential avoidance: A preliminary test of a working model. *The Psychological Record, 54,* 553–578.

Hoffman, S.G., & Smits, J.A.J. (2008). Cognitive–behavioral therapy for adult anxiety disorders: A meta-analysis of randomized placebo-controlled trials. *Journal of Clinical Psychiatry, 69,* 621–632.

Kabat-Zinn, J. (1990). *Full catastrophe living: Using the wisdom of your body and mind to face stress, pain, and illness.* New York: Delacorte.

Koons, C.R., Robins, C.J., Tweed, J.L., Lynch, T.R., Gonzalez, A.M., Morse, J.Q. et al. (2001). Efficacy of dialectical behavior therapy in women veterans with borderline personality disorder. *Behavior Therapy, 32,* 371–390.

Leahy, R.L. (2003). *Roadblocks in cognitive–behavioral therapy: Transforming challenges into opportunities for change.* New York: Guilford Press.

Levitt, J.T., & Cloitre, M. (2005). A clinician's guide to STAIR/MPE: Treatment for PTSD related to childhood abuse. *Cognitive and Behavioral Practice, 12,* 40–52.

Linehan, M.M. (1993a). *Cognitive behavioral treatment of borderline personality disorder.* New York: Guilford Press.

Linehan, M.M. (1993b). *Skills training manual for treating borderline personality disorder.* New York: Guilford Press.

Linehan, M.M., Armstrong, H.E., Suarez, A., Allmon, D., & Heard, H.L. (1991). Cognitive–behavioral treatment of chronically parasuicidal borderline clients. *Archives of General Psychiatry, 48,* 1060–1064.

Linehan, M.M., Dimeff, L.A., Reynolds, S.K., Comtois, K.A., Welch, S.S., Heagerty, P. et al. (2002). Dialectical behavior therapy versus comprehensive validation plus 12-step for the treatment of opioid dependent women meeting criteria for borderline personality disorder. *Drug and Alcohol Dependence, 67,* 13–26.

Linehan, M.M., Schmidt, H., Dimeff, L.A., Craft, J.C., Kanter, J., & Comtois, K.A. (1999). Dialectical behavior therapy for clients with borderline personality disorder and drug dependence. *American Journal on Addiction, 8,* 279–292.

Lynch, T.R., Morse, J.Q., Mendelson, T., & Robins, C.J. (2003). Dialectical behavior therapy for depressed older adults: A randomized pilot study. *American Journal of Geriatric Psychiatry, 11,* 33–45.

Mennin, D.S. (2004). Emotion regulation therapy for generalized anxiety disorder. *Clinical Psychology and Psychotherapy, 11,* 17–29.

Mennin, D.S. (2005). Emotion and the acceptance-based approaches to the anxiety disorders. In S.M. Orsillo & L. Roemer (Eds.), *Acceptance and mindfulness-based approaches to anxiety: Conceptualization and treatment* (pp. 37–68). New York: Springer.

Mennin, D.S. (2006). Emotion regulation therapy: An integrative approach to treatment-resistant anxiety disorders. *Journal of Contemporary Psychotherapy, 36,* 95–105.

Mennin, D.S., Heimberg, R.G., Turk, C.L., & Fresco, D.M. (2005). Preliminary evidence for an emotion dysregulation model of generalized anxiety disorder. *Behavior Research and Therapy, 43,* 1281–1310.

Orsillo, S.M., & Roemer, L. (Eds.). (2005). *Acceptance and mindfulness-based approaches to anxiety: Conceptualization and treatment.* New York: Springer.

Orsillo, S.M., Roemer, L., & Holowka, D.W. (2005). Acceptance-based behavioral therapies for anxiety: Using acceptance and mindfulness to enhance traditional cognitive–behavioral approaches. In S.M. Orsillo & L. Roemer (Eds.), *Acceptance and mindfulness-based approaches to anxiety: Conceptualization and treatment* (pp. 3–35). New York: Springer.

Pollard, C.A. (2007). Treatment readiness, ambivalence, and resistance. In M.M. Antony, C. Purdon, & L.J. Summerfeldt (Eds.), *Psychological treatment of obsessive–compulsive disorder: Fundamentals and beyond* (pp. 61–77). Washington, D.C.: American Psychological Association.

Roemer, L., & Orsillo, S.M. (2005). An acceptance-based behavior therapy for generalized anxiety disorder. In S.M. Orsillo & L. Roemer (Eds.), *Acceptance and mindfulness-based approaches to anxiety: Conceptualization and treatment* (pp. 213–240). New York: Springer.

Roemer, L., & Orsillo, S.M. (2007). An open trial of an acceptance-based behavior therapy for generalized anxiety disorder. *Behavior Therapy, 38,* 72–85.

Roemer, L., Orsillo, S.M., & Salters-Pedneault, K. (2008). Efficacy of an acceptance-based behavior therapy for generalized anxiety disorder: Evaluation in a randomized controlled trial. *Journal of Consulting and Clinical Psychology, 76*(6), 1083–1089.

Roy-Byrne, P.P., Craske, M.G., Stein, M.B., Sullivan, G., Bystritsky, A., Katon, W. et al. (2005). A randomized effectiveness trial of cognitive–behavioral therapy and medication for primary care panic disorder. *Archives of General Psychiatry, 62,* 290–298.

Safer, D.L., Telch, C.F., & Agras, W.S. (2001). Dialectical behavior therapy for bulimia nervosa. *American Journal of Psychiatry, 158,* 632–634.

Segal, Z.V., Williams, J.M.G., & Teasdale, J.D. (2002). *Mindfulness-based cognitive therapy for depression: A new approach to preventing relapse.* New York: Guilford Press.

Simpson, E.B., Pistorello, J., Begin, A., Costello, E., Levinson, J., Mulberry, S. et al. (1998). Use of dialectical behavior therapy in a partial hospital program for women with borderline personality disorder. *Psychiatric Services, 49,* 669–673.

Sookman, D., & Pinard, G. (1999). Integrative cognitive therapy for obsessive–compulsive disorder which focuses on multiple schemas. *Cognitive and Behavioral Practice, 6*(3), 351–361.

Sookman, D., & Pinard, G. (2007). Specialized cognitive behavior therapy for resistant obsessive compulsive disorder: Elaboration of a schema based model. In L.P. Riso, P.L. du Toit, D.J. Stein, & J.E. Young (Eds.), *Cognitive schemas and core beliefs in psychological problems: A scientist–practitioner guide* (pp. 93–109). Washington, D.C.: American Psychological Association.

Spoont, M.R., Sayer, N.A, Thuras, P., Erbes, C., & Winston, E. (2003). Adaptation of dialectical behavior therapy by a VA medical center. *Psychiatric Services, 54,* 627–629.

Description of generalized anxiety disorder

Generalized anxiety disorder is quite common, with 1-year prevalence rates of 3.1% and lifetime prevalence of 5.1% (Kessler, Keller, & Wittchen, 2001). This disorder is associated with significant distress and impairment (Kessler, DuPont, Berglund & Wittchen, 1999), which translate into considerable personal, social, and financial costs (Olfson & Gameroff, 2007). There is a high rate of comorbidity of GAD with other anxiety and mood disorders (Brown & Barlow, 1992). Moreover, GAD is typically chronic, with its onset in the late teens and early 20s (Kessler et al., 2001). It is not uncommon for clients with GAD to say that they have been a "worrier" for as long as they can remember.

The central feature of GAD is excessive and uncontrolled worry which is diffuse in nature (American Psychiatric Association, 1994). That is, those with GAD typically report worrying, often unrelentingly, about "everything." Worries can center on multiple themes including, but not restricted to, the health and well-being of oneself and others, work or school performance, finances, relationships, the future, world affairs, and relatively minor matters such as being on time or completing household tasks. Individuals with GAD report being unable to terminate their worry, despite their recognition of worry as irrational and unhelpful. Worry is often accompanied by other symptoms, including restlessness, fatigue, muscle tension, irritability, inability to concentrate, and sleep disturbance (American Psychiatric Association, 1994).

What is motivational interviewing?

Motivational interviewing was developed by William R. Miller and Stephen Rollnick. In 1991, they published the first edition of their classic book *MI: Preparing People to Change Addictive Behaviors.* (Miller & Rollnick, 1991). They have defined MI as "a client-centered directive method for enhancing intrinsic motivation to change by exploring and resolving ambivalence" (Miller & Rollnick, 2002, p. 25). It is client centered because of its strong roots in the therapeutic approach of Carl Rogers (1956). Both MI and client-centered therapies share an emphasis on understanding the client's internal frame of reference and working with discrepancies between behaviors and values. Both emphasize the importance of the therapist providing the conditions for growth and change by communicating attitudes of accurate empathy and unconditional positive regard.

Unlike client-centered therapy, however, MI is directive, with specific goals of reducing ambivalence and increasing intrinsic motivation for change. These goals are achieved in the context of the client-centered relationship stance described above. To achieve these goals, the MI therapist tries to create an atmosphere in which the client, rather than the therapist, is the main advocate for and primary agent of change.

The MI spirit of the therapist is central and consists of attitudes of collaboration, evocation, and respect for the client's autonomy. This approach also consists of specific principles and methods. The principles include expressing empathy, developing discrepancy between values and problem behaviors, rolling with resistance, and supporting self-efficacy. The methods are to ask open-ended questions, listen reflectively, affirm, and summarize. Although these are classic methods of client-centered therapy, one additional method—eliciting change talk—is specific to MI. The therapist intentionally works to elicit client statements reflecting interest in and commitment to change with questions such as, "How would your life be different if you no longer had this problem?" Other methods to increase change or commitment talk involve helping clients resolve ambivalence about change, increasing motivation to change, and facilitating the development of action plans to achieve desired changes. Throughout the entire process, the client is treated as the major change agent, with the therapist in the role of consultant to facilitate the client's movement toward change.

Miller and Rollnick (2002) divided MI into two phases. In the first phase, clients may be ambivalent about change, and motivation may be insufficient to accomplish change. Accordingly, the goals in this phase are to resolve ambivalence and build intrinsic motivation to change. Other clients come to therapy with little ambivalence about change. Once this is assessed, the therapist may move to the second phase discussed below, which involves the development and implementation of action strategies directed at changing the problem.

The second phase begins when the client shows signs of readiness to change. Such signs include increased verbalizations reflecting an interest in and commitment to change, questions about change, and envisioning a future that includes the desired changes. In this phase, the focus shifts to strengthening commitment to change and helping the client develop and implement a change plan. Even during this second phase, problems with motivation and resistance may arise. If they do, the therapist utilizes methods from phase one to address them.

How MI complements CBT

Arkowitz and Westra (2004) outlined several ways in which MI departs from traditional CBT and offers unique clinical strategies that can complement CBT. Differences between MI and CBT include the therapist's role, some aspects of the focus of therapy, the management of resistance, and the manner and timing of introducing change strategies.

Telch, C.F., Agras, W.S., & Linehan, M.M. (2001). Dialectical behavior therapy for binge eating disorder. *Journal of Consulting and Clinical Psychology, 69,* 1061–1065.

VanDyke, M.M., & Pollard, C.A. (2005). Treatment of refractory obsessive–compulsive disorder: The St. Louis model. *Cognitive and Behavioral Practice, 12,* 30–39.

Verheul, R., van den Bosch, L.M.C., Koeter, M.W.J., de Ridder, M.A.J., Stijnen, T., & van den Brink, W. (2003). Dialectical behavior therapy for women with borderline personality disorder: 12-month, randomized clinical trial in the Netherlands. *British Journal of Psychiatry, 182,* 135–140.

Welch, S.S., & Rothbaum, B.O. (2007). Emerging treatments for PTSD. In M.J. Freedman, T.M. Keane, & P.A. Resick (Eds.), *Handbook of PTSD: Science and practice* (pp. 469–496). New York: Guilford Press.

Wilhelm, S., & Steketee, G.S. (2006). *Cognitive therapy for obsessive compulsive disorder.* Oakland, CA: New Harbinger.

Williams, K.E., Chambless, D.L., & Ahrens, A. (1997). Are emotions frightening? An extension of the fear of fear construct. *Behaviour Research and Therapy, 35,* 239–248.

chapter seven

Combining motivational interviewing and cognitive–behavioral therapy to increase treatment efficacy for generalized anxiety disorder

Henny A. Westra
York University
Toronto, Ontario, Canada

Hal Arkowitz
University of Arizona
Tucson, Arizona

Contents

Resistance and the underlying ambivalence that often gives rise to it are common clinical realities in cognitive–behavioral therapy (CBT) and other therapies (Engle & Arkowitz, 2006). Newman (2002) outlined various behaviors that may constitute resistance in CBT, such as client actions that run counter to what was agreed upon in the session, high levels of expressed negative emotion toward the therapist, in-session avoidance such as silence or frequent use of "I don't know," gratuitous debates with the therapist, and misinterpretations of the therapist's comments. Resistance is among the most challenging of clinical issues to navigate successfully. It can result in frustration for both client and therapist and lead to deterioration in the working alliance. Because the quality of the client's engagement with treatment is among the most critical contributors to treatment outcomes (Orlinsky, Grawe, & Parks, 1994), it is likely that effective ways of reducing resistance, and increasing engagement may hold significant promise for improving the efficacy of CBT. One approach known as *motivational interviewing* (MI) (Miller & Rollnick, 2002) may hold promise for reducing resistance when combined with other therapies such as CBT (Arkowitz, Westra, Miller, & Rollnick, 2008). There is a great deal of empirical support for MI in the treatment of alcohol and drug addictions (Hettema, Steele, & Miller, 2005) and in the promotion of health behaviors (Rollnick, Miller, & Butler, 2008). Recently, several investigators have begun to explore the use of MI either integrated with CBT (i.e., a shift to MI within CBT when ambivalence or resistance arises) or in combination with CBT (e.g., as a pretreatment) in the treatment of other major mental health problems (Arkowitz et al., 2008).

In this chapter, we examine how MI has been added to CBT (i.e., as a pretreatment) or integrated with it (i.e., blended with CBT to form a unified treatment) to reduce resistance and to improve outcome in the treatment of generalized anxiety disorder (GAD). We describe MI and the rationale for applying it to GAD. This discussion is followed by an extended clinical example of the use of MI as a pretreatment to CBT for GAD. Finally, we present empirical work evaluating the impact of MI used with CBT in the treatment of anxiety disorders.

Description of generalized anxiety disorder

Generalized anxiety disorder is quite common, with 1-year prevalence rates of 3.1% and lifetime prevalence of 5.1% (Kessler, Keller, & Wittchen, 2001). This disorder is associated with significant distress and impairment (Kessler, DuPont, Berglund & Wittchen, 1999), which translate into considerable personal, social, and financial costs (Olfson & Gameroff, 2007). There is a high rate of comorbidity of GAD with other anxiety and mood disorders (Brown & Barlow, 1992). Moreover, GAD is typically chronic, with its onset in the late teens and early 20s (Kessler et al., 2001). It is not uncommon for clients with GAD to say that they have been a "worrier" for as long as they can remember.

The central feature of GAD is excessive and uncontrolled worry which is diffuse in nature (American Psychiatric Association, 1994). That is, those with GAD typically report worrying, often unrelentingly, about "everything." Worries can center on multiple themes including, but not restricted to, the health and well-being of oneself and others, work or school performance, finances, relationships, the future, world affairs, and relatively minor matters such as being on time or completing household tasks. Individuals with GAD report being unable to terminate their worry, despite their recognition of worry as irrational and unhelpful. Worry is often accompanied by other symptoms, including restlessness, fatigue, muscle tension, irritability, inability to concentrate, and sleep disturbance (American Psychiatric Association, 1994).

What is motivational interviewing?

Motivational interviewing was developed by William R. Miller and Stephen Rollnick. In 1991, they published the first edition of their classic book *MI: Preparing People to Change Addictive Behaviors.* (Miller & Rollnick, 1991). They have defined MI as "a client-centered directive method for enhancing intrinsic motivation to change by exploring and resolving ambivalence" (Miller & Rollnick, 2002, p. 25). It is client centered because of its strong roots in the therapeutic approach of Carl Rogers (1956). Both MI and client-centered therapies share an emphasis on understanding the client's internal frame of reference and working with discrepancies between behaviors and values. Both emphasize the importance of the therapist providing the conditions for growth and change by communicating attitudes of accurate empathy and unconditional positive regard.

Unlike client-centered therapy, however, MI is directive, with specific goals of reducing ambivalence and increasing intrinsic motivation for change. These goals are achieved in the context of the client-centered relationship stance described above. To achieve these goals, the MI therapist

tries to create an atmosphere in which the client, rather than the therapist, is the main advocate for and primary agent of change.

The MI spirit of the therapist is central and consists of attitudes of collaboration, evocation, and respect for the client's autonomy. This approach also consists of specific principles and methods. The principles include expressing empathy, developing discrepancy between values and problem behaviors, rolling with resistance, and supporting self-efficacy. The methods are to ask open-ended questions, listen reflectively, affirm, and summarize. Although these are classic methods of client-centered therapy, one additional method—eliciting change talk—is specific to MI. The therapist intentionally works to elicit client statements reflecting interest in and commitment to change with questions such as, "How would your life be different if you no longer had this problem?" Other methods to increase change or commitment talk involve helping clients resolve ambivalence about change, increasing motivation to change, and facilitating the development of action plans to achieve desired changes. Throughout the entire process, the client is treated as the major change agent, with the therapist in the role of consultant to facilitate the client's movement toward change.

Miller and Rollnick (2002) divided MI into two phases. In the first phase, clients may be ambivalent about change, and motivation may be insufficient to accomplish change. Accordingly, the goals in this phase are to resolve ambivalence and build intrinsic motivation to change. Other clients come to therapy with little ambivalence about change. Once this is assessed, the therapist may move to the second phase discussed below, which involves the development and implementation of action strategies directed at changing the problem.

The second phase begins when the client shows signs of readiness to change. Such signs include increased verbalizations reflecting an interest in and commitment to change, questions about change, and envisioning a future that includes the desired changes. In this phase, the focus shifts to strengthening commitment to change and helping the client develop and implement a change plan. Even during this second phase, problems with motivation and resistance may arise. If they do, the therapist utilizes methods from phase one to address them.

How MI complements CBT

Arkowitz and Westra (2004) outlined several ways in which MI departs from traditional CBT and offers unique clinical strategies that can complement CBT. Differences between MI and CBT include the therapist's role, some aspects of the focus of therapy, the management of resistance, and the manner and timing of introducing change strategies.

Role of the therapist

Cognitive–behavioral therapists are more likely than MI therapists to adopt a change-advocate role. In MI, the therapist specifically avoids becoming the advocate for change and instead tries to motivate the client to become his or her own advocate for change. In general, in self-report and observational studies, cognitive–behavioral therapists have been consistently found to employ significantly more direct guidance, instruction, education, structure, and directiveness than other therapies to which it has been compared (Watson & McCullen, 2005; for a review, see Blagys & Hilsenroth, 2002).

Research has demonstrated that directive approaches tend to elicit more resistance than supportive ones (e.g., Moyers & Martin, 2006; Patterson & Chamberlain, 1994) which may be mediated by the arousal of reactance (as described later). For example, in the context of parent management training, Patterson and Forgatch (1985) found a higher likelihood of noncompliance following therapist teach and confront behaviors, while support and facilitate behaviors were associated with increased client cooperation. Similarly, Miller, Benefield, and Tonigan (1993) reported that feedback on alcohol use delivered to problem drinkers in a directive style elicited more client defensiveness and greater post-intervention drinking, compared with the same feedback delivered in a supportive style.

Brehm and Brehm (1981) have developed reactance theory, which asserts that when important personal freedoms are threatened (as in the case of someone being very directive toward the person) a state of reactance is aroused to reassert these freedoms. Further, people are motivated to reduce this state by various means, such as by behaving oppositionally. Consistent with reactance theory, Shoham, Trost, and Rohrbaugh (2004) have found that some clients are more sensitive to therapist directiveness than others. Clients high in reactance, compared to those lower on this trait, tend to resist others' attempts at control and have been found to respond relatively poorly to more directive therapies such as CBT and more favorably to self-directed approaches (Beutler, Rocco, Moleiro, & Talebi, 2001; Shoham-Salomon, Avner, & Neeman, 1989).

It has also been suggested that motivation for change may show important interactions with therapist directiveness. For example, Huppert, Barlow, Gorman, Shear, and Woods (2006) found that higher therapist adherence in panic control treatment with less motivated clients was associated with poorer outcomes compared with lower adherence. In short, therapist directiveness may promote client reactance and resistance, which have consistently been associated with poorer outcome (Beutler et al., 2001; Bischoff & Tracey, 1995; Mahalik, 1994). To the extent that MI is more supportive and less directive than CBT, it may be beneficial for CBT therapists to consider adopting a more supportive and less directive relational style in therapy, particularly with resistant clients.

Management of resistance

Until recently, CBT models have been relatively silent on the management of resistance; however, ways of understanding and working with resistance in CBT are beginning to appear in the CBT literature (e.g., Beck, 2005; Leahy, 2001, 2003; Sookman & Pinard, 2007). In CBT models, characteristics of clients such as treatment-interfering behaviors (Pollard, 2007; VanDyke & Pollard, 2005) and client schemas and beliefs, particularly those presenting obstacles to treatment collaboration (Leahy, 2001, 2003; Sookman & Pinard, 2007), are identified and addressed in an effort to increase cooperation with CBT interventions. These approaches require further empirical scrutiny and are not yet widely implemented in nonspecialized mainstream CBT.

The recommendations for managing resistance in CBT diverge considerably from those of MI. Rather than confronting resistance directly, the MI therapist is encouraged to "roll with resistance," including using empathic reflections and preserving client autonomy to hold beliefs that may run counter to the goals of the therapist or the therapy. Consider a client who has made obvious and tangible progress in therapy but repeatedly claims that the therapy is not helping. In such a situation, a therapist who is rolling with resistance would respect the client's experience of therapy rather than stating that progress is being made. The therapist might say something like, "So, you feel that we're not making progress, and I suspect you don't feel very good about that. Usually when that happens there are good reasons for it that we need to explore. Can you tell me more about this feeling?" In other words, within MI resistance is not viewed as a problem to be defeated or an obstacle to therapy requiring removal, but rather as information to be understood from the perspective of the client, which can advance the therapy. MI also places great emphasis on the relational context between client and therapist. The continuing presence of resistance in MI is considered primarily a therapist skill error rather than a client problem (Miller & Rollnick, 2002; Moyers & Rollnick, 2002). Because the focus of MI is on a supportive rather than directive therapist style and on the resolution of ambivalence to increase motivation, it is more likely to bypass resistance that might otherwise occur in more directive approaches (Engle & Arkowitz, 2006).

The timing of introducing change strategies

In MI, the collaborative development and use of change strategies are timed to coincide with the client's readiness to change, as indexed by signs of low ambivalence and high intrinsic motivation. Some contemporary CBT approaches to GAD do include a focus on conflicting beliefs about worry (Wells, 1997, 1999) and ambivalence about worry (Koerner & Dugas, 2006; Ladouceur et al., 2000) as a component of treatment. To some extent, this overlaps with an MI approach; however, the focus on ambivalence and the use of specific MI methods to help resolve it are defining features of MI, while this is not the case in CBT approaches.

The manner of introducing change strategies

Because MI is more of a clinical style, rather than a set of techniques, it may offer alternatives for conducting CBT in a more client-centered manner. Central to MI is an explicit emphasis on evocation and preserving client autonomy. That is, the therapist regards the client as already possessing the requisite wisdom about how change can best be accomplished. The role of the therapist is to draw out this wisdom rather than to install what is missing (Miller & Rollnick, 2002); that is, the MI therapist regards the client as the leader of the change process, with the therapist being more of a consultant to the client and this process. Often, clients will come up with change strategies that are very similar to CBT techniques (e.g., changing unreasonable thoughts, exposure to avoided situations). In MI, the therapist is also free to provide feedback, information, and suggestions regarding the client's change plan as input for the client to consider. The client may accept, reject, or modify the suggestions of the therapist. In this way, respect for the client's autonomy is communicated, and internal attributions for change may be facilitated.

Although CBT therapists certainly value the client's input in defining and working with the problem, the approach differs from MI in that the emphasis in CBT is on the therapist as the expert in charge of the change process, with the client providing input and suggestion. Stated more concisely, in MI the client is more the expert and the therapist more of a consultant, whereas these roles are reversed in CBT. Our impression is that overall CBT is more directive than MI, although there may be a range of therapist styles employed by CBT therapists. To the extent that CBT is in fact more directive than MI, there is potentially a greater likelihood of internal attributions for change that have shown to lead to greater maintenance of change (e.g., Davison and Valins, 1969).

It is important to note that in MI the issue is not *whether* the therapist can provide feedback and suggestions, but *how* this is done. For example, Miller and Rollnick have explained the process for providing feedback to the client. In this style, the therapist first asks the client for permission to offer feedback (e.g., "I have some ideas, based on what others have done, about how to manage worry. Would you like me to hear about some of these?"). Next, the therapist provides the information or feedback and finally elicits the client's reaction. In this manner, the therapist operates as a consultant to the client's change plan, regarding the client as the principal agent for developing the plan. While CBT certainly seeks the client's input and feedback and emphasizes collaboration, MI places relatively more emphasis on explicitly recognizing and respecting the client's wisdom and views the client, rather than the therapist, as the main formulator and decision maker for the change plan.

Rationale for using MI with GAD

Motivational interviewing can be adapted to address ambivalence and motivation across different populations and presenting problems. A number of observations suggest that integrating MI into the treatment of GAD may be useful. These include: (1) the need to improve response rates to CBT for GAD, (2) significant rates of noncompliance with CBT, (3) the presence of ambivalence in GAD, and (4) empirical support for MI. Each of these rationales is discussed below.

The need to improve response rates

Although cognitive–behavioral therapies have demonstrated efficacy in the treatment of GAD compared to wait-list control groups (Barlow, Rapee, & Brown, 1992) or to other comparison groups controlling for therapist contact (Borkovec & Costello, 1993; Covin, Ouimet, Seeds, & Dozois, 2008), response rates are generally modest at best. The recent Cochrane review of 25 studies of psychological therapies for GAD concluded that, although CBT was more effective than wait-list control groups, there was significant heterogeneity of response, and only 46% of participants across studies showed clinically significant responses on posttreatment diagnostic interview (Hunot, Churchill, Teixeira, & Silva de Lima, 2007).

In their multidimensional meta-analysis of CBT for mood and anxiety disorders, Westen and Morrison (2001) reported that 48% of completers and 56% of the intent-to-treat sample of those with GAD were not improved at follow-up. Recommendations for improving response rates center on the need to target specific central components of GAD (Barlow, Raffa, & Cohen, 2002), such as beliefs about worry or metacognitive processes (Wells, 2006), intolerance of uncertainty (Ladouceur et al., 2000), or the presence of interpersonal problems (Borkovec, Newman, & Castonguay, 2003).

In short, although CBT has demonstrated efficacy in reducing worry and related symptoms in GAD, a significant number of individuals fail to show substantive benefit, leaving us with a need to improve response rates in the treatment of GAD. In reflecting on existing treatment outcome studies for GAD, Borkovec, Newman, Pincus, and Lytle (2002) concluded: "Our clinical research program has now spent 16 years attempting to refine, develop, and evaluate behavioral and cognitive therapy methods for GAD. Outcomes suggest that we need to look elsewhere for ways of incrementing the effectiveness of psychological treatments for this disorder" (p. 296). This is consistent with the recent Cochrane review, which recommended the evaluation of approaches other than CBT for the treatment of GAD (Hunot et al., 2007). In this context, MI may be particularly useful, as it can be used as an adjunctive therapy that can facilitate engagement with other established treatments and improve outcomes by building on rather than replacing existing treatments for GAD.

Noncompliance in CBT

Homework assignments are frequently recommended across various types of psychotherapy (Kazantzis & Ronan, 2006) and are widely hypothesized to be essential to the efficacy of CBT (Kazantzis, Deane, Ronan, & L'Abate, 2005). Nonetheless, homework noncompliance is a commonly acknowledged problem in CBT (Huppert & Baker-Morissette, 2003; Kazantzis, Deane, & Ronan, 2004; Leahy, 2003; Schmidt & Woolaway-Bickel, 2000). For example, Helbig and Fehm (2004) surveyed practicing CBT therapists regarding their clients' homework compliance. Problems in assigning homework (e.g., client doubts about ability to complete the task or client worries about the difficulty of the task) were noted for 74.5% of clients. Deviations from the assigned task were commonplace, with only 38.9% of cases being identified as totally compliant. The authors concluded that homework noncompliance in CBT seems to be the rule rather than the exception. This conclusion is supported by other therapist surveys (Hansen & Warner, 1994; Kazantzis, Lampropoulos, & Deane, 2005).

Despite the significance of motivation to engage in therapy and homework compliance, the CBT literature is relatively silent on the conceptualization and management of motivational issues (Engle & Arkowitz, 2006), with some notable exceptions (Burns & Auerbach, 1996; Kazantzis et al., 2005a; Leahy, 2001, 2003). Suggestions for enhancing adherence are beginning to appear in the CBT literature (e.g., Antony, Roth Ledley, & Heimberg, 2005; Kazantzis et al., 2005; VanDyke & Pollard, 2005); however, empirical support for their efficacy in reducing resistance and enhancing treatment engagement is needed.

Ambivalence about worry

Studies have found that individuals with GAD hold conflicting beliefs about worry, including both negative and positive perceptions of the value of worry (Borkovec & Roemer, 1995; Freeston et al., 1994). Although GAD clients do see worry as a problem (e.g., that it interferes with concentration and memory), they also hold *positive* beliefs about it (e.g., that worry is motivating, that it ensures that one is prepared for negative events) and are therefore ambivalent about reducing or relinquishing their excessive worry. Moreover, worry itself has been found to have an important avoidant and self-reinforcing function, protecting the individual from experiencing frightening emotional arousal (Borkovec, 1994). Finally, Wells (1997, 1999) identified an important role for metacognitive processes in GAD such as beliefs about the worry itself (both negative and positive perceptions of worry) and the management of conflicting beliefs about worry are a component of the CBT approach of Dugas and his colleagues to GAD (Koerner & Dugas, 2006; Ladouceur et al., 2000). Thus, converging conceptualizations and data from a variety of sources identify ambivalence about worry as an important feature of GAD.

In employing MI with GAD clients, it is necessary to elicit and work with GAD clients' perceptions of the advantages and disadvantages of worrying. It may seem odd to ask about perceived advantages of having the problem. Clients are more forthcoming about the value of worrying when therapists explore these advantages in a nonjudgmental way and without holding an *a priori* conclusion that the advantages of change outweigh the disadvantages. If the therapist is open to such information, the sources of client resistance to change and ambivalence can be better understood. In addition, they can also be addressed as ambivalence in a decisional balance exercise. An understanding and appreciation of *both* sides of the client's ambivalence can greatly facilitate therapy. It can be very challenging to fully integrate and understand the part of the client which argues for the *status quo*, because often in our role as helpers we are much better at hearing the problems associated with worry and the reasons to change. But, to practice MI, we must also become proficient at understanding and integrating the opposing side which argues for the *status quo*.

Benefits of worry and fears of change

Individuals with GAD hold various fears about the prospect of relinquishing worry. As long as these are present, the client with GAD will likely be less receptive to taking action toward change; that is, a client who is concerned that eliminating worry will lead to serious negative consequences will be less likely to pursue change. Given the chronicity of GAD in most clients, worry can become a central part of their identities (e.g., "I can't imagine my life without worry. I've worried my whole life. Who would I be?"). In some cases, clients attribute positive qualities to their worrying, identifying themselves as highly responsible, caring, and reliable individuals. In more extreme cases, there is sometimes an element of moral superiority in the self-identification as a worrier. As one client stated, "I think other people should worry more. It's usually me who catches problems because I'm always thinking about what could happen. People count on me to be alert." Given that many GAD clients positively value their worrying, it is understandable that they are often reluctant to change it. In fact, worry has often become a very familiar and well-practiced strategy for coping with stress for many GAD clients. And, although it may have some negative consequences, worry is often regarded as "the devil one knows." Change is unpredictable and anxiety laden. Maintaining the *status quo* may be uncomfortable, but its predictability makes it less anxiety-arousing than change.

Fears of the interpersonal consequences of being a non-worrier are also common. The first author worked with a GAD client who also presented with memory complaints. The client held a very demanding management position and was responsible for coordinating large-scale military exercises abroad. She denied experiencing any memory impairment at work; however, she complained that when it came to "simple" matters such as keeping appointments, doing household tasks, or arriving on time, she was virtually helpless and needed to rely heavily on her husband's assistance for even the most basic household and personal management tasks. It was noteworthy that her husband had an extramarital affair some time prior to the onset of her memory complaints. In this case, even though the client was distressed by her memory problems, she worried that her husband might withdraw the closeness and support she needed due to her memory problems. Her husband's possible withdrawal and possible abandonment were far more important priorities for her than relief from her cognitive difficulties. Moreover, when asked what she envisioned if worry were absent from her life, she quickly responded with, "But how would my children know I love them? A good mother should worry." She seemed to equate not worrying about her children with loving them less. Advocating for strategies to reduce her worrying would likely be ineffective unless these perceptions of her worry changed.

Many GAD clients are also concerned that, if they do successfully relinquish their worry, they will be less motivated to act in important areas of their lives. In addition, they are concerned that without worrying they would be poorly prepared for dealing with stressful situations, or perhaps even inviting bad things to happen (thought–action fusion). One client with GAD reported that she felt compelled to worry when her husband traveled abroad for work, stating: "I know it's crazy to think that my thoughts will keep the plane in the sky. So I tell myself not to worry. But then I think, 'What if it really is true?' For the sake of a little worry, I'd much rather not chance it." GAD clients may fear reducing excessive worry because they believe that such change would negatively impact fundamental needs for control, connection, support, and protecting loved ones.

We have observed a long-standing interpersonal style in GAD of anticipating the needs of others, being overly protective and excessively giving, with a concomitant diminishment of the importance of one's own needs. Such individuals often report attachment histories in which their own feelings and needs were neglected by important figures. For example, Hale, Engels, and Meeus (2006) found that adolescents with GAD reported greater parental alienation and rejection. Under these conditions, one can become adept at vigilantly anticipating the needs of others and attempting to fulfill them to ensure that vital connections with important others are maintained. These individuals may fear that if they set interpersonal boundaries, reduce their helpfulness, or become more focused on managing their own needs then significant others will withdraw from them.

Clients with GAD often believe that they are not capable of dealing with stress and other problems effectively. They may feel a strong sense of responsibility for others but simultaneously have little confidence in their ability to respond effectively to problems that arise. This is consistent with an emphasis on problem-solving training in Dugas and colleagues' approach to the management of GAD (Koerner & Dugas, 2006). One client, for example, brought her husband along to her first individual therapy session. She asked if it would be okay if they met together with the therapist, explaining that "he is so much better than me at knowing what my problems are and would do a better job of explaining them to you." The therapist, not wishing to reinforce this potentially problematic dependency on her husband, suggested that they first meet without her husband to see how it went, with the option of including the husband in the therapy if it seemed necessary. The client and her husband agreed; however, the therapist took note that the husband seemed more reluctant to agree to this proposal than the client. Central to this client's difficulties was a feeling that she had "no voice" and had never developed any confidence in her own thoughts or abilities. Using the MI method of empathic listening to deepen understanding, the dialogue went something like this:

C. Whenever I have a problem, my husband and father are right there to help me out.

T. And it's wonderful to have that kind of support. At the same time, and I could be wrong about this, I hear you saying, "If it were left up to me, nothing good could come of that. So it's a good thing I have others who can solve problems well because I can't."

C. (long pause) Yes, that's true. I don't have a lot of confidence in myself or my opinions about things. I guess somehow it's easier to trust other people to figure things out.

T. So it's safer in a way. And that's very important. What do you think or fear would happen if it were left to you to solve problems?

C. I would make a mess of things. It would turn out really badly.

T. And you certainly wouldn't want that. If you can avoid something negative from happening, then by all means you should do that. It makes a lot of sense that you would rely on others for help, especially if it means preventing disaster.

C. But, at the same time, it's not always about important things.

T. Can you think of a specific example of what you mean?

C. Well, my husband tells me how to manage everything—even the littlest things, like what groceries to buy.

T. And you're thinking that the world wouldn't collapse if you didn't buy the right brand of peanut butter. It sounds like his helpfulness, even though it's much appreciated, might be a little frustrating at times.

C. (pause) Yes. I love him, but sometimes he goes overboard.

Worry in GAD clients is also a way of feeing prepared for inevitable negative and stressful events. Particularly in people with low confidence in their ability to manage stress and other problems, it makes sense to anticipate problems to potentially avoid them, or at least be prepared when they do happen. One client we worked with continually envisioned the death of her mother, even visualizing herself at her mother's funeral. When asked about why she would do this, she reported that, "If I picture her death, I'll be better prepared to handle it when it eventually does happen." Stated differently, this client viewed her anticipatory rehearsal of negative events as proactive coping with seemingly devastating disappointment and loss. Another client referred to her excessive planning as "forward thinking" that helped her to be better equipped for managing stressful situations. From this perspective, the solution of worrying less becomes the problem. Inviting her to worry less might be regarded as "backward thinking," something that would be naturally resisted.

In MI, client ambivalence is elicited and examined in depth before embarking on a change program. Providing an atmosphere in which clients are free to discuss and elaborate their fears of relinquishing worry allows them to reflect critically on the utility of worry and to consider other options for meeting core needs. Given the prevalence and significance of ambivalence about change in GAD and other problems, treatments such as MI, which specifically address ambivalence, may hold promise for engaging people more productively to take action toward change.

Empirical support for MI

In their meta-analytic review, Burke, Arkowitz, and Menchola (2003) found strong evidence for the efficacy of MI as a brief pretreatment to other treatments for alcohol and drug addiction, even when subsequent treatments were quite directive. MI pretreatments were associated with better attendance in subsequent therapy and larger improvements. Burke et al. (2003) reported that effect sizes for MI as a prelude were substantially higher than for MI as a stand-alone treatment. These findings are consistent with a later meta-analytic review by Hettema et al. (2005). Given the strong empirical support for MI, its application to populations outside of addictions is indicated, and investigations with mental health populations such as anxiety are beginning. Much of the existing data in this area are reviewed by Arkowitz et al. (2008).

Extended clinical example

Carol, a 55-year-old divorced woman with two adult children, sought therapy for severe GAD. She described a chronic pattern of worrying, never being relaxed, having "no peace or happiness," and feeling constantly busy and rushed. She further complained of chronic tiredness and exhaustion, yet was puzzled because "there's nothing major going on, yet my mind is busy all the time." This is a classic pattern in GAD where activity often serves as a distraction from relentless worrying. Carol also received diagnoses of major depressive episode, panic disorder, and social phobia. On the Penn State Worry Questionnaire (PSWQ) (Meyer, Miller, Metzger, & Borkovec, 1990), she scored 72 out of a possible score of 80, reflecting extremely high levels of worry. Her scores on the Depression, Anxiety, and Stress Scale (DASS) (Lovibond & Lovibond, 1995) were in the "very severe" range, and she showed "marked disability" in work, social, and family life on the Sheehan Disability Scale (Sheehan, 1983).

Carol reported worrying about "everything," especially her relationships with other people and the well-being of her family members. She stated that her worry caused her distress and reported difficulties with insomnia, tension, and an inability to concentrate. In fact, she had to take a leave from her job due to the severe concentration problems associated with her worry. She described herself as a "lifelong worrier" and had previously been treated with psychotherapy and antidepressant medication with little improvement.

She described a history of feeling continually alone and rejected by others. As a child, she felt distant from her parents because her father had a major accident which left him disabled and her mother was largely preoccupied with her father's care. She left home at a young age to attend boarding school. She described a chronic pattern of excessive pleasing regarding others, fearful of setting boundaries or saying "no" because this might engender disapproval and abandonment, perpetuating her feelings of loneliness.

Carol was seen in the context of a randomized controlled trial examining MI as a pretreatment to CBT for GAD (Westra et al., 2007). She received 4 weekly individual sessions of MI with one therapist prior to participating in 14 individual therapy hours of CBT (2 hours per week for 6 weeks, then 1 hour per week for 2 weeks) with another. Quantitative MI adherence measures were taken on her therapist using the Motivational Interviewing Treatment Integrity Code (Moyers, Martin, Manuel, Hendrickson, & Miller, 2005). The scores reflected that she received exceptional quality MI.

Early in the MI sessions, Carol began articulating the many downsides of her severe anxiety, including extreme fatigue, inability to relax, and no sense of joy, among others. The MI therapist worked to elaborate these as well as the barriers to change (i.e., worrying less) and, more generally, the overall landscape of Carol's ambivalence. The following dialogue was taken from the first session of MI when the therapist used empathic listening to understand the nature of Carol's concerns and to begin to explore her ambivalent feelings about worry. The particular strategies the therapist used appear in parentheses.

> T. So, you've had this sense of pleasing others. It's very important to try to meet their needs (*summary*), and it sounds like you've been very good at that. (*affirmation*)
>
> C. I think so.
>
> T. Worry can be very helpful in meeting the needs of others, because a lot of your energy goes into anticipating what they want or need. (*reflection linking worry with the strong desire to please others*)
>
> C. Exactly. But, sometimes I don't agree that I have to please them. It's eating me inside. I didn't do anything wrong, you know, but still I had to apologize just to keep the peace.
>
> T. Yeah, and that's happened a number of times. (*reflection*)

C. I get angry at myself so many times. I'm aware of this but I can't stop doing it. It's just automatic.

T. I can understand that. Connections with other people are so important. It's very scary to think about being without that (*validation*). But, another voice is saying … what is it saying? (*evoking downside to the client's pleasing style*)

C. I was okay. I didn't do anything to break the relationship. Why do I have to be the one to say "I'm sorry"?

T. That's unfair (*reflection*). So, there are these two voices inside. One is saying, "This is scary. Do whatever you can to make sure there's not a problem." The other one says, "Don't do that. It's unfair. Stand up for yourself. This is not your fault." (*summary of ambivalence*)

C. (heavy sigh) It's horrible. I have this constant monologue in my head. I don't know why I'm like this.

T. So, there's this sense of being stuck in this place? (*reflection of feelings underlying ambivalence*)

C. I feel like I'm in a circle. I can't get out from this. I can't find myself. I don't know who I am even. I'm so confused.

T. That's really understandable when you feel stuck in the middle here, going around and around and around. (*validation*)

In this interview, the therapist maintained an attitude of exploration of the client's ambivalence, recasting her predictable and normal responses to ambivalence (responses that the client found confusing and nonsensical) as valid and understandable given her situation. For example, the therapist reframed the client's pleasing style as functional, understandable, and even useful in meeting the goal of maintaining critical connections with others.

In the second session, the therapist continued to explore the client's ambivalence, seeking to deepen the understanding of both the change and non-change voices. In particular, the therapist continued to work to understand the ambivalence and expressly sought to help the client accept and understand the positive motives underlying her worry and its associated interpersonal style.

C. I'm always giving the image to people that I'm happy, I'm okay, I'm calm, I'm good and helpful and nice, but that's not the truth. My image is different from what's going on inside. People think I'm very strong, that I always have some solution … that I'm happy. But, I know it's not the truth. Inside it's the opposite, and it's bothering me.

T. So, it's sounding like you're getting tired of playing that role. You're wondering, "What do I need? What do I feel? When is it my time to be me?" (*complex reflection summarizing change talk*)

C. Yes. I'm frustrated. Why do I have to be off work and not able to concentrate or anything? I want to be able to show my real self. Why do I have to play this role with people?

T. And, maybe that's a really good place to spend a little time. There might be some good things about playing this role. Would there be some good things about it? (*inviting exploration of benefits of client existing style*)

C. Umm. I don't know. Sometimes I hide a lot of things.

T. So, when you play this role, it helps hide some feelings inside—maybe difficult feelings. (*complex reflection encouraging client to continue exploring this identified advantage of the status quo*)

C. Yes, sometimes I'm embarrassed or ashamed and then I can hide this.

T. Right, I'm really good at playing this role! And when I play this role I don't have to show these embarrassing feelings. And that's kind of a good thing, because it prevents me from having to feel them. (*summary and validation*)

C. … Or judgment. They'll look at me or whatever they think about me.

T. So I can avoid their judgments—that fear of not measuring up, that fear of them not liking me. So, the role is really helpful for that. (*validation*) What are the other good things? (*open question encouraging elaboration of the benefits of the status quo*)

C. I don't have any enemies. People like me.

T. So that makes life a lot smoother. There's not many conflicts. I'm pleasing others. I'm helping them. (*validation*)

C. Yes, no conflict.

T. And how important is that? (*exploring significance of the identified advantage of status quo*)

C. Extremely important. I really don't handle conflict well, so I try to avoid it as much as I can.

T. So, pleasing others accomplishes something really critical. No wonder you're doing it. And you would worry that if you stopped pleasing others there might be a lot more tension, more conflict. (*summary and validation*)

This excerpt illustrates the importance of the therapist's attitude of accepting and reframing aspects of the client that she regards as unacceptable. That is, the therapist works to understand and explore the reasonable and important needs that the deferential style and worry about others help meet (e.g., avoidance of aversive encounters or difficult feelings which the client feels are unendurable). In the following excerpt, the therapist goes a bit further by explicitly drawing attention to an aspect of the client that the therapist finds genuinely laudable. This seems to have the effect of deepening their bond as well as eliciting more change talk. The therapist is empathically attuned to the client's core issues—being honest and being known and seen for her true self in all its complexity. The therapist offers genuine gratitude to the client for being honest with her. The following excerpt occurred just after the client had disclosed, with difficulty, her frequent feelings of resentment toward others.

> T. Well, I really appreciate you being able to share these stories with me … and the chance to see you! Because that seems to be very important. It takes a lot of courage to come here and share these things. (*affirmation*)
> C. (tearful, quiet). Thank you (softly).
> T. What's going on inside right now? (*open question exploring client's reaction*)
> C. I would like to be helped. So I can be more myself or try to be more myself in interactions with people, so I can find myself in this world because I feel completely lost.
> T. I'm also hearing "it's time." It feels like it's time. (*guessing at implicit meaning and reflecting change talk*)

This next excerpt is taken from the third MI session. Having attained a basic understanding of the client's concerns, the therapist sought to further deepen the client's understanding of her dilemma and to move toward bringing the two sides together to facilitate resolution.

> C. People ask me, "Do you have hobbies?" No, I don't.
> T. And how could you, Carol, when you have this voice in your head that says "Do the garage, mow the lawn, …"? (*validation*)
> C. Yes, this stuff is occupying my mind all the time. "What would you like to do?" they ask me. And I really don't know.
> T. Because I don't even have a moment when I'm allowed to think about that. If you were to do that, it would have to be, well, after the garage and … . (*validation*)
> C. Yes, I would feel so guilty.
> T. Guilty. Right. If we were to look at the upsides and the downsides of worry and how it takes over, I would guess that one of the upsides of worry and guilt is "Boy, you get a lot done." That garage gets cleaned and the house gets straightened up. Carol does a lot. Is that true? (*reflection, reframing, asking for accuracy of reflection*)
> C. (laughs) Yes.
> T. Yes, it is true. And you've told me too that you've learned English and gotten yourself a good education and job and a home. You take very good care of your children. So guilt kind of drives a lot of this? (*affirmation and validation*)

C. Even toward my husband. I always feel guilty.

T. Towards your *ex*-husband. What's this guilty feeling? (*open question encouraging elaboration of feelings*)

C. I just left him. So, whenever it's Thanksgiving or Christmas I have to invite him because I would feel so bad if I didn't.

T. There's that sense of "I'm responsible." (*complex reflection*)

C. Yes. Or, if he doesn't call, then I think maybe something happened to him and I have to find out if he's okay (laughing slightly and sounding disgusted with herself).

T. (picks up on nonverbals) And, there's another part of you going, "What is that about?" (*encouraging exploration of downside of status quo*)

C. Yes, because you know, who is asking me? Why do I always have to worry about the other person?

T. So, you give exceptional care to others. It sounds like you're a wonderful caregiver for other people and their needs. But, on the other side, it's robbing you. (*summary*) What's the downside? (*encouraging further exploration of problems with existing style*)

C. Sometimes I just feel like I'm doing everything for others. Just to please them, to make sure they are okay, that I don't have any conflicts with anybody or that I don't insult anybody.

T. So this is a lot of work! (Client laughs.) No insults, no conflicts, making sure they're safe, they're not lonely. (*summary*)

C. I cannot even say ... when a man calls me for a date, I can't say "no." Sometimes I just go even though I don't want to.

T. So somehow it's easier to sacrifice me. (*complex reflection*)

C. Yes. I feel like I am sacrificing a lot in my life.

T. Sacrificing me so no one is hurt or insulted or unsafe or ... that's all ...

C. (sounding exasperated) It's all about others! How are my kids doing? Are they okay? Constantly thinking about others, so I don't even have a moment for me.

T. And you're saying, "Boy, there's sure some costs to that for me, eh?" What are some of the costs? (*further elaborating down sides and eliciting change talk*)

C. Depression.

T. What is that? (*open question elaborating feelings*)

C. So sad ... and lonely ... and not able to do anything. I'm surrounded by people but actually I feel so alone inside.

This excerpt illustrates strong empathic attunement to the client. The therapist gauges which side of the ambivalence the client is expressing and moves with her in elaborating her thoughts and feelings. When the therapist expresses understanding and validation of the powerful and understandable reasons for the client's pleasing style, the client begins to spontaneously critique her interpersonal style and begins expressing change talk, which is then further reflected and elaborated by the therapist. The therapist's reflections allow the client to continue to elaborate her experience and move the dialogue forward to deepen the client's self-understanding and form the foundation for the client's own self-evaluation and decision-making regarding change.

Carol showed significant improvements with four sessions of MI, even before the following CBT began. Her scores on the Penn State Worry Questionnaire (PSWQ) dropped from 72 at baseline to 50 post-MI (a reduction of over 2.5 standard deviations). Although this is speculative because the mechanisms of MI have not been sufficiently investigated, perhaps the therapist's interest in and exploration of the client's needs allowed Carol to begin to appreciate these needs as legitimate and worthy of consideration and expression. Moreover, the therapist remained open to hearing both sides of her ambivalence (the arguments for being unassertive and the arguments for being assertive), which allowed the client to explore her own position on her interpersonal style and work through her ambivalence, informed by a clearer understanding of her own wants and needs.

Immediately after completing the MI, Carol received 14 sessions of CBT which involved a multi-component anxiety management package including relaxation training, self-monitoring, cognitive therapy, and worry exposure. She participated very actively and cooperatively in the CBT, receiving a high homework compliance rating from her CBT therapist. Over the course of the subsequent CBT, Carol's worry score on the PSWQ dropped to a 35, which is at the 30th percentile of scores for non-clinical samples (Gillis, Haaga, & Ford, 1995). She also showed significant improvements in depression, anxiety, stress, and disability from anxiety. All treatment gains were maintained at the 1-year follow-up. At that point, she no longer met DSM criteria for GAD, having only mild residual symptoms. She continued to meet criteria for social phobia, although with reduced severity from the pretreatment assessment.

Carol's subjective report of treatment and change

As part of the larger clinical trial, clients were interviewed immediately following their participation in each treatment, using a semi-structured interview (Angus & Westra, 2005). All interviews were recorded. Clients were asked about their experience of change, the process of therapy, and helpful and unhelpful aspects of the sessions. Carol reported a very positive experience with the MI sessions. She said that the sense of safety she experienced with the therapist was particularly important for her. She described this as follows: "I felt so free and without any fear about what I'm saying or feeling. I could share my experiences for the first time in my life with somebody." Her subjective report matched results from quantitative indices in reflecting significant change with MI alone. In particular, she said that, "The role that I used to play with others is not so strong. And I think that all this honesty I had with myself, it's really influenced my relationships with others. I have this hope or belief that I can be more honest with myself and with others. I feel lighter and like I would like to enjoy my life." These comments reflect both significant change with MI and increased readiness for more change. Interestingly, she also noted that she had already implemented some ideas about how to manage her anxiety such as working on the tension in her body more effectively and "finding other ways in which I can cope." Even though specific techniques for anxiety management were not discussed in the MI sessions, Carol's reflections and the evocative style of MI appeared to have facilitated her spontaneous generation of solutions to her anxiety problems.

Consistent with a major goal of MI, Carol also expressed feeling more engaged and curious about the CBT, noting that, "I'm looking forward to the other part. It made me feel more interested in how I can cope differently. I'm looking forward to not only talking about my feelings and thoughts but also learning how to implement practical new skills in my daily life." Interestingly, her reflections on the process of therapy and her experience of the MI sessions were consistent with core facilitative conditions outlined by Rogers (1957), such as empathy, the importance of the person of the therapist, and unconditional positive regard which also form the foundation of MI. For example, in reflecting on what stood out for her in her experience, she stated, "[The therapist] was really with me, really listening to what I said and what I was trying to say. She really moved all my thoughts and feelings forward so I was able to continue. … I felt she really feels me … what I'm going through and what I really want to change in my life." Here, the client experiences empathy, not as a passive process but as an enriching, healing experience enabling deeper self-understanding. Carol also experienced her therapist as warm: "I feel she likes me and that she enjoys the time," and as nonjudgmental: "I have this really nice feeling that she wanted to help me … or to feel okay with her, that it's nothing to be scared about. She makes sure she isn't hurtful when she talks with people. She's very careful about that."

In her post-CBT interview, Carol described numerous positive changes, recounting examples of expressing herself more openly without fear of judgment and being more assertive without guilt. She also reported feeling much more control over her worry and being "more realistic about my thoughts and the situations that cause me worry or depression." In terms of helpful aspects of CBT, she noted the specific exercises and the homework as being very useful in practicing the new concepts she was learning in therapy. She reported the exposure exercises as something that she did not anticipate would be helpful, but in fact proved very beneficial. She also reported experiencing the CBT therapist as nonjudgmental, empathetic, and genuinely interested in her and her progress. She reported being pleasantly surprised at this because she initially expected that the therapist would be less collaborative, more directive and controlling: "I thought her role would be more like a teacher ... like, give a task, I do it, and then she can see what's going on with me. But it wasn't like that ... she was fully with me and very concerned about how I progressed and really trying to understand what bothers me and what I would like to gain from this therapy." In contrasting the two therapies, this client noted that the MI therapist "understood me more" and "went deeper," while the CBT therapist was "more scientific."

Efficacy of adding MI to CBT for GAD and other anxiety disorders

Studies examining MI and related motivational enhancement strategies combined or integrated with CBT for anxiety disorders are just beginning to emerge. Consistent with the early stage of this research, much of this work involves case studies and controlled pilot studies with small sample sizes. Buckner, Roth Ledley, Heimberg, & Schmidt (2008) have provided case study data supporting the adjunctive use of motivational enhancement therapy to treat comorbid alcohol use disorder in social anxiety clients. MI is also being used successfully to increase treatment seeking among those with social anxiety who are not yet seeking care (Buckner & Schmidt, 2008). MI and related techniques have been reported to increase receptivity to exposure and response prevention (ERP) for obsessive–compulsive disorder (OCD). In a group of seven ERP refusers, Tolin and Maltby (2008) piloted a readiness intervention (RI) conducted in the MI style which included psychoeducation, viewing an ERP session, constructing an exposure hierarchy, a phone conversation with a client who completed ERP, and MI methods of increasing motivation and decreasing ambivalence about treatment. MI strategies were explicitly used in two of the four RI sessions, and the spirit of MI guided the therapist's style in all of the sessions. The RI group was compared to another group of ERP refusers (n = 5) who were put on a waiting list. Results indicated that the RI treatment significantly reduced fears of ERP as judged by scores on an expectancy scale (Borkovec & Nau, 1972) and, most importantly, a significantly higher rate of agreement to ERP treatment compared to the wait-list group. Those former treatment refusers who received the RI improved with the subsequent ERP as much as clients who initially did not refuse treatment (Tolin & Maltby, 2008). Related findings with OCD clients were obtained by McCabe, Rowa, Antony, Yong, and Swinson (2008). They found that a motivational enhancement pretreatment for OCD clients led to increased confidence and readiness to engage in ERP compared to a relaxation control. In a series of six case studies, Simpson, Zuckoff, Page, Franklin, and Foa (2008) reported significant decreases in OCD as measured by the Yale–Brown Obsessive Compulsive Scale (Y-BOCS) (Goodman et al., 1989) when using MI throughout ERP for OCD.

New motivational enhancement therapies are also being piloted in the area of PTSD. Preliminary findings show evidence of increased problem recognition and treatment attendance in those who received these therapies compared to those who received a pyschoeducational intervention (Murphy, 2008). In six case studies of individuals with various anxiety disorders, our research group found consistent evidence of symptom improvement when MI was integrated within a CBT approach for those demonstrating resistance at different points before and during CBT (e.g., Arkowitz & Westra, 2004; Westra, 2004; Westra & Phoenix, 2003). A manual outlining our application of MI to anxiety disorders is available (Westra & Dozois, 2003).

To date, two larger randomized controlled trials have been conducted of an MI pretreatment for CBT for anxiety disorders. Both found evidence supporting the combination. These studies are briefly reviewed below.

MI for a heterogeneous anxiety disorders group

In a preliminary study, Westra and Dozois (2006) randomly assigned 55 individuals with a variety of anxiety disorders (panic disorder, social phobia, and/or generalized anxiety disorder) to either a MI–CBT group, in which clients received 3 individual sessions of an MI pretreatment followed by group CBT for anxiety disorders, or a NPT–CBT group that received no pretreatment followed by group CBT. The pretreatment group showed significantly higher client-rated homework compliance throughout CBT (effect size of $d = .38$) than the group that did not receive a pretreatment. Additionally, the MI pretreatment group showed significantly greater increases over the MI pretreatment period in positive expectancies for change compared to the NPT group ($d = .60$). We also found that more subjects in the MI pretreatment group versus the NPT group completed CBT ($n = 21/25$ or 84% and $n = 19/30$ or 63%, respectively). Although both groups showed clinically significant reductions in anxiety symptoms, the addition of the MI pretreatment yielded a 25% increase in the number of individuals classified as treatment responders using the criteria for clinical significance proposed by Jacobson and Truax (1991): MI, $n = 19/25$ or 75% versus NPT, $n = 15/30$ or 50%. Gains in both groups were maintained at 6-month follow-up assessment.

The results of this study suggested that adding an MI pretreatment to CBT for mixed anxiety disorders had promise for enhancing treatment engagement and improving outcomes in CBT for anxiety disorders. Our findings suggested that the impact of MI may occur by increasing treatment engagement which in turn was associated with better outcome in the subsequent CBT. We also found that those individuals with GAD compared to those with other anxiety disorders showed the greatest symptom reductions in the MI–CBT condition compared to the NPT–CBT condition ($d = 1.29$). Effect sizes for the other anxiety disorders were $d = .69$ for panic disorder and $d = .44$ for social phobia; however, interpretation of these results is limited by the small sample of GAD subjects available for this analysis.

Although results of this study did suggest that adding MI to CBT may be beneficial, it had several limitations that preclude drawing a strong conclusion from these results. These include failure to control for concomitant treatments, no control for the additional sessions received by the pretreatment group, no assessment of treatment integrity, the use of a single MI therapist, and the use of a heterogeneous anxiety population. Next, we report on a controlled follow-up to this study that was designed to address most of these limitations.

MI for GAD: preliminary results of a randomized controlled trial

Westra, Arkowitz, and Dozois (2007) conducted a randomized controlled trial in which GAD clients were randomly assigned to a MI–CBT condition in which GAD clients first received 4 individual MI pretreatment sessions followed by 14 hours of individual CBT. This group was compared to a NPT–CBT condition in which clients did not receive any pretreatment but did receive 14 hours of individual CBT. Although 22% ($n = 15/67$) of the participants were stabilized on antidepressant medication, they were not permitted to use benzodiazepines or to receive other psychotherapy during the study. The majority of participants had a long history of problems with worry (mean chronicity of 20.9 years) and had received previous treatment for anxiety (70% some type of counseling, unspecified; 47% psychotropic medications). Almost half of the sample had at least one additional current diagnosis of an anxiety or depressive disorder. MI was delivered by one set of therapists and CBT by another. The results of treatment integrity checks on both therapies showed very good therapist adherence.

Findings from 67 treatment completers to date (34 MI–CBT and 33 NPT–CBT clients) revealed a posttreatment between-group effect size for worry reduction of $d = .47$ in favor of the MI–CBT group. In addition, the MI–CBT group showed greater therapist-rated homework compliance than did the NPT–CBT group (posttreatment between-group effect size of $d = .59$). Thus, the addition of MI to CBT substantially increased the effects of treatment on symptoms of worry and on homework compliance.

We also examined severity of worry as a possible moderator. For the more severe worriers, the between-group (NPT–CBT vs. MI–CBT) post-treatment effect size was a large $d = .97$, whereas for the moderate worriers it was small at $d = .20$. Clearly, the addition of an MI pretreatment to CBT was of much greater benefit to the severe versus moderate worriers. It is important to note that a large number of studies and meta-analyses comparing the efficacy of two viable treatments for a disorder have found little or no differences between them (Luborsky et al., 2002; Wampold et al., 1997). By contrast, we found large differences between our two treatment groups, both of which received the same active CBT treatment that has been found efficacious in other studies (e.g., Borkovec & Costello, 1993).

Our results are noteworthy in another respect, as well. A recent meta-analysis of CBT for GAD by Covin et al. (2008) used the PSWQ as the criterion outcome measure. In these studies, CBT was compared mainly to no-treatment wait-list control groups and in a few cases to a nonspecific supportive control group not intended to be therapeutic. They found a between-group posttreatment effect size of 1.15 favoring CBT over no treatment or presumably inert treatments. Our effect size of .97 for the severe worriers is of a roughly similar magnitude, but it is based on a comparison of two groups, both of which received empirically supported CBT, with the only difference between them being that one received the MI pretreatment and one did not. Although we need to rule out the effects of the four extra sessions received by the MI–CBT group, we believe that these results point to the possibility of a powerful effect for the MI pretreatment.

We also examined end-state functioning on a variety of indices, including worry, depression, anxiety (tension), stress (nervous energy, tendency to overreact to stress), disability associated with anxiety, positive and negative beliefs about worry, and clinician-rated severity. High end-state functioning was defined stringently as being within the normal range on at least 6 of these 7 indices. Using this measure, 85% ($n = 29/34$) of the MI–CBT group showed high end-state functioning compared with 65% ($n = 21/33$) of the NPT–CBT group. In summary, this study found evidence that an MI pretreatment can lead to substantially better outcomes in a variety of areas than the same exact CBT treatment without MI.

We further examined the effects of four sessions of MI without subsequent CBT compared to no treatment during the same period of time, Interestingly, the group that received four sessions of MI showed significant reductions in worry ($d = .59$) and stress ($d = .71$) compared to the group that received no pretreatment. This finding suggests that MI may not only influence motivation and ambivalence but may also lead directly to symptom reduction, as well, even without CBT. No significant effects of MI alone compared to no pretreatment were found for depression or overall disability.

We also examined whether initial problem severity influenced the response to the MI pretreatment. Similar to the results for the combined group presented earlier, we found that the four sessions of MI were of greatest value for clients with the most severe worry problems. In particular, among those of high severity, the posttreatment (four sessions of MI vs. no pretreatment) between-group effect sizes on worry (PSWQ) reduction were quite large ($d = 1.13$). This effect size is almost exactly the same as that found in the Covin et al. (2008) meta-analysis for the comparison between CBT versus no or presumably inert treatments. This finding further highlights that even a brief course of MI can have substantial effects on worry in GAD clients.

In general, the findings of this study are consistent with findings from the less well-controlled studies in demonstrating significant benefits of augmenting CBT with MI in the treatment of anxiety disorders. Our results stand in contrast to the generally modest success rates for CBT for GAD obtained by some other studies (e.g., Campbell & Brown, 2002). Benchmarked against response rates for CBT in the treatment of GAD from previous trials, which range from 46 to 60% high end-state functioning (Hunot et al., 2007), our results clearly suggest that an MI pretreatment may enhance the efficacy of CBT for GAD.

Our strong findings on worry severity as a moderator of outcome raise the question of what is there about high-problem-severity clients that renders them so much more responsive to the addition of the MI pretreatment? Interestingly, other studies of MI have also found that it is particularly effective for high severity subjects with other problems, such as problem gambling (Hodgins & Diskin, 2008) and alcohol use during pregnancy (Handmaker, Miller, & Manicke, 1999). Some of our results provide some clues to help answer this question; for example, we found that clients high in worry severity perceived their worry as more uncontrollable and dangerous compared to lower severity clients and tended to have more comorbid diagnoses. They also showed significantly greater increases in intrinsic motivation over the course of MI compared to those of lesser worry severity. In short, more severe GAD may have certain problematic characteristics that may interfere with the progress of therapy and that may be effectively addressed by MI.

Although our results suggest that MI can significantly enhance the efficacy of CBT for GAD, many questions remain. First, because the combination group in our study received four more sessions than the CBT-only group, we cannot conclude with certainty that our effects were attributable to the MI or simply to more sessions. We also need to know how MI pretreatment fares when compared with another pretreatment, a question we will be examining in our next study.

Future research is needed to examine several questions, such as to what degree can MI enhance CBT for other clinical problems? Although many studies, including our own, have shown that MI is efficacious, we have relatively few data regarding how and why it works. To do this research, measures of possible variables that may mediate the efficacy of MI are required. Some promising starts have already been made in this direction on constructs that Miller and Rollnick (2002) hypothesized to be some of the mechanisms of action of MI—intrinsic motivation (Pelletier, Tuson, & Haddad, 1997) and ambivalence (Brody, Arkowitz, & Allen, 2008). We hope to see more outcome and process research on MI in the near future.

Summary

We hope we have illustrated the value of MI in the cognitive–behavioral treatment of GAD. In our experience, combining MI with CBT for anxiety disorders is clinically helpful, particularly for some cases, and this is beginning to receive research support. Based on empirical data collected to date, GAD may represent a particularly MI-responsive population, especially those with more severe worry problems. The combination of MI and CBT is promising yet challenging clinically because the MI style deviates somewhat from the therapist style in CBT.

We hope that the future will bring further well-designed studies to examine how MI might increase the efficacy of CBT, not only for other anxiety disorders but also for a range of other clinical problems, as well. Some promising starts have been made in this direction (Arkowitz et al., 2008). Future research is also needed to elucidate how and why MI works. Research on and the practice of MI are beginning to move from the areas of problem drinking, drug addiction, and health behaviors to wider applications to other clinical disorders. As we extend our MI research and practice, many interesting and clinically relevant questions arise which we look forward to being addressed in the near future.

References

American Psychiatric Association. (1994). *Diagnostic and statistical manual of mental disorders* (4th ed.). Arlington, VA: American Psychiatric Association.

Angus, L., & Westra, H.A. (2005). *The narrative interview: Assessing client experiences of psychotherapy.* Unpublished measure.

Antony, M.M., Roth Ledley, D., & Heimberg, R.G. (2005). *Improving outcomes and preventing relapse in cognitive–behavioral therapy.* New York: Guilford Press.

Arkowitz, H., & Westra, H.A. (2004). Integrating motivational interviewing and cognitive behavioral therapy in the treatment of depression and anxiety. *Journal of Cognitive Psychotherapy, 18*(4), 337–350.

Arkowitz, H., Westra, H.A., Miller, W.R., & Rollnick, S. (2008). *Motivational interviewing in the treatment of psychological problems.* New York: Guilford Press.

Barlow, D.H., Raffa, S.D., & Cohen, E.M. (2002). *Psychosocial treatments for panic disorders, phobias, and generalized anxiety disorder.* New York: Oxford University Press.

Barlow, D.H., Rapee, R.M., & Brown, T.A. (1992). Behavioral treatment of generalized anxiety disorder. *Behavior Therapy, 23*(4), 551–570.

Beck, J.S. (2005). *Cognitive therapy for challenging problems: What to do when the basics don't work.* New York: Guilford Press.

Beutler, L.E., Rocco, F., Moleiro, C.M., & Talebi, H. (2001). Resistance. *Psychotherapy, 38*, 431–436.

Bischoff, M.M., & Tracey, J.J. (1995). Client resistance as predicted by therapist behavior: A study of sequential dependence. *Counseling Psychology, 42*, 487–495.

Blagys, M.D., & Hilsenroth, M.J. (2002). Distinctive activities of cognitive–behavioral therapy: A review of the comparative psychotherapy process literature. *Clinical Psychology Review, 22*, 671–706.

Borkovec, T.D. (1994). The nature, functions, and origins of worry. In G.C.L. Davey & F. Tallis (Eds.), *Worrying: Perspectives on theory, assessment and treatment* (pp. 5–33). New York: John Wiley & Sons.

Borkovec, T.D., & Costello, E. (1993). Efficacy of applied relaxation and cognitive–behavioral therapy in the treatment of generalized anxiety disorder. *Journal of Consulting and Clinical Psychology, 61*(4), 611–619.

Borkovec, T.D., & Nau, S.D. (1972). Credibility of analogue therapy rationales. *Journal of Behavior Therapy and Experimental Psychiatry, 3*, 257–260.

Borkovec, T.D., & Roemer, L. (1995). Perceived functions of worry among generalized anxiety disorder subjects: Distraction from more emotionally distressing topics? *Journal of Behavior Therapy and Experimental Psychiatry, 26*(1), 25–30.

Borkovec, T.D., Newman, M.G., & Castonguay, L.G. (2003). Cognitive–behavioral therapy for generalized anxiety disorder with integrations from interpersonal and experiential therapies. *CNS Spectrums, 8*(5), 382–389.

Borkovec, T.D., Newman, M.G., Pincus, A.L., & Lytle, R. (2002). A component analysis of cognitive–behavioral therapy for generalized anxiety disorder and the role of interpersonal problems. *Journal of Consulting and Clinical Psychology, 70*(2), 288–298.

Brehm, S.S., & Brehm, J.W. (1981). *Psychological reactance: A theory of freedom and control.* New York: Academic Press.

Brody, A.E., Arkowitz, H., & Allen, J.J.B. (2008). *Development and validation of a self-report measure of ambivalence toward change.* Poster presented at the annual meeting of the Association for Psychological Science, May 22–25, Chicago, IL.

Brown, T.A., & Barlow, D.H. (1992). Comorbidity among anxiety disorders: Implications for treatment and DSM-IV. *Journal of Consulting and Clinical Psychology, 60*(6), 835–844.

Buckner, J.D., & Schmidt, N.B. (2008). *Motivational enhancement therapy increases cognitive–behavior therapy utilization among non-treatment-seekers with social anxiety disorder.* Paper presented at the annual meeting of the Association for Behavioral and Cognitive Therapies, November 13–16, Orlando, FL.

Buckner, J.D., Roth Ledley, D., Heimberg, R.G., & Schmidt, N.B. (2008). Treating comorbid social anxiety and alcohol use disorders: Combining motivation enhancement therapy with cognitive–behavioral therapy. *Clinical Case Studies, 7*(3), 208–223.

Burke, B. L., Arkowitz, H., & Menchola, M. (2003). The efficacy of motivational interviewing: A meta-analysis of controlled clinical trials. *Journal of Consulting and Clinical Psychology, 71*(5), 843–861.

Burns, D.D., & Auerbach, A. (1996). Therapeutic empathy in cognitive–behavioral therapy: Does it really make a difference? In P.M. Salkovskis (Ed.), *Frontiers of cognitive therapy* (pp. 135–164). New York: Guilford Press.

Campbell, L.A., & Brown, T.A. (2002). Generalized anxiety disorder. In M.M. Antony & D.H. Barlow (Ed.), *Handbook of assessment and treatment planning for psychological disorders* (pp. 147–181). New York: Guilford Press.

Covin, R., Ouimet, A.J., Seeds, P.M., & Dozois, D.J.A. (2008). A meta-analysis of CBT for pathological worry among clients with GAD. *Journal of Anxiety Disorders, 22*(1), 108–116.

Davison, G.C., & Valins, S. (1969). Maintenance of self-attributed and drug-attributed behavior change. *Journal of Personality and Social Psychology, 11*, 25–33.

Engle, D.E., & Arkowitz, H. (2006). *Ambivalence in psychotherapy: Facilitating readiness to change.* New York: Guilford Press.

Frank, J.D. (1974). Therapeutic components of psychotherapy: A 25-year progress report of research. *Journal of Nervous and Mental Disease, 159*, 325–342.

Freeston, M.H., Rhéame, J., Letarte, H., Dugas, M.J., & Ladouceur, R. (1994). Why do people worry? *Personality and Individual Differences, 17*, 791–802.

Gillis, M.M., Haaga, D.A.F., & Ford, G.T. (1995). Normative values for the Beck Anxiety Inventory, Fear Questionnaire, Penn State Worry Questionnaire, and Social Phobia and Anxiety Inventory. *Psychological Assessment, 7*(4), 450–455.

Goodman, W.K., Price, L.H., Rasmussen, S.A., Mazure, C., Fleischmann, R.L., Hill, C.L. et al. (1989). The Yale–Brown Obsessive Compulsive Scale. I. Development, use, and reliability. *Archives of General Psychiatry, 46*, 1006–1011.

Haby, M.M., Donnelly, M., Corry, J., & Vos, T. (2006). Cognitive–behavioural therapy for depression, panic disorder and generalized anxiety disorder: A meta-regression of factors that may predict outcome. *Australian and New Zealand Journal of Psychiatry, 40*(1), 9–19.

Hale, W., Engels, R., & Meeus, W. (2006). Adolescent perceptions of parenting behavior and its relationship to adolescent generalized anxiety disorder symptoms. *Journal of Adolescence, 29*, 407–417.

Handmaker, N.S., Miller, W.R., & Manicke, M. (1999). Findings of a pilot study of motivational interviewing with pregnant drinkers. *Journal of Studies on Alcohol, 60*(2), 285–287.

Hansen, D., & Warner, J.E. (1994). Treatment adherence of maltreating families: A survey of professionals regarding prevalence and enhancement strategies. *Journal of Family Violence, 9*(1), 1–19.

Helbig, S., & Fehm, L. (2004). Problems with homework in CBT: Rare exception or rather frequent? *Behavioral and Cognitive Psychotherapy, 32*(3), 291–301.

Hettema, J., Steele, J., & Miller, W.R. (2005). Motivational interviewing. *Annual Review of Clinical Psychology, 1*(1), 91–111.

Hodgins, D., & Diskin, K.M. (2008). Motivational interviewing in the treatment of problem and pathological gambling. In H. Arkowitz, H.A. Westra, W.R. Miller, & S. Rollnick (Eds.), *Motivational interviewing in the treatment of psychological problems* (pp. 225–248). New York: Guilford Press.

Hunot, V., Churchill, R., Teixeira, V., & Silva de Lima, M. (2007). Psychological therapies for generalized anxiety disorder (review). *Cochrane Libraries, 4*.

Huppert, J.D., & Baker-Morissette, S.L. (2003). Beyond the manual: The insider's guide to panic control treatment. *Cognitive and Behavioral Practice, 10*(1), 2–13.

Huppert, J.D., Barlow, D.H., Gorman, J.M., Shear, M.K., & Woods, S.W. (2006). The interaction of motivation and therapist adherence predicts outcome in cognitive–behavioral therapy for panic disorder: Preliminary findings. *Cognitive and Behavioral Practice, 13*, 198–204.

Jacobson, N.S., & Truax, P. (1991). Clinical significance: A statistical approach to defining meaningful change in psychotherapy research. *Journal of Consulting and Clinical Psychology, 59*, 12–19.

Kazantzis, N., & Ronan, K.R. (2006). Can between-session homework activities be considered a common factor in psychotherapy? *Journal of Psychotherapy Integration, 16*(2), 115–127.

Kazantzis, N., Deane, F.P., & Ronan, K.R. (2004). Assessing compliance with homework assignments: Review and recommendations for clinical practice. *Journal of Clinical Psychology, 60*(6), 627–641.

Kazantzis, N., Deane, F.P., Ronan, K.R., & L'Abate, L. (2005a). *Using homework assignments in cognitive behavior therapy*. New York: Routledge.

Kazantzis, N., Lampropoulos, G.K., & Deane, F.P. (2005b). A national survey of practicing psychologists' use and attitudes toward homework in psychotherapy. *Journal of Consulting and Clinical Psychology, 73*(4), 742–748.

Kessler, R., DuPont, R.L., Berglund, P., & Wittchen, H.U. (1999). Impairment in pure and comorbid generalized anxiety disorder and major depression at 12 months in two national surveys. *The American Journal of Psychiatry, 156*(12), 1915–1923.

Kessler, R.C., Keller, M.B., & Wittchen, H. (2001). The epidemiology of generalized anxiety disorder. *Psychiatric Clinics of North America, 24*(1), 19–39.

Koerner, N., & Dugas, M.J. (2006). A cognitive model of generalized anxiety disorder: The role of intolerance of uncertainty. In G.C.L. Daey & A. Wells (Eds.), *Worry and its psychological disorders: theory, assessment and treatment* (pp. 201–216). Hoboken, NJ: John Wiley & Sons.

Ladouceur, R., Dugas, M.J., Freeston, M.H., Léger, E., Gagnon, F., & Thibodeau, N. (2000). Efficacy of a cognitive–behavioral treatment for generalized anxiety disorder: Evaluation in a controlled clinical trial. *Journal of Consulting and Clinical Psychology, 68*(6), 957–964.

Leahy, R.L. (2001). *Overcoming resistance in cognitive therapy.* New York: Guilford Press.

Leahy, R.L. (2003). *Roadblocks in cognitive–behavioral therapy: Transforming challenges into opportunities for change.* New York: Guilford Press.

Lovibond, P.F., & Lovibond, S.H. (1995). The structure of negative emotional states: Comparison of the depression anxiety stress scales (DASS) with the Beck Depression and anxiety inventories. *Behaviour Research and Therapy, 33*(3), 335–343.

Luborsky, L., Rosenthal, R., Diguer, L., Andrusyna, Berman, J.S, Levitt, J.T., Seligman, D.A., & Krause, E.D. (2002). The Dodo bird verdict is alive and well—mostly. *Clinical Psychology: Science and Practice, 9*, 2–12.

Mahalik, J.R. (1994). Development of the client resistance scale. *Journal of Counseling Psychology, 41*, 58–68.

McCabe, R.E., Rowa, K., Antony, M.M., Young, L., & Swinson, R.P. (2008). *Using motivational enhancement to augment treatment outcome following exposure and response prevention for obsessive compulsive disorder: Preliminary findings.* Paper presented at the Annual Meeting of the Association for Behavioral and Cognitive Therapies, November 13–16, Orlando, FL.

Meyer, T.J., Miller, M.L., Metzger, R.L., & Borkovec, T.D. (1990). Development and validation of the Penn State Worry Questionnaire. *Behaviour Research and Therapy, 28*(6), 487–495.

Miller, W.R., & Rollnick, S. (1991). *Motivational interviewing: Preparing people to change addictive behavior.* New York: Guilford Press.

Miller, W.R., & Rollnick, S. (2002). *Motivational interviewing: Preparing people for change* (2nd ed.). New York: Guilford Press.

Miller, W.R., Benefield, R.G., & Tonigan, J.S. (1993). Enhancing motivation for change in problem drinking: A controlled comparison of two therapist styles. *Journal of Consulting and Clinical Psychology, 61*, 455–461.

Moyers, T.B., & Martin, T. (2006). Therapist influence on client language during motivational interviewing sessions. *Journal of Substance Abuse Treatment, 30*, 245–251.

Moyers, T.B., & Rollnick, S. (2002). A motivational interviewing perspective on resistance in psychotherapy. *Journal of Clinical Psychology, 58*(2), 185–193.

Moyers, T.B., Martin, T., Manuel, J.K., Hendrickson, S.M.L., & Miller, W.R. (2005). Assessing competence in the use of motivational interviewing. *Journal of Substance Abuse Treatment, 28*(1), 19–26.

Murphy, R. (2008). Enhancing combat veterans' motivation to change post-traumatic stress disorder symptoms and other problem behaviors. In H. Arkowitz, H.A. Westra, W.R. Miller, & S. Rollnick (Eds.), *Motivational interviewing in the treatment of psychological problems* (pp. 57–84). New York: Guilford Press.

Newman, C.F. (2002). A cognitive perspective on resistance in psychotherapy. *Journal of Clinical Psychology, 58*, 165–174.

Olfson, M., & Gameroff, M.J. (2007). Generalized anxiety disorder, somatic pain and health care costs. *General Hospital Psychiatry, 29*(4), 310–316.

Orlinsky, D.E., Grawe, K., & Parks, B.K. (1994). Process and outcome in psychotherapy: Noch einmal. In A.E. Bergin, & S.L. Garfield (Eds.), *Handbook of psychotherapy and behavior change* (4th ed.) (pp. 270–376). New York: John Wiley & Sons.

Patterson, G.R., & Chamberlain, P. (1994). A functional analysis of resistance during parent training therapy. *Clinical Psychology: Science and Practice, 1*, 53–70.

Patterson, G.R., & Forgatch, M.S. (1985). Therapist behavior as a determinant for client noncompliance: A paradox for the behavior modifier. *Journal of Consulting and Clinical Psychology, 53*, 846–851.

Pelletier, L., Tuson, K.M., & Haddad, N.K. (1997). Client Motivation for Therapy Scale: A measure of intrinsic motivation, extrinsic motivation and amotivation for therapy. *Journal of Personality Assessment, 68*, 414–435.

Pollard, C.A. (2007). Treatment readiness, ambivalence, and resistance. In M.M. Antony, C. Purdon, & L. Summerfeldt (Eds.), *Psychological treatment of obsessive compulsive disorder: Fundamentals and beyond*. Washington, D.C.: APA Books.

Rogers, C.R. (1956). Client-centered therapy. *Journal of Counseling Psychology, 3*, 115–120.

Rogers, C.R. (1957). The necessary and sufficient conditions of therapeutic personality change. *Journal of Consulting Psychology, 21*(2), 95–103.

Rollnick, S., Miller, W.R., & Butler, C.C. (2008). *Motivational interviewing in health care*. New York: Guilford Press.

Schmidt, N.B., & Woolaway-Bickel, K. (2000). The effects of treatment compliance on outcome in cognitive–behavioral therapy for panic disorder: Quality versus quantity. *Journal of Consulting and Clinical Psychology, 68*(1), 13–18.

Shaw, B. F., Elkin, I., Yamaguchi, J., Olmsted, M., Vallis, T.M., Dobson, K.S. et al. (1999). Therapist competence ratings in relation to clinical outcome in cognitive therapy of depression. *Journal of Consulting and Clinical Psychology, 67*(6), 837–846.

Sheehan, D.V. (1983). *The anxiety disease*. New York: Scribner.

Shoham, V., Trost, S.E., & Rohrbaugh, M.J. (2004). From state to trait and back again: Reactance theory goes clinical. In R.A. Wright, J. Greenberg, & S.S. Brehm (Eds.), *Motivational analyses of social behavior: Building on Jack Brehm's contributions to psychology* (pp. 167–185). Mahwah, NJ: Lawrence Erlbaum.

Shoham-Salomon, V., Avner, R., & Neeman, R. (1989). You're changed if you do and changed if you don't: Mechanisms underlying paradoxical interventions. *Journal of Consulting & Clinical Psychology, 57*, 590–598.

Simpson, H.B., Zuckoff, A., Page, J.R., Franklin, M.E., & Foa, E.B. (2008). Adding motivational interviewing to exposure and ritual prevention for obsessive compulsive disorder: an open trial. *Cognitive Behavioral Therapy, 37*, 38–49.

Sookman, D., & Pinard, G. (2007). Specialized cognitive behavioral therapy for resistant obsessive compulsive disorder: Elaboration of a schema-based model. In L.P. Riso, P.L. du Toit, D.J. Stein, & J.E. Young (Eds.), *Cognitive schemas and core beliefs in psychological problems: A scientist–practitioner guide* (pp. 93–109). Washington, D.C.: American Psychological Association.

Tolin, D.F., & Maltby, N. (2008). Motivating treatment-refusing clients with obsessive–compulsive disorder. In H. Arkowitz, H.A. Westra, W.R. Miller, & S. Rollnick (Eds.), *Motivational interviewing in the treatment of psychological problems* (pp. 85–108). New York: Guilford Press.

Vallis, T.M., Shaw, B.F., & Dobson, K.S. (1986). The cognitive therapy scale: Psychometric properties. *Journal of Consulting and Clinical Psychology, 54*(3), 381–385.

VanDyke, M.M., & Pollard, C.A. (2005). Treatment of refractory obsessive–compulsive disorder: the St. Louis model. *Cognitive and Behavioral Practice, 12,* 30–39.

Wampold, B.E., Mondin, G.W., Moody, M., Stich, F., Benson, K., & Ahn, H. (1997). A meta-analysis of outcome studies comparing bona fide psychotherapies: Empirically, "all must have prizes." *Psychological Bulletin, 122,* 203–215.

Watson, J.C., & McMullen, E.J. (2005). An examination of therapist and client behavior in high and low alliance sessions in cognitive–behavioral therapy and process experiential therapy. *Psychotherapy: Theory, Research, Practice and Training, 42,* 297–310.

Wells, A. (1997). *Cognitive therapy of anxiety disorders: A practice manual and conceptual guide.* New York: John Wiley & Sons.

Wells, A. (1999). A cognitive model of generalized anxiety disorder. *Behavior Modification, 23,* 526–555.

Wells, A. (2006). The metacognitive model of worry and generalized anxiety disorder. In G.C.L. Davey & A. Wells (Eds.), *Worry and its psychological disorders: Theory, assessment and treatment* (pp. 179–199). Hoboken, NJ: John Wiley & Sons.

Westen, D., & Morrison, K. (2001). A multidimensional meta-analysis of treatments for depression, panic, and generalized anxiety disorder: An empirical examination of the status of empirically supported therapies. *Journal of Consulting and Clinical Psychology, 69*(6), 875–899.

Westra, H.A. (2004). Managing resistance in cognitive behavioural therapy: The application of motivational interviewing in mixed anxiety and depression. *Cognitive Behaviour Therapy, 33*(4), 161–175.

Westra, H.A., & Dozois, D.J.A. (2003). *Motivational interviewing adapted for anxiety.* Unpublished treatment manual (hwestra@yorku.ca).

Westra, H.A., & Dozois, D.J.A. (2006). Preparing clients for cognitive–behavioral therapy: A randomized pilot study of motivational interviewing for anxiety. *Cognitive Therapy and Research, 30*(4), 481–498.

Westra, H.A., & Dozois, D.J.A. (2008). Integrating motivational interviewing into the treatment of anxiety. In H. Arkowitz, H.A. Westra, W.R. Miller, & S. Rollnick (Eds.), *Motivational interviewing in the treatment of psychological problems* (pp. 26–56). New York: Guilford Press.

Westra, H.A., & Phoenix, E. (2003). Motivational enhancement therapy in two cases of anxiety disorder: New responses to treatment refractoriness. *Clinical Case Studies, 2*(4), 306–322.

Westra, H.A., Arkowitz, H., & Dozois, D.J.A. (2007). *Motivational interviewing as a pretreatment for cognitive behavioral therapy in generalized anxiety disorder: Preliminary results of a randomized controlled trial.* Paper presented at the annual meeting of the Association for Behavioral and Cognitive Therapies, November 15–18, Philadelphia, PA.

chapter eight

Using a compassionate mind to enhance the effectiveness of cognitive therapy for individuals who suffer from shame and self-criticism

Deborah A. Lee
Berkshire Traumatic Stress Service
University College
London, United Kingdom

Contents

Introduction

Jennifer lives in a tortured mind: "I can't report my rape to the police because it was my fault. I must have done something wrong to deserve to suffer in this way. What he did was so disgusting, I must be disgusting, too. If others find out what happened to me they will think badly of me and not want to know me. I don't deserve to be helped because I am a worthless piece of nothing. I brought this on myself. I am bad because I was born that way. I don't deserve a place in this world. My presence is toxic to others. I loathe myself and I just want to die. I don't deserve your help, and you make me angry when you try to be nice because you don't understand how loathsome I am." Jennifer is a 32-year-old who was raped and has a history of childhood sexual abuse. She presented for treatment with posttraumatic stress disorder (American Psychiatric Association, 2000) characterized by flashbacks to the adult rape and childhood sexual abuse. She suffered from very low self-esteem. She misused alcohol and engaged in deliberate self-harm. This was her third attempt at treatment.

Most individuals who experience profound levels of shame live with tortured minds. Typically, they believe that other people perceive them in a negative light. They are very self-critical and condemnatory of their perceived inadequacies. They often believe that they are different from others and that there is something fundamentally wrong with them. They invalidate their own distress in a hostile manner and believe they are undeserving of love, kindness, care, and help. They frequently experience unpleasant levels of anxiety associated with the fear of being exposed to others as bad and inadequate. They engage in various safety strategies (e.g., deliberate self-harm, alcohol or drug abuse, dissociation, avoidance of people, aggression) in an attempt to avoid painful emotions and being exposed to others. They do not believe they are deserving of help and appear to have little capacity to soothe themselves through self-talk which prevents them from accessing feelings of kindness, care, and self-acceptance.

This chapter explores some of the challenges encountered by clinicians who work with individuals experiencing such difficulties and draws on underlying processes that may underpin treatment resistance. The chapter explores recent developments in compassion-focused processes specifically developed to target self-acceptance and soothing abilities that could enhance the effectiveness of cognitive therapy with this group.

What is shame?

This chapter considers shame from a psychoevolutionary perspective (Gilbert, 1989). Shame is a distressing fear that other people hold you negatively in their minds and is often accompanied by a *belief* that such negative evaluations are true (e.g., "Other people think I am disgusting because of what I did, and I think I am disgusting, too"). Thus, shame can be seen as the response to people's evaluation of you (*external threat*) and your own self-evaluation (*internal threat*). As shame is experienced in the context of interpersonal relationships, it is considered to be a socially constructed emotion and the *perceived threat* is to one's social status within a group. The possible consequences of this may be rejection, abandonment, and isolation from the social group. Common experiences of those who suffer from shame are *shame flashbacks*. These are associated with reliving vivid, painful, and emotionally intense memories linked to experiences of feeling exposed, degraded, and inadequate in the eyes and minds of others. These flashbacks may link to self-defining memories (Conway & Holmes, 2004; Conway & Pleydell-Pearce, 2000), and they are readily triggered by sensory cues that match an aspect of the current experience. For example, you may experience a flashback of being mocked on the playground, triggered by a current experience of being criticized at work. Shame is associated with strong primary emotional responses such as fear, sadness, disgust, and anger, as well as a characteristic self-critical thinking style (Gilbert, 2000).

Social mentality theory

Compassion-focused therapy has its theoretical foundations in social mentality theory (Gilbert, 1989), which is based on a threat-focused evolutionary explanation of shame and self-criticism. Gilbert proposed that self-relevant information is often processed through information-processing systems (social mentalities) that were originally evolved for social relating. Self-focused thinking and feelings are forms of internal "self-to-self relating." Thus, a part of the self can enact a hostile, attacking, condemnatory, dominant role (e.g., "You are pathetic and weak"). Another part of the self responds and feels beaten down by being attacked. Thus, the evolutionary basis of self-criticism may come from innate drives to dominate in social groups. There are also other functions of self-criticism, such as motivating oneself (e.g., "Come on—you can do better than that"). Similarly, part of the self can recognize the need for nurturance and soothe the self, which enables the beaten-down self to then feel regulated and soothed (Gilbert & Irons, 2005).

Self-critical thinking styles typically develop in childhood (Blatt & Zuroff, 1992). Early onset of critical thinking styles has been shown to predict later psychological problems (Zuroff, Koestner, & Powers, 1994), and they are considered to be an important factor in the maintenance of shame (Gilbert, 1998; Gilbert & Miles, 2000; Tangney & Dearing, 2002). In brief, the problem with self-criticism (e.g., "You are a useless piece of nothing") is that we can threaten ourselves. Our brains respond in a similar way to being bullied by another person. Both experiences have the capacity to trigger shame (Gilbert & McGuire, 1998).

The capacity to internalize verbal attacks from other people (such as from critical and abusive parents) is thought to influence the nature of inner-working models of self–self relationships (Bowlby, 1969; Gilbert, 1989). Human brains have evolved to process threat stimuli from either internal (self-criticism) or external (hostile attacks from others) sources. Neurological research has shown that the amygdala (the brain's alarm system) is highly sensitive to both the tone and the content of speech. Thus, self-attacking thoughts such as "You are despicable and disgusting" will be registered by the amygdala as highly threatening stimuli. Consequently, brain structures located in the limbic system respond to the stimuli by mobilizing a threat response. Neurochemical signals are sent to the neocortex and cortex to orchestrate that response (LeDoux, 1998). The threat response involves the release of stress hormones (such as cortisol or noradrenaline), threat-focused thinking (narrowing of attention, rapid thinking), and safety-seeking behaviors (fight, flight, freeze response). This is a response similar to that which would be triggered by an external threat, such as a verbal threat (abusive insult) or a physical threat (man wielding knife).

Self-soothing

The amygdala, however, will also respond to stimuli that are associated with safe memories (e.g., of being supported and cared for) by generating positive affect, which is associated with self-soothing (Gilbert, 2000). These feelings are thought to be linked to the release of hormones such as oxytocin and opiates (Depue & Morrone-Strupinsky, 2005), and research suggests that this system also regulates the production of cortisol, the stress hormone (Wang, 2005). Thus, self-talk that is soothing, kind, supportive, and warm is thought to be associated with the release of positive affect (opiates) and may also be linked to emotional memories and experiences of being soothed. This system is activated by attachment behavior (e.g., a mother soothes and calms her distressed child) (Carter, 1998) and by signals of social interaction (Uvnäs-Morberg, 1998). It is this response that is thought to have a reciprocal inhibitory relationship with the threat system

(Wang, 2005) and thus has the effect of dampening the threat response which reduces the fear associated with the social threat.

Self-soothing promotes psychological well-being, as it allows us to deal with threats from our social world (e.g., what other people think of us, how they treat us) and our own self-criticism to end painful feelings of shame. The ability to self-soothe and be compassionate as an adult is proposed to come from the caregiving mentality and our experiences of receiving care in childhood (Gilbert, 1989). It is the quality of attachment relationships in early life, especially the relationship between the primary caregiver and the child that is thought to provide the building blocks for an inner sense of safeness and security and an ability to regulate our emotional world (Gilbert, 2000; Mikulincer & Sheffi, 2000; Pearlman & McCann, 1994; Repetti, Taylor, & Seeman, 2002; Ryff, Singer, Wing, & Lobe, 2001; Taylor, Dickerson, & Klein, 2002). For example, if the primary caregiver offers validation, empathic understanding, care, and soothing at times of distress, then this becomes an inner working model of self-soothing for the child (Bowlby, 1969; McCann & Pearlman, 1992). It is these emotional memories that an adult accesses to understand and *feel* that they are lovable and that they are safe.

Shame is a transdiagnostic phenomenon. It is prevalent in many psychological disorders, such as depression, psychosis, substance abuse, eating disorders, social anxiety, posttraumatic stress disorder, and personality disorders (Andrews, 1995; Brown, 1991; Gilbert & Trower, 1990; Gilbert, Pehl, & Allen, 1994; Kaufman, 1989), and for many years cognitive therapy has held a key position in the treatment of many of these difficulties (Beck, 1976; Beck & Emery, 1985; Beck, Brown, Berchick, Stewart, & Steer, 1990; Clark, 1986; Layden, Newman, Freeman, & Morse, 1993; Salkovskis, Forrester, Richards, & Morrison, 1998; Giesen-Bloo et al., 2006). This therapeutic approach is, of course, supported by a substantial evidence base (see www.nice.org.uk for a review of evidence), and cognitive–behavioral therapy (CBT) is the treatment of choice for many anxiety disorders (Roth & Fonagy, 2007).

Is cognitive therapy effective for individuals with shame-based difficulties?

We know that many people with chronic emotional difficulties are burdened with self-critical and condemnatory thoughts and overwhelmed with profound feelings of shame. There is evidence to suggest that this group may do less well with cognitive therapy (Gilbert & Irons, 2005; Rector, Bagby, Segal, Joffe, & Levitt, 2000). This may be due in part to a theme often observed that self-critics lack emotional warmth for themselves and reevaluate negative information in a cold, rational, and even hostile manner. This may be linked to findings that suggest that self-critics appear to have a reduced capacity to be empathetic to their own distress and to nurture themselves emotionally in a self-soothing and reassuring way (Gillath, Bunge, Shaver, Wendelken, & Mikulincer, 2005; Harman & Lee, in press; Irons, Gilbert, Baldwin, Baccus, & Palmer, 2006; Mikulincer & Shaver, 2005). Moreover, they may have had limited experiences of being cared for in childhood and thus lack access to emotional memories of being soothed (Greenberg, 1979, 2007; Greenberg, Rice, & Elliot, 1993; Savege Scharff & Tsigounis, 2003). Consequently, new perspectives and beliefs reached through cognitive therapy may be meaningless if they are not associated with helpful emotional memories. Thus, to feel lovable you have to believe that you are, and to believe it you have to know it through experience.

The implications of these observations are noteworthy, perhaps especially when using protocol-driven CBT to treat shame and self-criticism. They may even go some way to shed light on treatment-resistant cases for the very reasons stated above, perhaps because people may be able to reach new perspectives or access more balanced beliefs about themselves using cognitive therapy, but they are less able to access congruent emotional experiences associated with new beliefs. Thus, their emotional state may remain unchanged, which in itself can perpetuate the feelings of shame (e.g., "I know I shouldn't feel bad about myself, but I just can't help it and that actually makes me feel more stupid and ashamed about myself").

Jennifer, for example, was raped in a brutal stranger attack. Although objectively it was clear that Jennifer was not responsible for this horrific attack, she was consumed with feelings of shame and self-blame. She believed that this attack was a punishment for being bad, and she constantly spoke to herself in a punitive and self-denigrating way. She seemed immune to her own distress and pain and belittled herself all the time. She appeared virtually incapable of offering herself warmth and kindness and was at a loss to know how to self-soothe. After 16 sessions of trauma-focused CBT (Ehlers, Clark, Hackmann, McManus, & Fennell, 2005), she was able to see logically and objectively that this attack was not her fault, yet she struggled to accept the more balanced or helpful perspective being true for her. A Socratic method of guided discovery to facilitate a shift in perspective on self-blame led to dead ends, as Jennifer repeatedly reported that she was bad because she was born that way, that she had always felt that way, that she was different from everyone else, and that she deserved to be raped. The development of new beliefs (e.g., "I am okay, and I don't deserve this") did not appear to trigger congruent emotional memories of herself as deserving of or receiving care, so the development of this new perspective remained an intellectual exercise rather than an emotionally meaningful experience. Perhaps as a consequence of this incongruity between intellectual understanding and emotional experience, Jennifer's emotional distress did not decrease, and she continued to suffer from distressing flashbacks to the rape. Furthermore, Jennifer began to feel ashamed of not being "good enough at therapy to feel differently about myself," which in turn perpetuated her sense of being different and cut off from other people.

Conceivably, it is this experience of a client knowing something from a cognitive perspective but not being able to feel it to be meaningful on an emotional level that could lead to either limited progress or a lack of sustainable improvement in therapy when working with shame-based psychological distress.

Many psychotherapies have a shared understanding that helping people to develop a warm, soothing, and more accepting relationship with themselves is key to overcoming their difficulties (Fonagy & Target, 2006; Greenberg, 2007; Rogers, 1957; Ryle, 1990). Yet, it is also acknowledged that this task is incredibly difficult for most self-critics. The very nature of their self-reproach makes them reject any attempts at self-acceptance and self-soothing, while condemning themselves as undeserving of warmth, care, and understanding. Thus, the process of developing a soothing intrapersonal relationship may not engage them on an emotional or implicit level even if there is evidence of explicit, self-processing (Baldwin & Fergusson, 2001; Haidt, 2001; Power & Dalgleish, 1997; Teasdale & Barnard, 1993). For example, after 16 sessions of trauma-focused CBT, Jennifer was able to say: "I know objectively that I am not a bad person, but I still feel I deserve to feel bad about myself. I don't know how to feel any other way about myself, and even when I look at the evidence to support the belief that I am okay and it's not my fault it is like it doesn't touch me. I keep saying, 'Yes, but you know that is not true about you because you are rubbish.' I just don't feel reassured or comforted by the more helpful thoughts because if I am honest it makes me anxious to think nice things about myself, as I don't really deserve to."

In line with such clinical observations, new developments in cognitive therapy have emphasized an emotion-focused, rather than a cognition-focused, approach to work with a range of emotional difficulties (Leahy, 1999, 2007; Sookman & Pinard, 2007). Specifically, compassion-focused therapy (CFT) has been used to work with shame and self-criticism (Gilbert, 1989, 2000; Gilbert & Irons, 2005). These developments are complemented by an emerging evidence base to suggest that this approach may enhance clinical work with various clinical presentations such as borderline personality disorder (Gilbert & Proctor, 2006), depression (Gilbert & Irons, 2004), low self-esteem (MacFarlane, 2008), posttraumatic stress disorder (Lee, 2009a), and psychosis (Mayhew & Gilbert, 2008).

What is compassion-focused therapy?

Gilbert and Irons (2005) emphasized the value of focusing on self-compassion and generating new feelings in the self-evaluative process. Compassion-focused therapy (Gilbert, 1989, 2000, 2007) aims to help individuals facilitate an emotional shift toward a more caring and supportive relationship with the self that undermines self-attack, enhances self-acceptance, and reduces emotional disturbance, thus enabling a person to become more self-soothing and self-regulating of internal (self-evaluations) and external (other people's evaluations of you) threats. Gilbert and Irons (2005) highlighted the need to train clients to develop a compassionate mind to access the emotional experience of inner compassion and warmth. Given the observed difficulties and resistance that self-critics have to offering warmth and understanding to themselves, they suggest that repeated practice will aid the formation of or strengthen existing neuronal networks in the brain (thought to be associated with the affect of self-soothing) in a way that makes the networks sensitized and readily triggered when an individual engages in the process of self-soothing. They also suggest that this is a necessary prerequisite to cognitive challenging of critical thoughts. The cognitive focus alone may not create or stimulate the emotional experience associated with self-acceptance, self-soothing, and the ability to tolerate distress.

Integrating theory with practice

In this next section, I explore how one can use a compassionate focus in cognitive therapy to work with shame and self-attack. We return to Jennifer and use her case to illustrate the key approaches.

Developing a compassionate mind

Being compassionate to yourself is a state of mind, just as feeling threatened is a state of mind. States of mind are related to physiological responses in the body that govern behaviors, thought processes, and attention that are compatible with the needs and goals of the individual at that time. CFT targets the development of a compassionate mentality by the stimulation of physiological responses associated with self-soothing in three stages: (1) by modeling key characteristics of a compassionate mind (behavior, thoughts, attention, and affect) in the context of a therapeutic relationship and by developing a compassion-focused formulation; (2) by decentering from the critical voice and explicitly teaching and training clients in the practice of being compassionate to the self; and (3) by using compassionate imagery, compassionate letter writing, and third-chair practice to aid access to the physiological state of self-soothing and to help individuals access compassionate reframes to their self-critical dialogues. These three key phases are explored next.

Phase 1. Therapeutic relationship

The therapeutic relationship provides the foundation for this work, and a compassionate mind is demonstrated, modeled, encouraged, and reinforced by the therapist. Specific focus is given to (1) the ability to tolerate painful emotions and validate the distress experienced; (2) the ability to be sensitive and recognize being upset and distressed; (3) the ability to be moved by one's own distress; (4) the ability to have warmth, kindness, and genuine care for one's well-being; (5) the ability to be noncondemning of one's thoughts, actions, and feelings; and (6) the ability to understand the nature of the distress. It is these qualities, Gilbert suggested, that create opportunities for growth and change in an individual through the development of a supporting, caring, kind, and warm relationship with the self.

The therapy focus is explicit in developing empathy for the non-intentionality of their difficulties and struggles in life and the understanding that their problems are not their fault. For example, the therapist may encourage statements such as, "I did not intend for my life to work out like this. This would not have been the script I would write for my life." Indeed, the therapist may gently repeat at appropriate times, "This is not your fault," as Socratic questioning can be limited in generating a more balanced and meaningful perspective on the issue of fault and blame (e.g., "I was just born bad; I just am fundamentally different and I can't feel any other way"). It is common for clients to find a compassionate relationship aversive at first. They will struggle to accept that they deserve help, kindness, and understanding. It can take many months before clients are able to connect emotionally with the fact that their difficulties are not their fault. Yet, this experience is a milestone in the journey of developing a compassionate mind. When individuals are able to accept that their struggles are not their fault, they can begin to grieve for their loss, validate their pain, and take responsibility for changing their life. This process begins by helping the client understand the evolutionary model of human functioning that is embedded in seeking to understand the function of threat and safety-seeking behaviors as part of human survival.

Formulating cases with a compassionate mind

Similar to other therapies, clients are encouraged to make sense of their difficulties by using a shared formulation. Compassion-focused therapy helps clients link their current difficulties to their personal history, life-time struggles, and key fears. Clients are encouraged to adopt a nonjudgmental, wise, and empathic stance to help them gain insight into: "It's not my fault that I am having difficulties." Sometimes it can be helpful to begin your discussion by looking at safety strategies as behaviors designed to avoid both internal and external threats. This is because presenting problems are often safety strategies (e.g., alcohol abuse, bingeing/purging, deliberate self-harm, social avoidance, withdrawal). Before taking a look at Jennifer's formulation, I have outlined below a suggested sequence to explore an individual's experience using a threat-focused, transdiagnostic formulation (Gilbert & Irons, 2005):

1. *Explore the safety strategies*—Ask your client to explain his or her presenting problems; for example, "I can't go out. I avoid people, I drink too much, I make myself sick, and I put everyone else's needs first." Emphasize to them that these behaviors make sense as ways to avoid feelings of shame and anxiety.
2. *Identify external and internal threats and key memories*—Inquire what triggers the client's safety strategies (e.g., "I think people know what happened to me") and what the client fears would happen if people found out about him or her (e.g., "They will think I am disgusting, they will not want to know me, and they will reject me"). Is the client able to recall key memories from childhood or adulthood that convey a similar threat, such as a key memory of abuse or being bullied? Emphasize the sadness of the client's experiences and the validation of the fear the client feels as an adult.
3. *Unintended consequences*—Explore with your client the fact that it is understandable that the client engages in safety strategies to avoid the feared consequences of internal or external threats. Explain that the client's best efforts to keep safe have unintended consequences (e.g., loss of identity, feeling of social isolation, poor physical health).
4. *Self-criticism*—Explore the fact that your client criticizes his or her own best efforts to keep safe (e.g., "You're so weak and pathetic; why can't you just talk normally to people?"). Explain that the brain responds to self-attacks by mobilizing the threat response. Explore the fact that the client is trapped in a cycle of shaming self-attack that maintains the client's safety strategies. Thus, the client is more likely to engage in self-defeating behaviors when feeling shame or distress.
5. *Childhood experiences*—Help your client put a historical perspective on his or her struggles by exploring childhood experiences and key memories. Use compassion and empathic validation to promote an understanding that, given what they have been through as a child, it is understandable that the client is fearful and behaves the way he or she does.

Jennifer's compassion-focused formulation

A compassion-focused formulation was helpful in treating Jennifer. The focus of the shared formulation was to assist her in developing the insight that the rape and childhood abuse were not her fault and that it was understandable that she blamed herself given her previous experiences of childhood. We explored the notion that her self-attack could be seen as a safety behavior in that, if she blamed herself for her attack, she could perhaps keep it from happening again. We also hypothesized that the flashbacks both to the rape and childhood sexual abuse were maintained by thoughts of self-loathing and self-attack ("I am bad; I am disgusting and a worthless piece of nothing"). This in turn was associated with overwhelming feelings of shame. We explored how Jennifer found these feelings so painful that she engaged in attempts to avoid thoughts and feelings related to the attack by cutting herself and misusing alcohol.

Using an evolutionary focused formulation (Gilbert & Irons, 2005), we discussed that, as a result of Jennifer's early experiences of abuse and parenting, it made sense that she had real fears about being hated and rejected by others. It made sense that she believed that she was a disgusting, bad person who deserved to have bad things happen to her (i.e., she deserved to be raped). We explored how difficult and frightening it must have been for Jennifer when her mother was emotionally absent and unable to protect Jennifer from both physical and psychological threat. We discussed how frightened and alone Jennifer felt as a child. We explored how frightening and confusing it must have been to be touched by her uncle in a sexual way. We discussed how sad and confusing it must have been for Jennifer's dad to die when she was 4 years old. We explored how, as a result of these childhood experiences, her brain was highly threat focused and that it responded to threat-related stimuli (such as fear of attack, other people's opinions of her, and her own thoughts about herself) by releasing stress hormones and mobilizing the body's resources to manage the threat by, for example, avoidance of others and not wanting to go out, deliberate self-harm, and misuse of alcohol.

We developed a shared understanding that Jennifer's attempts to regulate the exposure to threat and experience of shame by withdrawing from others and deliberate self-harm made sense and were not her fault. However, they had unintended consequences for her, such as feeling isolated and disconnected from others, physical health problems from alcohol and drug abuse, and embarrassing scarring from self-harm. We hypothesized that Jennifer needed to develop other, more helpful ways to self-soothe, to manage threat by developing a compassionate and supportive self dialogue, to end the cycle of self-attack that was maintaining her flashbacks.

Phase 2. Ending maintenance cycles by working with critical dialogues

As discussed above, Jennifer was very self-critical. Similar to cognitive therapy, helping Jennifer to decenter from her critical dialogues was a key process to help her understand that her inner dialogue is learned (i.e., it is opinion, not fact). So, to develop this insight I asked Jennifer:

T. What exactly do you say to yourself in your head?

J. "You deserve to suffer. You are disgusting. No one wants you. You are a worthless piece of nothing. You are bad. You are toxic."

T. Whose voice do you hear? Has anyone ever said those things to you?

J. Well, it's a mixture of my uncle, my mum, and the boys who bullied me at school.

T. What do you make of that?

J. That's interesting, as I never realized that before, but I can see my uncle saying things to me in my head now.

T. What do you think is the function of your critical voice? Is it trying to protect you, motivate you, or destroy you?

J. It's definitely trying to bring me down and make me feel bad, like it's my fault.

T. Is it your fault?

J. Well, I feel like it is, because I feel it in my memories.

T. What makes you believe what it says without question?

J. I don't know. I just always have thought it was who I am.

T. What qualities and personal attributes does your critic have?

J. My uncle was creepy. He always made me feel bad and uncomfortable. Those boys at school were just plain mean.

T. Are their qualities ones that you admire in people?

J. No, not at all.

T. Is their opinion worth accepting unchallenged?

J. No, I suppose not, but I hadn't really realized that they were the ones who were making me think these things about myself. I just always thought it was me.

T. Can you imagine the critical part of yourself if you close your eyes? What does it look like, facial expression, tone of voice, size, characteristics, qualities?

J. Oh, I can see him winking at me and telling me I deserve this. His eyes freak me out. It's definitely my uncle.

T. Okay, what does that tell you?

J. I speak to myself like my uncle used to speak to me, but the problem is that I feel it is true.

T. Yes, I can see that, and are you able to hold onto the fact that you were made to believe these things about yourself?

J. Yes, I can.

We used another useful strategy to help Jennifer decenter from the critic—the two-chairs technique (Greenberg et al., 1993; Whelton & Greenberg, 2005). One chair represents the bully and the other represents the bullied. In one chair, Jennifer demonstrated what her critical voice might say to her, and in the other chair Jennifer explored how it felt to be on the receiving end of such condemnatory thoughts. This technique allowed Jennifer to see that her critical voice was a form of self–self relating. This exercise was quite a revelation to her, as she was able to see the extent of the hostility she directed at herself.

Developing self-soothing relationships

Next we embarked on a path of teaching Jennifer to self-soothe using the model of compassionate mind to stimulate a care-focused mentality associated with self-soothing and warmth. Although I had already been modeling and demonstrating the qualities of compassion (outlined in the previous section), we spent some time together discussing the qualities in terms of what they meant and how Jennifer would demonstrate them to herself. We paid particular attention to Jennifer's fears about being compassionate to herself and worked with these fears by offering empathic validation rather than challenging them. I helped Jennifer to develop a more supportive relationship with herself by training her, using the following pointers when she was struggling (Gilbert & Irons, 2005):

- What would compassionate attention attend to or focus on?
- What would compassionate thinking reflect?
- What would be a compassionate way to behave?
- How could you bring warmth, understanding, and acceptance into your experience?
- What would help you feel supported?
- What would you say to or do for someone you cared for?
- What would someone who cared for you say or do to help soothe you?

Helping Jennifer develop a compassionate reframe to the rape

The compassionate reframe is not about dismantling the evidence that supports the self-blame and building up a body of new evidence to support an alternative belief. Rather, it is about generating an alternative way of being with the self that is accepting, warm, caring, understanding, and supportive. For example, a compassionate reframe for the belief "I am worthless" may be "I understand why you want to blame yourself. It makes sense given what you have been through in the past and how hard you have found it to be kind to yourself. It's understandable that you are so sad and distressed, but this is not your fault. Focus on the warmth, care, and kindness you have for yourself. Allow yourself to accept the support you have for yourself. Allow yourself to feel the warmth you have for yourself in your body. This is not your fault."

Once Jennifer was able to develop and use self-soothing dialogues, we were able to revisit the memories of the rape and specifically reevaluate the meaning using Jennifer's compassionate part of her mind. Jennifer was able to update her thoughts of "You are dirty and disgusting" with a compassionate reframe: "This is so sad that you have suffered like this. You don't deserve this. Focus on the feelings of warmth and kindness you have for yourself." This new emotional experience became meaningful to Jennifer because it seemed to trigger a physiological response in her body that felt warm and soothing. We then revisited the flashback by using the technique of reliving (Ehlers, Michael, Chen, Payne, & Shan, 2006; Grey, Young, & Holmes, 2002) and updated the emotional experience of the flashback by asking Jennifer "What do you know now?" while she kept the image in mind, to which Jennifer responded, "This is so sad that you have suffered like this. You don't deserve this. Focus on the feelings of warmth and kindness you have for yourself." Jennifer focused on the feelings of warmth, compassion, and safeness while still reliving the flashback. Thus, the memory of the rape was experienced as a sad memory as opposed to a shameful one (Lee, 2009b). Jennifer was then able to begin to get in touch with the sadness and grief she felt for herself having been through such a painful experience. Her flashbacks to this event resolved within two sessions once she was able to access the feeling of self-soothing.

Phase 3. Using compassionate imagery to develop self-soothing

Jennifer was still struggling with thoughts of being dirty and deserving of punishment. Although she had successfully resolved her thoughts and feelings abut the rape, she still struggled to come to terms with her memories of childhood sexual abuse. These memories still had a powerful influence on how she felt about herself, and Jennifer was pugnacious with her compassionate mind on the issue of self-blame. At this stage, we decided to develop a compassionate image to help her revisit memories of abuse while being able to access the affect of self-soothing.

The use of imagery in cognitive therapy has become widespread and popular in recent years, as it appears to be highly effective in changing emotional states (Giesen-Bloo et al., 2006; Gilbert, 2005; Hackmann, 2005; Hirsch, Clark, & Mathews, 2006; Holmes & Hackmann, 2004; Smucker,

Dancu, Foa, & Niederie, 1995; Wheatley, Brewin, Hackmann, & Wells, 2007). The use of compassionate imagery is also proving effective in generating positive affect and feelings of self-soothing (Gilbert, Baldwin, Irons, Baccus, & Palmer, 2006). Perfect nurturer imagery (Lee, 2005) is a form of compassionate imagery that is based on a fantasy notion of an inner helper created especially to meet needs perfectly—the need for caring, kindness, emotional nurturing, strength, and connectedness. It is created to be beyond human failing; it can never let you down or fail to say what you need to hear when you are distressed. It is has your mind in mind, and care for your well-being is paramount to it. Perfect nurturer imagery is not prescriptive, and clients are encouraged to generate their own image. Some clients develop images of animals such as lions, some conjure up angelic images or Mother Earth images, while others come up with cartoon-like characters (for examples of perfect nurturer images, see Lee, 2005).

It is used with the specific purposes of stimulating positive affect associated with a sense of safeness, increasing access to internalized images of loving others, and increasing a sense of connectedness with humanity. The image can be used to work with critical dialogues and shame-based flashbacks. Also, the two-chairs practice (discussed earlier) can be enhanced by introducing a third chair to represent the compassionate mind. The client is then asked to respond to the bully and the bullied by offering a compassionate response that demonstrates the qualities of the compassionate mind.

Developing perfect nurturer images

In this phase of therapy prior to developing perfect nurturing imagery, we establish with the client the characteristics they would want in a fantastical image or inner helper that would always be able to nurture them and provide help and support when needed. Jennifer, for example, said she wanted her image to be unconditionally loving, strong, wise, accepting, and warm; it should understand her struggles and genuinely care about her. I asked her to identify a distinctive smell associated with positive feelings, and we used this smell during the imagery rehearsal with the specific intent to encourage a conditioned emotional response to the trigger smell. I then guided her through the development of this imagery using the following instructions:

- Sit comfortably and close your eyes.
- Focus on your breathing for a minute or so.
- Allow an image to come to mind that represents a "perfect nurturer" for you—an image that would always have your best interests at heart and that would never let you down, an image that would

support and comfort you when you are distressed and offer you warmth and wisdom to deal with your struggles.

- Focus on the physical appearance of the image (size, color), the texture of the image, and the smell of your image.
- Focus on the sound of the voice as it speaks to you and the relationship you would like to have with the perfect nurturer.
- Focus on the empathy and understanding your image has for you, focus on the feelings of warmth for you, and focus on the fact that your image can tolerate your distress with you and that it is valid to feel this way.
- Focus on the feeling in your body generated by the image.

Using perfect nurturer images to work with shame flashbacks

When Jennifer was well rehearsed in the art of accessing the feelings associated with self-soothing using her perfect nurturer image, we agreed to revisit a painful memory of childhood abuse. This time, however, Jennifer brought this positive affect into the memory. To achieve this, we followed the steps outlined below:

- We began by identifying the shame-triggering memory.
- We discussed the key threat and affect associated with the memory.
- We discussed what Jennifer would need to be different about the memory to help her feel soothed and safe.
- Jennifer worked out what she would like her perfect nurturer to say to soothe her.
- We discussed how Jennifer would like to feel in the memory.
- We decided to use her suggested smell of soap as a trigger for the self-soothing affect while bringing the flashback to mind.
- Jennifer began to recount the memory using a reliving paradigm.

I asked Jennifer to bring up the image and affect (triggered by smelling soap) and allow her image to speak to her and comfort her by bringing in a compassionate reframe (Lee, 2009b). She had worked out how she wanted her perfect nurturer to support her and help her feel soothed and safe in the flashback.

In total, Jennifer attended 30 sessions. The first 16 sessions used trauma-focused CBT and cognitive therapy to work with her symptoms of posttraumatic stress disorder and to address her deliberate self-harm and alcohol abuse. Jennifer made good progress in these sessions and was able to reduce many unhelpful safety strategies and develop new beliefs about the rape and to some extent about the childhood sexual abuse; however, she was unable to feel reassured or comforted by these thoughts, as they did not make her feel differently about herself. Although she understood that she was not to blame, she could not let herself fully believe this. She continued to suffer from distressing flashbacks to these events. Fundamentally, Jennifer did not believe she deserved to be let off the hook as she still felt bad and worthless. When we began to reconsider her difficulties from a threat-focused perspective and helped her develop a compassionate mind, she began to make some progress again. In some respects, this work progressed relatively quickly given the extent of her difficulties. The turning point in therapy was when Jennifer realized the extent of the sadness and pain locked in her childhood memories. When she was able to accept that her experiences in childhood were not her fault, she began to care for herself, validate her pain, and treat herself with kindness. Then, she was able to truly believe that she was not raped and abused because she was bad. The latter part of therapy focused on working directly with flashbacks by using her compassionate imagery. This approach seemed to help Jennifer experience a more helpful and soothing emotion in the flashback, and her flashbacks resolved within weeks.

Conclusions

This chapter described the role of shame and self-attack in psychological distress, which may prove difficult to treat with standard approaches to cognitive therapy. A framework for using compassionate mind to enhance the effectiveness of cognitive therapy has been presented. In particular, the client's ability to self-soothe using compassionate self-talk and the use of compassionate imagery are highlighted as important ways of working with shame and self-attack. This is because those who struggle to self-soothe often struggle to feel the congruent emotional valence of new perspectives and beliefs that have been developed using more traditional cognitive therapy techniques. The use of compassionate imagery appears particularly effective when working with shame-based difficulties, especially if individuals have shame-based flashbacks and vivid sensory memories of shameful experiences. Facing painful memories and multiple losses endured throughout a lifetime is sometimes overwhelming for clients, especially when they feel so undeserving of love and kindness. Such beliefs of undeservedness can present a significant block to developing compassion for the self as it is always difficult to accept things you do not think you deserve.

Acknowledgments

I would like to thank my clients who kindly gave me permission to write about them and Professor Paul Gilbert for his knowledge, support, and guidance in my development of his work in my clinical practice.

References

American Psychiatric Association. (2000). *Diagnostic and statistical manual of mental disorders* (4th ed., revised). Arlington, VA: American Psychiatric Association.

Andrews, B. (1995). Bodily shame as a mediator between childhood sexual abuse and depression. *Journal of Abnormal Psychology, 104,* 277–285.

Andrews, B., Brewin, C.R., Rose, S., & Kirk, M. (2000). Predicting PTSD symptoms in victims of violent crime: the role of shame, anger, and childhood abuse. *Journal of Abnormal Psychology, 109,* 69–73.

Arntz, A., & Weertman, A. (1999). Treatment of childhood memories: Theory and practice. *Behaviour Research and Therapy, 37,* 715–740.

Baldwin, M.W., & Fergusson, P. (2001). Relational schemas: The activation of inter-personal knowledge structures in social anxiety. In W.R. Crozier & L.E. Alden (Eds.), *International handbook of social anxiety: Concepts, research and interventions to the self and shyness* (pp. 235–257). New York: John Wiley & Sons.

Beck, A.T. (1976). *Cognitive therapy and the emotional disorders.* New York: International Universities Press.

Beck, A.T., & Emery, G. (1985). *Anxiety disorders and phobias: A cognitive perspective.* New York: Basic Books.

Beck, A.T., Brown, G.K., Berchick, R.J., Stewart, B.L., & Steer, R.A. (1990). Relationship between hopelessness and ultimate suicide: A replication with psychiatric outpatients. *American Journal of Psychiatry, 147*(2), 190–195.

Blatt, S.J., & Zuroff, D.C. (1992). Interpersonal relatedness and self-definition: Two prototypes for depression. *Clinical Psychology Review, 12,* 527–562.

Bowlby, J. (1969). *Attachment and loss* (Vol. 1). London: Hogarth Press.

Brown, H. (1991). Shame and relapse issues in the chemically dependent client. *Alcoholism Treatment Quarterly, 8,* 77–82.

Carter, C.S. (1998). Neuroendocrine perspectives on social attachment and love. *Psychoneuroendrocrinology, 23,* 779–818.

Clark, D.M. (1986). A cognitive approach to panic. *Behaviour Research and Therapy, 24,* 461–170.

Conway, M.A., & Holmes, E.A. (2004). Autobiographical memory and the working self. In N.R. Braisby & A.R.H. Gellatly (Eds.), *Cognitive psychology.* Oxford, U.K.: Oxford University Press.

Conway, M.A., & Pleydell-Pearce, C.W. (2000). The construction of autobiographical memories in the self-memory system. *Psychology Review, 107*(2), 261–288.

Depue, R.A., & Morrone-Strupinsky, J.V. (2005). A neurobehavioural model of affiliative bonding. *Behavioural and Brain Sciences, 28,* 313–395.

Ehlers, A., Clark, D.M., Hackmann, A., McManus, F., & Fennell, M. (2005). Cognitive therapy for PTSD: Development and evaluation. *Behaviour Research and Therapy, 43,* 413–431.

Ehlers, A., Michael, T., Chen, Y.P., Payne, E., & Shan, S. (2006). Enhanced perceptual priming for neutral stimuli in a traumatic context: A pathway to intrusive memories? *Memory, 12,* 316–328.

Fonagy, P., & Target, M. (2006). The mentalisation-focused approach to self pathology. *Journal of Personality Disorders, 20,* 544–576.

Giesen-Bloo, J., van Dyck, R., Spinhoven, P., van Tilburg, W., Dirksen, C., van Asselt, T. et al. (2006). Outpatient psychotherapy for BPD: randomised trial of schema focused therapy vs. transference focused psychotherapy. *Archives of General Psychiatry, 63*(6), 649–658.

Gilbert, P. (1989). *Human nature and suffering*. Hove, U.K.: Psychology Press.

Gilbert, P. (1998). What is shame? Some core issues and controversies. In B. Andrews (Ed.), *Shame: interpersonal behaviour, psychopathology and culture* (pp. 3–38). New York: Oxford University Press.

Gilbert, P. (2000). Social mentalities: Internal social conflicts and the role of inner warmth and compassion in therapy. In P. Gilbert and K.G. Bailey (Eds.), *Genes on the couch: Explorations in evolutionary psychotherapy* (pp. 118–150). Hove, U.K.: Psychology Press.

Gilbert, P. (2005) *Compassion: Conceptualisations, research and use in psychotherapy*. London: Routledge.

Gilbert, P. (2007). *Psychotherapy and counselling for depression* (3rd ed.). London: Sage Publications.

Gilbert, P., & Irons, C. (2004). A pilot exploration of the use of compassionate images in a group of self-critical people. *Memory, 12*, 507–516.

Gilbert, P., & Irons, C. (2005). Focused therapies and compassionate mind training for shame and self attacking. In *Compassion and psychotherapy: Theory, research and practice*. London: Routledge.

Gilbert, P., & McGuire, M. (1998). Shame, social roles, and status: The psychobiological continuum from monkey to human. In P. Gilbert & B. Andrews (Eds.), *Shame: Interpersonal behavior, psychopathology, and culture* (pp. 99–125). New York: Oxford University Press.

Gilbert, P., & Miles, J. (2000). Sensitivity to social putdown: Its relationship to perceptions of shame, social anxiety, depression, anger and self–other blame. *Personality and individual differences, 29*, 757–774.

Gilbert, P., & Proctor, S. (2006). Compassionate mind training for people with high shame and self criticism: Overview and pilot study of a group therapy approach. *Clinical Psychology and Psychotherapy, 13*, 353–379.

Gilbert, P., & Trower, P. (1990). The evolution and manifestation of social anxiety. In W.R. Crozier (Eds.), *Shyness and embarrassment: Perspectives in social psychology*, Cambridge, U.K.: Cambridge University Press.

Gilbert, P., Baldwin, M., Irons, C., Baccus, J., & Palmer, M. (2006). Self-criticism and self-warmth: An imagery study exploring their relation to depression. *Journal of Cognitive Psychotherapy: An International Quarterly, 20*, 183–200.

Gilbert, P., Pehl, J., & Allen, S. (1994). The phenonemology of shame and guilt: An empirical investigation. *British Journal of Medical Psychology, 67*, 23–36.

Gillath, O., Bunge, S.A., Shaver, P.R., Wendelken, C., & Mikulincer, M. (2005). Attachment-style differences in the ability to suppress negative thoughts: Exploring the neural correlates. *NeuroImage (Special Issue, Social Cognitive Neuroscience), 28*, 835–847.

Greenberg, L.S. (1979). Resolving splits: Use of two chair technique. *Psychotherapy, Theory, Research and Practice, 16*, 316–324.

Greenberg, L.S. (2007). Emotion in the therapeutic relationship in emotion focused therapy. In P. Gilbert & R. Leahy (Eds.), *The therapeutic relationship in the cognitive behavioural psychotherapies* (pp. 43–62). London: Routledge.

Greenberg, L.S., Rice, L.N., & Elliot, R. (1993). *Facilitating emotional change: The moment-by-moment process*. New York: Guilford Press.

Grey, N., Young, K.A., & Holmes, E.A. (2002). Cognitive restructuring within reliving: A treatment for peritraumatic emotional "hotspots" in post-traumatic stress disorder. *Behavioural and Cognitive Psychotherapy, 30*, 37–56.

Hackmann, A. (1998). Working with images in clinical psychology. In A. Bellack and M. Herson (Eds.), *Comprehensive clinical psychology* (pp. 301–317). London: Pergamon Press.

Hackmann, A. (2005). Compassionate imagery in the treatment of early memories in Axis I anxiety disorders. In P. Gilbert (Ed.), *Compassion: Conceptualisations, research, and use in psychotherapy* (pp. 352–368). Hove, U.K.: Brunner-Routledge.

Haidt, J. (2001). The emotional dog and its rational tail: A social intuitionist approach to moral judgement. *Psychological review, 108*, 814–834.

Harman, R., & Lee, D.A. (in press). The role of self-attack and self-soothing in the maintenance of shame-based PTSD. *Psychology and Psychotherapy: Theory, Research, and Practice.*

Hirsch, C.R., Clark, D.M., & Mathews, A. (2006). Imagery and interpretations in social phobia: Support for the combined cognitive biases hypothesis. *Behavior Therapy, 37*, 223-236.

Holmes, E.A., & Hackman, A. (2004). A healthy imagination? [editorial]. *Memory: Mental Imagery and Memory in Psychopathology, 12*(4), 387–388.

Holmes, E.A., Grey, N., & Young, K.A. (2005). Intrusive images and "hotspots" of trauma memories in posttraumatic stress disorder: An explanatory investigation of emotions and cognitive themes *Journal of Behaviour Therapy and Experimental Psychiatry 36*(1), 3–17.

Irons, C., Gilbert, P., Baldwin, M.W., Baccus, J., & Palmer, M. (2006). Parental recall-attachment relating and self-attacking/self-reassurance: Their relationship with depression. *British Journal of Clinical Psychology, 45*, 297–308.

Kaufman, G. (1989). *The psychology of shame: Theory and treatment of shame-based syndromes*. New York: Springer.

Layden, M.A., Newman, C.F., Freeman, A., & Morse, S.B. (1993). *Cognitive therapy of borderline personality disorder*. Boston, MA: Allyn & Bacon.

Leahy, R.L. (1999). *Overcoming resistance in cognitive therapy*. New York: Guilford Press.

Leahy, R.L. (2007). Schematic mismatch in the therapeutic relationship: A social–cognitive model. In P. Gilbert & R.L. Leahy (Eds.), *The therapeutic relationship in the cognitive behavioral psychotherapies* (pp. 229–254). New York: Routledge.

LeDoux, J.E. (1998). *The emotional brain*. London: Weidenfeld & Nicolson.

Lee, D.A. (2005). The perfect nurturer: A model to develop compassion within cognitive therapy. In P. Gilbert (Ed.), *Compassion and psychotherapy: Theory, research and practice* (pp. 326–351). Hove, U.K.: Brunner-Routledge.

Lee, D.A. (2006). Case conceptualisation in complex PTSD: Integrating theory with practice. In N. Tarrier, (Ed.), *Case formulation in cognitive behaviour therapy: The treatment of challenging and complex cases*. London: Routledge.

Lee, D.A. (2009a). Compassion-focused cognitive therapy for shame-based trauma memories and flashbacks in posttraumatic stress disorder. In N. Grey (Ed.), *A casebook of cognitive therapy for traumatic stress reactions* (pp. 230–246). Hove, U.K.: Brunner-Routledge.

Lee, D.A. (2009b). *Using compassion in cognitive therapy.* Oxford, U.K.: Oxford Cognitive Learning Center.

Lee, D.A., Scragg, P., & Turner, S.W. (2001). The role of shame and guilt in traumatic events: A clinical model of shame based and guilt-based PTSD. *British Journal of Medical Psychology, 74*, 451–466.

MacFarlane, F. (2008). *Compassionate mind training in adolescents: A pilot study.* Doctoral dissertation, University College London, University of London.

Mayhew, S.L., & Gilbert, P. (2008). Compassionate mind training with people who hear malevolent voices: A case series report. *Clinical Psychology and Psychotherapy, 15*, 113–138.

McCann, I.L., & Pearlman, L.A. (1992). Constructivist self development theory: A theoretical model of psychological adaptation to severe trauma. In D.K. Sakheim & S.E Devine (Eds.), *Out of darkness: Exploring satanism and ritual abuse* (pp. 185–206). New York: Lexington Books.

Mikulincer, M., & Shaver, P. R. (2005). Attachment security, compassion, and altruism. *Current Directions in Psychological Science, 14*, 34–38.

Mikulincer, M., & Sheffi, E. (2000). Adult attachment style and cognitive reactions to positive affect: A test of mental categorisation and creative problem solving. *Motivation and Emotion. 24*, 149–174.

Mikulincer, M., Shaver, P.R., & Pereg, D. (2003). Attachment theory and affect regulation: The dynamics, development and cognitive consequences of attachment-related strategies. *Motivation and Emotion, 27*, 77–102.

Pearlman, L.A., & McCann, L.L. (1994). Integrating structured and unstructured approaches to taking a trauma history. In M.B. Williams & J. Sommer, Jr. (Eds.), *Handbook of post-traumatic therapy* (pp. 38–48). Westport, CT: Greenwood Press.

Power, M., & Dalgleish, T. (1997). *Cognition and emotion.* Hove, U.K.: Psychology Press.

Rector, N.A., Bagby, R.M., Segal, Z.V., Joffe, R.T., & Levitt, A. (2000). Self-criticism and dependency in depressed patients treated with cognitive therapy or pharmacotherapy. *Cognitive Therapy and Research, 24*, 571–584.

Repetti, R.L., Taylor, S.E., & Seeman, T.E. (2002). Risky families: family social environments and the mental and physical health of offspring. *Psychological Bulletin, 128*, 330–366.

Rogers, C. (1957). The necessary and sufficient conditions of therapeutic change. *Journal of Consulting Psychology, 21*, 95–103.

Roth, A., & Fonagy, P. (2007). *What works for whom: A critical review of psychotherapy research.* New York: Guilford Press.

Ryff, C.D., Singer, B.H., Wing, E., & Lobe, G.D. (2001). Elective affinities and uninvited agonies: Mapping emotion with significant others onto health. In C.D. Ryff & B.H. Singer (Eds.), *Relationship experience and emotional wellbeing* (pp. 133–174). Oxford, U.K.: Oxford University Press.

Ryle, A. (1990). *Cognitive–analytic therapy: Active participation in change.* Chichester: John Wiley & Sons.

Salkovskis, P.M., Forrester, E., Richards, H.C., & Morrison, N. (1998). The devil is in the detail: conceptualising and treating obsessional problems. In N. Tarrier (Ed.), *Cognitive behaviour therapy for complex cases.* New York: John Wiley & Sons.

Savege Scharff, J., & Tsigounis, S.A. (Eds.) (2003). *Self hatred in psychoanalysis: Detoxifying the persecutory object*. New York: Routledge.

Smucker, M.C., Dancu, C., Foa, E.B., & Niederie, J.L. (1995). Image rescripting: A new treatment for survivors of childhood sexual abuse suffering from post-traumatic stress disorder. *Journal of Cognitive Psychotherapy, 9*, 3–17.

Sookman, D., & Pinard, G. (2007). Specialized cognitive behavior therapy for resistant obsessive compulsive disorder: Elaboration of a schema-based model. In L.P. Riso, P.L. du Toit, D.J. Stein, & J.E. Young (Eds.), *Cognitive schemas and core beliefs in psychological problems: A scientist–practitioner guide* (pp. 93–109). Washington, D.C.: American Psychological Association.

Tangney, J.P., & Dearing, R.L. (2002). *Shame and guilt*. New York: Guilford Press.

Taylor, S.E., Dickerson, S.S., & Klein, L.C. (2002). Toward a biology of social support. In C.R. Snyder & S.J. Lopez (Eds.), *Handbook of positive psychology* (pp. 556–569). Oxford, U.K.: Oxford University Press.

Teasdale, J.D., & Barnard, P.J. (1993). *Affect, cognition and change: Remodelling depressive affect*. Mahwah, NJ: Lawrence Erlbaum.

Uvnäs-Morberg, K. (1998). Oxytocin may mediate the benefits of positive social interaction and emotions. *Psychoneuroendocrinology, 23*, 819–835.

Wang, S. (2005). A conceptual framework for integrating research related to the physiology of compassion and the wisdom of Buddhist teachings. In P. Gilbert (Ed.), *Compassion and psychotherapy: Theory, research, and practice* (pp. 75–120). Hove, U.K.: Brunner-Routledge.

Wheatley, J., Brewin, C.R., Hackmann, A., & Wells, A. (2007). Imagery rescripting of intrusive sensory memories in depression. *Behaviour therapy and experimental psychiatry, 38*, 371–385.

Whelton, W.J., & Greenberg, L.S. (2005). Emotion in self-criticism. *Personality and Individual Differences, 38*, 1583–1595.

Zuroff, D.C., Koestner, R., & Powers, T.A. (1994). Self-criticism at age 12: A longitudinal study of adjustment. *Cognitive Therapy and Research, 18*, 367–385.

chapter nine

Suggestions from acceptance and commitment therapy for dealing with treatment-resistant obsessive–compulsive disorder

Michael P. Twohig
Utah State University
Logan, Utah

Jennifer C. Plumb
Dahlia Mukherjee
Steven C. Hayes
University of Nevada
Reno, Nevada

Contents

Introduction and definition

Obsessive–compulsive disorder (OCD), classified as an anxiety disorder, is characterized in the *Diagnostic and Statistical Manual of Mental Disorders* (DSM-IV-TR) (American Psychiatric Association, 2000) by distressing intrusive thoughts and unwanted repetitive behaviors that cause functional interference. A functional relationship exists between obsessions and compulsions, with almost 90% of people with OCD engaging in the compulsion in response to the obsession (Foa & Kozak, 1995). Current estimates indicate that 1% of the U.S. population (or 2.2 million people) meet criteria for OCD each year (Kessler, Chiu, Demler, & Walters, 2005). The age of onset ranges between early adolescence and early adulthood, usually with an earlier onset in men than women (Rasmussen & Eisen, 1992); a slightly greater percentage of women are diagnosed with OCD, although pediatric clinical cases show a 2:1 male-to-female ratio (Hanna, 1995). Approximately 50 to 75% of those diagnosed with OCD are simultaneously diagnosed with another psychological disorder, with anxiety and mood disorders being the most common (Antony, Downie, & Swinson, 1998). Other psychological disorders that may commonly co-occur with OCD include substance dependence, eating disorders, body dysmorphic disorder, and Tourette's disorder and other tic-related disorders (Antony et al., 1998).

Obsessive–compulsive disorder as defined in the DSM-IV is based on functional criteria without regard for the form the disorder takes or the cognitive processes involved, but those who work with this disorder have found that approach to be too limiting. Attempts have been made to better categorize subtypes of OCD without agreement on the best way to do so. One approach has been to divide them by topographical categories, such as cleaning and washing, checking, symmetry, hoarding, obsessional slowness, and primary obsessions, among others (Taylor, McKay, & Abramowitz, 2008). Although there is usually a predominant obsession and corresponding compulsion, most people with OCD have multiple obsessions and compulsions and variations in severity and intensity. The Obsessive Compulsive Cognitions Working Group (1997) identified a number of beliefs and appraisals hypothesized to be associated with the etiology and maintenance of OCD (e.g., overimportance and need to control thoughts, overestimation of threat, inflated responsibility). Contemporary cognitive treatments for OCD directly target these appraisals and beliefs (e.g., Wilhelm & Steketee, 2006) throughout treatment.

Even though the field has progressed in the treatment of OCD, there are still areas where mental health professionals struggle with its treatment. This chapter offers insights and suggestions from acceptance and commitment therapy (ACT, said as one word) (Hayes, Strosahl, & Wilson, 1999) in the management of some of these issues. In order to accomplish this, we provide a brief description of the philosophy, research, and model of psychopathology that informs ACT and the corresponding treatment model.

This chapter does not focus heavily on the similarities and differences between ACT and currently empirically supported approaches to the treatment of OCD. This is an important issue, but it is complicated by the fact that most of these methods come from cognitive–behavioral therapy (CBT). ACT is part of the CBT family of interventions; it is essentially a model of how to do CBT. So far as we know, all of the empirically supported individual components or elements of CBT approaches for OCD (e.g., exposure) are compatible with an ACT model. Distinguishing an ACT model from other models of CBT raises issues that go beyond the current topic, but there are theoretical papers on this topic (e.g., Arch & Craske, 2008; Hayes, 2008; Hayes, Levin, Plumb, Boulanger, & Pistorello, in press; Hayes, Luoma, Bond, Masuda, & Lillis, 2006; Hoffman, 2008; Hoffman & Asmundson, 2008). Thus, our focus will be on describing how ACT targets some of the issues that are encountered in the treatment of OCD with the hope that clinicians find useful ideas or procedures and researchers can be motivated to continue to address them.

ACT's philosophy of science: functional contextualism

Acceptance and commitment therapy, and much of the research that informs it, is based on a philosophy of science called *functional contextualism* (e.g., Hayes, Hayes, & Reese, 1988). There are multiple aspects to this philosophical position, but only a few of the central areas are addressed here, and then primarily in terms of their linkage to ACT. The manner in which scientists view the world is often affected by their goals. Many researchers are interested in how things work—much like a mechanic and a car. These researchers assume that the world is already divided up into parts, relations, and forces. They wish to model this complexity and consider themselves to be successful if they can predict how all the pieces work together—like components of a car engine. Functional contextualism varies from this approach in that it is primarily interested in predicting and influencing behavior with precision, scope, and depth (Hayes & Brownstein, 1986). In this view, truth is pragmatic and local. It is an issue of accomplishing goals, not modeling reality. Because as therapists we only have environmental variables at our hands, achieving a goal of predicting and influencing behavior ultimately is accomplished through the manipulation of environmental events. Psychological treatments performed by functional contextualists share similarities to the practices of behavior analysts, which is the tradition from which ACT emerged.

The goals of a functional contextualist are evident in the goals of ACT: to help the client function in a way more consistent with their values rather than symptom reduction *per se*. For example, a client might say, "I have disturbing thoughts that my presence can harm people," and the therapist might say, "Does that thought get in the way for you?" This can at times be at odds with some measures and diagnoses that are largely focused on symptom reduction, as ACT has less of a focus on symptom reduction and a greater focus on increasing quality of life. Interestingly, the DSM is consistent with this goal in that obsessions or compulsions can occur and not warrant a diagnosis of OCD if there is no impairment in functioning or heightened distress. Most clients ultimately want increased quality of life, and they just assume that obsessions and compulsions must be reduced first. Thus, ACT can be experienced as different and novel for some clients, but most clients find this approach to be consistent with their ultimate treatment goals.

Functional contextualists are holistic. They focus on the entire event and break it up only for pragmatic purposes. The whole event includes historical and current contexts and future expectations. From this perspective, OCD is not made up of obsessions, compulsions, cognitive misinterpretations, avoidance, thought–action fusion, and so on. These are constructions. Whether they are useful or not depends on context, both for the clients and the therapists. For example, if a client says, "I have thoughts that I am as bad as the devil and that I have to pray to make them go away," the therapist would not automatically assume this is a problem. The therapist would see where the thought fits in the larger part of the client's life to determine its function. The therapist could analyze the whole event and the function that thought serves by asking, "Is this an old thought?"; what conditions bring up the thought by asking, "When does this thought occur for you?"; how the thought is experienced by asking, "Is this a thought that you can have in your life?"; what else comes up when the thought occurs by asking, "What bodily sensations, memories, or feelings show up with this thought?"; how the person responds to this thought by asking, "How much do you fight against this thought?"; and what this entire pattern of action is in the service of by asking, "What is the focus of your life?" Therapeutically, this is useful because it keeps the door open to many areas of intervention depending on the function of the thought. These questions are asked within multiple therapeutic approaches, but why they are asked and how they are responded to may differ.

Relational frame theory

The approach of ACT to cognition is based on a behavioral account of language and cognition called *relational frame theory* (RFT) (Hayes, Barnes-Holmes, & Roche, 2001). According to RFT, verbal human beings respond to stimuli based not only on histories of interaction with them, as was originally studied in behavior analysis, but also on their mutual relations to other events. To simplify this concept, a rat must interact with stimuli to learn their functions, but a human can be told or assume that a novel stimulus is "the same as" or "different than" something that he or she has interacted with, and that the new stimulus will already have a meaning and a function based on the relational network that these cues establish. Consistent with the functional contextual model of science, this approach is not true with a capital "T" but may be true in the sense that it informs useful practices.

Relational framing has only been seen unequivocally in verbal human beings (Hayes, 1989). It develops as the person develops (Lipkens, Hayes, & Hayes, 1991), is under contextual control (e.g., Dymond & Barnes, 1995), is controlled by consequences (Wilson & Hayes, 1996), and can be directly trained when it is deficient (Berens & Hayes, 2007). As seen in children with developmental disabilities, the inability to relational frame is associated with higher level cognitive deficits (O'Hora, Pelaez, Barnes-Holmes, & Amesty, 2005), and training in relational framing increases higher order skills such as perspective taking and empathy (e.g., McHugh, Barnes-Holmes, & Barnes-Holmes, 2004). Training in perspective taking involves training in three specific relational frames: I/you, here/there, and now/then. As individuals acquire these three generalized operants, they are more able to take the perspective of others.

Relational framing is an evolutionary useful behavior in that it allows verbal humans to respond to events without having to necessarily interact with them first (Wulfert & Hayes, 1988). It changes the reinforcing and punishing functions of events without the need for direct experience by allowing the individual to respond to one stimuli in terms of another (e.g., Whelan & Barnes-Holmes, 2004), and it can produce emotional functions for novel events that exceed those that have been directly conditioned (e.g., Dougher, Hamilton, Fink, & Harrington, 2007). It has been shown that there are numerous forms of relational framing, including similarity, opposition, distinction, comparison, hierarchical, time, space, causality, and relationship and perspective (Hayes et al., 2001).

Relational frame theory is used by ACT theorists to illustrate the process through which cognition plays a role in psychopathology. Because it is a contextual theory, it puts less emphasis on cognitive and emotional content but instead stresses the context in which thinking and emotions occur and the additional contextual features that regulate how this has an effect on action (Olatunji, Forsyth, & Feldner, 2007). That is why, from this perspective, the primary clinical concern is the verbal context in which relational framing takes place rather than the type of relational framing itself. When cognitive activity/relational framing occurs in a literal context it dominates with and interferes with one's ability to experience the actual function of internal or external stimuli without verbal regulation. This results in behavior that is less flexible in adapting to environmental contingencies because it is governed by verbal rules regarding contingencies and not the actual contingencies (e.g., Hayes, 1989; Shimoff, Catania, & Matthews, 1981).

One of the more harmful verbal rules is one specifying that private events cause behaviors, as well as the corollary that negative private events are dangerous and must be controlled (as reviewed in Hayes et al., 2004b, 2006). This leads to a problematic response style called *experiential avoidance*, where people avoid negatively labeled thoughts, feelings, and bodily sensations at the cost of quality of life (Hayes, Wilson, Gifford, Follette, & Strosahl, 1996). This response style is a central problem of almost all anxiety disorders (Barlow, 2002), and aspects of the concept have long been integrated into traditional cognitive–behavioral approaches (Rachman & Shafran, 1998; Salkovskis, 1998).

In summary, RFT views psychopathology as primarily a problem in the verbal context (or the way) that one experiences private events and not a problem of the content, form, or frequency of those private events. Consistent with other therapies, ACT views the root of most forms of psychopathology as in part cognitive, but it defines *cognitive* to mean "based on relational framing," and it focuses on the context in which the cognitive events occur and have behavior regulatory functions. This stance is largely consistent with other acceptance- and mindfulness-based therapies such as mindfulness-based cognitive therapy (MBCT) in which "there is little emphasis ... on changing the *content* of thoughts; rather, the emphasis is on changing the *awareness of* and relationship to thoughts, feelings, and bodily sensations" (Segal, Teasdale, & Williams, 2004).

Current state of evidence of ACT for OCD

The current body of ACT as a treatment for OCD is limited but growing. To date, all research on ACT as a treatment for OCD has deliberately excluded other empirically supported procedures, including in-session exposure.

Exposure procedures can and should be incorporated into the clinical use of ACT (as described by Eifert & Forsyth, 2005), but initial research has been aimed at determining if the additional processes targeted in ACT are useful on their own, thus the protocols used have been deliberately limited. In the first treatment of ACT for OCD, a protocol of 8 weekly 1-hour sessions of ACT was used to treat 4 adults with OCD in a multiple-baseline, across-participants design (Twohig, Hayes, & Masuda, 2006a). The participants included two individuals with checking, one with cleaning, and one with hoarding compulsions. A battery of assessments given at pretreatment, posttreatment, and 3-month follow-up included measures of OCD severity, depression, anxiety, and ACT process measures, as well as a measure of treatment acceptability. Participants also self-monitored compulsions throughout the study. Results showed near zero levels of compulsions by the end of treatment, with results maintained at follow-up. Overall, scores moved from the clinical range to the nonclinical range for OCD as measured by the Obsessive–Compulsive Inventory (average scores were 57, 21, and 15 at pretreatment, posttreatment, and follow-up, respectively, for frequency and 59, 15, and 7, respectively, for distress), and reductions were seen on depression and anxiety. The ACT process measures suggested that ACT processes moved consistent with the model, and all participants found the treatment to be highly acceptable.

Next, a small randomized clinical trial comparing the same ACT protocol to progressive relaxation training (PRT) was conducted (Twohig, 2007). This study also included all subtypes of OCD including hoarding and primary obsessions. In the study, 34 participants (18 ACT, 16 PRT) completed outcome measures of OCD severity (Yale–Brown Obsessive Compulsive Scale, or Y-BOCS) and quality of life. Process measures involved a measure of psychological flexibility, thought–action fusion, and thought control. Additionally, weekly measures of OCD severity and ACT process measures were completed. Assessments were conducted by a rater who was blind to the treatment conditions, and treatments were delivered by therapists with allegiance to the respective treatments. Results showed that ACT had superior reductions on the Y-BOCS over PRT at posttreatment and follow-up. Pretreatment scores on the Y-BOCS were 23 and 24 for ACT and PRT, respectively; they reduced to 11 and 17 and were maintained at 9 and 14 for ACT and PRT, respectively. Additionally, 55% of the ACT group were considered treatment responders at posttreatment versus 12% in the PRT group, with these results maintained at follow-up (62% vs. 26%) using scores below 12 and at least a 6-point decrease as the clinical cut-off. Significant differences favoring ACT were seen at posttreatment on a measure of quality of life, but the difference was not present at follow-up. There were significantly greater reductions on all process measures at posttreatment and follow-up for the ACT group. Additionally, lag analyses on the weekly measures suggest that changes in ACT processes drove changes in OCD severity. Finally, there were no significant differences in treatment acceptability or treatment withdrawal between the two groups.

Single case designs have shown that ACT was successful in treating two cases of OCD (checking and primary obsessions) (Twohig & Whittal, 2008). This study also highlighted that ACT, cognitive therapy (CT), and exposure and response prevention (ERP) processes could be distinguished from each other, although these findings are preliminary because there were only six participants in the study. Additionally, there is a body of empirical support for ACT (with and without behavioral methods) in the treatment of OC-spectrum disorders of skin picking and trichotillomania (Twohig & Woods, 2004; Twohig, Hayes, & Masuda, 2006b; Woods, Wetterneck, & Flessner, 2006). Randomized trials have been conducted showing ACT to be effective for a variety of disorders, including psychosis, social phobia, smoking cessation, polysubstance abuse, depression, chronic pain, worksite stress and innovation, dealing with end-stage cancer, managing diabetes, stigma and burnout, agoraphobia, epilepsy, and trichotillomania (as reviewed in Hayes, Masuda, Bissett, Luoma, & Guerrero, 2004a; Hayes et al., 2006). Importantly, changes in processes specified in the ACT model generally predict outcomes (Hayes et al., 2006) which allows clinicians and researchers to target these processes when clients show problems in these areas. To these processes we now turn.

ACT conceptualization of OCD

An ACT conceptualization of OCD includes the target processes of experiential avoidance, cognitive fusion, attachment to a conceptualized self, lack of contact with the present moment, unclear values, and lack of engagement in valued activity, all of which may lead to psychological inflexibility (see Figure 9.1). ACT aims to foster converse treatment processes of acceptance, defusion, self as context, contact with the present moment, values clarification, and engagement in valued activity—all of which may promote behavioral flexibility (see Figure 9.2). (For a more complete description of ACT for OCD, see Twohig, Moran, & Hayes, 2008.) ACT is not a set of techniques, but a model. All therapeutic techniques that target these processes can be integrated into an ACT protocol without having to be invented by ACT clinicians.

Cognitive fusion versus defusion

Cognitive fusion refers to the domination of verbal/cognitive events over other sources of behavioral regulation. From an RFT perspective, fusion is due to the overextension of contexts that establish verbal control,

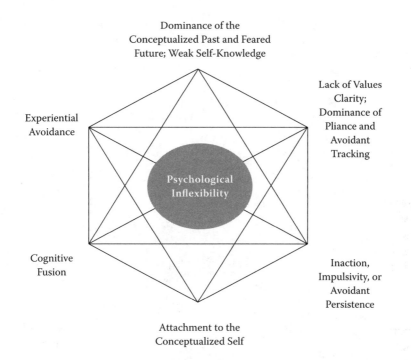

Figure 9.1 The ACT model of psychopathology.

including literal, reason-giving, and evaluative contexts. In the OCD area, the general term *cognitive fusion* can readily be confused with thought–action fusion (TAF). TAF means that negative thoughts are experienced to be as bad as the actual action and that thinking something can make it more likely to occur (Shafran, Thordarson, & Rachman, 1996). Fusion and TAF are not the same thing, but from the RFT perspective cognitive fusion is the process through which TAF is likely to occur. RFT indicates that TAF would occur in verbal contexts (e.g., literal) that promote a similarity between actions and thoughts and in functional contexts that cause the functions specified in the relations to be transferred. For example, in verbal contexts of literality, the functions of specific thoughts are much more likely to be experienced as actual events and not thoughts about those events. The process of fusion can apply in principle to all cognitive activity, including obsessions themselves.

Defusion techniques reduce the dominance of the literal functions of inner experiences and foster more flexible actions by broadening stimulus control over behavior. Some examples include watching obsessions go by as if they were written on leaves floating down a stream, repeating feared

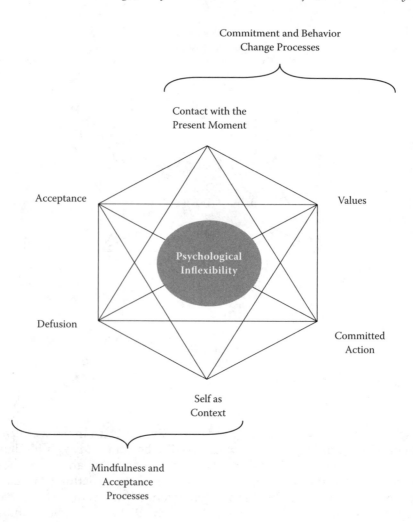

Figure 9.2 The ACT model of treatment.

words out loud until only the sound remains, or giving the obsessive thought a shape, size, color, texture, or form. Clients can practice labeling the process of thinking (e.g., "I am having the thought that I need to wash my hands right now") or thanking their mind for a thought. Similar concepts exist within more modern forms of CT, and ACT clinicians have developed scores of such methods, some of which have been individually evaluated in experimental research (e.g., Masuda, Hayes, Sackett, & Twohig, 2004). The aim of defusion is to decrease believability of, or attachment to, thoughts or other private events rather than an immediate change in their frequency, form, or situations in which they occur, and research shows that these defusion methods do have such an effect (e.g., Masuda et al., 2004). Believability is also targeted in traditional cognitive–behavioral approaches to these problems, but that goal is pursued by correcting faulty appraisals (e.g., Freeston, Rhéaume, & Ladouceur, 1996) with methods that are largely distinct despite the overlap in purpose.

Experiential avoidance and acceptance

Cognitive fusion and experiential avoidance may go hand in hand for clients with OCD. The more that private experiences are negatively evaluated and fused, the less willing clients may be to experience them. OCD is riddled with experiential avoidance as seen in the ways clients respond to obsessions, anxiety, and fearful situations. It appears in the form of compulsions and behavioral avoidance and in cognitive activities such as rationalizing and distracting. These behaviors may often adversely affect quality of life. Experiential avoidance is evident when the avoidance behavior is carried out in the service of controlling a private event and results in negative long-term effects. Written another way, avoidance is not always a problem; it is a problem when it causes problems. Most of the time compulsions are a problem. Thought suppression (actively attempting to not think a thought) has been found to be problematic in OCD (Tolin, Abramowitz, Przeworski, & Foa, 2002) and is only one type of avoidance. Many other more subtle forms of avoidance also exist, including avoiding situations and challenging thoughts, for example. Nevertheless, both ACT and modern CT have a strong focus on reducing attempts to control or regulate these inner experiences (e.g., Wilhelm & Steketee, 2006).

Acceptance is offered as an alternative response to experiential avoidance. Acceptance is best defined as a behavior, rather than a disposition or belief. Acceptance involves experiencing private events as they are and not taking steps to regulate or control them. It involves an active embrace of one's inner experiences—not a passive tolerance or type of resignation to fate. Acceptance procedures have been shown to increase the client's willingness to make contact with feared events, including panic sensations (Levitt, Brown, Orsillo, & Barlow, 2004), and as a useful response to obsessive-like thoughts (Marcks & Woods, 2005, 2007).

Lack of contact with the present moment versus contact with the present moment

From an ACT perspective, some ability to be in touch with what is happening moment to moment is necessary to be able to respond adaptively to one's experience and environment. Lack of *contact with the present moment* can lead to problems recognizing that one is thinking or feeling, even though such experiences may guide a client's overt behavior. Further, lack of contact with the present moment can be problematic in general, as clients may be less likely to respond effectively to other people or situations. Being in contact with one's private experiences and environment is central to many mindfulness-based therapies (e.g., Segal et al., 2004). Additionally, even though the data are somewhat unclear on this, it appears that the more clients are in contact with their obsessions and fears—as seen in ERP—the more effective exposure therapy is likely to be (e.g., Abramowitz, 1996; Abramowitz, Franklin, & Foa, 2002a).

Self as content versus self as context

Humans construct stories of "who we are" that are maintained over time—labeled *self as content*. Evidence that confirms such conceptualizations of self are emphasized, and evidence that does not cohere with these conceptualizations is discounted. It is logical that humans would construct such statements about the self as it can help us predict and control our behavior; however, from this stance, we can be attached to or invested in particular experiences over other experiences. In clients with OCD, attachment to a conceptualized self can be problematic if there is a struggle against the obsession, because it is experienced as threatening to the conceptualized self, or if changing OCD behaviors is resisted to stay consistent with a conceptualization of the self (e.g., as someone with OCD). Either way, the client is not responding flexibly to the thoughts. This is somewhat similar to conceptions underlying schema-focused cognitive therapy, which emphasizes the importance of multiple cognitive domains and levels of cognition (e.g., Sookman & Pinard, 1999; Sookman & Steketee, 2007).

Acceptance and commitment therapy promotes the development of the self as context through awareness of a sense of perspective that RFT is showing emerges from the deictic relational frames of I/you, here/there, and now/then. This sense of self supports contact with the present moment that is undefended, effective, and open. Clients are helped to develop a sense of perspective in which experiences are noticed from an open and accepting stance, not judged as either "good" or "bad." Observing and non-evaluative description can help to foster a sense of perspective for which thoughts and other private experiences have less power. This transcendent sense of self can help clients recognize that they are not defined by or controlled by their private experiences or their OCD symptoms; they may learn to contain those experiences and observe them nonthreateningly.

Unclear chosen values versus clear values

Values are defined within ACT as chosen qualities of living that are present moment to moment. Unlike goals, values can never be fulfilled but rather function as directions for ongoing patterns of action. Clients are also encouraged to consider what they want their lives to stand for and how they may be able to set goals within each of several valued-living domains such as family, career, friendships, and personal growth, just to name a few. In ACT, values serve a motivating function for such clients; approaching feared events and a willingness to experience private events are in service of these valued domains. It is important that values have a chosen quality—if they are fused with, become a method of avoidance, or are in the service of mere social compliance they can narrow rather than broad repertoires. Over time, clients are encouraged to build larger and larger patterns of action consistent with these valued domains, but their successful outcome is not the goal; rather, values bring vitality and meaning to the moment. Clients are encouraged to flexibly choose these behaviors and to continue to persist or choose to desist particular behaviors when it is effective to do so. Consistent with the functional contextual model, there is no correct way to live, including how to respond to obsessions and compulsions.

Behavioral inaction or impulsivity versus committed action

Many people have difficulty living consistently with their chosen values. Clients with OCD commonly report a lack of values-consistent living when entering therapy where OCD symptoms, not their values, tend to guide behavior. The time spent cleaning or checking, for example, can make the person late for class or work and can take away from quality time with loved ones. Clients may also attempt to avoid particular situations in service of reducing the risk of obsessions occurring (e.g., a client with contamination fears avoiding a hospital). Further, clients with OCD may believe that they must remove or manage anxiety associated with obsessions *before* they can attempt to live a more values-consistent life. They may spend time attempting to manage anxiety at the expense of engaging in behaviors consistent with valued directions. ACT aims to refocus the client's energy from regulating or controlling private events to pursuing areas of life that are meaningful without regard for the effects on private experiences. This leads to natural forms of exposure, but the purpose of exposure is not to diminish anxiety but to live more fully. Therapy becomes about increasing quality of life over emotional regulation. Clients are commonly asked to make behavioral commitments to engage in valued activities or engage in actions that are steps toward engaging in larger patterns of valued behaviors. Committed action can also include almost any other behavioral method, including skills building, contingency management, relationship enhancement, and the like. Often, these actions are counter to compulsive actions and naturally result in a reduction in compulsive behavior, and perhaps for that reason the impact of ACT on compulsions seems particularly strong (Twohig, 2007).

Behavioral inflexibility versus behavioral flexibility

The result of problems in each of these six areas is what is termed *psychological inflexibility* (Hayes et al., 2006). Psychological inflexibility refers to a rigid, narrow repertoire of behavior that is not directed by one's values but rather by experiential avoidance and fusion. Responding to obsessions by engaging in compulsions, avoiding particular triggering situations, creating elaborate rules for behavior that reduce anxiety or obsessions, and rationalizing or distracting from the current setting can all indicate psychological inflexibility. In an ACT model, psychological inflexibility (and its inverse) is the core target of therapeutic work.

These therapeutic processes and their common target together offer a focus that might inform the treatment of difficult cases of OCD. In the following section, we outline some of the difficulties seen in the treatment of OCD and illustrate how treatments focusing on these processes might prove to be useful.

Issues of treatment resistance in OCD

There are generally two supported treatment approaches for OCD: exposure and response prevention (ERP) (e.g., Abramowitz et al., 2002a) and cognitive–behavioral therapy (CBT) (e.g., Wilhelm & Steketee, 2006). The data on the use of ACT with OCD are limited but growing (e.g., Twohig, 2007; Twohig et al., 2006a). We do not yet know if an ACT model contributes above and beyond these existing models; therefore, most of what is known regarding treatment nonresponse and resistance is based on outcome studies using ERP and traditional CBT (for reviews of the limitations, see Pollard, 2007; Sookman & Steketee, 2007).

Treatment refusal, dropout, and compliance

The most notable concern in the treatment of OCD is maintaining and fostering full participation in therapy. In a recent study comparing ERP to clomipramine, 22% of participants dropped out after learning that they had been randomly assigned to the ERP condition, and an additional 28%

dropped out of the ERP condition after treatment began (Foa et al., 2005); thus, a startling 50% of these participants were not willing to participate in an effective treatment. It should be noted that dropout rates were similarly problematic in the clomipramine condition (Foa et al., 2005), so this is a general problem in the treatment of OCD rather than a problem specific to ERP. Although there are specialized forms of CBT that target treatment-resistant clients (e.g., Sookman & Pinard, 1999), there appear to be no controlled studies that show a lower refusal or withdrawal rate for CBT over ERP. Aggregating the participants from all CBT versus ERP studies, however, yields a significantly lower dropout rate for CBT (Abramowitz, Taylor, & McKay, 2005). On the one hand, this suggests that CBT might be a superior treatment because significant differences have not been found in outcomes between these two treatments (e.g., Whittal, Thordarson, & McLean, 2005), but other analyses have found significantly greater outcomes in treatments that include greater exposure whether in the form of ERP or behavioral experiments as done in CBT (Abramowitz, 1996, 1998).

Even if clients agree to participate in therapy and attend therapy sessions, treatment compliance is still a significant problem. Fostering full participation in therapy (such as exposure exercises), limiting unwanted distraction and the moderation of affect during exercises, and completion of therapeutic homework assignments, including exposure exercises, are all areas that therapists struggle with. Empirical evidence suggests that greater compliance and participation result in better outcomes (Abramowitz et al., 2002b; O'Sullivan, Noshirvani, Marks, Montiero, & Lelliott, 1991).

All therapists have to deal with client withdrawal, treatment refusal, and noncompliance. Even though that might just be part of being a therapist, we can do our best to decrease their frequency and severity. As with all behaviors, there can be multiple functions to any one action. As in all therapies, therapists should evaluate the function of withdrawal, refusing therapy, or not fully participating. It is possible that reduction in the disorder would result in greater demands on the individual, or the client may fear treatment and avoiding or not participating fully in therapy simply reduces that fear. These issues are targeted a particular way in ACT.

If a client reports being interested in leaving treatment or not participating, an ACT therapist would likely tell the client that he or she is absolutely welcome to do so and that there will be no repercussions if that occurs but that the important question is what these behaviors are in the service of. It is stated this way to reduce compliance-based rule following (which is a specific target in ACT) and to help responses be experienced as a "free" choice. The therapist should help elicit the function behind the client's actions; for example, the client might report time restraints leading to withdrawal, when in actuality the issue is one of fear regarding the procedures in the treatment. Assuming the therapist can assist the client in reporting the actual function of the behavior, then useful therapy can begin.

First, the therapist should not discuss the accuracy or inaccuracy of the client's thoughts or emotions. For example, if the client says, "I am afraid that I will not be able to handle the emotions that will occur in therapy," the therapist should *not* help her realize that there is nothing to be afraid of because that will only strengthen fusion and lead to counter-argument. If fusion is a current struggle for the client and is supporting avoidance, the therapist should work to reduce the way in which the client interacts with thoughts. Treatment should reduce unnecessary rule-governed behavior in these areas: Thoughts and feelings cause behavior; thoughts and feelings are dangerous, and thoughts and feelings should be controlled. A simple response such as "I bet you have that thought a lot, and it pushes you around. Do you think you would be willing to try something different with that thought, such as letting it be there and not fighting with it?" reduces reliance on these rules. Such a response begins to take the content of the thought off the table and gets at its function. There are many other ACT techniques and procedures that can assist in increasing defusion and acceptance. Once defusion is in place, there is a significantly greater likelihood that acceptance of that private event will occur; the client will let the thought be there and fight with it less. After there is an increase in defusion and acceptance, therapy can focus on the client's values with regard to participating in therapy.

The process of increasing motivation is an issue that has received additional attention in CBT recently (e.g., Slagle & Gray, 2007). For example, Purdon and colleagues (Purdon, Rowa, & Antony, 2004, as reported in Rowa, Antony, & Swinson, 2007) found that "treatment ambivalence concerns were widely reported by individuals with OCD about to embark in ERP" (p. 96) and that participants who feared that the treatment would fail or succeed (resulting in greater social interactions or employment obligations) had increased anxiety or had general concerns about treatment.

Increasing motivation and participation in therapy is accomplished in ACT through targeting values. Usually clients focus on wanting to remove their OCD symptoms, but they are also usually in contact with what would be possible in life if they were not consumed by their OCD symptoms. Discussions of what is really important to the client can transform the function of particular aversive experiences (such as contacting feared stimuli) from one of "avoid" to one of "approach" in the service of meaningful areas of life. Regardless of the exact function, targeting values increases new responses.

Values serve not only to motivate but also to dignify the experience of discomfort. Any discussions about values may lead to fused statements about what a client wants (such as "I want to feel better" or "I don't want to have OCD anymore"). Although such desires are common, it is the therapist's job to dig deeper, looking for function, so a question for such a client may be "What would you do if you felt better or OCD was no longer a problem?" Then, the therapist may use the statements that come from such lines of questioning as the motivation for engaging in therapy. A therapist may say, "What if we made therapy about finding a way for you to spend time with your family rather than cleaning the house? Would you be willing to experience some difficult emotions and thoughts in here in service of that?" In a statement like that, the therapist is linking current actions to future-oriented goals. When values and possible avoidance moves that may get in the way of values are discussed, helping clients set up small tasks for committing to treatment may help clients be more likely to continue to engage. Setting small commitments that can be achieved can create a context where clients experience that change is possible. In this way, values can point to appetitive activities that establish competing contingencies for avoidance, fusion, and lack of commitment to engaging in therapy. When repertoires narrow during values work, usually this is because fusion is dominant. Thus, there is a kind of dance between the two sides of the model (Figure 9.2), with the left side creating enough flexibility that the right side can be pursued.

Difficult-to-treat subtypes of OCD

Unlike many diagnoses where the form of the disturbance is more or less defined, to meet criteria for OCD specific types of obsessions or compulsions are not required but rather their functions are specified (American Psychiatric Association, 2000). Clinicians and researchers who work with this population can attest that the variations in the form of obsessions and compulsions can be limitless and, for many clients, change over time. For pragmatic reasons, ERP and CBT therapists have identified subtypes of OCD because the subtypes affect the manner in which the therapy is conducted. The approach to categorizing subtypes of OCD is largely based on a cognitive model in which different cognitive problems require different cognitive approaches (Sookman, Abramowitz, Calamari, Wilhelm, & McKay, 2005). For example, if the client has an exaggerated sense of responsibility, therapy will involve exercises aimed at clarifying the client's actual level of responsibility in obsessive situations. Additionally, different topographies of OCD are treated using separate techniques; for example, hoarding cases are not regularly included in trials of OCD but are instead treated in separate trials and are generally found to be much more difficult to treat. Similarly, certain cognitive subtypes have been found to be particularly difficult to treat from an exposure perspective; for example, people for whom compulsions serve a magical purpose or who must perform compulsions until it "feels right" are hard to graduate from an exposure point of view (Summerfeldt, 2004). Additionally, patients with other cognitive characteristics such as strongly held or overvalued ideation find ERP to be less acceptable and effective (Veale, 2007; Wilhelm & Steketee, 2006). Finally, if the client is very cognitive (e.g., thinks through every response), a cognitive approach can add fuel to the fire and help the client become even more verbally entangled. We have also run into this issue while doing ACT with very cognitive clients. The issue of how to handle different types of OCD is very important, and ACT approaches might inform some practices.

At the most fundamental level, ACT largely targets the function of thoughts, feelings, and bodily sensations without regard for their content. This is accomplished through analysis of the six psychopathology processes that are illustrated in Figure 9.1. The degree to which each psychopathology process is present, the alternative ACT therapy process is addressed (illustrated in Figure 9.2). Targeting these processes is commonly done when working from an ACT approach, but this approach might also be a useful alternative when the CBT therapist is having difficulty moving the appropriate cognitive process. This is more apparent when cognitive and ACT processes have greater overlap, such as acceptance from ACT and importance of controlling one's thoughts from CT. In some areas, they are more different than alike, such as defusion as compared to cognitive restructuring techniques (Deacon, Fawzy, & Lickel, 2007), although defusion is likely useful for reducing TAF (Twohig, 2007).

Defusion might present an alternative path forward for clients who will not shift their levels of belief about the accuracy of the content of one of their obsessions through techniques such as targeting overestimation of the importance of thoughts and possibly attempts to help these clients reappraise their thoughts as being unsuccessful or making the client more focused on their obsessions (Freeston et al., 1996). Defusion would be useful because it sidesteps the troublesome cognitive issue. Instead of changing the accuracy of a client's thought, defusion aims to alter the literal context under which all obsessive thoughts are experienced. Thus, the client can still find the thought to be accurate but learn to experience it as just a thought that does not have to be followed on utilitarian grounds. Reductions on the TAF scale as a result of ACT suggest that ACT procedures would be useful to reduce over importance of thoughts (Twohig, 2007). If the CBT therapist cannot get the client to shift from believing that he is responsible for harm coming to his son because of his thoughts, even after participating in many Socratic discussions and behavioral experiments, then the therapist could shift therapy and say something such as, "What if we tried this a different way? What if we treat the thought that you are responsible for what happens to your son as just a thought—not accurate or inaccurate—but just a thought? Can we just let your obsession be there without fighting with it? Then, while it is there, we can practice doing things that are really important to you." Behind this rationale, a whole host of ACT defusion methods (e.g., Luoma, Hayes, & Walser, 2007) could then be applied. It is not necessary to conclude or argue that this procedure is superior to cognitive restructuring techniques (that is purely an empirical matter) in order to use it as an alternative when treatment resistance is encountered within traditional CBT approaches.

An additional useful aspect of this approach is that it targets the function of the obsessions and not the content. This can simplify treatment because only one approach is utilized regardless of the type or content of the thought. These same procedures are used with checkers, cleaners, primary obsessionals, and hoarders. There is insufficient research to suggest whether ACT methods may be effective with specific subtypes, but there is evidence that the same protocol can at least be helpful for various subtypes (Twohig, 2007; Twohig et al., 2006a).

Co-occurring issues and what is a good outcome?

In addition to the many varieties of OCD, clients are likely to present with co-occurring diagnoses, the most common of which are additional anxiety disorders and mood disorders. Research has found that both of these conditions negatively affect outcomes (Abramowitz, Franklin, Street, Kozak, & Foa, 2000). In addition, even after successful treatment, such as using a conservative cutoff of 50% reduction in symptoms or particular outcome score (e.g., Whittal et al., 2005), many participants still have symptoms present following therapy (Abramowitz, 1998). Although it is an important step, quantifying such clinically significant changes in this way creates a problem in that it does not leave room for other patterns of change to be represented. In some cases, for example, clients experience a large decrease in their symptoms over time but do not experience an increase in quality of life and *vice versa* (Norberg, Calamari, Cohen, & Reiman, 2008). This raises important questions regarding outcome measurement, such as: "What is a good outcome?" The importance of clinically significant change is not a new issue in applied psychology (Jacobson, Follette, & Revenstorf, 1984). This problem has led researchers to focus increasingly on quality-of-life issues in addition to symptom reduction in the treatment of OCD (Diefenbach, Abramowitz, Norberg, & Tolin, 2007).

Acceptance and commitment therapy focuses on the function of one's actions and the role of cognitive and emotional processes in these actions. The techniques used in ACT do not really differ whether one is treating OCD, psychosis, depression, substance abuse, or one of the other disorders for which ACT has been found to be useful (Hayes et al., 2006). At the onset of ACT, the client is assessed for level of functioning and the way in which the ACT psychopathology processes interfere with it; the client's functioning takes precedence over formal diagnoses. This clearly affects what an ACT therapist would consider a "successful" outcome because the focus would not be on reduction of OCD or depression *per se*; instead, the focus would be on the flexibility of action related to overall functioning.

The philosophy that underlies ACT, functional contextualism, reminds us to look at the whole context of any event and not focus on a particular aspect of it. Thus, the mere presence of obsessions and compulsions is not necessarily a health concern, but how they affect the person's quality of life and goals in life is stressed. If the obsessions are not a concern for the client, then they do not need to be targeted. If a client continued to experience obsessions and anxiety, but these private events were experienced in a context where they did not interfere with the client's daily functioning and quality of life, the client would be considered a successful therapy client. Offering improved functioning as the treatment goal may do interesting and useful things to how clients interact with their obsessions and anxiety.

If a client were referred for treatment because the amount of hoarded items was too excessive and eviction or legal penalty was possible, the motivation to change is likely limited. In a situation like this, an ACT therapist would work to find some aspect of therapy that would increase the client's motivation to participate, even though motivation to decrease OCD may be low or not present. For example, the client may be motivated by keeping the police or family from interfering in her life. She may also be motivated to reduce money spent on items or have more room in her house. The value of *freedom* may capture these issues and be the initial target in therapy. As therapy progresses, it is very likely that the client will come to find that hoarding has functioned as avoidance, that it is not a value, and that it actually interferes with other values. Later in therapy, larger long-term values can be discussed and worked toward.

Oftentimes, clients enter therapy with the goal of reducing their obsessions and anxiety, with that as a prerequisite to changing the way they live. It does not necessarily have to work that way. It may not be necessary to reduce these private events before meaningful life changes can occur; for example, all of us do things that are meaningful and cause stress and anxiety, such as giving talks before a large professional audience. The anxiety and stress experienced are experienced willingly—they are just part of engaging in that activity. Some clients can be taught to treat their obsessions and anxiety in a similar fashion. If quality of life is the goal, then a reduction in symptom severity is not a necessary first step. This is important because it affects how treatment is measured and what the client looks at in terms of symptom improvement. It is possible that clients should be asked how they are functioning at the beginning of therapy sessions rather than how much time they spent on obsessions and compulsions.

Procedural issues

Finally, issues such as time to deliver the therapy and confidentiality during exposure therapy are notable in the delivery of treatment for OCD. The amount of time that it takes to deliver treatment for OCD varies from study to study, but Kozak & Coles (2005) reported that assessment followed by 15 daily sessions (90 to 120 minutes) of ERP done over 3 weeks was found to be "very successful." Treatment duration for certain subtypes such as hoarding can be much longer (Cherian & Frost, 2007). ACT has been successfully delivered in relatively brief durations (e.g., 8 hours) (Twohig, 2007; Twohig et al., 2006a), but there is not enough research to know if that is optimal when delivering ACT.

Difficulties in training and delivery also need to be considered. ERP requires less tailoring for the treatment of OCD than do more complex forms of psychotherapy. When many staff members need to be trained in a procedure, it seems likely that ERP would be easier to teach than many other treatment types. Exposure raises difficulties of its own, however; for example, as noted by Wilhelm and Steketee (2006), confidentiality, legal, and staff management issues can be raised when exposure exercises must be conducted outside of the therapy office.

These concerns are less of an issue with CT, where the entire treatment can be delivered without the need for exposure exercises. More recent approaches that tailor CBT interventions to the beliefs and appraisals associated with subtypes of OCD may address more pertinent issues for the client (Wilhelm & Steketee, 2006), but they are not yet known to be more effective that ERP, and tailoring could raise issues of time and complexity that must be considered.

Acceptance and commitment therapy is a fairly efficient model because of its breadth of application, but it too can be more complex to learn and administer than exposure alone. Fortunately, it appears that ACT is effective even when delivered by therapists in training who are not confident in the model (Lappalainen et al., 2007). Whether these characteristics make ACT viable within systems of care is not yet known. Normally, ACT would be used in combination with exposure because the model itself calls for the use of empirically supported behavior change methods, but limited research on deliberately restricted protocols has shown that ACT does not *require* the use of exposure techniques in treatment for OCD (Twohig, 2007; Twohig et al., 2006a). Thus, if decreasing the concerns with explicit exposure is key, ACT methods may be useful.

An ACT case example

Chester is a 50-year-old male who came to the clinic as a last resort to manage his life-interfering OCD. Even though he had held jobs for a while, he was currently on Social Security disability. He reported that for much of his adult life he felt an irrepressible urge to keep track of any and all relevant information, and he reported needing to plan everything to the last detail in advance. His compulsions included writing down conversations, and holding onto pamphlets, papers, class notes, and any document he felt might be important. He reported having so many boxes of paper that his spare bedroom and garage were completely filled to the ceiling. He also reported several in-depth planning compulsions that interfered with his daily functioning. First, he reported overpreparing for all events; for example, even though he lived and had worked within a 3-mile radius of a moderately urban environment, the trunk of his car held everything he could ever need if his car broke down (e.g., a tent, two emergency kits, several gallons of water, sunscreen, a complete overnight kit, nonperishable food), and he reported checking that everything was in place every time he left his car. Also, Chester's planning extended to everyday activities such as making a doctor's appointment, or the conversation he would have with the pharmacist later that day. Before an interaction, he would take a few hours to write and revise several drafts of the conversation he wanted to have. Chester reported high amounts of anxiety when he wasn't able to plan or write things down.

Chester came to the clinic because he reported trying "everything" to manage his OCD. Upon reporting to therapy, he was taking fluoxetine (40 mg) and had been for several years. Prior to going on fluoxetine, he had been hospitalized twice for severe OCD and major depression; however, since starting the medication, he reported a small reduction in his obsessions, and he had not felt suicidal. He had also been to several different therapists and psychiatrists over the years. In each treatment, he found some relief for a short period of time (e.g., he reported clearing out his garage three times only to fill it up again 6 months after therapy ended), but he still struggled with his symptoms on a daily basis. Therapy was designed to include 8 1-hour sessions and weekly dependent measures of obsession and compulsion frequency, as well as reported believability of obsessions (fusion), distress associated with them, and reactivity to them. At the start of therapy, Chester reported being quite high on believability, distress, and reactivity and engaged in compulsions at least 2 hours a day. His pretreatment Y-BOCS score was 21.

In his first session, Chester was taking notes on everything his therapist (JCP) said. He reported a strong desire for his therapist to provide him with a "syllabus" of what would be covered in therapy each session.

Chester's therapist began by discussing everything Chester had tried to reduce his obsessions (including coming in to a new therapy) into the same functional class that she identified as "struggling to feel better." Chester seemed confused at first, wondering how all this could help him finally deal with his OCD once and for all. His therapist responded by asking him what he was missing in his life due to OCD. Below is an example of how asking about values can be part of creating an agenda for ACT:

C. So, I get it. I've been trying to dig myself out of this hole [trying to manage obsessions] for about 35 years. So, what now? I don't know what else to do!

T. And notice that your mind doesn't get this—it wants a solution, even now. How familiar is it to try figure this out?

C. Oh, I guess I do that a lot: planning and things. But, if I can't figure out how to know enough or plan enough to be comfortable ... that would just really be horrible. I would be SOOOO anxious that I don't know if I could breathe.

T. Have you tried that before? Figuring out how to do enough to prevent anxiety? (Chester nods.) How has that worked?

C. Hmmm, I've never really thought about how it worked before! Wow, I'm going to write that down!

T. Have you done that before? Written everything important down?

C. (Sarcastically) Why, yes, my dear, all the time! (laughing) I bet if you tried hard enough, you could piece together a complete transcript of my life within the walls of my house.

T. Let's say I did that. And from that transcript we could pull out the theme of your life—what you've been working at tirelessly for at least 35 years. Let's say you died today and your tombstone were to reflect your theme so far. What would it say? I'll start it: "Here lies Chester. He spent his life... ."

C. (a moment of silence, then speaking slowly) I suppose it would just say "planning." I've tried taking classes to keep my mind active but I get lost in taking notes and making my own schedules from the syllabus. I've tried dating, but I can't decide when to call, what to wear—ugh, it's just exhausting. I've spent hours organizing and planning, but I never seem to get to the good part. I spend my time planning for my life, but *life* never seems to happen.

T. What *do* you want your tombstone to say?

C. I would want it to say "Chester *lived* his *life* no matter what." I want more than anything to have the ability to happily glide through life like I see everyone else doing. I can't leave the car without checking, I can't just call for an appointment without planning for hours—so forget dating! I get physically sick if I don't write everything down because I know I will forget. I can't just live my life and do what I need to do. I make a big production out of it.

T. So, I see some glimmers of what matters to you—other people, just being able to do whatever needs to be done. Is that a good start?

C. I guess that pretty much sums it up.

T. What if we could make our work together about actually living life, not just planning for it? Just doing what *you* want to do in your life, not what your obsessions say is possible? Doing what you want, regardless of whether you feel anxious, or whether you actually remember everything?

C. Oh, I'm so tired. I don't know if I have the energy to work harder. What if I'm just no good at living life?

T. What if it's not you that's failed? You've worked darned hard and done your best, and still you're stuck. What if it's these strategies? (pauses) Check your experience here. Do you feel that you're actually *living* your life by trying *not* to feel anxious, *not* to forget, *not* to miss some important detail, *not* to worry about some feared outcome?

C. Oh, my gosh. I guess it never really works. Well, it does for a while. But then I'm stuck again.

T. What if it can't work?

C. I don't know, then. What's the solution?

T. What if it's like this—the more you try not to feel anxious, to try to calm your obsessions, the further away you get from the life you want? Your mind says, "If you just try hard enough, plan perfectly, organize everything, keep track of all possible important information, write out that conversation, you'll get what you want—everything will just fall into place." But your experience says something different, doesn't it? You've put all this energy into trying to feel better and get ready for life, but meanwhile life is passing by. What if the strategy of trying to manage your experience is what is keeping you from living your life? Would you be willing to work for the life you want, even if it meant doing some things differently?

C. I'm not sure I know how to do things differently.

T. That's what we'll practice in here. With your permission, first we'll look at how you've managed your obsessions and really critically look at whether it works. Then we'll see what else might be possible.

C. (cautiously) Okay, I'll give it a try.

In this segment, the therapist has set the stage for therapy. Though formally she focused mainly on values, if you look closely each of the ACT processes is present in this conversation. By calling out what Chester's mind tells him, she is making a subtle defusion move. By asking him what he cares about and what he has given up to manage his OCD, she is helping him identify his values, and by asking if the work can be about living his life she is setting the stage for practicing acceptance and willingness to experience anxiety and obsessions in the service of his values.

Next, Chester and his therapist focused on examining his obsessions and how he was trying to manage them, by pushing them away, doing his compulsions, making deals with himself that he would write down an important conversation later, or arguing with his obsessions—whatever got in the way of Chester living his life. At first, he had difficulty with the notion that his obsessions did not cause his compulsions, so much of the first session was spent helping Chester identify his obsessions and discriminate them from compulsive behavior. Also, the therapist began to introduce the idea of psychological flexibility with a concrete metaphor by asking him to walk across the room while repeating out loud "I cannot walk." Then, the therapist and Chester practiced doing the same thing in session by using his compulsive behaviors accessible to them in the session, such as "I cannot take notes." The therapist and Chester practiced this both when the urge was present and when it wasn't, helping Chester experience that he had the ability to control his overt behavior regardless of what his mind was doing, whether an obsession was present or not.

In the second session, Chester and his therapist discussed how trying to ignore or manage his obsessions only made them worse by comparing his relationship to his obsessions to that of a kid in the candy aisle of the grocery store. Chester reported that he was very much like a parent walking by a candy display with a young child in the cart, in that the child would start asking, then demanding, then screaming for some candy. If he walked on, the child would still scream and embarrass him. If he gave in, it was only teaching the child to scream again to get the candy on another trip. Chester very much identified with this metaphor and stated that he felt that he'd been giving the kid candy for so long that the kid didn't have to ask anymore, and he did so solely based on the fear that the kid might scream if he skipped the candy one day. This was also a nice way for the therapist to predict with Chester what might happen when he started choosing what *he* wanted to do rather than just appeasing the kid. Chester also said that he felt that feeding the kid candy wasn't helping him get closer to living his life (dating, enjoying his classes, just going on a trip without planning everything) and subsequently expressed some willingness to just "let the kid scream."

The therapist then introduced the difference between the "world outside the skin" and the "world inside the skin"—that we are able to control, change, or avoid things outside of ourselves but are rarely successful at doing so with our thoughts and feelings. In the *polygraph metaphor*, Chester was asked to imagine what would happen if he was hooked up to the world's best polygraph machine, which would tell the therapist if he felt even the slightest bit anxious. In this imagined scenario, he would be given the simple instruction of "Do not get anxious!" as the therapist placed a mock gun to Chester's head. Chester laughed instantly, reporting that it would be impossible not to get nervous without serious doses of valium. The therapist and Chester discussed how it makes sense that people try to control inner experiences, because we're such good problem solvers, but that directly trying to control his experience was not possible. Further, the therapist asked him if he'd be able to fall in love with a stranger if he was paid $1 million. Chester again laughed, realizing that just as trying to control his experiences didn't work neither did creating them. Spending his life looking for these types of solutions was certainly not for getting him closer to his value of "living life."

In the third session, the therapist introduced mindfulness work, helping Chester to identify his experience and then practicing acceptance of it using the *tin-can monster* exercise, where Chester practiced breaking down his experience into smaller pieces—thought, emotion, sensation, evaluation—as if it were a monster made up of tin cans. By doing so, Chester practiced noticing all that was happening for him in a given moment, rather than simply automatically responding to his obsessions and big, scary monsters that must be heeded.

Again, his value of just "living life" was the motivation for him to continue to slow down and notice all of his private experiences. When he was better able to contact the present moment rather than being carried away by his obsessions, he found that, while he noticed all of his sensations, he also noticed more around him. At the beginning of the next session Chester said, "I can't believe it. I was in class the other day and someone said something really profound. I normally would have stopped paying attention to write it down but instead I suddenly realized there is a lot happening when I stop to write things down, so I just kept listening and actually joined in the conversation! I've not had a chance to really connect with anyone in my classes, and I think it's because I've been so caught up in remembering everything." The next session, for the first time, Chester did not ask his therapist for a preview of the next therapy session. Also, at this point in therapy, Chester reported a significant reduction on obsession believability, reactivity, and distress from an average of 95% to an average of 50%, and he reported spending only a half-hour each day planning and checking.

In the fourth session, Chester and his therapist focused on helping Chester recognize that he was thinking by writing out his thoughts on cards and then choosing to take them with him as he went about his day. He was also instructed to deliteralize his thoughts by singing them in funny voices. To illustrate this further, Chester and his therapist engaged in an exercise called *passengers on the bus* (Hayes et al, 1999), which helped him recognize that he could continue to have his experiences and move forward in his life:

> T. So, Chester. Let's imagine that you are driving this big yellow bus with lots of passengers on it. You are driving on the road toward "Living Life" when all of a sudden, a particularly nasty passenger—let's call him "Planner"—moves to the front of the bus and starts yelling at you about all of the things you need to do: Get maps of the area! Write down the conversation you need to have with the hotel clerk in the next town! Keep track of the license plates you see going by in case someone has an accident! You tell him to sit down but then he starts up again, telling you how horrible things will be if you don't get it right. He tells you that you've never been good at doing things and that planning is the only way you can make it in this world. Now he's starting to panic, because he's counting the water bottles and there is an odd number of them! You tell him, "Fine! I will pull over and get some more water and take some time to write out the conversation I will have with the hotel clerk." But what just happened? You were headed toward "Living Life" and suddenly you're pulled over and taking notes. Who is driving this bus, anyway? If you are headed toward "Living Life," how's the journey so far?
>
> C. (laughing) I get it. I stopped the bus!
>
> T. Right! Who is the driver of this bus?
>
> C. Me, but I was listening to "Planner," and he always seems pretty convincing.
>
> T. Sure! You've usually done what he's said. What happens if you don't listen to him? Another passenger shows up, right? "Anxiety," maybe?
>
> C. Oh, yeah. I'll call him "Nerve-Wracked" because he's always freaking out.
>
> T. Great! So, "Nerve-Wracked" shows up and what happens?
>
> C. Well, he tells me that if I don't listen to "Planner" then everything will fall apart. He shakes and looks like he's going to have a heart attack.
>
> T. So what do you do when he shows up?
>
> C. Even if I was going to ignore "Planner" I always give in when "Nerve-Wracked" shows up.
>
> T. So it's like you automatically turn left when he shows up.
>
> C. Yeah, I guess so.
>
> T. So let me ask you this. These passengers—what would they do to you if you didn't do what they said? Have they ever really hurt you?
>
> C. I see what you're saying. They can't really do anything to me, but they sound so convincing!

T. I know. But it's like they've got you convinced that they'll hurt you, so you turn without even noticing. And you've even said that sometimes you stop believing them and you turn around in your driver's seat and start telling them that they are wrong—maybe even threatening to come back there to show them that you really mean it! But what happens? You have to stop the bus to argue with them.

C. Yup. I'd say I've spent a whole lot of my life either turning the bus or stopping it to make deals with them.

T. Sure, and what happens to moving toward "Living Life"?

C. I never get there. I wish I could kick them off or tell them to be quiet!

T. You've tried that, right? How does that work? Do they actually leave?

C. (sighs) Not really. They just hunker down and sulk for a little while but they're not really gone.

T. So what can you do? Who is actually driving the bus? Even though they are convincing, who's feet are touching the pedals?

C. I guess I can just notice them. I've always just felt like I had to wait for them to really quiet down before I could keep moving. Like they were distracting me too much.

T. Yeah, they'll do that, huh? Can you be willing, in service of moving your bus toward living your life, to just let them do what they'll do?

C. Yeah, I mean I am driving the bus for a reason, and I'm the one letting them slow me down—they can't actually control the bus. I just have a hard time choosing to drive it myself.

T. Well, let's continue to practice that with your homework this week. This isn't about just listening, giving in, or resigning yourself to them. This is about you moving your bus toward what you care about regardless of what the passengers say they'll do to you!

In this segment, the therapist and Chester further explored psychological flexibility around some of the toughest of Chester's compulsions, his strong urge to plan out every detail for important events. For homework, Chester committed to choosing to just go somewhere and not plan for it. He predicted that this would most likely take the form of his mother calling and asking him to come over. Rather than plan what to bring and agonize over whether he got the right dessert, he would just go. Chester seemed glad to commit to this, citing that he would be more likely to have more time with his mother this way.

In the fifth session Chester's therapist introduced the idea of *self as context*. Chester had said that he had spent most of his adult life identifying himself as someone with OCD, so the *chessboard metaphor* was introduced. Chester was asked to imagine that his thoughts, feelings, and urges were on one side, and all of his positive experiences were the pieces on the other side of a chessboard. Together, the therapist and Chester examined what happens when Chester lives his life as a chess piece, as a player, and finally as the chessboard itself. The advantage of being the board is that Chester doesn't have to be invested in which side is winning or which side is right or wrong; rather, he can contain the pieces. From this perspective, Chester thought he would be more willing to notice his experiences, including urges. Next, Chester practiced an eyes-closed exercise in which the therapist asked Chester to notice the perspective of observing his thoughts, feelings, sensations, life roles, and body throughout his life. He reported following the exercise that he never really noticed that he was much more than his experiences before. He continued to practice noticing this observer self (or transcendent sense of self) for homework.

In session six, Chester reported that over the past week, when obsessions did arise, he was able to notice them (at least some of the time) as if they were leaves floating by him on a stream. Chester and his therapist practiced additional defusion strategies as a way to undermine Chester's conceptualized self as someone who was trapped by OCD and who had difficulty living his values. Chester continued practicing mindful awareness of all of his experiences, and following these activities he reported gaining a sense of perspective on his obsessions. He reported great enjoyment in the practice of making behavioral choices each day in line with his value of "living life," and for homework he agreed to practice living his life without getting caught up in either his obsessions or the self-conceptualization of being limited by OCD.

In the seventh session, Chester reported a much decreased level of compulsions (he said he only checked and planned three times this week), and his ratings on believability, reactivity, and distress were down to about 20% each. During the previous week, he noticed that sometimes it made sense for him to make brief notes about an important conversation, but that he didn't feel that it was a "have to" but rather a choice. Though Chester's global value of "living life" had been guiding the therapy all along, now the therapist and Chester explored his values in depth. Chester described his values for relationships, career, creativity, and community. Together, the therapist and Chester prepared a homework plan for creating goals consistent with his values, looking for actions to help achieve those goals and the internal and external barriers that might arise. Chester predicted some difficulty but expressed willingness to engage in values-consistent living regardless of the outcome.

In the eighth session, Chester reported that, while he still experienced his obsessions, he was largely able to do what he wanted in his life. Sometimes he still engaged in behaviors that looked very much like compulsions, but Chester agreed that they didn't function like that anymore.

He could choose when it was important to take notes and when it interfered with his life. He also stated that he felt much freer to just go places even though he noticed that he still would be considered an "over-packer" by others. He said that in the past he had tried to clean out his garage by simply throwing everything away, but this time he decided that he would have his brother come over and help him organize his documents with a simple but effective filing system. He anticipated very high levels of anxiety in doing this, but he really felt this was a free choice and it wasn't just about getting rid of stuff, citing a value of wanting more space for engaging in art projects.

Overall, Chester was thrilled about his life after therapy. At 3-month follow-up, he reported that he had maintained his gains, only now and then doing more compulsions but soon after choosing to get back to doing what he wanted for his life. He had a Y-BOCS score of 0 at posttreatment and at 3-month follow-up.

Summary

The focus of this chapter has been to illustrate the possible utility of concepts taken from ACT to the treatment of specific issues that are noted in the treatment of OCD. Because outcome data are still limited, it is not yet clear whether these procedures will be more or less effective than alternative empirically based approaches, but there is some evidence that these procedures do indeed help some people with OCD (Twohig, 2007; Twohig et al., 2006a). ACT is hardly a panacea, but it has been shown in many studies to be effective in targeting problematic psychological processes which then leads to good outcomes, even for difficult-to-treat clinical problems (for a review, see Hayes et al., 2006). Given the nature of the processes involved in treatment-resistant clients and the evidence that ACT can successfully target these processes, ACT may have something to offer treatment-resistant OCD clients.

References

Arch, J.J., & Craske, M.G. (2008). ACT and CBT for anxiety disorders. *Clinical Psychology: Science & Practice, 5*, 263–279.

Abramowitz, J.S. (1996). Variants of exposure and response prevention in the treatment of obsessive–compulsive disorder: A meta-analysis. *Behavior Therapy, 27*, 583–600.

Abramowitz, J.S. (1998). Does cognitive–behavioral therapy cure obsessive–compulsive disorder? A meta-analytic evaluation of clinical significance. *Behavior Therapy, 29*, 339–355.

Abramowitz, J.S., Franklin, M.E., & Foa, E.B. (2002a). Empirical status of cognitive–behavioral therapy for obsessive–compulsive disorder: A meta-analytic review. *Romanian Journal of Cognitive and Behavioral Psychotherapies, 2,*
89–104.

Abramowitz, J.S., Franklin M.E., Street, G.P., Kozak, M.J., & Foa, E.B. (2000). Effects
of comorbid depression on response to treatment for obsessive–compulsive
disorder. *Behavior Therapy, 31,* 517–528.

Abramowitz, J.S., Franklin, M.E., Zoellner, L.A., & Dibernardo, C.L. (2002b).
Treatment compliance and outcome in obsessive–compulsive disorder.
Behavior Modification, 26, 447–462.

Abramowitz, J.S., Taylor, S., & McKay, D. (2005). Potential limitations of cognitive
treatments for obsessive–compulsive disorder. *Cognitive Behaviour Therapy,
34,* 140–147.

American Psychiatric Association. (2000). *Diagnostic and statistical manual of mental
disorders* (4th ed., revised). Arlington, VA: American Psychiatric Association.

Antony, M.M., Downie, F., & Swinson, R.P. (1998). Diagnostic issues and epidemiology in obsessive–compulsive disorder. In R.P. Swinson, M.M. Antony,
S. Rachman & M.A. Richter (Eds.), *Obsessive–compulsive disorder: Theory,
research, and treatment* (pp. 3–32). New York: Guilford Press.

Barlow, D.H. (2002). *Anxiety and its disorders: The nature and treatment of anxiety and
panic (second edition).* New York: Guilford Press.

Berens, N.M., & Hayes, S.C. (2007). Arbitrarily applicable comparative relations:
Experimental evidence for a relational operant. *Journal of Applied Behavior
Analysis, 40,* 45–71.

Cherian A.E., & Frost, R.O. (2007). Treating compulsive hoarding. In M.M. Antony,
C. Purdon, & L.J. Summerfeldt (Eds.), *Psychological treatment of obsessive
compulsive disorder: Fundamentals and beyond.* Washington, D.C.: American
Psychological Association.

Deacon, B.J., Fawzy, T.I., & Lickel, J.J. (2007). *Cognitive defusion versus cognitive restructuring for negative body-image thoughts.* Paper presented at the
annual meeting of the Association for Cognitive and Behavioral Therapies,
November 15–18, Philadelphia, PA.

Diefenbach, G.J., Abramowitz, J.S., Norberg, M.M., & Tolin, D.F. (2007). Changes
in quality of life following cognitive–behavioral therapy for obsessive–compulsive disorder. *Behavior Therapy, 45,* 3060–3068.

Dougher, M.J., Hamilton, D., Fink, B., & Harrington, J. (2007). Transformation of
the discriminative and eliciting functions of generalized relational stimuli.
Journal of the Experimental Analysis of Behavior, 88(2), 179–197.

Dymond, S., & Barnes, D. (1995). A transformation of self-discrimination response
functions in accordance with the arbitrarily applicable relations of sameness,
more than, and less than. *Journal of the Experimental Analysis of Behavior, 64,*
163–184.

Eifert G.H., & Forsyth, J.P. (2005). *Acceptance and commitment therapy for anxiety
disorders: A practitioner's treatment guide to using mindfulness, acceptance, and
value-guided behavior change strategies.* Oakland, CA: New Harbinger.

Foa, E.B., & Kozak, M.J. (1995). DSM-IV field trial: Obsessive–compulsive disorder. *American Journal of Psychiatry, 152,* 90–94.

Foa, E.B., Liebowitz, M.R., Kozak, M.J., Davies, S., Campeas, R., Franklin, M.E. et al. (2005). Randomized, placebo-controlled trial of exposure and ritual prevention, clomipramine, and their combination in the treatment of obsessive–compulsive disorder. *American Journal of Psychiatry, 162,* 151–161.

Freeston, M.H., Rhéaume, J., & Ladouceur, R. (1996). Correcting faulty appraisals of obsessional thoughts. *Behaviour Research and Therapy, 34,* 433–446.

Hanna, G.L. (1995). Demographic and clinical features of obsessive–compulsive disorder in children and adolescents. *Journal of American Academy of Child Adolescent Psychiatry, 34,* 19–27.

Hayes, S.C. (1989). Nonhumans have not yet shown stimulus equivalence. *Journal of the Experimental Analysis of Behavior, 51,* 385–392.

Hayes, S.C. (2008). Climbing our hills: A beginning conversation on the comparison of ACT and traditional CBT. *Clinical Psychology: Science and Practice, 5,* 286–295.

Hayes, S.C., & Brownstein, A.J. (1986). Mentalism, behavior–behavior relations, and a behavior analytic view of the purposes of science. *The Behavior Analyst, 9,* 175–190.

Hayes, S.C., Barnes-Holmes, D., & Roche, B. (2001). *Relational frame theory: A post-Skinnerian account of human language and cognition.* New York: Kluwer Academic.

Hayes, S.C., Hayes, L.J., & Reese, H.W. (1988). Finding the philosophical core: A review of Stephen C. Popper's world hypotheses. *Journal of Experimental Analysis of Behavior, 50,* 97–111.

Hayes, S.C., Levin, M., Plumb, J., Boulanger, J., & Pistorello, J. (in press). Acceptance and Commitment Therapy and contextual behavioral science: Examining the progress of a distinctive model of behavioral and cognitive therapy. *Behavior Therapy.*

Hayes, S.C., Luoma, J.B., Bond, F.W., Masuda, A., & Lillis, J. (2006). Acceptance and commitment therapy: Model, processes and outcomes. *Behaviour Research and Therapy, 44,* 1–25.

Hayes, S.C., Masuda, A., Bissett, R., Luoma, J., & Guerrero, L.F. (2004a). DBT, FAP, and ACT: How empirically oriented are the new behavior therapy technologies? *Behavior Therapy, 35,* 35–54.

Hayes, S.C., Strosahl, K.D., & Wilson, K.G. (1999). *Acceptance and commitment therapy: An experiential approach to behavior change.* New York: Guilford Press.

Hayes, S.C., Strosahl, K.D., Wilson, K.G., Bissett, R.T., Pistorello, J. et al. (2004b). Measuring experiential avoidance: A preliminary test of a working model. *The Psychological Record, 54,* 553–578.

Hayes, S.C., Wilson, K.G., Gifford, E.V., Follette, V.M., & Strosahl, K. (1996). Emotional avoidance and behavioral disorders: A functional dimensional approach to diagnosis and treatment. *Journal of Consulting and Clinical Psychology, 64,* 1152–1168.

Hofmann, S.G. (2008). Common misconceptions about cognitive mediation of treatment change: A commentary on Longmore and Worrell (2007). *Clinical Psychology Review, 28,* 67–70.

Hofmann, S.G., & Asmundson, G.J. (2008). Acceptance and mindfulness-based therapy: new wave or old hat? *Clinical Psychology Review, 28,* 1–16.

Jacobson, N.S., Follette, W.C., & Revenstorf, D. (1984). Toward a standard definition of clinically significant change. *Behavior Therapy, 17,* 308–311.

Kessler, R.C., Chiu, W.T., Demler, O., & Walters, E.E. (2005). Prevalence, sever-ity, and comorbidity of twelve-month DSM-IV disorders in the National Comorbidity Survey Replication (NCS-R). *Archives of General Psychiatry, 62,* 617–627.

Kozak, M.J., & Coles M.E. (2005). Treatment for OCD: Unleashing the power of exposure. In J.S. Abramowitz & A.C. Houts (Eds.), *Concepts and controversies in obsessive compulsive disorder* (pp. 283–304). New York: Springer.

Lappalainen, R., Lehtonen, T., Skarp, E., Taubert, E., Ojanen, M., & Hayes, S.C. (2007). The impact of CBT and ACT models using psychology trainee thera-pists: A preliminary controlled effectiveness trial. *Behavior Modification, 31,* 488–511.

Levitt, J.T., Brown, T.A., Orsillo, S.M., & Barlow, D.H. (2004). The effects of accep-tance versus suppression of emotion on subjective and psychophysiological response to carbon dioxide challenge in patients with panic disorder. *Behavior Therapy, 35,* 747–766.

Lipkens, G., Hayes, S.C., & Hayes, L.J. (1991). Longitudinal study of derived stimulus relations in an infant. *Journal of Experimental Child Psychology, 56,* 201–239.

Luoma, J.B., Hayes, S.C., & Walser, R.D. (2007). *Learning ACT. An acceptance and commitment therapy skills-training manual for therapists.* Oakland, CA: New Harbinger.

Marcks, B.A., & Woods, D.W. (2005). A comparison of thought suppression to an acceptance-based technique in the management of personal intrusive thoughts: A controlled evaluation. *Behaviour Research and Therapy, 43,* 433–445.

Marcks, B.A., & Woods, D.W. (2007). Role of thought-related beliefs and coping strategies in the escalation of intrusive thoughts: An analog to obsessive–compulsive disorder. *Behaviour Research and Therapy, 45,* 2640–2651.

Masuda, A., Hayes, S.C., Sackett, C.F., & Twohig, M.P. (2004). Cognitive defusion and self-relevant negative thoughts: Examining the impact of a ninety year old technique. *Behaviour Research and Therapy, 42,* 477–485.

McHugh, L., Barnes-Holmes, Y., & Barnes-Holmes, D. (2004). A relational frame account of the development of complex cognitive phenomena: Perspective-taking, false belief understanding, and deception. *International Journal of Psychology and Psychological Therapy, 4,* 303–323.

Norberg, M.N., Calamari, J.E., Cohen, R.J., & Riemann, B.C. (2008). Quality of life in obsessive–compulsive disorder: An evaluation of impairment and a preliminary analysis of the ameliorating effects of treatment. *Depression and Anxiety, 25,* 248–259.

Obsessive Compulsive Cognitions Work Group. (1997). Cognitive assessment of obsessive–compulsive disorder. *Behavior Research and Therapy, 35,* 667–681.

O'Hora, D., Pelaez, M., Barnes-Holmes, D., & Amesty, L. (2005). Derived rela-tional responding and human language: Evidence from the WAIS-III. *The Psychological Record, 55,* 155–174.

Olatunji, B.O., Forsyth, J.P., & Feldner, M.T. (2007). Implications of emotion regu-lation for the shift from normative fear-related learning to anxiety-related psychopathology. *American Psychologist, 62,* 257–259.

O'Sullivan, G., Noshirvani, H., Marks, I., Montiero, W., & Lelliott, P. (1991). Six-year follow-up after exposure and clomipramine therapy for obsessive–com-pulsive disorder. *Journal of Clinical Psychiatry, 52,* 150–155.

Pollard, A.C. (2007). Treatment readiness, ambivalence, and resistance. In M.M. Antony, C. Purdon, & C. Summerfeldt (Eds.), *Psychological treatment of obsessive–compulsive disorder: Fundamentals and beyond* (pp. 61–77). Washington, D.C.: American Psychological Association.

Purdon, C., Rowa, K., & Antony M.M. (2004). Treatment fears in individuals awaiting treatment for obsessive–compulsive disorder. In C.L. Purdon (chair), *Treatment ambivalence, readiness, and resistance in obsessive–compulsive disorder*. Symposium presented at the annual meeting of the Association for Advancement of Behavior Therapy, November 18–21, New Orleans, LA.

Rachman, S., & Shafran, R. (1998). Cognitive and behavioral features of obsessive–compulsive disorder. In R.P. Swinson, M.M. Antony, S. Rachman, & M.A. Richter (Eds.), *Obsessive–compulsive disorder: Theory, research, and treatment* (pp. 51–78). New York: Guilford Press.

Rasmussen, S.A., & Eisen, J.L. (1992). The epidemiology and clinical features of obsessive compulsive disorder. *Psychiatric Clinics of North America, 15,* 743–758.

Rowa, K., Antony, M.M., & Swinson, R.P. (2007). Exposure and response prevention. In M.M. Antony, C. Purdon, & L.J. Summerfeldt (Eds.), *Psychological treatment of obsessive compulsive disorder: Fundamentals and beyond* (pp. 79–111). Washington, D.C.: American Psychological Association.

Salkovskis, P.M. (1998). Psychological approaches to the understanding of obsessional problems. In R.P. Swinson, M.M. Antony, S. Rachman, & M.A. Richter (Eds.), *Obsessive–compulsive disorder: Theory, research, and treatment* (pp. 33–50). New York: Guilford Press.

Segal, Z.V., Teasdale, J.D., & Williams, J.M.J. (2004). Mindfulness-based cognitive therapy: Theoretical rationale and empirical status. In S.C. Hayes, V.M. Follette, and M.M. Linehan (Eds.), *Mindfulness and acceptance* (pp. 45–65). New York: Guilford Press.

Shafran, R., Thordarson, D., & Rachman, S. (1996). Thought–action fusion in obsessive–compulsive disorder. *Journal of Anxiety Disorders, 5,* 379–391.

Shimoff, E., Catania, A.C., & Matthews, B.A. (1981). Uninstructed human responding: Sensitivity of low-rate performance to schedule contingencies. *Journal of the Experimental Analysis of Behavior, 36,* 207–220.

Slagle, D.M., & Gray, M.J. (2007). The utility of motivational interviewing as an adjunct to exposure therapy in the treatment of anxiety disorders. *Professional Psychology: Research and Practice, 38,* 329–337.

Sookman, D., & Pinard, G. (1999). Integrative cognitive therapy for obsessive–compulsive disorder: A focus on multiple schemas. *Cognitive and Behavioral Practice, 6,* 351–362.

Sookman, D., & Steketee, G. (2007). Direction in specialized cognitive behavior therapy for resistant obsessive compulsive disorder: Theory and practice of two approaches. *Cognitive and Behavioral Practice, 14,* 1–17.

Sookman, D., Abramowitz, J.S., Calamari, J.E., Wilhelm, S., & McKay, D. (2005). Subtypes of obsessive–compulsive disorder: Implications for specialized cognitive behavior therapy. *Behavior Therapy, 36,* 393–400.

Summerfeldt, L.J. (2004). Understanding and treating incompleteness in obsessive–compulsive disorder. *Journal of Clinical Psychology, 60,* 1155–1168.

Taylor S., McKay, D., & Abramowitz, J.S. (2008). Making sense of obsessive–compulsive disorder: Do subtypes exist? In J.S. Abramowitz and D. McKay (Eds.), *Clinical handbook of obsessive–compulsive disorder and related problems* (pp. 5–17). Baltimore, MD: The Johns Hopkins University Press.

Twohig, M.P. (2007). *Acceptance and commitment therapy as a treatment for obsessive–compulsive disorder.* Doctoral dissertation, University of Nevada, Reno.

Twohig, M.P., & Whittal, M.L. (2008). *An evaluation of mechanisms of action in ACT, CT, and ERP for OCD.* Paper presented at the annual conference of the Association for Behavior Analysis, May 24–27, Chicago, IL.

Twohig, M.P., & Woods, D.W. (2004). A Preliminary investigation of acceptance and commitment therapy and habit reversal as a treatment for trichotillomania. *Behavior Therapy, 35,* 803–820.

Twohig, M.P., Hayes, S.C., & Masuda, A. (2006a). Increasing willingness to experience obsessions: Acceptance and commitment therapy as a treatment for obsessive–compulsive disorder. *Behavior Therapy, 37,* 3–13.

Twohig, M.P., Hayes, S.C., & Masuda, A. (2006b). A preliminary investigation of acceptance and commitment therapy as a treatment for chronic skin picking. *Behaviour Research and Therapy, 44,* 1513–1522.

Twohig, M.P., Moran, D.J., & Hayes, S.C. (2008). A functional contextual account of obsessive–compulsive disorder. In D.W. Woods & J. Kantor (Eds.), *A modern behavioral analysis of clinical problems.* Reno, NV: Context Press.

Tolin, D.F., Abramowitz, J.S., Przeworski, A., & Foa, E.B. (2002). Thought suppression in obsessive–compulsive disorder. *Behaviour Research and Therapy, 40,* 1251–1270.

Veale, D. (2007). Treating obsessive compulsive disorder in people with poor insight and overvalued ideation. In M.M. Antony, C. Purdon, & L.J. Summerfeldt (Eds.), *Psychological treatment of obsessive–compulsive disorder: Fundamentals and beyond* (pp. 267–280). Washington D.C.: American Psychological Association.

Whelan, R., & Barnes-Holmes, D. (2004). The transformation of consequential functions in accordance with the relational frames of same and opposite. *Journal of the Experimental Analysis of Behavior, 82,* 177–195.

Whittal, M.L., Thordarson, D.S., & McLean, P.D. (2005). Treatment of obsessive–compulsive disorder: Cognitive behavior therapy vs. exposure and response prevention. *Behavior Research and Therapy, 43,* 1559–1576.

Wilhelm, S., & Steketee, G.S. (2006). *Cognitive therapy for obsessive–compulsive disorder: A guide for professionals.* Oakland, CA: New Harbinger.

Wilson, K.G., & Hayes, S.C. (1996). Resurgence of derived stimulus relations. *Journal of the Experimental Analysis of Behavior, 66,* 267–281.

Woods, D.W., Wetterneck, C.T., & Flessner, C.A. (2006). A controlled evaluation of acceptance and commitment therapy plus habit reversal as a treatment for trichotillomania. *Behaviour Research and Therapy, 34,* 639–656.

Wulfert, E., & Hayes, S.C. (1988). The transfer of conditional sequencing through conditional equivalence classes. *Journal of the Experimental Analysis of Behavior, 50,* 125–144.

chapter ten

Treating anxiety disorders in the context of concurrent substance misuse

Sherry H. Stewart
Roisin M. O'Connor
Dalhousie University
Halifax, Nova Scotia, Canada

Contents

Decades of research have established that substance use disorders are far more common among those with anxiety disorders than can be explained by chance alone (see Stewart & Conrod, 2008a). Thus, it is the clinical reality for therapists working with anxiety disorder patients that they will encounter some patients who not only are dealing with a clinically significant anxiety disorder but are also suffering from substance abuse or dependence. On the surface, such anxiety patients can appear to be quite "treatment resistant," as concurrent substance use disorders (SUDs) are known to interfere with the efficacy of anxiety disorders treatment (e.g., Bruce et al., 2005). As will be evident throughout this chapter, substance misuse can be a part of the avoidance response profile typical of anxiety disorder patients, and substance abuse may, in some cases, serve as a safety behavior. Avoidance responses and safety behaviors are well known maintenance factors in anxiety disorders (Salkovskis, 1991). Thus, it should come as no surprise that anxiety disorder patients with concurrent SUD fare less well in anxiety disorder treatments and relapse to their anxiety disorder at higher rates than those with no concurrent SUD (e.g., Bruce et al., 2005).

Luckily, though, there are effective treatments for SUDs that can be readily integrated with anxiety disorder treatment. One type of treatment that has received considerable empirical support in the treatment of a wide variety of SUDs is cognitive–behavioral therapy (CBT). CBT is one of the most widely used and effective treatments in the case of alcohol use disorders (e.g., Finney & Monahan, 1996; Oei, Lim, & Young, 1991), and it has also been demonstrated effective in the treatment of cocaine dependence (Carroll et al., 2004), methamphetamine dependence (Rawson, Gonzales, & Brethan, 2002), and nicotine dependence (Hall, Muñoz, & Reus, 1994). CBT for SUDs also receives high ratings on patient satisfaction (Donovan, Kadden, DiClemente, & Carroll, 2002). Coping skills training is a core focus of CBT for SUDs (Monti, Kadden, Rohsenow, Cooney, & Abrams, 2002) to help clients prepare to deal with the intrapersonal (e.g., negative emotions) and interpersonal (e.g., conflict with others) triggers for their substance misuse. Skills such as listening, drinking and drug refusal, and assertiveness are taught, and clients are trained in techniques for managing urges, dealing with anger, and increasing their involvement in pleasant activities. Together, the goal of this skills training is to increase clients' self-efficacy to cope without the use of substances. Another commonly used technique in CBT for SUDs is cue exposure. This involves repeated exposures to individually relevant substance use triggers paired with practice of the previously learned skills for coping with urges to drink or take drugs (Monti et al., 2002).

In clinical practice, the most common method of treating comorbid anxiety disorders and SUDs is through a sequential approach, where the SUD is addressed first and the anxiety disorder is addressed second if it remains a concern. There are several problems with this approach. First, substance-induced anxiety disorders are actually quite rare (Grant et al., 2004), so the assumption that many anxiety disorders will disappear once the SUD is resolved is faulty in the large majority of cases. Second, because the anxiety disorder is motivating the substance abuse in many cases, the untreated anxiety disorder may serve as a factor that creates risk for relapse to substance misuse (Stewart, 1996). Expert opinion and emerging clinical data suggest that an integrated approach that targets the anxiety disorder, the SUD, and their interrelations simultaneously is the best course of action for the treatment of this form of comorbidity.

In this chapter, we examine the treatment of anxiety disorders in the context of SUDs. For each of the anxiety disorders in the *Diagnostic and*

Statistical Manual of Mental Disorders, 4th ed., text revision (DSM-IV-TR) (American Psychiatric Association, 2000), we examine: (1) rates of comorbidity with SUD, (2) theories of comorbidity, and (3) integrated treatment options available for simultaneously dealing with the two concurrent problems. For some of the anxiety disorders, integrated treatments have been developed and are fairly well studied (e.g., in the case of PTSD). In other cases, integrated treatments are just beginning to emerge (e.g., for panic disorder and social phobia). In cases where no integrated treatments have yet been developed (e.g., for specific phobia and generalized anxiety disorder), we offer treatment recommendations for providing integrated treatments based on the research on underlying mechanisms available to date. We conclude the chapter with consideration of a sample case and with some final clinical recommendations emerging from the review.

Posttraumatic stress disorder

Posttraumatic stress disorder (PTSD) is an anxiety disorder that can develop in response to a traumatic event (e.g., rape, combat, natural disaster). It involves symptoms of hyperarousal (e.g., excessive startle), avoidance (e.g., avoiding trauma reminders), numbing (e.g., sense of foreshortened future), and cognitive reexperiencing (e.g., flashbacks and nightmares about the trauma) (American Psychiatric Association, 2000). Estimates of the lifetime prevalence of PTSD in the general population range from 1 to 12% (Kessler, Sonnega, Bromet, Hughes, & Nelson, 1995; Resnick, Kilpatrick, Dansky, Saunders, & Best, 1993). Epidemiologic surveys have consistently found a high rate of comorbidity between PTSD and SUD (Chilcoat & Menard, 2003; Stewart, 1996). Adult men with PTSD are about 2 times more likely than those without PTSD to suffer from an alcohol use disorder and about 3 times more likely to suffer from a drug use disorder (Kessler et al., 1995). The comorbidity rates are even higher in adult women and in adolescents. Women with PTSD are about 2.5 times more likely than those without PTSD to suffer from an alcohol use disorder and about 4 times more likely to suffer from a drug use disorder (Kessler et al., 1995). Adolescents with PTSD are about 4 times more likely to have an alcohol use disorder than those without PTSD and about 8 times more likely to have a drug use disorder (Kilpatrick et al., 2000).

A variety of theories have been proposed to account for the high comorbidity of PTSD and SUD (see reviews by Coffey, Read, & Norberg, 2008; Stewart, 1996). First, it has been suggested that those who suffer from PTSD are at risk of attempting to self-medicate their aversive PTSD symptoms through the excessive use of alcohol or other drugs. Second, it has been suggested that substance abuse interferes with the processing of trauma, thus increasing risk for PTSD development in traumatized individuals. A third hypothesis, the "high-risk hypothesis," contends that substance abuse increases risk for trauma exposure (e.g., through a risky lifestyle), thus in turn increasing risk for PTSD development. Empirical evidence supports each of these positions in terms of the development of this form of comorbidity, with the majority of cases appearing to develop via the first pathway described above (see review by Stewart, 1996). However, the mutual maintenance hypothesis argues that, regardless of the order of causation, once the two disorders are established, functional relationships among the symptoms may form a vicious cycle in which PTSD symptoms and the SUD serve to maintain one another over time (Riggs & Foa, 2008; Stewart & Conrod, 2003, 2008b). Specifically, while patients may attempt to self-medicate for their distressing PTSD symptoms through the use of alcohol or drugs (e.g., attempting to quell traumatic memories through the use of drugs), the substance misuse can interfere with the process of natural recovery from trauma, serving to maintain the PTSD in the longer term.

We mentioned earlier in the chapter that the most common method of treating comorbid anxiety disorders and SUDs, in general, is through a sequential approach where the SUD is addressed first. This is very much the case in the specific area of PTSD–SUD treatment where the SUD is typically addressed first and the PTSD is not tackled until abstinence has been achieved for a significant period (Ouimette, Moos, & Brown, 2003a). There are many reasons why the sequential approach continues to be the norm in this area of comorbidity treatment, but one of the main reasons is the concern held by many practitioners that PTSD exposure treatment will lead to worsening of substance abuse if the substance problems are not treated first (Riggs & Foa, 2008). But, unfortunately, delaying treatment for PTSD can lead to poorer short-term outcome of substance use treatment (Ouimette, Ahrens, Moos, & Finney, 1997, 1998; Ouimette, Finney, & Moos, 1999) and greater relapse of the substance abuse in the longer term when using the sequential approach (Brown, Stout, & Mueller, 1996; Dansky, Brady, & Saladin, 1998; Ouimette, Moos, & Finney, 2003b). This is because patients remain at risk of returning to substance use to alleviate unresolved PTSD symptoms. Thus, some have argued that treatment of these comorbid patients might be achieved more effectively and efficiently if the two treatments were provided simultaneously (Ouimette et al., 2003a). Furthermore, comorbid PTSD and SUD patients themselves prefer concurrent treatment of their two problems (Brown, Stout, & Gannon-Rowley, 1998).

For these reasons, a number of concurrent treatments for comorbid PTSD and SUD have been developed, and preliminary data support their efficacy. In fact, of all of the anxiety disorders, PTSD–SUD comorbidity is the area that is furthest along in terms of effective treatment development (see review by Riggs & Foa, 2008). The existing treatment packages are integrated treatments that employ the following common cognitive–behavioral ingredients: training in effective coping skills, relapse prevention and managing substance use urges, education about the relations between PTSD and substance abuse/dependence, and PTSD management or reduction techniques (e.g., Brady, Dansky, Back, Foa, & Carroll, 2001; Najavits, Weiss, Shaw, & Muenz, 1998; Riggs, Rukstalis, Volpicelli, Kalmanson, & Foa, 2003; Triffleman, Carroll, & Kellogg, 1999; Zlotnick, Najavits, Rohsenow, & Johnson, 2003). Most of these treatments (e.g., Brady et al., 2001; Riggs et al., 2003; Triffleman et al., 1999) employ imaginal exposure techniques for the treatment of the PTSD (Foa & Rothbaum, 1998). However, some clinicians have expressed concern that substance use may increase in these patients in response to the arousal generated by exposure to traumatic memories and thus have explicitly omitted exposure therapy from the core treatment program. One such program is Najavits' (2003) "Seeking Safety" treatment, which focuses on establishing patients' safety through the achievement of substance abstinence, reduction in self-harm behaviors, and terminating dangerous or abusive relationships.

Despite concerns, the data available to date demonstrate that trauma-focused exposure techniques help reduce PTSD symptoms without interfering with recovery from the SUD (e.g., Brady et al., 2001; Riggs et al., 2003). In fact, a review of the treatment outcome literature by Riggs and Foa (2008) suggests that programs that incorporate extensive trauma-related exposure appear to produce greater improvement in PTSD symptoms than do programs that do not include extensive exposure. Thus, including trauma-related imaginal exposure as part of the integrated treatment for comorbid PTSD and SUD does appear to be a promising approach deserving of additional controlled research. However, it is important to note that exposure to trauma reminders often triggers craving and urges for substance use in patients with comorbid PTSD and SUD (Saladin et al., 2003). Thus, we recommend that substance use and craving be carefully monitored in such patients over the course of exposure therapy along with provision of frequent practice of effective coping skills and urge management techniques.

Panic disorder with and without agoraphobia

Panic disorder is an anxiety disorder characterized by frequent and severe panic attacks. Panic attacks are intense emotional reactions that often seem to come "out of the blue." They involve autonomic arousal symptoms (e.g., racing heartbeat, difficulty breathing, sweating), as well as psychological symptoms such as a feeling of losing control or worries that one is going crazy (American Psychiatric Association, 2000). Panic disorder may or may not occur concurrently with agoraphobia—a marked avoidance of situations where it might be difficult to escape or where the person might be embarrassed, if he or she were to experience a panic attack (e.g., avoidance of public transportation, movie theaters). The lifetime prevalence of panic disorder is about 3.5% (Eaton, Kessler, Wittchen, & Magee, 1994) and that of agoraphobia is about 5.3% (Kessler et al., 1994).

Together, these panic spectrum disorders have been found to be highly comorbid with SUD (see reviews by Kushner, Abrams, & Borchardt, 2000; Norton, Norton, Cox, & Belik, 2008; Zvolensky, Schmidt, & Stewart, 2003). For example, in the National Epidemiologic Survey of Alcohol and Related Conditions (NESARC), it was shown that alcohol dependence was 2.9 and 3.5 times more likely in those with panic disorder without agoraphobia (PD) and those with panic disorder with agoraphobia (PDA), respectively, relative to those without PD/PDA (Hasin, Stinson, Ogburn, & Grant, 2007). Drug dependence was 6.4 and 9.2 times more likely in those with PD and PDA, respectively, relative to those without PD/PDA (Compton, Thomas, Stinson, & Grant, 2007). In fact, in the NESARC, PDA was the anxiety disorder most strongly related to alcohol dependence. Moreover, people with panic spectrum disorders smoke more cigarettes (Pohl, Yeragani, Balon, Lycaki, & McBride, 1992) and drink alcohol more frequently (Regier et al., 1990) compared to controls.

This form of comorbidity has been shown to have a negative impact on prognosis (e.g., Burns, Teesson, & O'Neill, 2005; Willinger et al., 2002). This is not surprising, as patients with panic spectrum disorders experience more severe substance withdrawal symptoms (Breslau, Kilbey, & Andreski, 1991) and drop out of alcohol treatment (Labounty, Hatsukami, Morgon, & Nelson, 1992) and smoking cessation treatment (Covey, Hughes, Glassman, Blazer, & George, 1994) at higher rates than others. Moreover, PD patients with a comorbid SUD are at increased risk for suicide relative to PD patients without comorbid substance abuse/dependence (Hornig & McNally, 1995).

Several theories have been proposed to account for the high comorbidity between panic spectrum disorders and SUDs; for example, the self-medication theory (Khantzian, 1997) posits that patients with PD/PDA are attempting to manage their aversive panic symptoms by self-medicating with alcohol, tobacco, or other drugs. In fact, some lab-based data do suggest that panic-prone individuals are more sensitive than others to the effects of alcohol in dampening anxiety and catastrophic thoughts in response to arousal-related bodily sensations (MacDonald, Baker, Stewart, & Skinner, 2000). A questionnaire study also showed that the very large majority (83%) of a sample of inpatient alcoholics experiencing panic attacks reported that they used alcohol to prevent or reduce the intensity of panic attacks (Cox, Norton, Dorward, & Fergusson, 1989). Another theory points to the panicogenic effects of various drugs of abuse and argues that acute intoxication or repeated substance withdrawal experiences among those with an SUD can kindle the onset of panic attacks, leading to the development of PD (see reviews by Kushner et al., 2000; Norton et al., 2008). A third possibility is a common underlying predisposition to both PD and SUD (e.g., common genetic or personality predisposition). And, finally, regardless of the original pathway to the development of the comorbid problem, it is possible that, once established, the two disorders are mutually maintaining. A PD patient, for example, may frequently attempt self-medication of his or her panic attacks through alcohol use, smoking, "as-needed" benzodiazepine use, or other drug misuse. However, the escalating substance use to control the panic may result in more frequent and intense substance withdrawal symptoms. It is possible that these withdrawal symptoms are misperceived as panic attacks or impending panic which could in turn promote continued self-medication with substances, resulting in a vicious cycle (George, Nutt, Dwyer, & Linnoila, 1990).

Given the high prevalence and the negative impact of this form of comorbidity, it is surprising that little work has been done to develop and evaluate treatments for those with comorbid PD/PDA and SUD. Again, unfortunately, most existing treatments continue to focus on either the anxiety disorder or the SUD using a sequential or parallel treatment approach, rather than targeting their functional relations in an integrated approach (Toneatto & Rector, 2008). Recent data are encouraging that we may be on our way to the development of effective and efficient integrated treatments for this type of comorbid disorder.

One such treatment was developed by Kushner et al. (2006). They compared two groups of patients with a diagnosis of PD who were admitted for treatment of an alcohol use disorder ($n = 63$). The first group received an integrated 12-session intensive treatment for both the PD and alcohol disorder that was delivered over 2 weeks. The treatment consisted of psychoeducation, cognitive restructuring, and cue exposure. It was explicitly designed to treat behaviors and cognitions related to the anxiety–alcohol association. The second group received only the alcohol-focused treatment as usual. At 4-month follow-up, the integrated treatment was shown to be more effective than the treatment as usual on several outcome measures: diagnoses of PD and alcohol dependence, severity of alcohol relapse, total drinks, and number of heavy drinking episodes (Kushner et al., 2006).

Another example is an intervention developed by Otto, Jones, Craske, and Barlow (2004a) for treating patients with comorbid PD and benzodiazepine dependence. The theory underlying this approach suggests that, because panic factors and benzodiazepine use interact in clinically meaningful ways, it may be useful to concurrently target both in a single overarching treatment model (see also Otto, Safren, & Pollack, 2004b). In their integrated treatment approach, Otto and his colleagues have extended to the treatment of benzodiazepine dependence a technique that is known to help PD patients with their fear of their internal arousal sensations. This technique is called *interoceptive exposure* and involves repeated exposure to the arousal-related sensations that are so feared by those with PD (see Stewart & Watt, 2008). Tapering benzodiazepines produces many of these feared internal sensations. Thus, Otto et al. (2004a) reasoned that inclusion of interoceptive exposure prior to benzodiazepine tapering should allow for the effective reduction of panic while also facilitating benzodiazepine discontinuation. Their 10-week integrated group CBT program, which is illustrated through a case example presented later in this chapter, has been shown to be effective relative to a treatment-as-usual condition of gradual taper alone in a randomized controlled trial involving 33 dually diagnosed patients (Otto et al., 1993).

A final recent example is an integrated treatment developed by Zvolensky and colleagues for the treatment of concurrent PD and tobacco dependence. This treatment is based on the theoretical model developed by Zvolensky, Schmidt, and Stewart (2003) to explain the high rates of comorbidity between PD and smoking and on many of the same principles outlined above for Otto and colleagues' (1993) integrated treatment for PD and benzodiazepine dependence. Specifically, their Anxiety Sensitivity-Based Program for Targeting Panic and Smoking Problems model involves three key elements (see Zvolensky, Bernstein, Yartz, McLeish, & Feldner, 2008). First, they include psychoeducation to provide patients with knowledge of the interrelation of their two problems and to give them a rationale for the treatment. Second, there is a focus on decreasing emotional reactivity to and increasing tolerance of anxious emotions, bodily sensations, and nicotine withdrawal symptoms using cognitive–behavioral methods including interoceptive exposure. And, finally, this approach includes specialized smoking-oriented psychoeducation and relapse prevention training (e.g., learning to effectively cope with urges). It is important to emphasize that the interoceptive exposures are begun before the smoking quit date with a rationale that this will help patients learn to tolerate and manage those same sensations when they are experienced during nicotine withdrawal. Zvolensky and colleagues also incorporate "mini-withdrawals" as part of the interoceptive exposure plan, where patients are asked to perform the interoceptive exposures (e.g., hyperventilation) after increasing periods of smoking abstinence. A randomized controlled trial of this new intervention is ongoing. Zvolensky, Yartz, Gregor, Gonzalez, and Bernstein (2008) have recently reported success with this approach in a case series design. Specifically, the intervention was tested in three female daily smokers with moderately high levels of nicotine dependence and high levels of anxiety sensitivity (i.e., fear of arousal sensations) (Stewart

& Kushner, 2001). The pilot study showed that the integrated intervention had positive effects on smoking outcomes, decreased anxiety sensitivity, increased distress tolerance, and improved mood, suggesting promise for this new program.

Although each of these three empirically supported approaches can provide clinicians with a program for dealing with specific forms of PD–SUD comorbidity (i.e., comorbidity with alcohol dependence, benzodiazepine dependence, and smoking dependence), guidelines are also available for helping clinicians deal with PD comorbidity with substance abuse and dependence more generally. Specifically, Toneatto and Rector (2008) suggested an approach in which clinicians utilize a functional analysis to establish the interrelations between the substance use behaviors and the panic disorder symptoms in a given comorbid patient and develop their treatment approach accordingly. This functional analytic approach remains to be empirically tested.

Social phobia

Social phobia is the most prevalent anxiety disorder, occurring at a rate of 13.3% in the general population (Kessler et al., 1994). In the National Comorbidity Survey (NCS), the lifetime prevalence of alcohol abuse or dependence was nearly twice as high among those with social phobia as compared to those without (i.e., 24% vs. 14%) (Magee, Eaton, Wittchen, McGonagle, & Kessler, 1996). The relationship does not seem to be specific to alcohol but extends to other drugs as well. According to the NESARC, alcohol dependence is 2.7 times more likely and drug dependence 4.5 times more likely among those with social phobia as compared to those without (Compton et al., 2007; Hasin et al., 2007). Marijuana use problems seem to be particularly associated with social phobia. For example, the NCS indicated that those with social phobia were 7 times more likely to suffer from a marijuana use disorder relative to those without social phobia (Agosti, Nunes, & Levin, 2002). Recent longitudinal research suggests that social phobia (but not other anxiety disorders or depression) in adolescence was linked to greater rates of marijuana dependence at age 30 years (Buckner et al., 2008).

Anecdotal reports (Chambless, Cherney, Caputo, & Rheinstein, 1987; Schneier, Martin, Liebowitz, Gorman, & Fyer, 1989; Thomas, Randall, & Carrigan, 2003) suggest that socially anxious individuals intentionally use alcohol to self-medicate their social fears (see review by Morris, Stewart, & Ham, 2005). Several theories, including the tension reduction hypothesis (Conger, 1956) and the self-medication hypothesis (Khantzian, 1997), can be applied to explaining the relationship between social phobia and SUDs. These theories all purport that the repeated use of substances to relieve social anxiety ultimately results in dependence. While the use of substances is initially rewarding by providing relief from anxiety in feared social contexts, as tolerance develops greater amounts of the substance are needed to achieve social anxiety relief. As substance use escalates, it can maintain or even exacerbate the social anxiety (see Kushner et al., 2000).

It may be helpful to view substance abuse in socially anxious clients as a form of safety behavior. It is well established that socially phobic individuals regularly engage in a variety of systematic cognitive and behavioral strategies known as safety behaviors in an attempt to hide their anxiety from others and thus avoid negative social outcomes (Voncken, Alden, & Bögels, 2006). These behaviors include thinking carefully before speaking (to avoid stumbling over words), avoiding eye contact (to avoid having others view one's anxious expression), and putting hands in pockets (to hide one's shaking) (Pinto-Gouveia, Cunha, & Salvador, 2003). However, it is also established that these safety behaviors actually serve to maintain anxiety by interfering with anxiety habituation/extinction and by preventing socially anxious individuals from experiencing the disconfirmation of their negative beliefs and assumptions (Salkovskis, 1991). The use of safety behaviors has been shown to interfere with the efficacy of traditional exposure therapy, and exposure therapy for social phobia is more effective in reducing social anxiety and negative beliefs when the safety behaviors are simultaneously treated than when patients receive exposure therapy alone (Kim, 2005; Wells et al., 1995). Thus, interventions that have been developed for reducing safety behaviors in socially anxious individuals might be particularly useful for patients with comorbid social phobia–SUD.

It has also been suggested that those with comorbid social phobia and substance dependence are more psychologically dependent on alcohol or drugs than substance-dependent individuals without social phobia (see review by Tran & Smith, 2008). Compared to alcohol-dependent individuals without social phobia, those with social phobia report more drinking to enhance their social functioning (Thomas, Thevos, & Randall, 1999) and greater difficulty controlling their alcohol use (Lepine & Pelissolo, 1998). It has also been shown that elevated coping motives for drinking (i.e., drinking specifically to control negative mood states such as anxiety) mediate or help explain the relationship between social anxiety and alcohol problems (Stewart, Morris, Mellings, & Komar, 2006). Similar findings have been recently reported linking social anxiety, coping motives for marijuana use, and levels of marijuana-related problems (Buckner, Bonn-Miller, Zvolensky, & Schmidt, 2007). Such findings suggest that these characteristics (e.g., coping motives for substance use; substance use to enhance social functioning) should be targeted as specific treatment foci when working with socially phobic patients with a concurrent SUD.

Because concurrent substance misuse can serve as a maintenance factor for social anxiety, it makes intuitive sense to treat both disorders simultaneously. Unfortunately, very few studies have been conducted to validate expert opinion that simultaneous treatment is preferable (Smith & Book, 2008). Those studies that have been conducted have produced contradictory findings. Randall, Thomas, and Thevos (2001) conducted a controlled trial where patients with comorbid social phobia and alcohol dependence (n = 93) were randomized to one of two 12-week treatments: CBT for the alcohol disorder only or CBT for the alcohol disorder simultaneous with CBT for social phobia. The latter can be considered a parallel treatment approach in that established treatment protocols for each disorder were administered at the same time. In this particular case, the two treatments were delivered in the same treatment facility, by the same therapist, and within the same treatment session. The alcohol treatment included training in such skills as coping with urges to drink, problem solving, and drink refusal skills (Kadden et al., 1992). The dual-focused treatment included all of the above plus a focus on social anxiety through relaxation training, discussion of triggers for social anxiety, creation of a social fears hierarchy, and graduated exposure homework (Butler, 1989). No specific training in social skills was provided in the dual-focused treatment. The authors had expected that the dual-focused treatment would result in both better anxiety outcomes and better alcohol outcomes.

Contrary to hypotheses, both groups did equally well with social anxiety outcomes (with both groups showing only modest improvements), and the dual-focused treatment unexpectedly resulted in *increased* alcohol use. One possibility discussed by the authors was that encouraging exposure to feared situations in the dual-focused treatment may have resulted in participants engaging in more coping drinking, thus explaining the increased alcohol use in the dual-focused treatment relative to the alcohol-only treatment. This increased alcohol use, in turn, may have interfered with the anxiety being extinguished by exposure, thus explaining why the dual-focused treatment did not result in greater improvement in social anxiety than the alcohol-only treatment (Randall et al., 2001). Conrod and Stewart (2005) have provided another explanation for these unexpected findings by contrasting the parallel approach to treatment of comorbidity that was used by Randall et al. (2001) to a more integrated approach. Specifically, parallel treatment requires the simultaneous provision of two empirically supported treatments, which can be quite demanding of patients with complex problems relative to a single integrated treatment. Integrated treatments can be more efficient and can directly address the functional interrelations between the symptoms of the two disorders (Zahradnik & Stewart, 2008).

The only integrated treatment for social anxiety and substance misuse that has yet to be tested has shown promising initial results. Specifically, Tran (2008a) randomized college students with concurrent social anxiety and hazardous alcohol use ($n = 41$) to one of two treatments: a brief integrated treatment for social anxiety and alcohol misuse or a brief treatment for alcohol misuse alone. The integrated treatment used motivational interviewing and cognitive–behavioral strategies to reduce concurrent hazardous drinking and social anxiety. The control intervention was of the same duration (3 sessions totaling 280 minutes) and involved psychoeducation about hazardous drinking and alcohol skills building. Consistent with the hypothesis, the integrated treatment was found to be more successful in treating both the social anxiety and the hazardous drinking (Tran, 2008a). It was most successful relative to the control treatment in the following treatment outcome variables: coping drinking motives, relief expectancies, and drink refusal self-efficacy specific to social situations. These are variables that theoretically link social anxiety with hazardous drinking. Tran (2008b) has also noted that, at least for college students, offering a treatment that also helps them deal with social anxiety is more palatable than a treatment focusing solely on alcohol misuse. Thus, the results do seem encouraging in terms of the utility of a brief integrated approach to the treatment of comorbid social anxiety and alcohol abuse. Future studies are needed to determine if Tran's (2008a,b) integrated treatment performs better than CBT focusing on social anxiety alone, in terms of treatment of both the social anxiety and the alcohol misuse, as well as to determine if its efficacy extends beyond college students and to comorbidity with other drugs of abuse, such as marijuana.

Obsessive–compulsive disorder

The lifetime prevalence of obsessive–compulsive disorder (OCD) is approximately 2.5% in the general population (for a review, see Antony, Downie, & Swinson, 1998). The prevalence of OCD among those with SUDs seems to vary broadly, ranging from 3 to 11% (Compton et al., 2000; Eisen & Rasmussen, 1989; Fals-Stewart & Angarano, 1994). Thus, OCD seems to be somewhere between equally to more than 4 times as prevalent among those who abuse substances than in the general population. The discrepancy in prevalence rates may be attributable to a few key factors. As suggested by Fals-Stewart and Lucente (1994; see also Klostermann & Fals-Stewart, 2008), OCD may be underdiagnosed because symptoms are overlooked by substance abusing patients or not reported due to embarrassment and are either not part of the assessment at substance abuse treatment centers or are not detected by counselors due to lack of training. On the other hand, OCD may be overdiagnosed in SUD patients, as substance use, including cravings and behavior, may be conceptualized as obsessions and compulsions (Modell, Glaser, Mountz, Schmaltz, & Cyr, 1992). Thus, overdiagnosing may be an issue of differential diagnosis rather than comorbidity (Zohar & Pato, 1991). Finally, rates of comorbidity may vary depending on the substance abused and the subtype of OCD. Although there is a paucity of such research, a recent study found that alcohol dependence was most strongly associated with a subtype of OCD characterized by symmetry, ordering, and arranging (n = 418) (Hasler et al., 2007). The fact that OCD is equally or even more prevalent in those with SUD necessitates that treatment providers be equipped to address issues of co-occurring substance abuse or dependence when they are treating clients with OCD.

A theoretical conceptualization of OCD and SUD comorbidity is first needed to provide the groundwork for treatment planning. OCD is typically characterized by both obsessions, which include intrusive and distressing thoughts, and compulsions, which include repetitive behaviors that usually decrease the distress caused by the obsessions. Obsessions often include contamination fears and fears of harm to self or others, and compulsions often include cleaning (e.g., hand-washing) and checking (e.g., locks) rituals (Leckman, Zhang, Alsobrook, & Paul, 2001). Individuals need only meet criteria for either obsessions or compulsions to receive a DSM-IV-TR diagnosis of OCD; however, although 25% of those receiving a diagnosis of OCD meet the criteria for obsession only, meeting the criteria for compulsions only is very rare (e.g., Rachman, 2003; Stein, Forde, Anderson, & Walker, 1997; Welkowitz, Struening, Pittman, Guarding, & Welkowitz, 2000). Accordingly, most often obsessions are experienced and are responded to with attempts to avoid or suppress the distressing thoughts or neutralize them with compulsions. These safety behaviors only temporarily relieve the distress while sustaining the maladaptive cognition (Rachman, 2003). Thus, they play a central role in maintaining and escalating the obsessions, and ultimately perpetuate the cycle of obsessions and avoidance/compulsions.

Given this conceptualization of OCD, it is possible that substances may be used as a safety behavior by some. In the short term, use of substances may allow individuals to avoid or numb the distress that they are experiencing due to their obsessions, and consequently reduce the need for the time-consuming and often embarrassing neutralizing compulsive rituals. Substance use would provide temporary relief—serving as a coping mechanism—and thus be negatively reinforcing to the individual with OCD. There is a critical need for research testing this potential function of substance use in OCD, as it may well help explain the initial development of an SUD in clients with OCD. But, like other safety behaviors (Rachman, 2003), substance use may actually have longer term negative consequences for OCD, as they serve to maintain or even exacerbate the symptoms of the anxiety disorder with repeated substance misuse. In fact, there is some research showing that psychoactive substances do indeed exacerbate OCD symptoms (e.g., McDougle, Goodman, Delgado, & Price, 1989).

The effectiveness of treatments for OCD may also be hampered by concurrent SUD. Both cognitive therapy and exposure and response prevention (ERP) have demonstrated efficacy for treating OCD (e.g., McLean et al., 2001). Specifically, empirically supported cognitive therapy treatments incorporate cognitive challenges to modify maladaptive beliefs and behavioral experiments aimed at testing the validity of beliefs (e.g., Rachman, 2003). ERP uses repeated exposure to the feared stimuli pertaining to the obsessions while preventing compulsive rituals, with the goal of habituation (e.g., Foa & Kozak, 1996). It has been argued that to reduce fear using such therapeutic techniques as cognitive therapy and ERP, there must be full activation of the fear structure (Foa & Kozak, 1986). Consistent with this, Westra and Stewart (1998) review evidence showing that the use of arousal-dampening drugs (e.g., benzodiazepines) reduces the efficacy of both cognitive restructuring and exposures in the treatment of anxiety disorders. Although OCD was not examined specifically in this review paper, it is expected that, as with the treatment of these other anxiety disorders, substance use reduces the effects of cognitive therapy and ERP in OCD treatments by dampening anxiety. By self-medicating, individuals will not experience the high levels of anxiety caused by the obsessive thinking and thus will not have the opportunity to implement cognitive challenges *in vivo*. Although the focus of this chapter is on the effects of substance use on OCD, it should also be noted that OCD may also exacerbate substance use and interfere with SUD treatments. Also, there may be reluctance to engage in SUD treatments such as the easily accessible 12-step programs, as fears of contamination, particularly in these group settings, may predominate (for an interesting case illustrating this point, see Klostermann & Fals-Stewart, 2008).

Integrated treatments for individuals with comorbid OCD and SUD currently do not exist; however, Fals-Stewart and Schafer (1992) tested a parallel treatment approach for addressing both OCD and SUD symptoms in a sample of 60 dually diagnosed individuals. Clients were randomly assigned to one of three treatment conditions: concurrent ERP-focused OCD and substance abuse treatment, substance abuse treatment only, or a progressive muscle relaxation control condition. At the completion of the 6-week treatment, only those receiving the concurrent treatment showed a significant reduction in OCD symptom severity (as measured by the NIMH Obsessive Compulsive Rating Scale) (Rapoport, Elkins, & Mikkelsen, 1980). Also, those in the concurrent treatment condition had higher abstinence rates at 12-months posttreatment, as compared to those in the other two treatment conditions. Although these are promising results, the previously discussed bidirectional relationship between OCD and SUD symptoms suggests the need for development of a treatment that simultaneously addresses both disorders in an integrated fashion.

An integrated treatment may benefit from starting with psychoeducation on the cyclical relation between OCD symptoms and substance use and a functional analysis of relations between the client's obsessions and/or compulsions and their substance use. Should the functional analysis identify the substance use as a safety behavior, then this would become a central focus when doing the cognitive and ERP components of the treatment. For example, just as other safety behaviors are systematically reduced (Rachman, 2003), substance use will be targeted as a behavior that is to be refrained from during the exposures. A specific focus on the SUD may also be beneficial in an integrated treatment. By using a cognitive–behavioral framework for understanding the SUD, SUD-focused treatment can be readily integrated into the above-described cognitive–behavioral treatment for OCD. Cognitive–behavioral models of SUDs view a lack of effective coping skills as central to substance misuse (Marlatt & Gordon, 1985). Of particular importance is the low self-efficacy that individuals have in believing that they can successfully cope without the use of substances. Successful OCD-focused work described above will be paramount to increasing self-efficacy. For example, the aim of ERP is to provide clients with the success of experiencing heightened anxiety and not using either substances or neutralizing compulsive rituals to cope. Given the interlacing of obsessions/compulsions and substance use, there may be utility in building a hierarchy that incorporates the obsessions/compulsions that trigger substance use along with the feared stimuli that are usually of focus in ERP. In addition, drawing directly from coping-based CBT for SUDs, broader coping skills may be taught, such as drink refusal skills (Monti et al., 2002).

Specific phobia

The comorbidity of specific phobia (formerly *simple phobia*) with SUDs has received much less attention than the comorbidity of many of the other anxiety disorders with SUDs, as is evident throughout this chapter. One possible reason for this is that specific phobias are often not the primary reason why individuals seek treatment (Zimmerman & Mattia, 2000). Thus, not only may specific phobias go underdetected but the co-occurrence of SUD may also be linked to the primary presenting problem rather than the specific phobia. However, the lifetime prevalence of specific phobia is approximately 12.5% in the general population (Kessler et al., 2005a), and those with a specific phobia are twice as likely to have an alcohol use disorder and twice as likely to have a drug use disorder relative to those with no specific phobia diagnosis (Stinson et al., 2007). In addition, a 12-month prevalence study found that meeting DSM-IV-TR criteria for specific phobia was significantly and positively correlated with having an alcohol dependence diagnosis (*n* = 3199) (Kessler, Chiu, Demler, & Walters, 2005b). These statistics suggest that the co-occurrence of specific phobia with SUDs should be receiving increased attention in the treatment setting.

The DSM-IV-TR categorizes specific phobias into five subtypes: animal (e.g., fear of spiders), natural environment (e.g., fear of heights), blood/injection/injury (e.g., fear of needles), situational (e.g., fear of flying), and other (e.g., fear of choking). Although there does not appear to be empirical support linking substance use more strongly with any one of these subtypes of specific phobias, we most commonly hear about or even witness the use of substances in the context of flying anxiety. Indeed, a small body of research suggests that of those with a fear of flying (*flying phobia*)—which may be upwards of 10% of the general population (Van Gerwen & Diekstra, 2000)—20% use alcohol and/or anxiolytics when flying (e.g., Greist & Greist, 1981). Although 20% is the most commonly reported statistic, other prevalence data suggest even higher rates; for example, Wilhem and Roth (1997) found that 51% and 73% of a small sample (*n* = 37) of individuals with flying phobia reported taking anxiolytics and drinking, respectively, when flying. These variations in prevalence rates may reflect differences in how substance use is defined. Wilhem and Roth (1997) focused on any use, whereas other studies may be focusing on disordered use (i.e., meeting full criteria for abuse or dependence). Regardless of whether flying phobia is concurrent with a full-blown SUD, what seems important is that substances are being used preceding or during flights. This suggests a link between flying phobia and substance use. Moreover, this highlights the importance of those clinicians treating specific phobias, in particular, a flying phobia, being prepared to address concurrent substance misuse in their assessments and treatments.

Using flying phobia as an example, examining the theoretical conceptualization of specific phobia and the function of substance within this framework will allow us to understand the relationship between specific phobia and substance use. Broadly, a specific phobia is an excessive or unreasonable fear of an object or situation, exposure to which provokes anxiety (American Psychiatric Association, 2000). The feared stimulus is most often avoided or endured with extreme discomfort. Specific to flying phobia, the anticipation of a pending flight will often evoke anxiety, and anxiety will be quite intense with actual exposure to the aircraft, particularly during the initial stages of a flight (i.e., take-off) (Wilhem & Roth,

1997). In response to this anxiety, avoidance strategies, such as not flying at all, are often implemented. These avoidance strategies function by lowering the anxiety and associated discomfort; thus, the avoidance strategies are negatively reinforcing. For example, if a high level of anxiety is experienced with the anticipation of an upcoming flight and then the person cancels the flight, the immediate reduction of anxiety will reinforce use of the avoidance behavior (i.e., not flying). Substance use in the context of flying phobia seems to also function as an avoidance strategy. In support of this, research has found that those with a flying phobia who use substances before or during flights report doing so with the specific goal of reducing their anxiety (e.g., Greist & Greist, 1981; Wilhem & Roth, 1997). As with any avoidance behavior, and as previously described, substance use is also expected to maintain and escalate the specific phobia through the process of negative reinforcement.

Accordingly, the effectiveness of treatments for specific phobias may also be limited when substances are being used. In particular, one of the most widely used and supported treatments for specific phobia is exposure therapy (Wolitzky-Taylor, Horowitz, Powers, & Telch, 2008). As noted elsewhere in this chapter, the goal of exposure therapy is habituation, but it has been hypothesized that this goal can only be accomplished if the full fear structure is evoked (Foa & Kozak, 1986). This will not happen if substances are used to dampen the anxiety response. Accordingly, what is needed is an integrated treatment that simultaneously addresses both problems. Taking flying phobia once again as an example, this treatment may start off with a cognitive–behavioral-rooted psychoeducation to emphasize the long-term negative consequences substance use has on their fear of flying. Use of motivational interviewing may also have great utility at the onset of such a treatment. The use of substances is allowing these individuals to fly, which may be important or even critical to their personal life and career. Thus, it may be challenging to get the client on board with refraining from substance use as a way to reduce anxiety. Once the client is committed to treatment, a course of exposure therapy could be implemented. Here, the focus should be on refraining from substance use (and other avoidance behaviors) during imaginal, virtual reality, if available (for a review, see Parsons & Rizzo, 2008), and *in vivo* exposures to the feared stimuli. As noted earlier, it may be that the substance misuse is limited to the specific phobia, which may be a fairly infrequent concern. In this case, a course of therapy focused on the specific phobia while preventing substance use may suffice. However, if the substance misuse is a broader problem (e.g., frequent flying for business, substance use to dampen anticipatory anxiety of feared stimulus), an integrated treatment may also incorporate some of the strategies used in CBT for substance use, such as those outlined in Monti et al.'s (2002) treatment manual.

Generalized anxiety disorder

The lifetime prevalence rate of generalized anxiety disorder (GAD) in the general population was recently estimated at 5.7% (Kessler et al., 2005a). The specific prevalence rate of GAD–SUD comorbidity is somewhat difficult to identify. Some early work suggests that of those with a SUD approximately 23% have GAD (Kushner, Sher, & Beitman, 1990); however, because symptoms of GAD can mimic those of substance use withdrawal, such prevalence rates should be interpreted with caution. Moreover, caution should be taken when diagnosing GAD in the context of SUD. Despite the difficulty in pinpointing the exact rate of comorbidity, there is evidence to suggest that substance use in the context of GAD is a concern. For example, evidence from a 12-month prevalence study found a significant positive correlation between meeting DSM-IV-TR criteria for GAD and having an alcohol or drug use disorder, including DSM-IV-TR abuse or dependence ($n = 3199$) (Kessler et al., 2005b).

Generalized anxiety disorder is characterized by excessive and pervasive anxiety and worry, occurring more days than not for at least 6 months and related to various events or activities (American Psychiatric Association, 2000). According to the DSM-IV-TR classification of GAD, the anxiety or worry is associated with at least three of the following symptoms: restlessness or feeling keyed up or on edge, being easily fatigued, difficulty concentrating or mind going blank, irritability, muscle tension, and sleep disturbance. Thus, like many of the other anxiety disorders, the associated symptoms of GAD are both distressing and can cause social and occupational impairment (e.g., irritability with spouse, not being able to concentrate at work). Unlike many of the other anxiety disorders, however, the source of the anxiety is difficult to physically avoid; for example, in the case of specific phobias, the object or situation of distress can be avoided. Without the option of physical avoidance of the worries, substance use may become a viable option for providing immediate relief for those with GAD. Thus, as described in the context of the other anxiety disorders, substance use will be negatively reinforcing. Although empirical evidence is needed to clearly elucidate this link between GAD and substance use as a coping mechanism, there is some work supporting a link. Bolton, Cox, Clara, and Sareen (2006) found that 35.6% of their study sample who were diagnosed with GAD ($n = 295$) reported using substances for the specific purpose of relieving worry and anxiety. Moreover, Romach, Busto, Somer, Kaplan, and Sellers (1995) found that, of their benzodiazepine-dependent sample, 33% ($n = 117$) met GAD criteria, and these individuals tended to shift away from using benzodiazepines as prescribed to using them on an as-needed basis. This suggests use for self-medication purposes.

Given this functional role of substances as a coping mechanism by those with GAD, as with the other anxiety disorders, substance use may also impede success in GAD treatments. In fact, the presence of an SUD has been shown to impact the course of GAD. Specifically, a 12-year prospective study by Bruce et al. (2005) showed that the presence of an SUD reduced the recovery rate from GAD (n = 179 meeting GAD at baseline) and increased the likelihood of recurrence of GAD. Why might this be the case? CBT treatments for GAD, which have been shown to be among the most efficacious treatments for GAD (Brown, O'Leary, & Barlow, 2001), incorporate both cognitive techniques such as cognitive restructuring and behavioral techniques such as relaxation and worry exposure. Central to cognitive restructuring for GAD treatments is identifying automatic thoughts and challenging these thoughts. If substances are used in response to excessive worry, clients will not have the opportunity to practice what can be quite difficult thought challenging. This could lead to low client self-efficacy with regard to their ability to be successful at cognitive restructuring. In terms of the behavioral strategies, practice and the use of relaxation techniques, such as progressive muscle relaxation, may be limited if substances are used in response to worry. Again, these are difficult techniques that require much practice, and with limited use the client may underestimate their ability to use them effectively. Finally, as mentioned elsewhere in this chapter, habituation to the discomfort associated with worrying will not be accomplished if clients use substances in response to distressing worries outside of the clinical setting.

Accordingly, an integrated treatment that simultaneously addresses both the GAD and SUD is needed; however, to our knowledge, such a treatment is not currently available. As with treating comorbidity of any of the anxiety disorders and SUDs, it is recommended that when a client presents with both GAD and substance misuse or an SUD that a functional analysis first be done. Also, as with the other recommended CBT treatments in this chapter, it may be beneficial to include a psychoeducation component at the start of the treatment that emphasizes how the client's continued substance use could interfere with GAD treatment success. With the goal of simultaneously addressing both the GAD and SUD, this cognitive–behavioral approach to treating GAD has great utility, as it integrates well with the empirically supported CBT treatment for SUDs (Monti et al., 2002). Specifically, CBT for SUDs stresses the importance of building a client's self-efficacy to successfully cope without the use of substances. The components of the GAD treatment aim to accomplish this very goal. By increasing self-efficacy, the inclusion of GAD treatment components should theoretically lead to reduced coping-related substance use.

Case example

We now turn to a case example to illustrate first how the presence of a comorbid SUD may result in an apparently treatment-resistant anxiety disorder if only traditional anxiety treatment is utilized without attention to the substance misuse. This case will also illustrate how an integrated approach utilizing both cognitive–behavioral and motivational enhancement interventions can be helpful not only in improving anxiety-related outcomes but also in effectively and efficiently treating the substance misuse.

Michelle was a 38-year-old divorcee who presented with a 15-year history of panic disorder with agoraphobia (PDA). She was a moderately successful novelist. Michelle was seeking treatment because she was realizing that her anxiety was interfering with the success of her writing career; for example, she felt that her agoraphobia was preventing the travel necessary to promote her books. Furthermore, she had observed that her panic attacks worsened around crucial writing deadlines.

Clinical assessment revealed that Michelle suffered from moderately intense panic attacks that typically occurred several times a week. The panic attacks had recently increased in frequency to several times per day as she was attempting to finish her latest novel. Many of these attacks appeared to come on without warning. Her attacks were characterized by sudden onset of shortness of breath, pounding heart, dizziness, and a very intense feeling of dread. Shortly after her panic attacks had started, Michelle began restricting her activities to avoid situations where she might panic and be embarrassed by her loss of control or where she might find it difficult to escape should she feel the need to flee. At the time of the onset of her panic attacks, she had been living in a large urban center, and she began to avoid taking public transit such as the subway. Consequently, she eventually moved to a less populated city to avoid the crowds that she identified as the cause of her panic. In her new location, Michelle began to cut down on her driving and began to avoid several other public locations (e.g., grocery stores, movie theaters). She had come to rely more and more on her husband to do the driving or the grocery shopping, given her increasing mobility restrictions. This put quite a strain on the marriage, and the couple had divorced 3 years ago. She found she was increasingly reliant on friends to help her out with such activities (e.g., running grocery errands for her) or to accompany her when she needed to enter her feared agoraphobic situations (e.g., accompanying her when she needed to drive in the city). Michelle had sought treatment several times in the past but reported that her prior attempts at recovery from her anxiety disorder had not been successful. She had tried several types of treatment including CBT and medications. In fact, she was still taking benzodiazepines (lorazepam) for the treatment of her panic attacks, but Michelle noted that she was only taking lorazepam "as needed" to help manage her anxiety.

The therapist began a course of cognitive–behavioral treatment for her PDA. In terms of *in vivo* exposure exercises, Michelle and her therapist agreed to begin with compiling a hierarchy of her feared agoraphobic situations from least to most anxiety provoking (e.g., going to the corner store, going to the grocery store, attending a movie at the theater, driving in the city, taking the bus in the city) and that Michelle would need to confront these in succession. They also agreed that the exposures would later move on to "interoceptive exposure"—exposure to her feared arousal-related sensations (e.g., shortness of breath, pounding heart, dizziness)—through exercises such as voluntary hyperventilation, running, and breathing through a straw (Stewart & Watt, 2008). Although Michelle agreed to trying these exercises, she indicated strong doubt that they would work, as she noted that she had tried them both (*in vivo* exposure and interoceptive exposure) with a previous therapist and they had not shown much benefit in helping her get past her anxiety disorder. The therapist pondered whether Michelle might represent a true case of treatment-resistant anxiety.

For the first exposure, Michelle and her therapist took a trip together to the convenience store close to Michelle's home, which Michelle had rated as moderately anxiety provoking on her fear hierarchy. The therapist was surprised that Michelle's peak anxiety ratings were quite low on this first exposure, and the therapist attributed this to her own reassuring presence during the exposure. The therapist recommended that Michelle try to undertake her next exposure on her own to optimize the likelihood that Michelle would experience sufficient peak anxiety to experience therapeutic benefits.

Thus, during the next week Michelle attempted her first *in vivo* exposure homework exercise on her own. Specifically, she attempted a solo grocery shopping trip. She dutifully completed her exposure homework sheets and brought them to the therapist's office at the next session. Contrary to her prediction that she would find this exercise very stressful, her peak anxiety rating during the exposure was again surprisingly low. The therapist queried whether Michelle had escaped the grocery trip before she experienced her expected high level of anxiety and Michelle denied this. It was also determined that she had not brought along a trusted companion to the grocery store, which might have served to dampen the anxiety. Michelle and her therapist chose another exposure activity for the coming week that was higher up on the anxiety hierarchy—namely, driving in the city. At her next therapy session, Michelle reported that she was still markedly avoiding grocery stores despite the outcome of her last exposure; she noted that she was still terrified that she would have a panic attack in the grocery store if she were to attempt the exposure again. An examination of her homework sheet revealed a pattern very similar to the pattern seen the week before. Contrary to Michelle's prediction that she would find the activity of driving in the city very stressful, her reported peak anxiety rating was low. Querying revealed that Michelle had conducted the full exposure as planned; she had not escaped nor had she brought along a trusted companion as she typically did to help her manage her anxiety when driving. The therapist queried further about why Michelle thought that she had not experienced the expected high anxiety and strong physical arousal sensations during the last two exposures. Michelle reported that she believed it was because she had taken lorazepam before each exposure to better help her cope with the anxiety she was expecting to experience in the convenience store and grocery store and while driving. She felt that her success in being able to confront those feared situations was entirely due to the medication rather than her own efforts. She noted an extreme reluctance to attempt exposure to these situations without lorazepam.

Further querying revealed an additional problem that Michelle had developed during the course of her anxiety disorder—namely, benzodiazepine dependence. It turns out that Michelle had been taking lorazepam for nearly as long as she had been experiencing panic attacks. On her doctor's instructions, she had been using it "as needed" to prevent an oncoming panic attack or to help her face her feared agoraphobic situations. She reported that such occasions had been occurring quite regularly. Michelle acknowledged that she was currently taking a 2-mg lorazepam tablet two to three times a day. Michelle had attempted several times to stop taking the lorazepam altogether; however, she had experienced severe physical and emotional symptoms on attempting sudden discontinuation and had always quickly returned to the benzodiazepine use, leading the therapist to diagnose a comorbid condition of benzodiazepine dependence. Further inquiry revealed that the benzodiazepine use had not been a focus of treatment in her last, failed attempt at cognitive–behavioral therapy. Michelle admitted that her prior CBT therapist had probably not been aware of the extent of her reliance on her medication.

The therapist hypothesized that the benzodiazepine use had been contributing to the maintenance of Michelle's anxiety and that it would be crucial to address both the benzodiazepine dependence and the PDA simultaneously. Such an approach to treatment would allow Michelle to fully benefit from her anxiety treatment. The therapist also believed that it would not make sense for Michelle to get separate treatment for her SUD because her benzodiazepine use was so tightly linked with her anxiety disorder. Thus, an integrated approach appeared warranted. Given Michelle's initial reluctance to engage in CBT for her anxiety disorder without the use of her lorazepam, the first step in the integrated treatment was enhancing her motivation to change her substance use behavior. Specifically, the therapist embarked on a short course of motivational interviewing (Miller & Rollnick, 1991). Using a nonconfrontational approach, the therapist was able to draw from Michelle examples from the patient's own experience that illustrated how her benzodiazepine use was ultimately interfering with, rather than assisting with, her anxiety recovery (O'Connor & Stewart, in press). Through exercises such as decisional balancing Michelle carefully considered the advantages and disadvantages of continuing with her benzodiazepine use versus attempting to change this pattern of safety behavior. Michelle eventually came to the decision that she should attempt to tackle both problems simultaneously. She and her therapist discussed this decision with her family physician who agreed to assist with the gradual benzodiazepine taper.

Then Michelle and her therapist, in collaboration with the family physician, embarked on a course of cognitive–behavioral therapy designed to simultaneously target both her benzodiazepine dependence and PDA based on the treatment developed by Otto et al. (1993) that was discussed earlier in the PD and SUD section of this chapter. In the past, Michelle had unsuccessfully attempted to address each problem (her PDA and her benzodiazepine dependence) in isolation. In contrast, the Otto et al. approach targets both problems simultaneously in a single treatment. Specifically, the patient is encouraged to experience internal cues associated with panic (e.g., dizziness, racing heart) without defensive responses such as benzodiazepine use (see review in Toneatto & Rector, 2008). As Michelle had experienced previously, the tapering of benzodiazepines produces many of the internal sensations that are so feared by PDA patients (Otto et al., 1993). Thus, Michelle was offered a rationale for beginning her interoceptive exposure exercises to help her prepare for the discomfort associated with benzodiazepine discontinuation. She reported that one of the most intolerable aspects of benzodiazepine discontinuation for her in the past had been symptoms of dizziness. Thus, the therapist selected interoceptive exposure exercises that are known to bring on sensations of dizziness, such as chair spinning. After several sessions of practice of interoceptive exposure exercises both with the therapist and on her own at home, Michelle was set to begin her slow benzodiazepine taper. She continued with her *in vivo* exposure exercises, but agreed with the therapist and her family physician that she would include in the hierarchy a gradual fading out of the use of her benzodiazepines prior to these exposures.

This approach to Michelle's treatment was much more successful during the course of the treatment in eliciting the anxiety necessary for effective exposure. By the end of the 11 session treatment (Otto et al., 2004a), Michelle no longer met diagnostic criteria for either PDA or benzodiazepine dependence. Moreover, the frequency and intensity of her panic attacks had markedly decreased as had her level of agoraphobic avoidance. She no longer felt the need to use benzodiazepines to manage her panic or confront various agoraphobic situations. At a 1-year follow-up, Michelle reported that she had experienced a couple of panic attacks over the last year, but they had not caused her much distress, and she was pleased to report that she continued to live medication free.

Conclusion

This case illustrates how an established integrated treatment for comorbid anxiety disorder and SUDs can be effective in an apparently treatment-resistant case. In cases where no evidence-based treatment is available (e.g., patients with comorbid flying phobia and substance abuse), we recommend the use of a functional analysis in treatment planning. It is also important to note that in cases with severe substance dependence, the patient may be in medical need of detoxification before he or she is ready to undertake an integrated cognitive–behavioral treatment. In such cases, it is very important to ensure that the patient is moved quickly from the detoxification program into the integrated treatment for the anxiety and SUD to avoid having the untreated anxiety prompt a quick relapse to substance abuse (Ouimette et al., 2003a). Finally, as is illustrated in the case above, some patients are reluctant to change their substance use behavior but are quite motivated and willing to work on their anxiety. In such cases, motivational interviewing techniques can be quite helpful in moving clients toward increased readiness to change their substance use behavior (O'Connor & Stewart, in press), particularly if they are able to see how the substance abuse is contributing to the maintenance of their aversive anxiety symptoms in the long run (Stewart & Conrod, 2008b).

We are at an exciting time in the development of this field of treatment. Emerging data do appear to support the efficacy of integrated treatments for intervening with anxiety disorder patients with comorbid substance use disorders. Nonetheless, much more research is needed before we can develop best practice guidelines on how to most effectively treat patients with concurrent anxiety and substance use disorders.

References

Agosti, V., Nunes, E., & Levin, F. (2002). Rates of psychiatric comorbidity among U.S. residents with lifetime cannabis dependence. *American Journal of Drug and Alcohol Abuse, 28,* 643–652.

American Psychiatric Association. (2000). *Diagnostic and statistical manual of mental disorders* (4th ed., text revision). Arlington, VA: American Psychiatric Association.

Antony, M.M., Downie, F., & Swinson, R.P. (1998). Diagnostic issues and epidemiology in obsessive-compulsive disorder. In R.P. Swinson, M.M. Antony, S. Rachman, & M.A. Richter (Eds.), *Obsessive–compulsive disorder: Theory, research, and treatment* (pp. 3–32). New York: Guilford Press.

Bolton, J., Cox, B., Clara, I., & Sareen, J. (2006). Use of alcohol and drugs to self-medicate anxiety disorders in a nationally representative sample. *The Journal of Nervous and Mental Disease, 194*, 818–825.

Brady, K.T., Dansky, B.S., Back, S.E., Foa, E.B., & Carroll, K.M. (2001). Exposure therapy in the treatment of PTSD among cocaine-dependent individuals: Preliminary findings. *Journal of Substance Abuse Treatment, 21*, 47–54.

Breslau, N., Kilbey, M., & Andreski, P. (1991). Nicotine dependence, major depression, and anxiety in young adults. *Archives of General Psychiatry, 48*, 1069–1074.

Brown, P.J., Stout, R.L., & Gannon-Rowley, J. (1998). Substance use disorder—PTSD comorbidity: Patients' perception of symptom interplay and treatment issues. *Journal of Substance Abuse Treatment, 15*, 445–448.

Brown, P.J., Stout, R.L., & Mueller, T. (1996). Posttraumatic stress disorder and substance abuse relapse among women: A pilot study. *Psychology of Addictive Behaviors, 10*, 124–128.

Brown, T.A., O'Leary, T.A., & Barlow, D.H. (2001). Generalized anxiety disorder. In D.H. Barlow (Ed.), *Clinical handbook of psychological disorders: A step-by-step treatment manual* (3rd ed.). New York: Guilford Press.

Bruce., S.E., Yonkers, K.A., Otto, M.W., Eisen, J.L., Weisberg, R.B., Pagano, M. et al. (2005). Influence of psychiatric comorbidity on recovery and recurrence in generalized anxiety disorder, social phobia, and panic disorder: A 12-year prospective study. *American Journal of Psychiatry, 162*, 1179–1187.

Buckner, J.D., Bonn-Miller, M.O., Zvolensky, M.J., & Schmidt, N.B. (2007). Marijuana use motives and social anxiety among marijuana using young adults. *Addictive Behaviors, 32*, 2238–2252.

Buckner, J.D., Schmidt, N.B., Lang, A.R., Small, J.W., Schlauch, R.C., & Lewinsohn, P.M. (2008). Specificity of social anxiety disorder as a risk factor for alcohol and cannabis dependence. *Journal of Psychiatric Research, 42*, 230–239.

Burns, L., Teesson, M., & O'Neill, K. (2005). The impact of comorbid anxiety and depression on alcohol treatment outcomes. *Addiction, 100*, 787–796.

Butler, G. (1989). Issues in the application of cognitive and behavioral strategies to the treatment of social phobia. *Clinical Psychology Review, 9*, 91–106.

Carroll, K.M., Fenton, L.R., Ball, S.A., Nich, C., Frankforter, T.L., Shi, J. et al. (2004). Efficacy of disulfiram and cognitive behavior therapy in cocaine-dependent outpatients. *Archives of General Psychiatry, 61*, 264–272.

Chambless, D.L., Cherney, J., Caputo, G.C., & Rheinstein, B.J. (1987). Anxiety disorders and alcoholism: A study with inpatient alcoholics. *Journal of Anxiety Disorders, 1*, 29–40.

Chilcoat, H.D., & Menard, C. (2003). Epidemiological investigations: Comorbidity of posttraumatic stress disorder and substance use disorder. In P. Ouimette & P. Brown (Eds.), *Trauma and substance abuse: Causes, consequences, and treatment of comorbid disorders* (pp. 9–28). Washington, D.C.: American Psychological Association.

Coffey, S.F., Read, J.P., & Norberg, M.M. (2008). Posttraumatic stress disorder and substance use disorder: Neuroimaging, neuroendocrine, and psychophysiological findings. In S.H. Stewart & P.J. Conrod (Eds.), *Anxiety and substance use disorders: The vicious cycle of comorbidity* (pp. 37–57). New York: Springer.

Compton III, W.M., Cottler, L.B., Abdallah, A.B., Phelps, D.L., Spitznagel, E.L., & Horton, J.C. (2000). Substance dependence and other psychiatric disorders among drug dependent subjects: Race and gender correlates. *American Journal of Addictions, 9*, 113–125.

Compton III, W.M., Thomas, Y.F., Stinson, F.S., & Grant, B.F. (2007). Prevalence, correlates, disability, and comorbidity of DSM-IV drug abuse and dependence in the United States: Results from the National Epidemiologic Survey on Alcohol and Related Conditions. *Archives of General Psychiatry, 64*, 566–576.

Conger, J.J. (1956). Reinforcement theory and the dynamics of alcoholism. *Quarterly Journal of Studies on Alcohol, 17*, 296–305.

Conrod, P.J., & Stewart, S.H. (2005). A critical look at dual-focused cognitive–behavioral treatment for co-morbid substance abuse and psychiatric disorders: Strengths, limitations, and future directions. *Journal of Cognitive Psychotherapy, 19*, 265–289.

Covey, L.S., Hughes, D.C., Glassman, A.H., Blazer, D.G., & George, L.K. (1994). Eversmoking, quitting, and psychiatric disorders: Evidence from the Durham, North Carolina, epidemiologic catchment area. *Tobacco Control, 3*, 222–227.

Cox, B.J., Norton, G.R., Dorward, J., & Fergusson, P.A. (1989). The relationship between panic attacks and chemical dependencies. *Addictive Behaviors, 14*, 53–60.

Dansky, B.S., Brady, K.T., & Saladin, M.E. (1998). Untreated symptoms of PTSD among cocaine-dependent individuals: Changes over time. *Journal of Substance Abuse Treatment, 15*, 499–504.

Donovan, D.M., Kadden, R.M., DiClemente, C.C., & Carroll, K.M. (2002). Client satisfaction with three therapies in the treatment of alcohol dependence: Results from Project MATCH. *American Journal on Addiction, 11*, 291–307.

Eaton, W.W., Kessler, R.C., Wittchen, H.U., & Magee, W.J. (1994). Panic and panic disorder in the United States. *American Journal of Psychiatry, 151*, 413–420.

Eisen, J.L., & Rasmussen, S.A. (1989). Coexisting obsessive compulsive disorder and alcoholism. *Journal of Clinical Psychiatry, 50*, 96–98.

Fals-Stewart, W., & Angarano, K. (1994). Obsessive–compulsive disorder among patients entering substance abuse treatment: Prevalence and accuracy of diagnosis. *The Journal of Nervous and Mental Disease, 182*, 715–719.

Fals-Stewart, W., & Lucente, S. (1994). Treating obsessive–compulsive disorder among substance abusers: A guide. *Psychology of Addictive Behaviors, 8*, 14–23.

Fals-Stewart, W., & Schafer, J. (1992). The treatment of substance abusers diagnosed with obsessive–compulsive disorder: An outcome study. *Journal of Substance Abuse Treatment, 9*, 365–370.

Finney, J.W., & Monahan, S.C. (1996). The cost-effectiveness of treatment for alcoholism: A second approximation. *Journal of Studies on Alcohol, 57*, 229–243.

Foa, E.B., & Kozak, M.J. (1986). Emotional processing of fear: Exposure to corrective information. *Psychological Bulletin, 99*, 20–35.

Foa, E.B., & Kozak, M.J. (1996). Psychological treatment for obsessive-compulsive disorder. In M.R. Mavissakalian & R.F. Prien (Eds.), *Long-term treatments of the anxiety disorders* (pp. 285–309). Washington, D.C.: American Psychiatric Association.

Foa, E.B., & Rothbaum, B.O. (1998). *Treating the trauma of rape: Cognitive–behavioral therapy for PTSD*. New York: Guilford Press.

George, D.T., Nutt, D.J., Dwyer, B.A., & Linnoila, M. (1990). Alcoholism and panic disorder: Is the co-morbidity more than coincidence? *Acta Psychiatrica Scandinavica, 81,* 97–107.

Grant, B.F., Stinson, F.S., Dawson, D.A., Chou, P., Dufour, M.C., Compton, W. et al. (2004). Prevalence and co-occurrence of substance use disorder and independent mood and anxiety disorders: Results from the National Epidemiological Survey on Alcohol and Related Conditions. *Archives of General Psychiatry, 61,* 807–816.

Greist, J.H., & Greist, G.L. (1981). *Fearless flying: A passenger's guide to modern airline travel.* Chicago, IL: Nelson Hall.

Hall, S.M., Muñoz, R.F., & Reus, V.I. (1994). Cognitive–behavioral intervention increases abstinence rates for depressive-history smokers. *Journal of Consulting and Clinical Psychology, 62,* 141–146.

Hasin, D.S., Stinson, F.S., Ogburn, E., & Grant, B.F. (2007). Prevalence, correlates, disability and comorbidity of DSM-IV alcohol abuse and dependence in the United States: Results from the National Epidemiologic Survey on Alcohol and Related Conditions. *Archives of General Psychiatry, 64,* 830–842.

Hasler, G., Pinto, A., Greenberg, B.D., Samuels, J., Fyer, A.J., Pauls, D. et al. (2007). Familiarity of factor analysis-derived YBOCS dimensions in OCD-affected sibling pairs from the OCD collaborative genetics study. *Biological Psychiatry, 61,* 617–625.

Hornig, C.D., & McNally, R.J. (1995). Panic disorder and suicide attempt: A reanalysis of data from the Epidemiologic Catchment Area study. *British Journal of Psychiatry, 167,* 76–79.

Kadden, R., Carroll, K.M., Donovan, D., Cooney, N., Monti, P., Abrams, D. et al. (1992). *Cognitive–behavioral coping skills therapy manual: A clinical research guide for therapists treating individuals with alcohol abuse and dependence.* Rockville, MD: National Institute on Alcohol Abuse and Alcoholism. (NIAAA Project MATCH Monograph Series, Vol. 3, DHHS Publ. No. (ADM) 92-1895.)

Kessler, R.C., Berglund, P., Demler, O., Jin, R., Merikangas, K.R., & Walters, E.E. (2005a). Lifetime prevalence and age of onset distributions of DSM-IV disorders in the National Comorbidity Survey Replication. *Archives of General Psychiatry, 62,* 593–602.

Kessler, R.C., Chiu, W.T., Demler, O., & Walters, E.E. (2005b). Prevalence, severity, and comorbidity of 12-month DSM-IV disorders in the National Comorbidity Survey Replication. *Archives of General Psychiatry, 62,* 617–627.

Kessler, R.C., McGonagle, K.A., Zhao, S., Nelson, C.B., Hughes, M., Eshleman, S. et al. (1994). Lifetime and 12-month prevalence of DSM-III-R psychiatric disorders in the United States: Results from the National Comorbidity Survey. *Archives of General Psychiatry, 51,* 8–19.

Kessler, R.C., Sonnega, A., Bromet, E., Hughes, M., & Nelson, C.B. (1995). Posttraumatic stress disorder in the National Comorbidity Survey. *Archives of General Psychiatry, 52,* 1048–1060.

Khantzian, E.J. (1997). The self-medication hypothesis of substance use disorders: A reconsideration and recent applications. *Harvard Review of Psychiatry, 4,* 231–244.

Kilpatrick, D.G., Acierno, R., Saunders, B., Resnick, H.S., Best, C.L., & Schnurr, P.P. (2000). Risk factors for adolescent substance abuse and dependence: Data from a national sample. *Journal of Consulting and Clinical Psychology, 68,* 19–30.

Kim, E.J. (2005). The effect of decreased safety behaviors on anxiety and negative thoughts in social phobics. *Anxiety Disorders, 19*, 69–86.

Klostermann, K.C., & Fals-Stewart, W. (2008). Treatment of co-morbid obsessive–compulsive disorder and substance use disorders. In S.H. Stewart & P.J. Conrod (Eds.), *Anxiety and substance use disorders: The vicious cycle of comorbidity* (pp. 101–117). New York: Springer.

Kushner, M.G., Abrams, K., & Borchardt, C. (2000). The relationship between anxiety disorders and alcohol use disorders: A review of major perspectives and findings. *Clinical Psychology Review, 20*, 149–171.

Kushner, M.G., Donahue, C., Sletten, S., Thuras, P., Abrams, K., Peterson, J. et al. (2006). Cognitive–behavioral treatment of co-morbid anxiety disorder in alcoholism treatment patients: Presentation of a prototype program and future directions. *Journal of Mental Health, 15*, 697–707.

Kushner, M.G., Sher, K.J., & Beitman, B.D. (1990). The relation between alcohol problems and the anxiety disorders. *American Journal of Psychiatry, 1147*, 685–695.

Labounty, L.P., Hatsukami, D., Morgon, S.F., & Nelson, L. (1992). Relapse among alcoholics with phobic and panic symptoms. *Addictive Behaviors, 17*, 9–15.

Leckman, J.F., Zhang, H., Alsobrook, J.P., & Paul, D.L. (2001). Symptom dimensions in obsessive–compulsive disorder: Toward quantitative phenotypes. *American Journal of Medicine and Genetics, 105*, 28–30.

Lepine, J.P., & Pelissolo, A. (1998). Social phobia and alcoholism: A complex relationship. *Journal of Affective Disorders, 50*(Suppl. 1), 23–28.

MacDonald, A.B., Baker, J.M., Stewart, S.H., & Skinner, M. (2000). Effects of alcohol on the response to hyperventilation of participants high and low in anxiety sensitivity. *Alcoholism: Clinical and Experimental Research, 24*, 1656–1665.

Magee, W.J., Eaton, W.W., Wittchen, H.U., McGonagle, K.A., & Kessler, R.C. (1996). Agoraphobia, simple phobia, and social phobia in the National Comorbidity Survey. *Archives of General Psychiatry, 53*, 159–168.

Marlatt, G.A., & Gordon, J.R. (Eds.). (1985). *Relapse prevention.* New York: Guilford Press.

McDougle, C.J., Goodman, W.K., Delgado, P.L., & Price, L.H. (1989). Pathophysiology of obsessive–compulsive disorder. *American Journal of Psychiatry, 147*, 1350–1351.

McLean, P.D., Whittal, M.L., Söchting, I., Koch, W.J., Paterson, R., Thordarson, D.S. et al. (2001). Cognitive versus behavior therapy in the group treatment of obsessive–compulsive disorder. *Journal of Consulting and Clinical Psychology, 69*, 205–214.

Miller, W.R., & Rollnick, S. (1991). *Motivational interviewing: Preparing people to change addictive behavior.* New York: Guilford Press.

Modell, J.G., Glaser, F.B., Mountz, J.M., Schmaltz, S., & Cyr, L. (1992). Obsessive and compulsive characteristics of alcohol abuse and dependence: Quantification by a newly developed questionnaire. *Alcoholism: Clinical and Experimental Research, 16*, 266–271.

Monti, P.M., Kadden, R.M., Rohsenow, D.J., Cooney, N.L., & Abrams, D.B. (2002). *Treating alcoholic dependence: A coping skills training guide* (2nd ed.). New York: Guilford Press.

Morris, E.P., Stewart, S.H., & Ham, L.S. (2005). The relationship between social anxiety disorder and alcohol use disorders: A critical review. *Clinical Psychology Review, 25*, 734–760.

Najavits, L.M. (2003). Seeking safety: A new psychotherapy for posttraumatic stress disorder and substance use disorder. In P.C. Ouimette & P.J. Brown (Eds.), *Trauma and substance abuse: Causes, consequences, and treatment of comorbid disorders* (pp. 127–146). Washington, D.C.: American Psychological Association.

Najavits, L.M., Weiss, R.D., Shaw, S.T., & Muenz, L.R. (1998). "Seeking safety": Outcome of a new cognitive–behavioral psychotherapy for women with posttraumatic stress disorder and substance abuse. *Journal of Traumatic Stress, 11*, 437–456.

Norton, G.R., Norton, P.J., Cox, B.J., & Belik, S.-L. (2008). Panic spectrum disorders and substance use. In S.H. Stewart, & P.J. Conrod (Eds.), *Anxiety and substance use disorders: The vicious cycle of comorbidity* (pp. 81–98). New York: Springer.

O'Connor, R.M., & Stewart, S.H. (in press). Substance use disorders. In D.M. McKay, J. Abramowitz, & S. Taylor (Eds.), *The expanded scope of cognitive–behavior therapy: Lessons learned from refractory cases.* Washington, D.C.: American Psychological Association.

Oei, T.P.S., Lim, B., & Young, R.M. (1991). Cognitive processes and cognitive behavior therapy in the treatment of problem drinking. *Journal of Addictive Disorders, 10*, 63–80.

Otto, M.W., Jones, J.C., Craske, M.G., & Barlow, D.H. (2004a). *Stopping anxiety medication: Panic control therapy for benzodiazepine discontinuation.* Oxford, U.K.: Oxford University Press.

Otto, M.W., Pollack, M.H., Sachs, G.S., Reiter, S.R., Melzer-Brody, S., & Rosenbaum, J.F. (1993). Discontinuation of benzodiazepine treatment: Efficacy of a cognitive–behavior therapy for patients with panic disorder. *American Journal of Psychiatry, 150*, 1485–1490.

Otto, M.W., Safren, S.A., & Pollack, M.H. (2004b). Internal cue exposure and the treatment of substance use disorders: Lessons from the treatment of panic disorder. *Journal of Anxiety Disorders, 18*, 69–87.

Ouimette, P.C., Ahrens, C., Moos, R.H., & Finney, J.W. (1997). Posttraumatic stress disorder in substance abuse patients: Relationships to 1-year posttreatment outcomes. *Psychology of Addictive Behaviors, 11*, 34–47.

Ouimette, P.C., Ahrens, C., Moos, R.H., & Finney, J.W. (1998). During treatment changes in substance abuse patients with posttraumatic stress disorder: The influence of specific interventions and program environments. *Journal of Substance Abuse Treatment, 15*, 555–564.

Ouimette, P.C., Finney, J.W., & Moos, R.H. (1999). Two-year posttreatment functioning and coping of substance abuse patients with posttraumatic stress disorder. *Psychology of Addictive Behaviors, 13*, 105–114.

Ouimette, P.C., Moos, R.H., & Brown, P.J. (2003a). Substance use disorder—posttraumatic stress disorder comorbidity: A survey of treatments and proposed practice guidelines. In P.C. Ouimette & P.J. Brown (Eds.), *Trauma and substance abuse: Causes, consequences, and treatment of comorbid disorders* (pp. 91–111). Washington, D.C.: American Psychological Association.

Ouimette, P.C., Moos, R.H., & Finney, J.W. (2003b). PTSD treatment and five-year remission among patients with substance use and posttraumatic stress disorders. *Journal of Consulting and Clinical Psychology, 71*, 410–414.

Parsons, T.D., & Rizzo, A.A. (2008). Affective outcomes of virtual reality exposure therapy for anxiety and specific phobias: A meta-analysis. *Journal of Behavior Therapy, 39*, 250–261.

Pinto-Gouveia, J., Cunha, M.I., & Salvador, M.C. (2003). Assessment of social phobia by self-report questionnaires: The social interaction and performance
anxiety and avoidance scale and the social phobia safety behaviors scale.
Behavioral and Cognitive Psychotherapy, 31, 291–311.

Pohl, R., Yeragani, V.K., Balon, R., Lycaki, H., & McBride, R. (1992). Smoking in
patients with panic disorder. *Psychiatry Research, 43*, 253–262.

Rachman, S. (2003). *The treatment of obsessions.* Oxford, U.K.: Oxford University
Press.

Randall, C.L., Thomas, S., & Thevos, A.K. (2001). Concurrent alcoholism and
social anxiety disorder: A first step toward developing effective treatments.
Alcoholism: Clinical and Experimental Research, 25, 210–220.

Rapoport, J., Elkins, R., & Mikkelsen, E. (1980). Clinical controlled trial of clomipramine in adolescents with obsessive compulsive disorder. *Psychopharmacology
Bulletin, 80*, 61–63.

Rawson, R.A., Gonzales, R., & Brethen, P. (2002). Treatment of methamphetamine
use disorders: An update. *Journal of Substance Abuse Treatment, 23*, 145–150.

Regier, D.A., Farmer, M.E., Rae, D.S., Locke, B.Z., Keith, S.J., Judd, L.L. et al. (1990).
Co-morbidity of mental disorders with alcohol and other drug abuse: Results
for the Epidemiological Catchment Area (ECA) Study. *Journal of the American
Medical Association, 264*, 2511–2518.

Resnick, H.S., Kilpatrick, D.G., Dansky, B.S., Saunders, B.E., & Best, C.L. (1993).
Prevalence of civilian trauma and posttraumatic stress disorder in a representative national sample of women. *Journal of Consulting and Clinical Psychology,
61*, 984–991.

Riggs, D.S., & Foa, E.B. (2008). Treatment for comorbid posttraumatic stress disorder and substance use disorders. In S.H. Stewart & P.J. Conrod (Eds.), *Anxiety
and substance use disorders: The vicious cycle of comorbidity* (pp. 119–137). New
York: Springer.

Riggs, D.S., Rukstalis, M., Volpicelli, J.R., Kalmanson, D., & Foa, E.B. (2003).
Demographic and social adjustment characteristics of patients with comorbid posttraumatic stress disorder and alcohol dependence: Potential pitfalls
of PTSD treatment. *Addictive Behaviors, 28*, 1717–1730.

Romach, M., Busto, U., Somer, G., Kaplan, H.L., & Sellers, E. (1995). Clinical aspects
of chronic use of alprazolam and lorazepam. *American Journal of Psychiatry,
152*, 1161–1167.

Saladin, M.E., Drobes, D.J., Coffey, S.F., Dansky, B.S., Brady, K.T., & Kilpatrick,
D.G. (2003). PTSD symptom severity as a predictor of cue-elicited drug craving in victims of violent crime. *Addictive Behaviors, 28*, 1611–1629.

Salkovskis, P.M. (1991). The importance of behavior in the maintenance of anxiety
and panic: A cognitive account. *Behavioral Psychotherapy, 19*, 6–19.

Schneier, F.R., Martin, L.Y., Liebowitz, M.R., Gorman, J.M., & Fyer, A.J. (1989).
Alcohol abuse in social phobia. *Journal of Anxiety Disorders, 3*, 15–23.

Smith, J.P., & Book, S.W. (2008). Anxiety and substance use disorders: A review.
Psychiatric Times, 25(Suppl.), 19–23.

Stein, M., Forde, D., Anderson, G., & Walker, J. (1997). Obsessive–compulsive
disorder in the community: An epidemiological survey with clinical reappraisal. *American Journal of Psychiatry, 154*, 1120–1126.

Stewart, S.H. (1996). Alcohol abuse in individuals exposed to trauma: A critical
review. *Psychological Bulletin, 120*, 83–112.

Stewart, S.H., & Conrod, P.J. (2003). Psychosocial models of functional associations between post-traumatic stress disorder and substance use disorder. In P. Ouimette & P.J. Brown (Eds.), *Trauma and substance abuse: Causes, consequences, and treatment of comorbid disorders* (pp. 29–55). Washington, D.C.: American Psychological Association.

Stewart, S.H., & Conrod, P.J. (Eds.). (2008a). *Anxiety and substance use disorder: The vicious cycle of comorbidity*. New York: Springer.

Stewart, S.H., & Conrod, P.J. (2008b). Anxiety disorder and substance use disorder comorbidity: Common themes and future directions. In S.H. Stewart & P.J. Conrod (Eds.), *Anxiety and substance use disorder: The vicious cycle of comorbidity* (pp. 239–257). New York: Springer.

Stewart, S.H., & Kushner, M.G. (2001). Introduction to the special issue on anxiety sensitivity and addictive behaviors. *Addictive Behaviors, 26*, 775–785.

Stewart, S.H., & Watt, M.C. (2008). Introduction to the special issue on "Interoceptive exposure in the treatment of anxiety and related disorders: Novel applications and mechanisms of action." *Journal of Cognitive Psychotherapy, 22*, 291–302

Stewart, S.H., Morris, E.P., Mellings, T., & Komar, J. (2006). Relations of social anxiety variables to drinking motives, drinking quantity and frequency, and alcohol-related problems in undergraduates. *Journal of Mental Health, 15*, 671–682.

Stinson, F.S., Dawson, D.A., Chou, S.P., Smith, S., Goldstein, R.B., Ruan, W.J. et al. (2007). The epidemiology of DSM-IV specific phobia in the USA: Results from the National Epidemiologic Survey on Alcohol and Related Conditions. *Psychological Medicine, 37*, 1047–1059.

Thomas, S.E., Randall, C.L., & Carrigan, M.H. (2003). Drinking to cope in socially anxious individuals: A controlled study. *Alcoholism: Clinical and Experimental Research, 27*, 1937–1943.

Thomas, S.E., Thevos, A.K., & Randall, C.L. (1999). Alcoholics with and without social phobia: A comparison of substance use and psychiatric variables. *Journal of Studies on Alcohol, 60*, 472–479.

Toneatto, T., & Rector, N.A. (2008). Treating co-morbid panic disorder and substance use disorder. In S.H. Stewart & P.J. Conrod (Eds.), *Anxiety and substance use disorders: The vicious cycle of comorbidity* (pp. 157–175). New York: Springer.

Tran, G.Q. (2008a). Efficacy of a brief intervention for college hazardous drinkers with social anxiety: A randomized controlled pilot study. *Alcoholism: Clinical and Experimental Research, 32*(Suppl.), 190A.

Tran, G.Q. (2008b). Effects of an integrated alcohol and anxiety intervention on college hazardous drinkers' social anxiety: Implications for intervention dissemination on college campuses. In J.D. Buckner (Chair), *Addressing anxiety in psychosocial treatments for addiction: implications for advancing the dissemination of CBT*. Symposium presented at the annual convention of the Association for Behavioural and Cognitive Therapies, Orlando, FL.

Tran, G.Q., & Smith, J.P. (2008). Comorbidity of social phobia and alcohol use disorders: A review of psychopathology research findings. In S.H. Stewart, & P.J. Conrod (Eds.), *Anxiety and substance use disorders: The vicious cycle of comorbidity* (pp. 59–79). New York: Springer.

Triffleman, E., Carroll, K., & Kellog, S. (1999). Substance dependence posttraumatic stress disorder therapy: An integrated cognitive–behavioral approach. *Journal of Substance Abuse Treatment, 17*, 3–14.

Van Gerwen, L.J., & Diekstra, R.F. (2000). Fear of flying treatment programs for passengers: An international review. *Aviation, Space, and Environmental Medicine, 71,* 430–437.

Voncken, M.J., Alden, L.E., & Bögels, S.M. (2006). Hiding anxiety versus acknowledgement of anxiety in social interaction: Relationship with social anxiety. *Behavior Research and Therapy, 44,* 1673–1679.

Welkowitz, L.A., Struening, E.L., Pittman, J.P., Guarding, M., & Welkowitz, J. (2000). Obsessive–compulsive disorder and comorbid anxiety problems in a national anxiety screening sample. *Journal of Anxiety Disorders, 14,* 471–482.

Wells, A., Clark, D.M., Salkovskis, P., Ludgate, J., Hackmann, A., & Gelder, M. (1995). Social phobia: The role of in-situation safety behaviors in maintaining anxiety and negative beliefs. *Behavior Therapy, 26,* 153–161.

Westra, H.A., & Stewart, S.H. (1998). Cognitive behavioural therapy and pharmacotherapy: Complementary or contradictory approaches to the treatment of anxiety? *Clinical Psychology Review, 18,* 307–340.

Wilhem, F.H., & Roth, W.T. (1997). Clinical characteristics of flight phobia. *Journal of Anxiety Disorders, 11,* 241–261.

Willinger, U., Lenzinger, E., Hornik, K., Fischer, G., Schonbeck, G., Aschauer, H.N. et al. (2002). Anxiety as a predictor of relapse in detoxified alcohol-dependent patients. *Alcohol and Alcoholism, 37,* 609–612.

Wolitzky-Taylor, K.B., Horowitz, J.D., Powers, M.B., & Telch, M.J. (2008). Psychological approaches in the treatment of specific phobias: A meta-analysis. *Clinical Psychology Review, 28,* 1021–1037.

Zahradnik, M., & Stewart, S.H. (2008). Anxiety disorders and substance use disorder co-morbidity: Epidemiology, theories of interrelation, and recent treatment approaches. In M. Antony & M. Stein (Eds.), *Handbook of anxiety and the anxiety disorders* (pp. 565–575). Oxford, U.K.: Oxford University Press.

Zimmerman, M., & Mattia, J.I. (2000). Principal and additional DSM-IV disorders for which outpatients seek treatment. *Psychiatric Services, 51,* 1299–1304.

Zlotnick. C., Najavits, L.M., Rohsenow, D.J., & Johnson, D.M. (2003). A cognitive–behavioral treatment for incarcerated women with substance abuse disorder and posttraumatic stress disorder: Findings from a pilot study. *Journal of Substance Abuse Treatment, 25,* 99–105.

Zohar, J., & Pato, M.T. (1991). Diagnostic considerations. In M.T. Pato & J. Zohar (Eds.), *Current treatments of obsessive–compulsive disorder* (pp. 1–12). Washington, D.C.: American Psychiatric Association.

Zvolensky, M.J., Bernstein, A., Yartz, A.R., McLeish, A.C., & Feldner, M.T. (2008). Cognitive-behavioral treatment of comorbid panic psychopathology and tobacco use and dependence. In S.H. Stewart & P.J. Conrod (Eds.), *Anxiety and substance use disorders: The vicious cycle of comorbidity* (pp. 177–200). New York: Springer.

Zvolensky, M.J., Schmidt, N.B., & Stewart, S.H. (2003). Panic disorder and smoking. *Clinical Psychology: Science and Practice, 10,* 29–51.

Zvolensky, M.J., Yartz, A.R., Gregor, K., Gonzalez, A., & Bernstein, A. (2008). Interoceptive-exposure based cessation intervention for smokers high in anxiety sensitivity: A case series. *Journal of Cognitive Psychotherapy, 22,* 346–365.

chapter eleven

The pharmacotherapy of treatment-resistant anxiety disorders in adults in the setting of cognitive–behavioral therapy

Theodore T. Kolivakis
Howard C. Margolese
Simon Ducharme
McGill University Health Centre
Montreal, Quebec, Canada

Contents

Approximately one out of three people will meet DSM-IV-TR (American Psychiatric Association, 2000) criteria for an anxiety disorder at some point in their lifetime. Response rates from randomized controlled trials (RCTs) are on the order of 40 to 90% for pharmacotherapy and psychotherapy. Reported remission rates are significantly lower (20 to 47%) (Ballenger, 1999). A majority of patients suffer from residual symptoms that are associated with poor functional outcomes, as well as comorbidity with other disorders, particularly major depression and alcohol abuse (Sanderson, DiNardo, Rapee, & Barlow, 1990).

    The burden of the illness of anxiety disorders is enormous, especially when one considers lost productivity, decreased quality of life, and societal costs. Greenberg et al. (1999) estimated that the annual cost of anxiety disorders in the United States was approximately $42 billion in 1990. People with an anxiety disorder are more likely to visit the doctor in general, and seven times more likely to visit their physicians if they suffer from panic disorder (Siegel, Jones, & Wilson, 1990).

Over the last decade there has been increasing emphasis placed on the practice of evidence-based medicine. This approach has gradually gained a great deal of importance in mental health research (Audet, Greenfield, & Field, 1990; Mellman et al., 2001) and is aimed at reducing inappropriate variation in clinical practice, improving outcomes, facilitating cost management, and disseminating research findings. Unfortunately, studies (Andrews, Henderson, & Hall, 2001; Bebbington, Brugha et al., 2000; Bebbington et al., 2000a; Jenkins et al., 1997) estimate that a minority of people (<25%) with anxiety disorders receive interventions of proven efficacy. More recent data from the Australian National Survey of Health and Well-Being (Issakidis, Sanderson, Corry, Andrews, & Lapsley, 2004) showed that receipt of evidence-based interventions ranged from 32% for social phobia to 64% for posttraumatic stress disorder. The authors performed an economic analysis and concluded that evidence-based care for anxiety disorders would result in improved health outcomes and a substantial increase in the cost effectiveness of treatment.

Many guidelines on the management of anxiety disorders have been published in the last few years. We reviewed publications from the major psychiatric associations, including the American Psychiatric Association (American Psychiatric Association, 1998; Koran, Hanna, Hollander, Nestadt, & Simpson, 2007; Ursano et al., 2004), the Canadian Psychiatric Association (2006), the British Association for Psychopharmacology (Baldwin et al., 2005), the World Federation of Societies of Biological Psychiatry (Bandelow, Zohar, Hollander, Kasper, & Moller, 2002), and the European College of Neuropsychopharmacology (Montgomery, 2002; Montgomery & Bech, 2000; Montgomery et al., 2004). Unfortunately, none of these guidelines deals specifically with treatment-resistant anxiety disorders, which is not surprising given the limited number of RCTs that include treatment-resistant patients. Despite this difficulty, all guideline algorithms include options for the management of patients with anxiety disorders who fail recommended first-line treatments. Most guidelines place greater emphasis on pharmacological treatments, but cognitive–behavioral therapy (CBT) is unanimously recognized as being a well-demonstrated, efficacious, first-line treatment for all anxiety disorders. Due to the limited available evidence, there is little emphasis on the interactions between pharmacotherapy and CBT in either first-line or treatment-resistant cases.

First-line treatment in anxiety disorders

Before focusing on treatment resistance, it would be appropriate to briefly review the evidence-based, first-line treatment options. A consensus among all published guidelines states that medication, mainly antidepressants and notably selective serotonin reuptake inhibitors (SSRIs), and CBT are both statistically more efficacious than placebo for all subtypes of anxiety disorders. Most studies, including a recent meta-analysis (Mitte, 2005a), have not found significant superiority of one form of treatment over the other in measured outcomes. In that context, all guidelines recommend SSRIs, the serotonin–norepinephrine reuptake inhibitor (SNRI) venlafaxine, or CBT as equally acceptable first-line treatments, with an emphasis on starting first with a trial of CBT where resources are available.

One notable exception is specific phobias, for which the overwhelming response to exposure therapy makes pharmacological intervention unnecessary in the great majority of cases (Antony & Barlow, 2002). Nonetheless, there is some evidence suggesting that paroxetine might have beneficial effects in the acute treatment of specific phobias (Benjamin, Ben-Zion, Karbofsky, & Dannon, 2000).

In terms of specific medication recommendations, there are variations in efficacy for the different anxiety disorders, and clinicians should try to choose drugs that have been well studied for each specific diagnosis. A further consideration would be to choose a medication with proven efficacy for any comorbidity that may be present in a particular patient. Once efficacy is established, treatment must also be individualized based on the acceptability of a particular medication's side-effect profile. SSRIs and SNRIs are usually well tolerated. Headaches, gastrointestinal symptoms, and sleep perturbations are the most frequent complaints but tend to be self-limited. Patients may even experience a transient increase in anxiety upon initiation of medication that can be lessened by starting with lower, subtherapeutic doses for 1 to 2 weeks. Patients should be made aware of the potential adverse effects, as their presence may interfere with initial treatment compliance. Longer term problems can include weight gain and sexual dysfunction, which tend to persist and may require a reevaluation of treatment.

In addition, on attempting to stop or reduce medication, patients may experience a discontinuation syndrome consisting of dizziness, insomnia, paresthesias, and flu-like symptoms lasting a few days, depending on the half-life of each medication. Although a class effect, the frequency of the syndrome is higher for SSRIs with shorter half-lives and in one study ranged from 7.2% for paroxetine and fluvoxamine to as low as 2.2% for sertraline and fluoxetine (Coupland, Bell, & Potokar, 1996). Discontinuation syndrome symptoms can be reduced by very slow taper of SSRIs—for example, decreasing paroxetine by 5 to 10 mg every 2 to 3 weeks (Bhanji, Chouinard, Kolivakis, & Margolese, 2006). Contrary to the first generation of antidepressants (tricyclics and monoamine oxidase inhibitors), dangerous side effects are rare with SSRIs. One notable exception is the serotonin syndrome occasionally seen in patients being treated with multiple medications or abusing substances that increase central and peripheral serotonergic activity (Boyer & Shannon, 2005). This syndrome consisting typically of mental status changes, neuromuscular signs, autonomic symptoms, and changes in vital signs is seen in 0.4 cases per 1000 patient-months of regular treatment (Looper, 2007). Signs of excess serotonin range from tremor and diarrhea in mild cases to delirium, neuromuscular rigidity, and hyperthermia in life-threatening cases.

When implementing psychological or pharmacological interventions, both benefits and tolerability issues must be considered when choosing a specific therapy for a patient. Clinicians must bear in mind that CBT may understandably produce a transient worsening of anxiety as exposure to anxiety-provoking situations is central to therapeutic outcome (Baldwin et al., 2005). Strategies to adaptively cope with emotional distress are addressed in specialized CBT (e.g., Leahy, 2003, this volume, Chapter 5; Sookman & Pinard, 1999; Sookman & Steketee, this volume, Chapter 2).

As a general rule, clinicians should decide which form of intervention is most likely to help a specific patient based on the patient's motivation, capacity for and previous response to each treatment, comorbidities, and the local availability of psychological treatments. CBT alone is recommended as a first-line treatment for patients without significant comorbid depression or severe medical illness that would prevent cooperation with this treatment modality (Koran et al., 2007). Medication would likely be indicated in cases of very severe disorders in which extensive symptomatology might prevent good collaboration with CBT or for patients with psychiatric comorbidities that could be improved with pharmacological treatment. Patient preference is often cited as a reason to choose one modality over another (Canadian Psychiatric Association, 2006; Koran et al., 2007); however, there is very little research as to what factors constitute patient preference (e.g., lack of knowledge and education regarding treatment differences, a preference for medication representing a wish to avoid any feelings of anxiety).

In this context, the clinician must take great care to present both psychotherapy and pharmacotherapy as nonconflicting and potentially complementary treatment options. This allows patients to make informed decisions they are comfortable with and strengthens the therapeutic alliance. One study on depression showed that patients who actively chose psychotherapy rather than medication had better treatment adherence and better outcomes than those randomly assigned to psychotherapy (Chilvers et al., 2001). Administration of pharmacotherapy requires some psychotherapeutic interventions to improve patient adherence and properly assess functional treatment outcomes. These include, but are not limited to, frank discussion regarding potential side effects of medication and the potential duration of treatment, setting and evaluating treatment goals at regular intervals, identifying and challenging cognitive distortions such as unrealistic expectations about medication, psychoeducation regarding the role of medication in the overall context of treatment, and behavioral approaches to encourage exposure and tolerance to previously anxiety-provoking situations.

The treating clinician should be able to present a basic (even if as yet incomplete) conceptualization of anxiety disorders that integrates the biological and psychological models of illness through discussion of a "top–down" (cognitive) or "bottom–up" approach through neurotransmitter modulation by psychotropic medications. A unified model may assist patients in making sense of the various treatment modalities offered to them.

Treatment resistance in anxiety disorders

No universally accepted definition of treatment resistance exists, and there is potential discordance between the CBT and pharmacological research views. In terms of defining *remission*, it should be emphasized that the absence of anxiety is not necessarily synonymous with recovery if patients can successfully avoid the anxiety-provoking stimulus. It is therefore important to include some functional parameters in the evaluation of remission (Brown & Barlow, 1995).

In a review on the topic (Ballenger, 2001), the authors proposed a set of criteria for remission that includes both symptom reduction and the absence of functional impairment in terms of no longer avoiding anxiety-provoking situations, being able to return to work, and resuming a premorbid level of activities and interpersonal experiences. The common proposed general endpoints for remission across anxiety disorders include Hamilton Rating Scale for Anxiety (HAM-A) scores of ≤7 to 10, Sheehan Disability Scale (SDS) scores of ≤1 (mildly disabled), and Hamilton Rating Scale for Depression (HAM-D) scores of ≤7. In addition, disorder-specific remission criteria include reduction in the Panic Disorder Severity Scale (PDSS) to <3 for panic disorder (with no individual item score >1), Liebowitz Social Anxiety Scale score to ≤30 for social anxiety disorder (SAD), Treatment Outcome for Posttraumatic Stress Disorder (TOP-8) score to ≤5 or 6 for posttraumatic stress disorder (PTSD), and Yale–Brown Obsessive Compulsive Scale (Y-BOCS) (Goodman et al., 1989a,b) ≤8 for obsessive–compulsive disorder (OCD) (see Chapter 2 for updated and comprehensive criteria for recovery in OCD).

In a recent review, Pollack et al. (2008) further examined the concept of treatment resistance in anxiety disorders. They noted that the criteria proposed by Ballenger have little empirical validation and have not been universally adopted. The authors concluded that treatment resistance may be due to multiple factors: (1) treatment-related factors (including incorrect or incomplete diagnosis, inadequate dosing, and short duration of treatment); (2) patient-related factors (poor compliance, comorbidity); and (3) logistical factors (lack of well-trained treatment providers, inadequate insurance coverage).

Given that CBT is a well-demonstrated effective treatment of anxiety disorders, most recent guidelines regard a failed CBT trial as an equivalent of a failed medication trial in their definition. Because the guidelines suggest the use of two first-line agents before switching to second-line agents, treatment resistance would therefore be defined as failure of adequately administered CBT and an SSRI or SNRI (given in series or concomitantly). Pharmacological resistance may be defined as a trial of two SSRIs or SNRIs (given in series or concomitantly).

A recent Cochrane review of treatment-resistant anxiety disorders used a less stringent criterion, defining treatment resistance as failure to respond to one first-line intervention. Those who did not respond to multiple interventions were classified as treatment-refractory (Ipser et al., 2006). This definition is more indicative of the lack of RCTs for interventions on treatment resistance in anxiety disorders rather than a clinically useful definition, as there are many potential reasons to fail a single trial of medication (see Chapter 2 for criteria for CBT-resistant OCD).

Evidence-based management of treatment-resistant anxiety disorders

It is clear that treatment response of anxiety disorders is suboptimal despite the increasing therapeutic arsenal. The percentage of patients meeting response criteria to first-line pharmacological intervention in terms of symptom reduction has been estimated to range from 40 to 60% in OCD and 60 to 80% in panic disorder (Bandelow & Ruther, 2004; Pallanti et al., 2002). Even though it is not as well documented as for major depression, it seems obvious clinically that the pharmacological management of treatment-resistant anxiety disorders suffers from diminishing returns as one proceeds through multiple medication trials. Additionally, relapse rates following discontinuation of pharmacotherapy alone are high (Liebowitz, 1998).

There are basic principles that clinicians generally adhere to when confronted with a partial response to an initial course of treatment for anxiety disorders. After reconfirming the diagnosis and addressing any comorbidity, every effort must be made to assess and ensure adherence to treatment. Reasons for poor compliance will obviously differ between pharmacotherapy and CBT. The clinician may then opt to maximize the dose of the initial medication based on the premise that there may be significant inter-individual variability in how a medication is metabolized (pharmacokinetic) and how it modulates neurotransmitter activity (pharmacodynamic). The next step would be to maximize the duration of therapy, as some data suggest that nonresponders may convert to responders over a longer period of time. In a study on PTSD, 54% of patients who did not respond to an initial 12-week trial of the SSRI sertraline converted to responders following a 24-week continuation phase (Londborg et al., 2001); however, it is difficult to convince most patients suffering from an anxiety disorder to stay with the current course of treatment if they see no improvement. If there is little or no response on the initial medication, a common strategy is to switch to another medication of similar or different class. There is little empirical evidence for the efficacy of this intervention in anxiety disorders, although it is supported from the data on depression. Poor tolerability may be another reason to change the original medication. If the patient exhibits partial response, augmenting with a second agent from a different class is warranted and may help maintain therapeutic optimism. Here, again, the evidence is limited and is reviewed below. The potential benefits from augmentation must be weighed against the risks of polypharmacy, namely cumulative side effects and decreased tolerability. It is important to remember that a poor response to an initial trial of pharmacotherapy may be an opportunity to reassess motivation and explore initial resistance to a course of CBT in patients who initially refused psychotherapy. These principles are important to keep in mind when assimilating all the evidence-based strategies reviewed below in the treatment of resistant anxiety.

A recent Cochrane review (Ipser et al., 2006) included 28 short-term RCTs (average of 7 weeks; $n = 740$). Twenty studies that investigated augmentation of medication for treatment-resistant OCD looked at two primary outcome measures: treatment response and reduction in symptom severity. Treatment resistance was defined as a lack of response on the primary outcome measures employed in the studies. This broad definition of treatment resistance was employed in anticipation of differences across trials in the operational definition of resistance. Trials that described their sample as treatment resistant, without providing evidence of the lack of response on a validated outcome measure against which to assess this claim, were not included in the meta-analyses. Treatment response was determined from the improvement item of the Clinical Global Impression scale (CGI-I) as a change item score of 1 ("very much") or 2 ("much") improved.

Only data from OCD trials (n = 9 trials) were available for treatment response comparison. Globally, response has occurred in more than twice as many patients treated with medication (31.8%) than with placebo (13.6%). Augmentation with any medication used in these 9 trials was significantly more likely to result in treatment response compared to placebo, as determined by the CGI-I, with an odds ratio of 3.16 (95% confidence interval, 1.08 to 9.23; sample size, n = 250). The authors noted a number needed to treat (NNT) of 5.5, meaning that it would take approximately six additional patients on augmentation to yield one extra responder relative to placebo. More specifically, augmentation of SSRIs with antipsychotics as a group for OCD (n = 6 out of 9 trials) increased treatment response compared to placebo with an odds ratio of 5.43 (95% confidence interval, 2.13 to 13.87; sample size, n = 146). None of the three remaining trials (two with lithium augmentation and one with buspirone augmentation of SSRIs) showed a significant effect on treatment response.

A recent 8-week pilot study (Maina, Pessina, Albert, & Bogetto, 2008) investigated the efficacy and tolerability of risperidone versus olanzapine augmentation in OCD resistant to previous medication trials (<35% decrease in the Y-BOCS score after 16 weeks of SSRI treatment). Of the 96 subjects who entered the open-label prospective phase, 50 (52%) were resistant after 16 weeks and were randomized to receive risperidone (1 to 3 mg/day) or olanzapine (2.5 to 10 mg/day) for 8 weeks. Both groups had significant improvement in CGI-S and the Y-BOCS (30.1 ± 4.3 to 22.6 ± 7.2 for risperidone and 30.6 ± 4.2 to 22.2 ± 7.4 for olanzapine), and there were no differences in treatment response. It should be noted that, on average, patients were still moderately ill following treatment. Adverse events were reported by 52% (13/25) of patients receiving risperidone addition, the most common being tension/inner unrest (24%) and amenorrhea (66.7%); 64% (16/25) of patients receiving olanzapine reported adverse events, the most common (52%) being weight gain (2.80 ± 3.10 kg; range, –2.6 to 8.9 kg). However, as is discussed below, research indicates that, for optimal clinical management of OCD, pharmacotherapy, if needed, should be combined with specialized CBT.

Apart from OCD, atypical antipsychotics have been studied most frequently in PTSD. A recent meta-analysis (Pae et al., 2008) of 7 RCTs (n = 192 patients) using risperidone or olanzapine in the treatment of PTSD as either monotherapy or as augmentation of SSRIs showed general beneficial effects of this class of medications as measured by improvement in the Clinician Administered PTSD Scale (CAPS) (Blake et al., 1995). On analysis of subscales it appears that reduction in the symptom of "intrusion" was mainly responsible for the improvement noted. In a recent RCT, Rothbaum et al. (2008) studied risperidone augmentation in civilians with PTSD currently receiving sertraline without an optimal response (CAPS score ≥ 50). Participants were treated for 8 weeks with open-label sertraline. Those who did not remit (defined as a 70% decrease in PTSD symptoms as measured by the CAPS) remained on sertraline and were randomly assigned to augmentation with risperidone or placebo for 8 weeks. Of the 45 patients enrolled, 34 completed the initial 8-week trial with sertraline, and 25 of those patients were randomly assigned to risperidone or placebo; 20 patients completed the trial. PTSD symptoms improved (as measured by a decrease in the CAPS scores from randomization to endpoint) by a mean of 23.1 (SD = 12.9) in the risperidone group and 23.5 (SD = 19.6) in the placebo group, with no significant differences between groups. In *post hoc* analyses, the group that received risperidone augmentation had significantly more improvement than the placebo group on the Davidson Trauma Scale (DTS) sleep item ($p = .03$) and demonstrated a trend toward significantly more improvement on the CGI-I ($p = .066$); however, the sample size in this trial (as in others) was too small to examine this clinical question. Future trials with a larger number of patients are warranted. Finally, the alpha-blocker prazosin could be useful for PTSD, mainly for decreasing nightmares and sleep disturbances (Raskind et al., 2003). Nightmares in PTSD may be related to disrupted rapid eye-movement (REM) sleep which is normalized by prazosin (Pickworth, Sharpe, Nozaki, & Martin, 1977; Woodward, Arsenault, Murray, & Bliwise, 2000).

Two positive RCTs have used adjunctive risperidone (Brawman-Mintzer, Knapp, & Nietert, 2005) and olanzapine (Pollack et al., 2006) in generalized anxiety disorder (GAD). In the first study, 40 patients with pharmacotherapy-resistant GAD (i.e., HAM-A ≥ 18 and CGI severity of moderate or greater despite 4 weeks of anxiolytic treatment) were randomized to 5 weeks of risperidone (0.5 to 1.5 mg/day; mean dose, 1.1 ± 0.4 mg) vs. placebo augmentation. The risperidone group showed greater reductions in HAM-A total (−9.8 ± 5.5 vs. −6.2 ± 4.9; $p = .034$) and psychic anxiety factor scores (−6.3 ± 3.7 vs. −3.8 ± 4.0; $p = .047$) compared with placebo; however, differences in other outcome measures did not achieve significance: HAM-A somatic anxiety, CGI-S, Montgomery–Åsberg Depression Rating Scale (MADRS), SDS, and Quality of Life Enjoyment and Satisfaction Questionnaire (Q-LES-Q) (Endicott, Nee, Harrison, & Blumenthal, 1993). One review of this study (Kopecek, Mohr, & Novak, 2006) pointed out that differences in rates of somnolence between the two groups may have accounted for a nonspecific effect on anxiety in the risperidone group.

In the second study, patients remaining symptomatic after 6 weeks of fluoxetine (20 mg/day) were randomized to 6 weeks of olanzapine (mean dose, 8.7 ± 7.1 mg/day; $n = 24$) or placebo ($n = 22$) augmentation.

Olanzapine resulted in a greater proportion of treatment responders based on a CGI severity score of ≤ 2—$n = 6/9$ (67%) for olanzapine versus $n = 1/12$ (8%) for placebo—or a 50% reduction in the HAM-A score—$n = 5/9$ (56%) for olanzapine versus $n = 1/12$ (8%) for placebo. There were no statistically significant differences for olanzapine compared with placebo augmentation in other outcome measures. Average weight gain for completers was greater with olanzapine than placebo (11.0 ± 5.1 vs. -0.7 ± 2.4 lb). The authors concluded that olanzapine may further reduce anxiety for some GAD patients remaining symptomatic despite initial treatment with an SSRI, but the emergence of significant weight gain represents an important clinical consideration.

Both olanzapine and quetiapine have been studied as monotherapy in RCTs of social anxiety disorder (Barnett, Kramer, Casat, Connor, & Davidson, 2002; Vaishnavi, Alamy, Zhang, Connor, & Davidson, 2007). Olanzapine was superior to placebo in the primary outcome measures: Brief Social Phobia Scale (BSPS) and Social Phobia Inventory (SPIN). Quetiapine (up to 400 mg/day) failed to differentiate from placebo on the BSPS at endpoint, but 20% ($n = 2/10$) of the quetiapine patients had a 50% or greater drop in BSPS score at the end of the trial compared to baseline, while 0% had such a drop in the placebo group. In addition, although there was no significant difference in responders (CGI-I score of 1 or 2) versus nonresponders (CGI-I score ≥ 3) across the groups, 40% ($n = 4/10$) of quetiapine patients and 0% of the placebo patients showed much or very much improvement on the CGI-I. Perhaps a subgroup of patients with SAD who are resistant to first-line treatment with CBT or SSRIs may preferentially benefit from atypical antipsychotics. There is, however, no indication that the patients in these two studies were treatment resistant. The other possibility remains of misdiagnosis due to syndrome overlap. If patients with a cluster A personality disorder (paranoid, schizoid, or schizotypal) are misdiagnosed as having SAD due to social avoidance, they may conceivably show benefit from treatment with low-dose antipsychotic medication.

No RCTs have used atypical antipsychotics in treatment-resistant panic disorder. One open-label trial ($n = 10$) examining the efficacy of olanzapine in refractory panic disorder (Hollifield, Thompson, Ruiz, & Uhlenhuth, 2005) found that the average number of panic attacks decreased from 6.1/week at baseline to 1.1/week at the end of treatment, and anticipatory anxiety decreased from 32% of the day to 8% of the day. At the end of treatment, 50% of the patients were panic free, and 60% of the patients were anticipatory anxiety free. Weight gain was seen in 60% of patients.

Two RCTs have studied augmentation in treatment-resistant panic disorder (Hoffart et al., 1993; Hirschmann et al., 2000). The first study examined clomipramine augmentation (up to 150 mg/day) in a crossover design over 12 weeks in 18 patients with panic disorder with agoraphobia who were judged to be nonresponders (score of ≥1.5 on the Phobic Avoidance Rating Scale, or PARS) 1 year following an 11-week inpatient behavioral–psychodynamic treatment program for agoraphobia (exposure-based supportive psychotherapy). Study completers ($n = 17$) had significantly ($p < .05$) lower symptom scores on the PARS (separation avoidance subscale) on clomipramine than following the placebo period; however, the clinical gains were modest as there was no significant difference on the behavioral avoidance test (BAT). Interestingly, the authors noted that only 29% of the subjects improved at least 50% on the PARS separation avoidance subscale following a trial of clomipramine, whereas 47% of patients from the initial cohort had achieved the same response from behavioral therapy alone. The authors set out to examine whether patients with panic disorder with agoraphobia whose response to behavioral therapy was not sustained after 1 year ($n = 36/100$) would improve with a trial of clomipramine. Their response was weaker than the initial response to behavioral therapy, and, as the crossover design demonstrated (going from active drug to placebo), the response was not sustained with a short trial of clomipramine, either. The authors speculated on the long-term use of clomipramine but did not consider employing long-term or booster sessions of behavioral therapy as an alternative.

The second study examined the efficacy of pindolol augmentation of fluoxetine in patients with treatment-resistant panic disorder ($n = 25$). These patients had not responded to two different trials with antidepressants and an 8-week trial of fluoxetine at 20 mg/day. Treatment resistance was defined as a less than 20% reduction in score on the Panic Self-Questionnaire (PSQ) and the Clinical Anxiety Scale with Panic Attacks (CAS + PA). Patients taking 20 mg/day fluoxetine were randomly assigned to additionally receive either pindolol (2.5 mg three times daily) or placebo for 4 weeks. The pindolol augmentation group ($n = 13$) showed significant improvement over placebo on all rating scales, with the exception of HAM-D. The significance was notable on the HAM-A (11.1 ± 5.5 to 3.4 ± 2.5 at week 4 on pindolol vs. 12.7 ± 3.7 to 9.9 ± 3.4 on placebo; $p < 0.001$), CAS + PA (15.9 ± 2.9 to 6.5 ± 3.1 vs. 17.9 ± 2.3 to 15.8 ± 1.3 on placebo; $p < 0.001$), Present State Questionnaire (6.6 ± 1.9 to 1.0 ± 1.5 vs. 6.3 ± 1.4 to 5.0 ± 1.5 on placebo; $p < 0.001$), and CGI-Global Improvement (4.0 ± 0.4 to 2.2 ± 0.7 vs. 4.1 ± 0.5 to 3.4 ± 0.7 on placebo; $p < 0.001$). The clinical changes noted with pindolol were evident by the second week of the study.

Finally, it is also important to mention where the evidence in the literature shows no benefit from a particular pharmacological strategy that may be commonly employed. Several RCTs of adjunctive medications in treatment-resistant anxiety disorders failed to show any benefit. A 2-week ($n = 20$) and a 4-week ($n = 10$) double-blind, placebo-controlled trial of lithium added to fluvoxamine in patients with fluvoxamine-refractory OCD (defined as <35% improvement on Y-BOCS or a score ≥16 and minimal improvement on the CGI-I or primary caregiver consensus of a lack of improvement) did not produce any clinically meaningful response (McDougle et al., 1991). This finding is important in light of the evidence-based support of lithium augmentation in treatment-resistant depressed patients (Crossley & Bauer, 2007), suggesting pathophysiological differences between OCD and depression. This does not necessarily mean that serotonergic abnormalities are not involved in the pathophysiology of OCD but that the ability of lithium to enhance serotonin release may be limited to brain areas involved in depression such as the hippocampus and not in areas involved in OCD such as the fronto-orbital cortex and the striatum (Blier & de Montigny, 1992). A 6-week trial of buspirone in 33 patients resistant (defined as <35% improvement on Y-BOCS or a score of ≥16 and minimal improvement on the CGI-I or primary caregiver consensus of a lack of improvement) to an initial 8-week trial of fluvoxamine augmentation was ineffective in OCD (McDougle et al., 1991, 1993). Pindolol added to paroxetine for social phobia yielded no significant improvement (Stein, Sareen, Hami, & Chao, 2001). Another recent study (Simon et al., 2008) examined paroxetine CR augmentation to prolonged exposure therapy in PTSD and found no incremental benefit.

In extreme cases of refractory OCD, nonpharmacological treatments, including deep-brain stimulation or neurosurgical interventions, in carefully selected cases have success rates (as defined by treatment response) of approximately 30% in small clinical trials (Lipsman, Neimat, & Lozano, 2007). It should be stressed that the increased availability of these invasive treatment modalities makes it all the more important to properly define treatment resistance and behooves us to adhere to a rigorous treatment algorithm that includes an adequate trial of intensive inpatient CBT prior to being eligible for such procedures (Calvocoressi et al., 1993).

Overall, pooled data from the Cochrane meta-analysis confirm that most pharmacological augmentation strategies are useful, more than doubling the proportion of responders to medication (31.8%) compared to placebo (13.6%). The number needed to treat (NNT) of 5.5 justifies the clinical use of these combinations, especially given the similar dropout rates in control groups (Ipser et al., 2006). It is difficult to determine the minimal effective duration of an augmentation strategy; however, rates of relapse following discontinuation of medication are high (83%), usually within 2 months. In some cases, long-term pharmacological combination treatment is warranted (Maina, Albert, Ziero, & Bogetto, 2003), but it is important to provide CBT to achieve sustained effects (see below). Despite proving statistical and clinical improvement in treatment response, the limited evidence thus far has failed to clearly demonstrate an improvement in overall level of function following pharmacological augmentation strategies. Scales focusing on quality of life and functional status must be included in future trials to make study results more meaningful.

Combined CBT and pharmacotherapy in treatment-resistant anxiety disorders

Another as yet poorly investigated topic in the field of anxiety disorders is the combination of pharmacological and psychological approaches. Unfortunately, scientific data supporting this practice are scarce or lacking for most anxiety disorders. Clinicians commonly combine the two interventions for refractory cases based on the hypothesis that they could be complementary (working through different mechanisms) or have a synergistic effect. A putative mechanism underlying this synergistic effect may be a reduction in anxiety with medication that allows a patient to tolerate the amount of exposure necessary for adequate CBT. However, the same argument can be turned against combining treatments (adding medication to CBT), particularly in the case of panic disorder, where the acute reduction of anxiety (i.e., by a benzodiazepine) may cause faulty associations in the patient such as the belief that the feared outcome (dying or "going crazy") was prevented by the medication. In these clinical scenarios, there is little motivation to do work in a CBT context as the anxiety has been avoided, but the faulty assumptions remain intact. The absence of anxiety does not allow for a situation where the dysfunctional cognitions can be challenged in the context of feared situations. In an interesting study (Powers, Smits, Whitley, Bystritsky, & Telch, 2008), investigators examined the effect of attributional processes concerning taking medication on return of fear following exposure-based treatment. Subjects with severe claustrophobia ($n = 95$) were randomly assigned to several different treatments, including a one-session, exposure-based treatment given in conjunction with an inactive pill. The subjects in the exposure-based treatment plus pill condition were further randomly assigned to one of three instructional sets following treatment completion: (1) The pill was described as a sedating herb that likely made exposure treatment easier, (2) the pill was described as a stimulating herb that likely made exposure treatment more difficult, or (3) the pill was described as a placebo that had no effect on exposure treatment. Return-of-fear rates for the three conditions were 39%, 0%, and 0%, respectively. The authors concluded that the poor results in the sedation instructions group were mediated by reduced self-efficacy and misattribution of improvement to the pharmacotherapy.

In a comprehensive meta-analysis, Foa, Franklin, and Moser (2002) reviewed 9 studies (out of a possible 26) that met criteria for a well-designed RCT to evaluate the effects of combination therapy in anxiety disorders. Of the 17 studies that were excluded in this analysis, 5 did not permit for a test of combination treatment versus monotherapy, 9 failed to use adequate methodology, 4 failed to include blind independent evaluation, and 10 failed to present essential statistics for calculating within-group effect sizes. Out of the 9 studies reviewed, 4 of them were on OCD. From these data, the authors concluded that the effect of CBT for OCD was not impeded by medication; however, there was no incremental benefit from the addition of medication to the results achieved with CBT alone. Administration of CBT alone was more effective compared with pharmacotherapy alone. The authors recommended that CBT alone should be a first-line treatment for OCD. In one of the studies reviewed (Hohagen et al., 1998), patients with comorbid depression and OCD who received combination treatment had better outcomes than those receiving CBT alone; this benefit was not seen in patients without depression. The presence of comorbid depression may warrant an initial combination treatment.

In a 12-week comparative study comparing clomipramine with exposure and response prevention therapy, Foa et al. (2005) randomized 149 patients with OCD into 4 groups: exposure + ritual prevention (EXP + RP), clomipramine alone (CMI), EXP + RP + CMI, and placebo. The therapy consisted of daily exposure sessions, each lasting 2 hours, conducted on weekdays over a 3-week period (15 sessions total). Daily exposure and ritual prevention homework (≤ 2 hours/day) were assigned. Therapists visited the patients' homes twice (4 hours total) in the fourth week to promote generalizability of treatment gains by conducting exposures in contexts relevant to the patient's functioning. For the remaining 8 weeks, 45-minute sessions were conducted weekly to promote maintenance.

Intent-to-treat analysis was performed on the 122 patients who entered treatment. Response rates were significantly higher for EXP + RP + CMI (70%) and for EXP + RP alone (62%) than for CMI alone (42%) or placebo (8%). Response rates were higher for completers. The dropout rate did not differ across treatments (29%). Importantly, EXP + RP alone was as effective as EXP + RP + CMI. The authors further suggested that the addition of CBT to medication could decrease relapse rates when medication is discontinued.

It is important to note that the therapy offered in this study was particularly intense, and its impressive success rate may not have allowed for significant incremental improvement from the pharmacotherapy. As access to this type of intensive therapy may unfortunately be limited outside specialized clinics, it would be interesting to examine the interaction between pharmacotherapy and less intensive CBT to improve the generalizability of the findings.

The data from this trial were reanalyzed (Simpson, Huppert, Petkova, Foa, & Liebowitz, 2006) focusing specifically on rates of response and remission. Again, comparisons were made among exposure and ritual prevention (EX/RP), clomipramine (CMI), their combination (EX/RP + CMI), or placebo. The results showed that EX/RP + CMI and EX/RP each produced significantly more responders and remitters than placebo. When remission was defined as a Y-BOCS score of ≤12, significantly more EX/RP + CMI (18/31, or 58%) and EX/RP (15/29, or 52%) patients achieved remission than in either the CMI (9/36, or 25%) or placebo groups (0/26, or 0%). The authors concluded that EX/RP + CMI and EX/RP alone were superior to CMI alone in OCD patients without comorbid depression. It is important to remember, however, that depression in the context of OCD is often a secondary reaction to the chronic obsessions and persistent rituals. We may postulate that successful CBT for OCD symptoms would relieve the depression in the majority of these cases.

In a more recent RCT, Simpson et al. (2008) examined the effects on OCD of augmenting SSRIs with exposure and ritual prevention versus stress management training. Participants ($n = 108$) had a Y-BOCS total score of ≥16, despite a therapeutic SSRI dose for at least 12 weeks. They received 17 sessions of CBT (either exposure and ritual prevention or stress management training) twice a week while continuing their pharmacotherapy. Results showed that exposure and ritual prevention were superior to stress management training in reducing OCD symptoms. At week 8, significantly more patients receiving exposure and ritual prevention than patients receiving stress management training attained minimal symptoms (Y-BOCS ≤ 12): 47% ($n = 22$) versus 22% ($n = 12$); NNT = 4; confidence interval, 2–6. The authors concluded that exposure and ritual prevention is an effective strategy for further reducing OCD symptoms in patients already on an SSRI; however, 17 sessions were insufficient to help the majority of patients achieve minimal symptoms. This corroborates the finding that a substantial number of OCD patients show persistent disabling symptoms at long-term follow-up in spite of combined pharmacologic and behavioral treatments (Alonso et al., 2001). However, in those patients with OCD whose symptoms do remit on pharmacotherapy combined with CBT, discontinuation of the SSRI did not prompt a recurrence of symptoms at 2-year follow-up (Kordon et al., 2005). This important finding needs to be further explored as it points to a long-lasting process of active learning from CBT that appears to be protective of future relapse.

In the meta-analysis by Foa et al. (2002), the data from three studies on panic disorder were more difficult to synthesize. Combined treatment was found to be superior to CBT alone in one study (Barlow, Gorman, Shear, & Woods, 2000), but not in the other two (Cottraux et al., 1995; Marks et al., 1993). In two of the studies (Barlow et al., 2000; Marks et al., 1993), combination treatment was associated with greater risk of relapse at treatment discontinuation than CBT alone. This suggests that the medication may have decreased the long-term impact of CBT through several potential mechanisms—namely, reduced self-efficacy, misattribution of improvement to the pharmacotherapy, safety behavior, return of physical symptoms following medication sensation, and the possibility that learning processes during CBT (particularly state-dependant learning) may be negatively influenced by medication. A recent follow-up to the Barlow study (Raffa et al., 2008) indicated that almost all of the patients thought they were receiving imipramine, thus reducing the likelihood that misattribution of improvement to medication and reduced self-efficacy are the main factors related to greater relapse in the imipramine group versus the placebo group.

Mitte (2005b) published another meta-analysis that demonstrated only a small benefit of combination treatment for all symptom categories except quality of life; however, the number of studies that used quality-of-life measures was low. It is important to note that this result was not maintained in long-term follow-up. There was no significant difference between combining CBT and pharmacotherapy and using CBT alone in follow-up (the author used the last available assessment in the analysis; mean = 16.8 months); however, only half of the studies included a follow-up. To conduct a meaningful analysis of the evidence comparing CBT to combination treatment it is important to examine the difference between short-term and long-term effects.

In a more recent meta-analysis from Bandelow et al. (2007), the combination of CBT and pharmacotherapy was more effective than CBT plus placebo for both clinician and self-reported ratings; however, the effect size of combination treatment for panic disorder ranged between 0.23 and 0.61, corresponding to small and medium impact, respectively. In two studies that did not utilize a placebo, the difference between combined treatment and CBT alone was not significant.

Some preliminary data support combination treatment for social anxiety, but the evidence is not strong enough to make any recommendation at this point (Bandelow et al., 2007). In a study on GAD (Power et al., 1990), 113 patients were randomized to one of five treatment conditions: CBT + diazepam (responders = 90.5%), CBT + placebo (83%), CBT alone (86%), diazepam alone (68%), and placebo (37%). Response (reduction ≥ 2 SD on pretreatment HAM-A) rates were assessed at 10 weeks. All active treatment arms fared better than placebo but did not differ statistically from one another. At 6-month follow-up, treatment arms that included CBT were superior to diazepam alone. As a corollary to this, CBT has been shown to improve the success rate of benzodiazepine discontinuation for patients with GAD who were treated for more than one year with medication (Gosselin, Ladouceur, Morin, Dugas, & Baillargeon, 2006).

Cognitive–behavioral therapy has also been used successfully in open studies to improve response for patients who have failed previous medication trials for PTSD and panic disorder (Heldt et al., 2006; Otto, Pollack, Penava, & Zucker, 1999; Otto et al., 2003). For example, Heldt et al. obtained sustained clinical response at 1 year with CBT in nearly two-thirds of a small sample of 63 patients with panic disorder who had previously failed an adequate treatment with antidepressant medication.

Finally, novel approaches include the use of D-cycloserine, a partial agonist at the *N*-methyl-D-aspartate receptor, in combination with psychological treatment. When given prior to exposure therapy, it is postulated to facilitate the extinction of fears by strengthening extinction memories so they might be more easily retrieved during subsequent exposure to fear-relevant cues. D-Cycloserine has no direct effect on symptoms of anxiety when administered chronically (Heresco-Levy et al., 2002), but studies suggest that it may enhance treatment outcome when administered acutely in combination with exposure-based procedures. This medication has significantly improved outcomes in phobias, obsessive–compulsive disorder, and social anxiety disorder in some studies (Guastella et al., 2008; Ressler et al., 2004; Wilhelm et al., 2008), although not in others (Storch et al., 2007). Effect sizes on most outcome measures in the positive studies were in the moderate range. This study by Guastella et al. suggests that the amount of adaptive learning between exposure treatment sessions was closely associated with the overall effect of D-cycloserine in social anxiety disorder. Specifically, for patients receiving D-cycloserine, a positive relationship was found between improvements (from sessions 2 to 5) on appraisals about participants' speech performance and reported improvements in social fear and avoidance symptoms.

It should be noted that few of the combined treatment studies discussed were designed to specifically focus on treatment-resistant anxiety disorders. Most studies analyzed the effects of monotherapies versus combined therapy in all patients who presented for treatment. Finally, guidelines on anxiety disorders do not address the optimal sequence of treatments. There are unfortunately very few studies so far that attempt to provide an evidence-based rationale for the timing of CBT *vis-à-vis* pharmacotherapy.

This opens the field to many clinically important questions: Is there an optimal medication dosing so the patient can learn during CBT? What is the optimal timing during combined treatment for a medication reduction schedule as the patient learns alternative CBT strategies? How should the clinician manage medication dependence? To what extent is the probability of relapse increased following medication discontinuation if the patient on combined treatment has not received, or collaborated sufficiently in, optimal CBT? How can treating clinicians collaborate to improve the patient's collaboration in CBT?

In summary, clinicians must use an evidence-based approach in treating resistant anxiety disorders. This will increase and hasten the likelihood of achieving response or remission and avoid time-wasting, low-impact trials. More research is required to examine which patients would respond better to a combination of CBT and pharmacotherapy and how these should be administered. Despite available evidence-based treatments clinicians often have to manage patients with severe anxiety disorders, with significant comorbidity, who seem to be resistant or refractory to multiple trials of medications and therapy. Clinicians may resort to experimental treatment strategies in these cases, such as the use of carefully selected "polypharmacy cocktails" with complementary mechanisms of action (Bystritsky, 2006); however, great care must be taken so that exhausting multiple sequential medication trials, even if justified, do not become a barrier to referral for specialized CBT. There may be a bias toward pharmacotherapy in treatment-resistant disorders that interferes with early referral for specialized CBT.

References

Alonso, P., Menchon, J.M., Pifarre, J., Mataix-Cols, D., Torres, L., Salgado, P. et al. (2001). Long-term follow-up and predictors of clinical outcome in obsessive–compulsive patients treated with serotonin reuptake inhibitors and behavioral therapy. *Journal of Clinical Psychiatry, 62*(7), 535–540.

American Psychiatric Association. (1998). Practice guideline for the treatment of patients with panic disorder. *American Journal of Psychiatry, 155*(5 Suppl.), 1–34.

American Psychiatric Association. (2000). *Diagnostic and statistical manual of mental disorders* (4th ed., text revision). Arlington, VA: American Psychiatric Association.

Andrews, G., Henderson, S., & Hall, W. (2001). Prevalence, comorbidity, disability and service utilisation: Overview of the Australian National Mental Health Survey. *British Journal of Psychiatry, 178*, 145–153.

Antony, M.M., & Barlow, D.H. (2002). Specific phobias. In D.H. Barlow (Ed.), *Anxiety and its disorders: The nature and treatment of anxiety and panic*. New York: Guilford Press.

Audet, A.M., Greenfield, S., & Field, M. (1990). Medical practice guidelines: current activities and future directions. *Annals of Internal Medicine, 113*(9), 709–714.

Baldwin, D.S., Anderson, I.M., Nutt, D.J., Bandelow, B., Bond, A., Davidson, J.R. et al. (2005). Evidence-based guidelines for the pharmacological treatment of anxiety disorders: recommendations from the British Association for Psychopharmacology. *Journal of Psychopharmacology, 19*(6), 567–596.

Ballenger, J.C. (1999). Current treatments of the anxiety disorders in adults. *Biological Psychiatry, 46*(11), 1579–1594.

Ballenger, J.C. (2001). Treatment of anxiety disorders to remission. *Journal of Clinical Psychiatry, 62*(Suppl. 12), 5–9.

Bandelow, B., & Ruther, E. (2004). Treatment-resistant panic disorder. *CNS Spectrums*, *9*(10), 725–739.

Bandelow, B., Seidler-Brandler, U., Becker, A., Wedekind, D., & Ruther, E. (2007). Meta-analysis of randomized controlled comparisons of psychopharmacological and psychological treatments for anxiety disorders. *World Journal of Biological Psychiatry*, *8*(3), 175–187.

Bandelow, B., Zohar, J., Hollander, E., Kasper, S., & Moller, H.J. (2002). World Federation of Societies of Biological Psychiatry (WFSBP) guidelines for the pharmacological treatment of anxiety, obsessive–compulsive and posttraumatic stress disorders. *World Journal of Biological Psychiatry*, *3*(4), 171–199.

Barlow, D.H., Gorman, J.M., Shear, M.K., & Woods, S.W. (2000). Cognitive–behavioral therapy, imipramine, or their combination for panic disorder: A randomized controlled trial. *Journal of the American Medical Association*, *283*(19), 2529–2536.

Barnett, S.D., Kramer, M.L., Casat, C.D., Connor, K.M., & Davidson, J.R. (2002). Efficacy of olanzapine in social anxiety disorder: a pilot study. *Journal of Psychopharmacology*, *16*(4), 365–368.

Bebbington, P.E., Brugha, T.S., Meltzer, H., Jenkins, R., Ceresa, C., Farrell, M. et al. (2000). Neurotic disorders and the receipt of psychiatric treatment. *Psycholological Medicine*, *30*(6), 1369–1376.

Bebbington, P.E., Meltzer, H., Brugha, T.S., Farrell, M., Jenkins, R., Ceresa, C. et al. (2000). Unequal access and unmet need: neurotic disorders and the use of primary care services. *Psycholological Medicine*, *30*(6), 1359–1367.

Benjamin, J., Ben-Zion, I.Z., Karbofsky, E., & Dannon, P. (2000). Double-blind placebo-controlled pilot study of paroxetine for specific phobia. *Psychopharmacology (Berlin)*, *149*(2), 194–196.

Bhanji, N.H., Chouinard, G., Kolivakis, T., & Margolese, H.C. (2006). Persistent Tardive rebound panic disorder, rebound anxiety and insomnia following paroxetine withdrawal: a review of rebound–withdrawal phenomena. *Canadian Journal of Clinical Pharmacology*, *13*(1), e69–74.

Blake, D.D., Weathers, F.W., Nagy, L.M., Kaloupek, D.G., Gusman, F.D., Charney, D.S. et al. (1995). The development of a clinician administered PTSD scale. *Journal of Traumatic Stress*, *8*, 75–90.

Blier, P., & de Montigny, C. (1992). Lack of efficacy of lithium augmentation in obsessive–compulsive disorder: The perspective of different regional effects of lithium on serotonin release in the central nervous system. *Journal of Clinical Psychopharmacology*, *12*(1), 65–66.

Boyer, E.W., & Shannon, M. (2005). The serotonin syndrome. *New England Journal of Medicine*, *352*(11), 1112–1120.

Brawman-Mintzer, O., Knapp, R.G., & Nietert, P.J. (2005). Adjunctive risperidone in generalized anxiety disorder: a double-blind, placebo-controlled study. *Journal of Clinical Psychiatry*, *66*(10), 1321–1325.

Brown, T.A., & Barlow, D.H. (1995). Long-term outcome in cognitive–behavioral treatment of panic disorder: clinical predictors and alternative strategies for assessment. *Journal of Consulting and Clinical Psychology*, *63*(5), 754–765.

Bystritsky, A. (2006). Treatment-resistant anxiety disorders. *Molecular Psychiatry*, *11*(9), 805–814.

Calvocoressi, L., McDougle, C.I., Wasylink, S., Goodman, W.K., Trufan, S.J., & Price, L.H. (1993). Inpatient treatment of patients with severe obsessive–compulsive disorder. *Hospital & Community Psychiatry*, *44*(12), 1150–1154.

Canadian Psychiatric Association. (2006). Clinical practice guidelines: Management of anxiety disorders. *Canadian Journal of Psychiatry*, 51(8, Suppl. 2), 9S–91S.

Chilvers, C., Dewey, M., Fielding, K., Gretton, V., Miller, P., Palmer, B. et al. (2001). Antidepressant drugs and generic counselling for treatment of major depression in primary care: randomised trial with patient preference arms. *British Medical Journal*, 322(7289), 772–775.

Cottraux, J., Note, I.D., Cungi, C., Legeron, P., Heim, F., Chneiweiss, L. et al. (1995). A controlled study of cognitive–behaviour therapy with buspirone or placebo in panic disorder with agoraphobia. *British Journal of Psychiatry*, 167(5), 635–641.

Coupland, N.J., Bell, C.J., & Potokar, J.P. (1996). Serotonin reuptake inhibitor withdrawal. *Journal of Clinical Psychopharmacology*, 16(5), 356–362.

Crossley, N.A., & Bauer, M. (2007). Acceleration and augmentation of antidepressants with lithium for depressive disorders: two meta-analyses of randomized, placebo-controlled trials. *Journal of Clinical Psychiatry*, 68(6), 935–940.

Endicott, J., Nee, J., Harrison, W., & Blumenthal, R. (1993). Quality of life enjoyment and satisfaction questionnaire: A new measure. *Psychopharmacology Bulletin*, 29(2), 321–326.

Foa, E.B., Franklin, M.E., & Moser, J. (2002). Context in the clinic: how well do cognitive–behavioral therapies and medications work in combination? *Biological Psychiatry*, 52(10), 987–997.

Foa, E.B., Liebowitz, M.R., Kozak, M.J., Davies, S., Campeas, R., Franklin, M.E. et al. (2005). Randomized, placebo-controlled trial of exposure and ritual prevention, clomipramine, and their combination in the treatment of obsessive–compulsive disorder. *American Journal of Psychiatry*, 162(1), 151–161.

Goodman, W.K., Price, L.H., Rasmussen, S.A., Mazure, C., Delgado, P., Heninger, G.R. et al. (1989a). The Yale–Brown Obsessive Compulsive Scale. II. Validity. *Archives of General Psychiatry*, 46(11), 1012–1016.

Goodman, W.K., Price, L.H., Rasmussen, S.A., Mazure, C., Fleischmann, R.L., Hill, C.L. et al. (1989b). The Yale–Brown Obsessive Compulsive Scale. I. Development, use, and reliability. *Archives of General Psychiatry*, 46(11), 1006–1011.

Gosselin, P., Ladouceur, R., Morin, C.M., Dugas, M.J., & Baillargeon, L. (2006). Benzodiazepine discontinuation among adults with GAD: A randomized trial of cognitive–behavioral therapy. *Journal of Consulting and Clinical Psychology*, 74(5), 908–919.

Greenberg, P.E., Sisitsky, T., Kessler, R.C., Finkelstein, S.N., Berndt, E.R., Davidson, J.R. et al. (1999). The economic burden of anxiety disorders in the 1990s. *Journal of Clinical Psychiatry*, 60(7), 427–435.

Guastella, A.J., Richardson, R., Lovibond, P.F., Rapee, R.M., Gaston, J.E., Mitchell, P. et al. (2008). A randomized controlled trial of D-cycloserine enhancement of exposure therapy for social anxiety disorder. *Biological Psychiatry*, 63(6), 544–549.

Heldt, E., Gus Manfro, G., Kipper, L., Blaya, C., Isolan, L., & Otto, M.W. (2006). One-year follow-up of pharmacotherapy-resistant patients with panic disorder treated with cognitive–behavior therapy: Outcome and predictors of remission. *Behavior Research and Therapy*, 44(5), 657–665.

Heresco-Levy, U., Kremer, I., Javitt, D.C., Goichman, R., Reshef, A., Blanaru, M. et al. (2002). Pilot-controlled trial of D-cycloserine for the treatment of post-traumatic stress disorder. *International Journal of Neuropsychopharmacology*, 5(4), 301–307.

Hirschmann, S., Dannon, P.N., Iancu, I., Dolberg, O.T., Zohar, J., & Grunhaus, L. (2000). Pindolol augmentation in patients with treatment-resistant panic disorder: A double-blind, placebo-controlled trial. *Journal of Clinical Psychopharmacology, 20*(5), 556–559.

Hoffart, A., Due-Madsen, J., Lande, B., Gude, T., Bille, H., & Torgersen, S. (1993). Clomipramine in the treatment of agoraphobic inpatients resistant to behavioral therapy. *Journal of Clinical Psychiatry, 54*(12), 481–487.

Hohagen, F., Winkelmann, G., Rasche-Ruchle, H., Hand, I., Konig, A., Munchau, N. et al. (1998). Combination of behaviour therapy with fluvoxamine in comparison with behaviour therapy and placebo: Results of a multicentre study. *British Journal of Psychiatry, 173*(Suppl. 35), 71–78.

Hollifield, M., Thompson, P.M., Ruiz, J.E., & Uhlenhuth, E.H. (2005). Potential effectiveness and safety of olanzapine in refractory panic disorder. *Depression and Anxiety, 21*(1), 33–40.

Ipser, J.C., Carey, P., Dhansay, Y., Fakier, N., Seedat, S., & Stein, D.J. (2006). Pharmacotherapy augmentation strategies in treatment-resistant anxiety disorders. *Cochrane Database Systematic Reviews, 4*, CD005473.

Issakidis, C., Sanderson, K., Corry, J., Andrews, G., & Lapsley, H. (2004). Modelling the population cost-effectiveness of current and evidence-based optimal treatment for anxiety disorders. *Psychological Medicine, 34*(1), 19–35.

Jenkins, R., Bebbington, P., Brugha, T., Farrell, M., Gill, B., Lewis, G. et al. (1997). The national psychiatric morbidity surveys of Great Britain: strategy and methods. *Psychological Medicine, 27*(4), 765–774.

Kopecek, M., Mohr, P., & Novak, T. (2006). Sedative effects of low-dose risperidone in GAD patients and risk of drug interactions. *Journal of Clinical Psychiatry, 67*(8), 1307–1308; author reply, 1308–1309.

Koran, L.M., Hanna, G.L., Hollander, E., Nestadt, G., & Simpson, H.B. (2007). Practice guideline for the treatment of patients with obsessive–compulsive disorder. *American Journal of Psychiatry, 164*(7 Suppl.), 5–53.

Kordon, A., Kahl, K.G., Broocks, A., Voderholzer, U., Rasche-Rauchle, H., & Hohagen, F. (2005). Clinical outcome in patients with obsessive–compulsive disorder after discontinuation of SRI treatment: results from a two-year follow-up. *European Archives of Psychiatry and Clinical Neuroscience, 255*(1), 48–50.

Leahy, R.L. (2003). Emotional schemas and resistance in cognitive therapy, in R.L. Leahy (Ed.), *Roadblocks in cognitive–behavioral therapy: Transforming challenges into opportunities for change*, New York: Guilford Press.

Liebowitz, M.R. (1998). Anxiety disorders and obsessive compulsive disorder. *Neuropsychobiology, 37*, 69–71.

Lipsman, N., Neimat, J.S., & Lozano, A.M. (2007). Deep brain stimulation for treatment-refractory obsessive–compulsive disorder: The search for a valid target. *Neurosurgery, 61*(1), 1–11; discussion, 11–13.

Londborg, P.D., Hegel, M.T., Goldstein, S., Goldstein, D., Himmelhoch, J.M., Maddock, R. et al. (2001). Sertraline treatment of posttraumatic stress disorder: Results of 24 weeks of open-label continuation treatment. *Journal of Clinical Psychiatry, 62*(5), 325–331.

Looper, K.J. (2007). Potential medical and surgical complications of serotonergic antidepressant medications. *Psychosomatics, 48*(1), 1–9.

Maina, G., Albert, U., Ziero, S., & Bogetto, F. (2003). Antipsychotic augmentation for treatment-resistant obsessive–compulsive disorder: What if antipsychotic is discontinued? *International Clinical Psychopharmacology, 18*(1), 23–28.

Maina, G., Pessina, E., Albert, U., & Bogetto, F. (2008). 8-week, single-blind, randomized trial comparing risperidone versus olanzapine augmentation of serotonin reuptake inhibitors in treatment-resistant obsessive–compulsive disorder. *European Neuropsychopharmacology, 18*(5), 364–372.

Marks, I.M., Swinson, R.P., Basoglu, M., Kuch, K., Noshirvani, H., O'Sullivan, G. et al. (1993). Alprazolam and exposure alone and combined in panic disorder with agoraphobia: A controlled study in London and Toronto. *British Journal of Psychiatry, 162*, 776–787.

McDougle, C.J., Goodman, W.K., Leckman, J.F., Holzer, J.C., Barr, L.C., McCance-Katz, E. et al. (1993). Limited therapeutic effect of addition of buspirone in fluvoxamine-refractory obsessive–compulsive disorder. *American Journal of Psychiatry, 150*(4), 647–649.

McDougle, C.J., Price, L.H., Goodman, W.K., Charney, D.S., & Heninger, G.R. (1991). A controlled trial of lithium augmentation in fluvoxamine-refractory obsessive–compulsive disorder: Lack of efficacy. *Journal of Clinical Psychopharmacology, 11*(3), 175–184.

Mellman, T.A., Miller, A.L., Weissman, E.M., Crismon, M.L., Essock, S.M., & Marder, S.R. (2001). Evidence-based pharmacologic treatment for people with severe mental illness: a focus on guidelines and algorithms. *Psychiatric Services, 52*(5), 619–625.

Mitte, K. (2005a). Meta-analysis of cognitive–behavioral treatments for generalized anxiety disorder: A comparison with pharmacotherapy. *Psychology Bulletin, 131*(5), 785–795.

Mitte, K. (2005b). A meta-analysis of the efficacy of psycho- and pharmacotherapy in panic disorder with and without agoraphobia. *Journal of Affective Disorders, 88*(1), 27–45.

Montgomery, D. (2002). ECNP consensus meeting March 19–22, 2000: Guidelines for investigating efficacy in GAD. *European Neuropsychopharmacology, 12*(1), 81–87.

Montgomery, S., & Bech, P. (2000). ECNP consensus meeting, March 5–6, 1999, Nice: Posttraumatic stress disorder—guidelines for investigating efficacy of pharmacological intervention. ECNP and ECST. *European Neuropsychopharmacology, 10*(4), 297–303.

Montgomery, S.A., Lecrubier, Y., Baldwin, D.S., Kasper, S., Lader, M., Nil, R. et al. (2004). ECNP consensus meeting, March 12–14, 2003: Guidelines for the investigation of efficacy in social anxiety disorder. *European Neuropsychopharmacology, 14*(5), 425–433.

Otto, M.W., Hinton, D., Korbly, N.B., Chea, A., Ba, P., Gershuny, B.S. et al. (2003). Treatment of pharmacotherapy-refractory posttraumatic stress disorder among Cambodian refugees: a pilot study of combination treatment with cognitive–behavior therapy vs. sertraline alone. *Behavior Research and Therapy, 41*(11), 1271–1276.

Otto, M.W., Pollack, M.H., Penava, S.J., & Zucker, B.G. (1999). Group cognitive–behavior therapy for patients failing to respond to pharmacotherapy for panic disorder: A clinical case series. *Behavior Research and Therapy, 37*(8), 763–770.

Pae, C.U., Lim, H.K., Peindl, K., Ajwani, N., Serretti, A., Patkar, A.A. et al. (2008). The atypical antipsychotics olanzapine and risperidone in the treatment of posttraumatic stress disorder: A meta-analysis of randomized, double-blind, placebo-controlled clinical trials. *International Clinical Psychopharmacology*, 23(1), 1–8.

Pallanti, S., Hollander, E., Bienstock, C., Koran, L., Leckman, J., Marazziti, D. et al. (2002). Treatment non-response in OCD: Methodological issues and operational definitions. *International Journal of Neuropsychopharmacology*, 5(2), 181–191.

Pickworth, W.B., Sharpe, L.G., Nozaki, M., & Martin, W.R. (1977). Sleep suppression induced by intravenous and intraventricular infusions of methoxamine in the dog. *Experimental Neurology*, 57(3), 999–1011.

Pollack, M.H., Otto, M.W., Roy-Byrne, P.P., Coplan, J.D., Rothbaum, B.O., Simon, N.M. et al. (2008). Novel treatment approaches for refractory anxiety disorders. *Depression and Anxiety*, 25(6), 467–476.

Pollack, M.H., Simon, N.M., Zalta, A.K., Worthington, J.J., Hoge, E.A., Mick, E. et al. (2006). Olanzapine augmentation of fluoxetine for refractory generalized anxiety disorder: A placebo-controlled study. *Biological Psychiatry*, 59(3), 211–215.

Power, K.G., Simpson, R.J., Swanson, V., Wallace, L.A., Feistner, A.T.C., & Sharp, D. (1990). A controlled comparison of cognitive- behaviour therapy, diazepam, and placebo, alone and in combination, for the treatment of generalised anxiety disorder. *Journal of Anxiety Disorders*, 4(4), 267–292.

Powers, M.B., Smits, J.A., Whitley, D., Bystritsky, A., & Telch, M.J. (2008). The effect of attributional processes concerning medication taking on return of fear. *Journal of Consulting and Clinical Psychology*, 76(3), 478–490.

Raffa, S.D., Stoddard, J.A., White, K.S., Barlow, D.H., Gorman, J.M., Shear, M.K., & Woods, S.W. (2008). Relapse following combined treatment discontinuation in a placebo-controlled trial for panic disorder. *Journal of Nervous and Mental Disease*, 196(7), 548–555.

Raskind, M.A., Peskind, E.R., Kanter, E.D., Petrie, E.C., Radant, A., Thompson, C.E. et al. (2003). Reduction of nightmares and other PTSD symptoms in combat veterans by prazosin: A placebo-controlled study. *American Journal of Psychiatry*, 160(2), 371–373.

Ressler, K.J., Rothbaum, B.O., Tannenbaum, L., Anderson, P., Graap, K., Zimand, E. et al. (2004). Cognitive enhancers as adjuncts to psychotherapy: Use of D-cycloserine in phobic individuals to facilitate extinction of fear. *Archives of General Psychiatry*, 61(11), 1136–1144.

Rothbaum, B.O., Killeen, T.K., Davidson, J.R., Brady, K.T., Connor, K.M., & Heekin, M.H. (2008). Placebo-controlled trial of risperidone augmentation for selective serotonin reuptake inhibitor-resistant civilian posttraumatic stress disorder. *Journal of Clinical Psychiatry*, 69(4), 520–525.

Sanderson, W.C., DiNardo, P.A., Rapee, R.M., & Barlow, D.H. (1990). Syndrome comorbidity in patients diagnosed with a DSM-III-R anxiety disorder. *Journal of Abnormal Psychology*, 99(3), 308–312.

Siegel, L., Jones, W.C., & Wilson, J.O. (1990). Economic and life consequences experienced by a group of individuals with panic disorder. *Journal of Anxiety Disorders*, 4, 201–211.

Simon, N.M., Connor, K.M., Lang, A.J., Rauch, S., Krulewicz, S., LeBeau, R.T. et al. (2008). Paroxetine CR augmentation for posttraumatic stress disorder refractory to prolonged exposure therapy. *Journal of Clinical Psychiatry, 69*(3), 400–405.

Simpson, H.B., Foa, E.B., Liebowitz, M.R., Ledley, D.R., Huppert, J.D., Cahill, S. et al. (2008). A randomized, controlled trial of cognitive–behavioral therapy for augmenting pharmacotherapy in obsessive–compulsive disorder. *American Journal of Psychiatry, 165*(5), 621–630.

Simpson, H.B., Huppert, J.D., Petkova, E., Foa, E.B., & Liebowitz, M.R. (2006). Response versus remission in obsessive–compulsive disorder. *Journal of Clinical Psychiatry, 67*(2), 269–276.

Sookman, D., & Pinard, G. (1999). Integrative cognitive therapy for obsessive–compulsive disorder which focuses on multiple schemas. *Cognitive and Behavioral Practice, 6*(3), 351–361.

Stein, M.B., Sareen, J., Hami, S., & Chao, J. (2001). Pindolol potentiation of paroxetine for generalized social phobia: a double-blind, placebo-controlled, crossover study. *American Journal of Psychiatry, 158*(10), 1725–1727.

Storch, E.A., Merlo, L.J., Bengtson, M., Murphy, T.K., Lewis, M.H., Yang, M.C. et al. (2007). D-Cycloserine does not enhance exposure–response prevention therapy in obsessive–compulsive disorder. *International Clinical Psychopharmacology, 22*(4), 230–237.

Ursano, R.J., Bell, C., Eth, S., Friedman, M., Norwood, A., Pfefferbaum, B. et al. (2004). Practice guideline for the treatment of patients with acute stress disorder and posttraumatic stress disorder. *American Journal of Psychiatry, 161*(11 Suppl.), 3–31.

Vaishnavi, S., Alamy, S., Zhang, W., Connor, K.M., & Davidson, J.R. (2007). Quetiapine as monotherapy for social anxiety disorder: a placebo-controlled study. *Progress in Neuro-Psychopharmacology and Biological Psychiatry, 31*(7), 1464–1469.

Wilhelm, S., Buhlmann, U., Tolin, D.F., Meunier, S.A., Pearlson, G.D., Reese, H.E. et al. (2008). Augmentation of behavior therapy with D-cycloserine for obsessive–compulsive disorder. *American Journal of Psychiatry, 165*(3), 335–341; quiz, 409.

Woodward, S.H., Arsenault, N.J., Murray, C., & Bliwise, D.L. (2000). Laboratory sleep correlates of nightmare complaint in PTSD inpatients. *Biological Psychiatry, 48*(11), 1081–1087.

chapter twelve

Conclusions

Robert L. Leahy
The American Institute for Cognitive Therapy
New York, New York

Contents

Cognitive–behavioral therapists have well-established treatment modules for each of the anxiety disorders. We know that exposure and response prevention (ERP) is effective for the treatment of obsessive–compulsive disorder (Foa & Franklin, 2001; Foa et al., 2005) and that structured cognitive–behavioral therapy (CBT) is effective for the treatment of social anxiety disorder (Turk, Heimberg, & Hope, 2001). Several different but effective CBT approaches have been advanced for the treatment of post-traumatic stress disorder involving gradual exposure to feared intrusive images and memories and cognitive restructuring of beliefs that have led to demoralization, distrust, and defeat (Ballenger et al., 2000; Foa et al., 1999; Resick, 2001). But, as any clinician who has had considerable experience treating patients with anxiety disorders knows, there are problems getting patients to follow through on exposure, to continue in therapy, to be persistent in self-help homework, and to modify their beliefs that they have improved.

We have chosen to use the term *treatment resistant* in order to reflect the common perception among clinicians that some manifestations of anxiety are more difficult to treat using standard techniques and some patients appear to have difficulty complying with the guidelines or "rules" of CBT.

Moreover, I believe that some patients actively resist treatment because of their fears that exposure and response prevention or the elimination of safety behaviors will only make matters worse. Indeed, resistance may be a strategy to minimize risk. Unlike psychodynamic theory, resistance to therapy may reflect attempts to protect the self from "unnecessary" danger rather than as a personal affront to the therapist, as dynamic therapists have suggested.

Cognitive–behavioral therapy requires considerable change for patients, relying on the use of exposure techniques that intentionally increase anxiety and discomfort and encouraging the patient to actively initiate change that appears risky and unpleasant. CBT is structured and here and now, thereby setting up certain demands or expectations that the patient will be directly responsive to inquiries; will consider a problem-solving, self-help approach; and will be willing to take initiatives. I have suggested in the past that the concept of resistance depends on the implicit expectations of the therapeutic modality, such that in psychodynamic therapy resistance might be formulated as an unwillingness or inability to access memories or emotions, whereas in CBT resistance might be viewed as rejection of the agenda of an active or "agentic" patient (Leahy, 2001).

The goal of this book is to provide the reader with innovative conceptualizations, strategies, and techniques that can enhance more traditional cognitive–behavioral approaches for a wide range of treatment-resistant anxiety. In this volume, we have brought together leading proponents of metacognitive theory, integrative CBT for obsessive–compulsive disorder (OCD), acceptance and commitment therapy, emotional schema therapy, compassionate mind therapy, dialectical behavioral therapy, motivational interviewing, skills training in affective and interpersonal regulation for trauma victims, treatment for comorbid substance abuse, and the use of pharmacotherapy in the treatment of anxiety disorders. In addition, Bruce and Sanderson provide data on the factors that clinicians have found problematic in achieving compliance in the treatment of anxiety disorders. Our hope is that these contributions will enrich the understanding that clinicians and researchers will have in assisting more promising outcomes using CBT.

In reviewing these contributions, I thought it would be helpful to examine how they address common issues that clinicians encounter in developing and providing a treatment approach. As many practicing clinicians know, abstract and theoretical papers on research and "models of psychopathology" do not always translate into practical application. When the next treatment-resistant patient comes in, what will you do differently as a result of reading this book? To facilitate an answer to that question, I have identified five areas that I believe are relevant in using the material in this book to achieve better outcomes.

Developing a conceptualization of resistance

What accounts for resistance? Each of the contributors to this volume has advanced a model of how resistance to change *makes sense* to the patient. Wells views resistance to change in worry as based on metacognitive beliefs about the positive function of worry and the risk of losing control of worry. According to the metacognitive model, resistance is based on faulty appraisals of the function of thought and attentional deployment to detect and manage risk (both externally and internally). Thus, resistance is risk avoidance, and the patient attempts to control thinking. The ironic process of looking for risk to reduce risk only exacerbates overestimation of risk, which then leads to attempts to eliminate the worry because worry is viewed as dangerous in itself. The conceptualization here is that therapeutic attempts that might naïvely encourage worrisome patients to abandon worry only activate resistance from the patient who believes he or she is being asked to make the self even more vulnerable. The metacognitive approach addresses resistance by collaborating with the patient to identify and test out these self-defeating metacognitive appraisals and strategies.

Leahy's model of emotional schemas is a form of metacognitive therapy in that this model also helps patients identify their theory of how emotions function, the duration and controllability of emotions, and faulty strategies for managing emotion. In the emotional schema model, resistance to exposure follows the strategy that "emotions need to be avoided," which is based on problematic theories of how emotions will "get out of hand." Again, therapy follows from the conceptualization by helping the patient collect evidence and test out the logic of these theories of emotion and to normalize and temporize emotional experiences rather than attempt to escape or avoid them.

Similarly, the acceptance and commitment therapy (ACT) model, which stresses experiential avoidance and the over-reliance on problematic strategies to control thoughts, emotions, and sensations, shares with the foregoing two models the view that problematic risk-avoidance strategies ironically perpetuate and maintain anxiety. The conceptualization that is developed with the patient is to recognize that past attempts to solve the problem of anxiety through suppression, escape, or avoidance have failed. By building on a recognition of "creative hopelessness," the ACT therapist joins with the patient in recognizing that attempts to resist experience are doomed. This then leads to an elaboration of longer term and superordinate goals such as a "valued life" and tolerance for experiential distress rather than avoidance of uncomfortable experiences.

Sookman and Steketee provide a complex model of resistance that addresses multiple reasons for treatment failure, including intervention inadequacies as well as patient characteristics. The authors propose criteria for an adequate trial of specialized CBT for OCD, as well as criteria for recovery/remission and for CBT resistance in OCD, foundational both to clinical work and to design of controlled outcome trials with treatment-resistant patients. Relevant patient characteristics discussed include dysfunctional appraisals of intrusions, cognitive and emotional processing of events, beliefs about how change can be achieved (e.g., simply talking should be sufficient rather than facing difficult feelings and avoided events integral to exposure), overvalued ideas, intolerance of distress, risk aversion, and other factors.

The model of OCD developed by Sookman and colleagues provides a conceptual frame for individualized case formulation of comprehensive factors that may be relevant to etiology and maintenance of current symptoms. Cognitive, experiential, and behavioral strategies are described to identify and modify dysfunctional schemas. The aim of the specialized CBT approach for OCD described is to improve collaboration with ERP, foster adaptive change in cognitive and emotional processing of inner and external experiences, and improve generalization and maintenance of change.

The skills training in affective and interpersonal regulation (STAIR) program, proposed by Jackson, Nissenson, and Cloitre, views trauma memory processing as "an activity that recruits, reinforces, and consolidates emotion regulation capacities and allows exploration and meaningful reworking of highly charged emotional memories." The STAIR program views resistance in terms of emotional processing/regulation and interpersonal and personal schemas that complicate the lives of those who have had repeated or chronic experiences with trauma. Consequently, the step-wise program for trauma begins with emotion awareness, regulation skills, and an emphasis on emotionally meaningful living and then moves to interpersonal and personal strategies and schemas. This preparatory work on emotional regulation sets the stage for ERP and development of newer more adaptive narratives. Because cases of complex PTSD usually involve impairment of interpersonal relations, the therapy employs a hybrid, step-wise approach to first establish sufficient emotion regulation skills and then attempts to move on to address and repair interpersonal functioning.

Similarly, Welch, Osborne, and Pryzgoda view conceptualization in terms of emotion regulation and experiential avoidance and take a skills-based approach based on the dialectical behavior therapy (DBT) model. In this approach, resistance is viewed as a manifestation of the lack of skills and interpretations to handle the difficult emotions that arise through exposure. As several of these contributors note, emotional dysregulation may underpin resistance to exposure and may make the experience of exposure even more difficult to tolerate. This reflects a growing trend within CBT that we need to address emotional processing issues in the treatment of a wide range of forms of psychopathology (Barlow, Allen, & Choate, 2004; Mennin & Farach, 2007).

Compassionate mind therapy, developed by Gilbert (2007) and here applied by Lee, proposes that for some patients shameful and self-loathing feelings about the self undermine effective CBT. Thus, before effective ERP can be initiated, the therapist can assist the patient in identifying the origin and function of these self-loathing thoughts and feelings, help develop a compassionate and soothing self-caring voice, and utilize this to help with emotional dysregulation and feelings of demoralization.

Motivational interviewing places less stress on the conceptualization of the problem and more stress on the conditions for enhancing change. Westra and Arkowitz view resistance as part of reactance motivation for some patients, such that a greater emphasis by the therapist on change can lead to an opposing demand for autonomy on the part of the patient. The motivational interview attempts to gently identify disparities between the patient's goals and the current situation while exploring the patient's reasons why change appears difficult. Rather than challenging or testing the patient's beliefs, the motivational interview approach is more nondirective (at times) while also revealing disparities as they arise. Finally, Stewart and O'Connor identify how substance abuse may complicate the therapeutic process by preventing the patient from utilizing the tools of CBT. Here there is less emphasis on conceptualization of resistance and more emphasis on reducing the reliance on substances that impede progress.

Appraisals of thoughts

In recent years, there has been considerable progress in identifying the beliefs about intrusive thoughts or images that characterize the range of anxiety disorders (Harvey, 2001; Purdon & Clark, 1994; Purdon, Rowa, & Antony, 2005; Salkovskis, Forrester, & Richards, 1998). For example, patients with obsessive–compulsive disorder appraise their intrusive thoughts in terms of personal responsibility, relevance, danger, and control, thus leading to a belief that they must eliminate these thoughts through neutralizing rituals (Obsessive Compulsive Cognitions Working Group, 1997; Sookman & Pinard, 2002). A similar pattern of appraisal is engaged in the metacognitive model of worry, outlined by Wells. The metacognitive therapist helps the patient identify beliefs about the positive function of worry ("Worry prepares and protects") and beliefs about the danger and uncontrollability of worry—beliefs that actually maintain the ongoing process of worry. Sookman and Steketee indicate that many patients with OCD fear, and report that they experience, that their intrusive thoughts and anxiety will worsen if neutralization rituals are not performed. Strategies are described to improve tolerance and reappraisal of urges and emotional distress associated with response prevention and to foster more adaptive responses to a myriad of thoughts and feelings. Twohig, Plumb, Mukherjee, and Hayes suggest that relational frame theory is helpful in understanding the *function* of thoughts by helping patients change their relationship to thoughts, recognizing how thoughts may lead to unnecessary suffering.

The ACT model stresses the claim that the content of the thought is not important—it is how thoughts function. Traditional cognitive therapy models, such as Beck's and Ellis's, have long evaluated the function of thoughts by examining the costs and benefits of having a thought or belief (Beck, Rush, Shaw, & Emery, 1979; Ellis, 1962; Ellis, David, & Lynn, 2010). This is the pragmatic aspect of cognitive therapy. However, ACT has elaborated an intriguing set of interventions that simply change the way one relates to thoughts, without addressing the content. The ACT model recognizes the importance of thought–action fusion (Rachman, 1993), which they claim is a result of fusion—that is, confounding a thought with reality. Of course, this is consistent with earlier approaches in CBT, such as Rachman's description of thought appraisal and concepts of inflated responsibility (Rachman, 1993, 1997). The relational frame model attempts to modify how the individual responds or relates to a thought by engaging in recognition that "this is just a thought," repeating a thought until it becomes boring or relating to the thought in a playful way. Many of these techniques have been used in more traditional cognitive therapy for quite some time; for example, in Beckian therapy, one of the first interventions in socializing a patient to the cognitive model is to distinguish a thought from reality and from emotions (Beck et al., 1979; Ellis, 1962). The technique of repeating a thought endlessly was introduced by Freeston and colleagues (1997) some years ago, using thought flooding to desensitize a feared intrusion.

Nonetheless, anxiety disorders appear to be amenable to modifying the patient's evaluation of what a thought is and how it functions, with the contributors to the present volume placing far less emphasis on "disputation" of the content of thoughts. It is unclear if disputation of thoughts is unhelpful, as the proponents of ACT have suggested (Longmore & Worrell, 2007). Yet, the current trend in CBT appears to focus more on exposure, behavioral activation, emotional processing and dysregulation, acceptance, mindfulness, appraisal of thoughts and emotions, and developing new relationships with one's internal sensation and experience.

Building motivation

The very nature of treatment resistance raises the issue of motivation. How do these contributors address this important issue? Traditional cognitive therapy raises the question of the costs and benefits of beliefs and actions ("I need to suppress my thoughts") and should always be part of a cognitive module. Westra and Arkowitz suggest that structured and directive approaches run the risk of creating more resistance—the well-known reactance effect. Motivational interviewing (MI) relies on empathy and unconditional positive regard, but unlike Rogerian client-centered therapy the therapist following the MI approach also develops discrepancy between values and problem behaviors, rolls with resistance, and supports self-efficacy. Although this approach is consistent with traditional cognitive therapy, the emphasis is less on testing or challenging (as in the Ellis model) and more on eliciting discrepancies that the patient can see are in conflict with goals. The metacognitive model advanced by Wells elicits the patient's theory of how worry functions to protect and prepare. This metacognitive approach addresses motivation by attempting to modify the patient's belief about how thinking can function to help him cope. This motivational question then leads to behavioral or cognitive experiments to examine what happens when worry is postponed or when worry is practiced *ad nauseam* to evaluate the need to worry or to control worry. Motivation is addressed, then, by examining the need to worry to stay safe or the need to suppress worry to keep worry from getting worse.

The ACT model has a strong motivational component in that it helps clarify values that trump the discomfort and ambivalence of the patient who is considering the wisdom of exposure and consequent increases in anxiety. Hayes and his colleagues have expanded significantly on this important issue of a "valued life" that can help patients tolerate discomfort and direct them in their self-help. While recognizing that exposure is an important component of treatment, the emphasis in ACT can focus on the quality of life that the patient is aiming for.

Leahy's emotional schema model views motivation as part of the patient's theory of the threat of emotional dysregulation; for example, the patient who believes that anxiety will increase, overwhelm him, and last forever will be motivated to resist exposure. Emotional schema therapy uses the apparently paradoxical instruction to make discomfort a goal to build the "mental muscle" to do what needs to be done. Concepts such as "constructive discomfort" and "successful imperfection" assist the patient to be motivated to use discomfort as a tool or a means to an end.

Similar concepts are reflected in the DBT and ACT models of stress tolerance. The ACT model emphasizes the role of emotional avoidance as a demotivator in the treatment of anxiety and encourages the use of mindfulness as a way to increase tolerance and acceptance of experience. Interestingly, in a recent study, the Acceptance and Action Questionnaire (AAQ) and the Mindful Attention Awareness Scale (MAAS) were not independently predictive of anxiety on the Beck Anxiety Inventory (BAI).

Anxiety was better predicted by metacognitive and meta-emotional factors rather than dispositional mindfulness and acceptance (Leahy, Tirch, & Napolitano, 2009). Thus, it may be that mindfulness modifies emotional schemas which then leads to less experiential avoidance. The integration of so-called "third-wave" approaches with metacognitive and meta-emotional models may provide a more sophisticated model of how "thinking" functions. Indeed, as Wells demonstrates, mindfulness exercises can help modify the patient's belief that worry needs to be controlled. The interesting question from the theoretical model of how worry or suppression of thought and emotions function is how do mindfulness and acceptance actually work?

Does content matter?

There has been considerable interest in recent years as to whether modifying the content of thoughts really matters. The relational frame model proposed by ACT suggests that content is not relevant—it is the functionality of a thought and one's relationship to a thought. Thus, the therapy here would involve changing the relationship to the thought, such as noticing a thought, thanking your mind for its comments, playing with the thought, or taking a thought for a walk. The schematic content is not disputed.

Sookman and Steketee provide two sophisticated approaches to OCD in their chapter, recognizing the meaning, function, and perceived danger of intrusions. Wilhelm and Steketee (2006) used a variety of cognitive strategies and behavioral experiments to help patients test their (faulty) hypotheses. Modules are developed on a case conceptualization basis to address specific classes of beliefs identified as characteristic of OCD: overimportance and control of thoughts, overestimation of threat or harm, inflated responsibility, perfectionism, and need for certainty, as well as concerns of managing high anxiety and fears of positive experiences. The schema-based approach for CBT-resistant OCD developed by Sookman and colleagues additionally involves identification and modification of more core cognitive and emotional schemas that may be associated with perceived vulnerability, difficulty with strong emotions, risk aversion, and intransigence of symptoms.

Similarly, Jackson, Nissenson, and Cloitre address the content of schemas about self and others in the STAIR program, helping the patient identify and modify beliefs about relationships. Patients use the Interpersonal Schema Sheet and other evaluations to identify their beliefs and the source of their beliefs, and therapy focuses (at this stage) on developing new, more adaptive schemas. This sophisticated and complex approach to posttraumatic stress disorder incorporates many of the factors described in other chapters in the current volume—emotional

regulation, distress tolerance, identifying a valued life, personal schemas, and interpersonal functioning.

Are developmental origins important?

Cognitive–behavioral therapy is often viewed as being focused on the
present situation or the environmental contingencies that support current
behavior or beliefs. The popular view of CBT is that we do not examine
the developmental origins of beliefs or emotions—and certainly there
are many behavioral approaches, including acceptance and commitment
therapy, that appear to leave the past in the past. Treatment resistance in
anxiety disorders may lead some clinicians to consider how beliefs about
the self and one's emotions, as well as the ability to support oneself emotionally, can be rooted in the past. In cognitive therapy, for example, the
schema-focused models advanced by Beck, Freeman, Young, Klosko, and
their colleagues recognize that long-standing problems in interpersonal
and personal functioning may benefit from examining and even reworking earlier unresolved conflicts (Beck et al., 2003; Leahy, Beck, & Beck,
2005; Young, Klosko, & Weishaar, 2003).

What is especially interesting in most CBT approaches is that developmental origins are not generally addressed in the standard ERP model
of anxiety. In the current collection of papers, there are notable exceptions to this. For example, in their chapters Sookman and Steketee discuss the developmental origins of personal schemas that may underpin
beliefs in OCD; Leahy addresses the origins of beliefs about emotion
and its expression and validation focusing on emotional socialization;
Jackson, Nissenson, and Cloitre examine the developmental experiences
that originate with the narrative of repeated trauma affecting interpersonal and personal schemas; and Lee discusses compassionate mind
therapy, which addresses the narrative of self-loathing and shame as a
developmental experience of substantial importance. The DBT approach
can address the origin of the invalidating environment, thereby helping
the patient understand why emotions have not been soothed in the past
and why it is difficult to self-soothe or self-regulate emotions in the present. Motivational interviewing can, at times, examine the developmental origins of these problems, although MI is more of an interviewing
and motivational strategy rather than one that leads to a developmental
conceptualization.

Indeed, the authors whose chapters bring up developmental origins
address more complex cases of anxiety disorders. Perhaps it is the complexity of the case that will require a more complex, developmental analysis of the problem and its perpetuation. Perhaps the more complex the
problem, the more complex the conceptualization and the treatment.

A personal note

While recognizing the value of specific theoretical and clinical models, experienced clinicians often find themselves drawing on a variety of approaches. The current volume provides the reader with an opportunity to either commit oneself to a particular school of thought or to sample from a variety of approaches in an eclectic manner. I have commented on what I believe is the nature of clinical practice in a recent article, "The Confessions of a Cognitive Therapist" (Leahy, 2009b). Although I may be better known as a cognitive therapist or someone doing emotional schema therapy, in my daily practice with patients I am happy to say that every one of these chapters is helpful to me. Although I have been part of the debate with Hayes about acceptance and commitment therapy versus cognitive therapy, I am thankful to have his ideas affecting what I actually do. The same with DBT, compassionate mind therapy, behavioral activation, cognitive–behavioral analysis system (CBAS), mindfulness-based cognitive therapy, positive psychology, and whatever seems to be helpful at the time. Indeed, several of the contributors in this volume are boldly integrative, recognizing as they do the complexity and persistence of difficult problems in the lives of their patients.

A rather traditional defining characteristic of intelligence is the ability to adapt to given situations. Intelligence entails flexibility, the recognition that different problems require different solutions, and the creative integration of tools and conceptualizations that fit one situation but not all situations. The intelligent clinician should feel free to break from traditional schools of thought to adapt to the needs of the patient. Not all patients are the same. Indeed, as we debate in journals the relative merits of the content or function of thought, the role of directive versus nondirective approaches, or the importance of understanding the etiology of clinical problems, we may ironically find ourselves, behind closed doors in clinical practice, using everything that we know. And isn't that what our patients would want from us?

References

Ballenger, J.C., Davidson, J.R., Lecrubier, Y., Nutt, D.J., Foa, E.B., Kessler, R.C. et al. (2000). Consensus statement on posttraumatic stress disorder from the international consensus group on depression and anxiety. *Journal of Clinical Psychiatry*, 61(Suppl. 5), 60–66.

Barlow, D.H., Allen, L.B., & Choate, M.L. (2004). Toward a unified treatment for emotional disorders. *Behavior Therapy*, 35(2), 205–230.

Beck, A.T., Freeman, A., Davis, D.D., Pretzer, J., Fleming, B., Artz, A. et al. (2003). *Cognitive therapy of personality disorders* (2nd ed.). New York: Guilford Press.

Beck, A.T., Rush, A.J., Shaw, B.F., & Emery, G. (1979). *Cognitive therapy of depression.* New York: Guilford Press.

Ellis, A. (1962). *Reason and emotion in psychotherapy.* Secaucus, NJ: Citadel Press.

Ellis, A., David, D., & Lynn, S.J. (2010). Rational and irrational beliefs: A historical and conceptual perspective. In D. David, S.J. Lynn, & A. Ellis (Eds.), *Rational and irrational beliefs: Research, theory, and clinical practice.* New York: Oxford University Press.

Foa, E.B., & Franklin, M.E. (2001). Obsessive–compulsive disorder. In D.H. Barlow (Ed.), *Clinical handbook of psychological disorders: A step-by-step treatment manual* (3rd ed.) (pp. 209–263). New York: Guilford Press.

Foa, E.B., Dancu, C.V., Hembree, E.A., Jaycox, L.H., Meadows, E.A., & Street, G.P. (1999). A comparison of exposure therapy, stress inoculation training, and their combination for reducing posttraumatic stress disorder in female assault victims. *Journal of Consulting & Clinical Psychology, 67*(2), 194–200.

Foa, E.B., Liebowithz, M.R., Kozak, M.J., Davies, S., Campeas, R., Franklin, M.E. et al. (2005). Treatment of obsessive–compulsive disorder by exposure and ritual prevention, clomipramine, and their combination: A randomized, placebo controlled trial. *American Journal of Psychiatry, 162,* 151–161.

Freeston, M.H., Ladouceur, R., Gagnon, F., Thibodeau, N., Rheaume, J., Letarte, H. et al. (1997). Cognitive–behavioral treatment of obsessive thoughts: A controlled study. *Journal of Consulting and Clinical Psychology, 65,* 405–413.

Gilbert, P. (2007). Evolved minds and compassion in the therapeutic relationship. In P. Gilbert & R.L. Leahy (Eds.), *The therapeutic relationship in the cognitive behavioural psychotherapies* (pp. 106–142). London: Brunner-Routledge.

Harvey, A.G. (2001). I can't sleep, my mind is racing! An investigation of strategies of thought control in insomnia. *Behavioural and Cognitive Psychotherapy, 29*(1), 3–11.

Leahy, R.L. (2001). *Overcoming resistance in cognitive therapy.* New York: Guilford Press.

Leahy, R.L. (2009a). *Anxiety free: Unravel your fears before they unravel you.* New York: Hay House.

Leahy, R.L. (2009b). The confessions of a cognitive therapist. *The Behavior Therapist, 32*(1), 1–3.

Leahy, R.L., Beck, A.T., & Beck, J.S. (2005). Cognitive therapy of personality disorders. In S. Strack (Ed.), *Handbook of Personology and Psychopathology: Essays in honor of Theodore Millon* (pp. 442–461). New York: John Wiley & Sons.

Leahy, R.L., Tirch, D., & Napolitano, L. (2009). Meta-cognitive and meta-emotional processes affecting anxiety. Paper presented at Association of Behavioral and Cognitive Therapies meeting, New York, NY.

Longmore, R.J., & Worrell, M. (2007). Do we need to challenge thoughts in cognitive behavior therapy? *Clinical Psychology Review, 27*(2), 173–187.

Mennin, D.S., & Farach, F.J. (2007). Emotion and evolving treatments for adult psychopathology. *Clinical Psychology: Science and Practice, 14*(4), 329–352.

Obsessive Compulsive Cognitions Working Group (OCCWG). (1997). Cognitive assessment of obsessive–compulsive disorder. *Behaviour Research and Therapy, 35*(7), 667–681.

Purdon, C., & Clark, D.A. (1994). Obsessive intrusive thoughts in nonclinical subjects. II. Cognitive appraisal, emotional response and thought control strategies. *Behaviour Research and Therapy, 32,* 403–410.

Purdon, C., Rowa, K., & Antony, M.M. (2005). Thought suppression and its effects on thought frequency, appraisal and mood state in individuals with obsessive–compulsive disorder. *Behaviour Research and Therapy*, 43(1), 93–108.

Rachman, S.J. (1993). Obsessions, responsibility and guilt. *Behaviour Research and Therapy*, 31, 149–154.

Rachman, S.J. (1997). A cognitive theory of obsessions. *Behaviour Research and Therapy*, 35, 793–802.

Resick, P.A. (2001). *Stress and trauma.* Philadelphia, PA: Psychology Press.

Salkovskis, P.M., Forrester, E., & Richards, C. (1998). Cognitive–behavioural approach to understanding obsessional thinking. *British Journal of Psychiatry*, 173(Suppl. 35), 53–63.

Sookman, D., & Pinard, G. (2002). Overestimation of threat and intolerance of uncertainty in obsessive compulsive disorder. In R.O. Frost & G. Steketee (Eds.), *Cognitive approaches to obsessions and compulsions: Theory, assessment, and treatment* (pp. 63–89). Amsterdam: Pergamon Press.

Turk, C.L., Heimberg, R.G., & Hope, D.A. (2001). Social anxiety disorder. In D.H. Barlow (Ed.), *Clinical handbook of psychological disorders: A step-by-step treatment manual* (3rd ed.) (pp. 114–153). New York: Guilford Press.

Wilhelm, S., & Steketee, G. (2006). *Cognitive therapy of obsessive–compulsive disorder: A guide for professionals.* Oakland, CA: New Harbinger.

Young, J.E., Klosko, J.S., & Weishaar, M. (2003). *Schema therapy: A practitioner's guide.* New York: Guilford Press.

Index

A

homework noncompliance, 207
homework review, 118
hopelessness, 147
  creative, 349
"how" mindfulness skills, 174
hyperarousal, 76, 77, 78, 293
hyperthyroidism, 120
hypervigilance, 78, 140, 144
hypochondriasis, 3, 24

I

imaginal exposure, 34, 52, 189, 295
  trauma-related, 295
imipramine, 338
inflexibility, psychological, 268, 282
inpatient residential treatment (IRT),
  37
interoceptive exposure, 108–109, 177,
  298, 311, 313
interpersonal behaviors, 91–92
interpersonal effectiveness, 176–177
  skills, 189–190
Interpersonal Schema Sheet, 84, 104,
  354
Interpretation of Intrusions Inventory,
  47
intrusions, 5, 10, 13, 21, 22, 35, 38, 39,
  42, 44, 46, 48, 49, 57, 139, 144,
  330–331, 350, 352, 354
  expression of, 145
  obsessions as, 41
  shame, and, 147
investing in discomfort, 142

J

joy, capacity for, 166

L

Liebowitz Social Anxiety Scale, 327
life events, negative, 124
life skills/life story, 80
lithium, 330
  fluvoxamine, and, 334
lorazepam, 311, 312

M

marijuana, social phobia and, 299, 300
marital therapy, 124
MCT, *see* metacognitive therapy
medication complications, 125–126
mental rehearsal, 4
metacognition, 46
  categories of, 4
  defined, 2, 46
  vs. negative thoughts, 7
Metacognitions Questionnaire (MCQ),
  13, 18
metacognitive therapy, 1–25, 45, 139,
  349, 351, 353, 354
  case illustration of, 14–18
  evidence for, 18–22
  vs. applied relaxation, 23
meta-worry, 19, 20, 22, 23
Meta-Worry Questionnaire (MWQ), 13
methamphetamine dependence, 292
Mindful Attention Awareness Scale
  (MAAS), 192, 353–354
mindfulness, 146, 165, 171–174, 178, 185,
  192, 283, 352, 353, 354, 356
mindfulness-based cognitive therapy
  (MBCT), 171, 260, 266
mindfulness-based stress reduction
  (MBSR), 171
mindfulness training, 144
modified prolonged exposure (MPE),
  80, 85–86, 92, 189, 190
monoamine oxidase inhibitors, 326
Montgomery–Åsberg Depression
  Rating Scale (MADRS), 331
mood regulation, 80
motivation, building, 352–354
motivational enhancement, 113–114,
  310–314
motivational interviewing, 351, 353,
  355
  clinical example, 212–220
  efficacy of, 220–225
  empirical support for, 212
  for generalized anxiety disorder,
    199–226
  for resistance management, 204